Social Theories of

Jacksonian Democracy

Representative Writings
of the Period 1825–1850

Edited, with an Introduction, by

JOSEPH L. BLAU

Associate Professor of the Philosophy of Religion
Columbia University

Hackett Publishing Company, Inc.
Indianapolis/Cambridge

This book was originally published as a volume in the American Heritage Series under the general editorship of Leonard W. Levy and Alfred Young.

Printed in the United States of America

09 08 07 06 05 04 03   1 2 3 4 5 6 7

For further information, please address:

> Hackett Publishing Company, Inc.
> P.O. Box 44937
> Indianapolis, IN   46244-0937
>
> www.hackettpublishing.com

Cover design by Rick Todhunter and Abigail Coyle
Printed at Sheridan Books, Inc.

Library of Congress Cataloging-in-Publication Data
Social theories of Jacksonian democracy: representative writings of the
  period 1825–1850/ edited, with an introduction, by Joseph L. Blau.
    p. cm.
  Originally published: Indianapolis: Bobbs-Merrill, c1954
  (The American heritage series).
  Includes index.
  ISBN 0-87220-690-4 (alk. paper)—ISBN 0-87220-689-0 (pbk.: alk. paper)
  1. United States—Politics and government—1815–1861—Sources.
  2. Unites States—Economic conditions—19th century—Sources.
  3. United States—Social conditions—19th century—Sources. I. Blau,
Joseph L. (Joseph Leon), 1909–1986. II. American heritage series (New
York, N.Y.)

E338.S64 2003
973.5—dc22

                                        2003056169

The paper used in this publication meets the minimum requirements of
American National Standard for InformationSciences—Permanence of
Paper for Printed Library Materials, ANSI Z39.48-1984

∞

PREFACE

There has been a great deal of attention given during the past few years to the redefinition and description of the theory of Jacksonian democracy. I have derived much from the treatments of this theme by Joseph Dorfman, Arthur M. Schlesinger, Jr., and Herbert W. Schneider. If the specimens of Jacksonian thought here collected contribute to the understanding and elucidation of the critical differences among these interpreters and furnish a reservoir of materials for teachers and students of American social thought, I shall be well satisfied.

In editing these selections, I have been guided by a desire to make them as readable as possible. I have therefore altered punctuation and spelling to conform to current American usage. For the most part, the titles given the selections and the subheadings used within each selection have been introduced by me to facilitate the reading of the volume. The original titles are given in full in the first footnote to each selection. Subheadings, passages, and footnotes inserted by the editor are marked by brackets, and deletions are consistently indicated by suspension points. With the exceptions noted, the texts are given as they were first printed.

The editor of a collection such as this is dependent upon libraries for much assistance; I have been fortunate in finding ready and capable aid in the staffs of the New York Public Library and the Columbia University Library. Oskar Piest, the editor of this series, and Herbert W. Schneider, one of the advisory editors, have listened to my problems and given sage advice. In the preparation of the manuscript for the press, Eleanor W. Blau and Lee Rubin have been my right and left hands. The selections from Walt Whitman's editorials appear as published in *The Gathering of the Forces*, edited by C. Rodgers and J. Black (G. P. Putnam's Sons, New York, 1920), by permission of the publishers. It is a pleasure to me to make public acknowledgement of my debt to all these who have helped me. In giving testimony of my gratitude to them, however, I absolve myself from no responsibility.

J. L. B.

COLUMBIA UNIVERSITY, June, 1947

BIBLIOGRAPHICAL NOTE

Recent treatments of the Jacksonian have so completely altered the earlier view of the movement that earlier studies may well remain unread. Of the recent works, Arthur M. Schlesinger, Jr., *The Age of Jackson* (Boston, 1945), is valuable for its correction of older works and for its resurrection of many forgotten figures in Jacksonian thought. It errs however in its acceptance of the equation of the Jacksonian "laboring" class with our "workers" and in its attempt to make a sermon for our times out of the movements of a past century. Joseph Dorfman, *The Economic Mind in American Civilization, 1606–1865* (New York, 1946), especially Chaps. XXIII and XXIV, supplies an excellent corrective to Schlesinger. Dorfman's study is limited to economic theory, however, and does not, therefore, stand by itself. Herbert W. Schneider, *A History of American Philosophy* (New York, 1946), Chaps. XI and XII, help to clarify the theoretical orientation of the Jacksonians, especially with reference to their belief in "The Common Man."

Other materials of value in the further study of the Jacksonian movement include Albert Post, *Popular Freethought in America, 1825–1850* (New York, 1943), which is suggestive of the extent to which religious radicalism entered into the Jacksonian picture, and Merle Curti, *The Growth of American Thought* (New York, 1943), Chap. XII, which sketches some of the factors in the American scene which influenced the Jacksonians in their "democratic upheaval."

Extensive bibliographies are available in all the books which have been mentioned.

CONTENTS

PART THREE

SOCIAL CRITICISM

INTRODUCTION

JACKSONIAN SOCIAL THOUGHT

WHO WERE THE JACKSONIANS?

The party of the Jacksonian Democrats was, in many respects, the first of the modern American political parties. In Jacksonian democracy, for the first time in our party history, the Washington "dynasty" lost its power to direct the Presidential nomination to one of their own group. John Adams and Jefferson had both served in the cabinet of George Washington; Madison was trained for the Presidency by acting as Jefferson's Secretary of State; Monroe held the same position under Madison; John Quincy Adams occupied this training ground under Monroe. A tradition was well on its way to being established. The President was to be a man who had learned what was demanded of him in his new position by being at the center of affairs in the cabinet of his predecessor. He was to be a man of national vision who had made a career of national affairs. Jacksonianism broke sharply with this tradition by entering for the Presidency men like Van Buren and Polk whose reputations and support were local or sectional. They were partisans as well as party men. Jackson himself, though he drew his support from all over the country, had never cut much of a figure on the national political stage prior to his election to the highest office within the gift of the people of the United States.

Yet it was his ability to gain popular support in all sections of the country which was Jackson's strong point. The rivalry between the Commonwealth of Massachusetts and the old Dominion of Virginia, each with its allies, had enlivened the politics of the early years of the American nation. To this open rivalry there succeeded an "era of good feeling," which was not so much the abandonment of sectional rivalry as its subordination to the mutual interests of northern industrialists and southern planters. There was a sentiment abroad for a movement which stood above sections, which united the North, the South, and the developing West. Of this unity the Jacksonian movement was the exponent, and Jackson himself was the symbol. The sense of national unity which the Jacksonians bequeathed to the United

ix

States has never been lost; it was for this unity that the Civil War was fought. Lincoln spoke in the Jacksonian tradition when he placed the preservation of the Union above the abolition of slavery.

Jackson stood forth as symbol in another sense, too. His predecessors in the Presidency came of the "best" families, were well educated men, and scorned, feared, or distrusted the "rabble." Jackson, though better educated than he has been given credit for being and wealthier and more aristocratic than most accounts of his times allow, came from the frontier, was an "outsider." Thus he came to symbolize for the American people the possibility that any citizen might become President. Again the similarity to Lincoln is clear. However rare such an elevation may be, the examples of Jackson and Lincoln can always be cited to prove the freedom of opportunity in America. The Jacksonians thus brought a new hope to the "common man."

Partly, too, the reason for this hope was that Jackson's appointments to Federal offices were based upon a frontiersman's ideal, the equicompetence of most men to most tasks. Thus, Jackson has been unjustly credited with inventing another characteristic of modern party government in the United States, the "spoils system." True, he made use of the system for his special end; he may even have been the first to apply to American politics the classic line, "To the victors belong the spoils." This method of guaranteeing administrative officers favorable to the point of view of the new President had, however, been used before. What was distinctive about Jackson's way was that his appointments were based not on proved competence but on party loyalty. He proclaimed the theory that any citizen was competent to the performance of any duty within the government. Perhaps, then, he should be credited with this continuing tradition rather than the one he did not originate.

There was another aspect of Jackson's party which foreshadows the parties of today. It was not so much a single, unified party, maintaining a single point of view, as it was an aggregation of diverse groups, covering well-nigh the entire spectrum of political, social, and economic thought. These groups were able to unite, more or less stably, for a time, in opposition to certain characteristics which were emerging in American life. They were unable, however, to find a more permanent basis for union than this opposition. The party's position, therefore, represented a compromise among the different views of the different component groups. It is for this reason that different writers, stressing the programs of different groups, can present such varying pictures of the Jacksonian party. Because of this variegation of views, the reader of this collection must be prepared for the discovery that no single epithet will describe the Jacksonian Democrats. They were by turns liberal and reactionary; it is possible to maintain that they were reactionary in their espousal of eighteenth-century Liberalism.

There is another, broader sense, however, in which the term Jacksonianism may be used if we consider ideas rather than party labels. In this use Jacksonianism is a general name for a current in American social thought of the second quarter of the nineteenth century which, more or less consciously, pushed back the boundaries of democratic thinking. There were men who believed that it was important to maintain a democratic way of thought and a democratic way of life in the face of the changing conditions which marked this quarter of a century of developing finance and industry. These men were not all members of the Jacksonian party; they may not have been political supporters of Jackson at all. Nor was the Jacksonian party always in accord with the ideas of the men whom I make bold to call the spokesmen of the *theory* of Jacksonian democracy, whoever may have been its *practical* exponents. The programs of these Jacksonian social thinkers represent the ideal which no political party, conscious of the need to compromise a program in order to win elections, could possibly maintain in its fullness. In the selections included in this volume this ideal can be seen in its strength and its weakness.

Sources of Jacksonian Social Theory

The sources of Jacksonianism were many and so intertwined as to make them virtually impossible to disentangle. Basically it must be said that the Jacksonians were trying to make their adjustment to the life of the nineteenth century in terms drawn either from the eighteenth century or from the economic liberals of the twenty-five years immediately preceding their times.

Politically, their chief saint was Jefferson, and their major guide was John Taylor of Caroline, who made the attempt to give systematic statement to Jefferson's political theories. Less often the Jacksonians derived their political views from Tom Paine, Jeremy Bentham, or other more radical eighteenth-century Democrats. Through Jefferson, however, they were in touch with one of the classical traditions in political thought, reaching back to Cicero in antiquity, and to John Milton, Algernon Sydney, and John Locke in the great century of the development of democratic theory in England. Where it is possible to distinguish the ethical views of the Jacksonians, these also seem to derive largely from English sources in the enlightenment; they adhered to the "moral sense" school which developed in England and Scotland in the eighteenth century. This summary statement of their sources in ethics and politics places the Jacksonians clearly in the line of political liberalism of the sort to which the English have given the name "philosophical radicalism," though in the light of today's problems the position seems far from radical.

In their economic views, the Jacksonians followed — and exaggerated — the views of the school of economic liberals. They criticized Adam Smith for having admitted any economic restrictions into his system of free trade at the same time as they idolized Smith for this system; they followed David Ricardo; they quoted John Ramsay M'Culloch. Of their American predecessors and contemporaries in economic theory, the only one they viewed with any approval was Daniel Raymond, who, like them, was a stalwart defender of free trade principles. In addition they had read and carefully considered James Madison's exposition of economic determinism in the *Federalist* papers and were in general agreement with the views there expressed. They were sympathetic to the movements for reform in England, such as Chartism. They thought highly of Robert Owen, not so much because of his economic "communalism," his community system, however, as because of his emphasis on education. The community system, they felt, violated their central tenet of individualism, and, therefore, despite its beneficial results, they would have none of it. In economic theory, too, they carried on the work of Thomas Jefferson; he had attacked and brought down to defeat the Virginia system of primogeniture and entail. The more extreme Jacksonians attacked the whole system of inheritance as an unwarranted interference with the "freedom of trade" of each individual in his own generation.

One other point remains to be noticed. Among the Jacksonians there was a strong tinge of deistic "infidelity," which was no longer fashionable in their period as it had been in Jefferson's. The Age of Reason and its reasonable God had lost favor together; the romantics regarded the world less as a machine running on orderly principles and more as a haphazard, chance affair. As the mathematical intellect gave way to a "reason" at the beck and call of man's emotions, the traditional God of unreason had returned to religion, and a new orthodoxy had developed. The out-and-out freethinkers who espoused the Jacksonian cause brought dismay into the political ranks because of the orthodox votes they lost; Frances Wright, for example, was politely requested not to try to help the Philadelphia Workingmen's Party because her publicized anticlerical and antichurch views would be a political handicap. Despite the careful conventionality of the party in religious matters, however, many of the Jacksonians were men of the reasonable religion of Jefferson and Paine, and perhaps even more of Elihu Palmer and the "deistical societies." It is noteworthy that, next to Jackson himself, the greatest popular hero of the Jacksonians was Colonel Richard M. Johnson of Kentucky, conqueror of Tecumseh, who as senator introduced bill after bill for the abolition of imprisonment for debt, but won the nomination for the vice-presidency by his report denying the petitions of many orthodox groups that transportation of the mails should be halted on Sunday. This report is in many ways the masterly document which the Jacksonians thought it, and deserves to stand beside Jefferson's Act establishing religious freedom in Virginia and Madison's Memorial and Remonstrance against the paying of religious teachers out of state funds in the front rank of defenses of the freedom of religion in the United States.

JACKSONIANISM A MIDDLE CLASS MOVEMENT

By 1824, it had become clear that the American public would not always cling to the political guidance of an aristocratic Washington clique. Though Fisher Ames and his political heirs might talk to the death about the "dangers of American liberty," the hounds were loose and were baying at the heels of their "betters." The Jacksonian struggle for power was a class struggle, and this was never far from the minds of its political and ideological leaders. Lest, however, there should be any misunderstanding about this statement, let it be made perfectly clear that the "classes" which were struggling against each other were actually the two divisions of the so-called middle class.

In the upper middle class were the growing group of large scale industrial and commercial capitalists and the smaller but politically significant number of financiers; this group was the beneficiary of the Hamiltonian program of subsidy, protection, and monopoly. In Jacksonian terminology it was called "the party of privilege." The major magazines and newspapers of the country were under the control of members of this group. Its program called for a high protective tariff, the building of roads and canals at government expense, and a strong central government.

Around the lower middle class there collected a motley aggregation of landowners and farmers, who were taxed for roads and canals they neither needed or wanted, "hard money" men who distrusted the banks and their paper money, artisans and master mechanics who resented the headstart that the "protected" industries had over their unprotected industries, "states rights" men, especially in the South, who feared that the concentration of power in the Federal Government might prove disastrous to the institution of slavery, faddists and fanatics of all sorts, and a few pure Democrats. This miscellaneous group was called by the Jacksonians "the democracy," "the people," "the working men," and various other similarly appealing names. The program of the Democratic party called for lowered tariffs, state banks of deposit with money-issuing powers reduced to a minimum, the removal of special privileges in the form of corporate charters, local control over local improvements, and, up to a point just short of nullification, the maintenance of states rights. Boldly they advocated the extension of the franchise, abolition of imprisonment for debt, and other such measures designed to attract the new industrial working class to their cause.

This was good practical politics. It was clear that this group of laborers could not forever be excluded from representation in a country whose revolution had been inaugurated with the slogan of "No taxation without representation." The time was bound to come when those whose rights had been gained by the revolution of their fathers would be confronted by a demand for the granting of rights directed against their position of privilege. Some of the scions of the older families recognized that this claim might well be enforced by violence if it were not granted as a right. A large part of the New Jersey Federalist party, an agrarian group, preferred to support the Jacksonians rather than to cast their lot with the rising industrial upper middle class. In New York, James Fenimore Cooper, whose father had been a leader of the New York Federalists, included in his too-little read *Notions of the Americans* an elaborate theoretical justification of broadening the base of the franchise in order to provide representation for the lower orders. To some extent, it must be recognized that Cooper spoke for a landowning class whose power had dwindled as the rising commercial oligarchy began to outnumber them. To some extent, too, Cooper's attitude was based upon a fear of revolution. This is evident in the selection included in this volume. But, though considerations such as these entered into the determination of his position, it is noteworthy that Cooper chose extension of the franchise rather than policing and restrictions as the means to achieve a renewed security for his group.

Cooper's position and, indeed, that of many of the Jacksonians, was tied to a criticism of the "stake in society" principle which was good Whig doctrine both in the United States and in England. This principle asserted simply that only those who were property owners should have the right to vote because only they had an interest or "stake" in good government. It is the application to government of the old proverb that "He who pays the piper calls the tune." In times when the pressure from the unfranchised was very great, it could be mitigated by a reduction in the amount of property deemed necessary to establish such a "stake," but it was a rare and extreme position to suggest, as did Cooper, that the principle itself was absurd. Another of his less familiar works, *The Monikins*, is a satiric novel dealing largely with this point.

The career of Colonel Richard M. Johnson of Kentucky has already been mentioned, and his constant attempt to outlaw imprisonment for debt has been noticed. This was also a major concern of the Jacksonian Democrats of Massachusetts. The victory of the Massachusetts Democracy was the culmination of a long-term tussle which originally involved only the commercial interests of the coast towns and the agrarian debtor class of the back country. Out of this contest Shays' Rebellion had developed as far back as 1786. The sympathy of the populace had been with Daniel Shays; the government dared not execute him or any of his followers. The state constitution of 1780, however, which John Adams had drafted, and which created the situation out of which the rebellion arose, was not altered. By its provisions the franchise and the right to office were restricted to property owners and taxpayers, and the richer commercial towns were over-represented in the state senate. Yet, despite this restrictive constitution, the Democratic party achieved a signal victory when imprisonment for debt was abolished on July 4, 1834. That was doubly Independence Day for the farmers and mechanics of Massachusetts. Their jubilation and their heightened hopes of further successes are revealed in the oration of Frederick Robinson which is included in this collection.

Proposals to extend the franchise, to abolish imprisonment for debt, and to decrease the high protective tariffs were designed to appeal to the laboring classes as well as to the lower middle class group among which they were originated. It is noteworthy that the attempts of the Democrats to achieve these ends brought victory in six of the eight Presidential elections between 1828 and the Civil War. In 1840, however, a weakness of the extended electorate was revealed; the very emphasis which had been given by the Democrats to the increase of popular power was turned against them in the demagogic Whig campaign for Harrison and Tyler. To some of the Jacksonians this was a disappointment and a shock. Orestes Augustus Brownson, whose review of Carlyle's *Chartism* in the *Boston Quarterly Review* for 1840 had been a clarion call against reformism and for revolution, the most radical of the pieces included in this collection, completely lost his faith in the political method of improving labor's position, and sought in religious institutions the key to a better future. Others, however, recognized the results of the 1840 election as a temporary setback, and did not lose faith as easily as the volatile Brownson.

THE AGE OF THE PEOPLE

Richard Hildreth, journalist, historian, and philosopher, was never a Democrat; during his earlier years he had been a Whig and had served the Whig cause in his formal writings and in his journalistic activities. In 1840, however, when Brownson broke with the Democrats, Hildreth broke with the Whigs. Those who know only his *History of the United States*, which he asserted he had written with complete objectivity but which emphasized the distinctive services of the Federalist party in the early years of the United States, have felt that Hildreth broke only with the party and not with its program. To those others who have read his *Theory of Politics* it is clear that on some points Hildreth had come to a position close to that of the Jacksonians. Nowhere is this clearer than in the concluding section of the *Theory of Politics*, titled "Hopes and Hints for the Future." In this chapter, which is here reprinted as the concluding selection, the author points to the coming "age of the people," an age in which the questions, particularly of economic equality, raised by the socialists, will come in for full and detailed consideration and a non-socialist solution. Hildreth's route to this conclusion was unique, yet many of the Jacksonians agreed with him in the hope that American democracy would truly yield an age of the people.

This theme appears and reappears in many guises in this collection. In the earliest form in which it is included here, Charles Stewart Daveis — another who was by politics not a Democrat, but who is included because his thought was Jacksonian even before the era of Jacksonianism — defended the ideal of popular sovereignty, of the ability of the people to govern themselves, against the attacks of such men as Fisher Ames, whose most typical work was entitled *The Dangers of American Liberty*. For Daveis, even the geographical features of the United States favored the extension of self-government by the entire people. The suggestion that the whole people were not capable of self-government seemed to him to strike at the very roots of everything which the United States represented in the world. He placed his trust in the power of education; his interpretation of Machiavelli's *Prince* is especially interesting in this connection. Machiavelli, he said, had been concerned with the political education of the sovereign; inasmuch as, in the United States, the entire people was the sovereign, the application of Machiavelli's scheme of political education to the whole people would produce a capable sovereignty as well in a democracy as under an autocracy.

Another whose faith was placed on an educational program was Frances Wright. This freethinking disciple of Jeremy Bentham, who was a close friend of the aged Lafayette, believed that only a democratic education could create democrats. In her view the schools had to be "nationalized" in order to provide an educational program which would eliminate from the minds of the young the prejudices of caste and wealth which their parents held and instilled in them. She advocated taking children from their homes, dressing them uniformly, feeding them uniformly, giving to all alike the same training. This "rational" plan, she thought, would establish a "national" character of belief in social equality. Her crusade for national education was a failure, but in the workmen's associations and unions which objected to the extremism of her program there grew a strong movement for public education which has finally produced an approximation to the ideal for which she strove as the "remedy" for the evils of American society.

In the internecine warfare for control of the Massachusetts Democratic party, the sympathy which has been given to George Bancroft has tended to throw suspicion on the character and motives of his chief opponent for party control, Benjamin Franklin Hallett. This suspicion is in a large measure undeserved; Hallett as politician was no better and no worse than his rival. He was a lawyer and journalist who left no systematic statement of his theoretical position; his two chief works were legal arguments in defense of the rights of the underprivileged. The earlier of these concerned *The Rights of the Marshpee Indians* (1834) at a time when little concern was being manifested for the redskinned aborigines. Parenthetically it should be noted here that Jackson considered that his administration had "solved" the Indian problem by pushing the Indians out of white territory into a backwoods which he thought unlikely to become "civilized." Hallett's later argument, sections of which are here reprinted, defended the legality of the government established in Rhode Island by the Dorr Revolution. The broad ground on which Hallett argued was that the people could not by any act alienate their ultimate sovereignty. Unfortunately the Court ruled that the considerations which Hallett had introduced were political rather than judicial; in giving decision against Hallett's clients, Chief Justice Taney failed to consider the fundamental issues which were raised.

Bancroft himself presents a strange pattern. Of all men, he seems one of the least likely to have been a political leader. He went to Germany as a young man with the intention of studying theology, one of the earliest of the many American youths who took this educational path. There his interest shifted towards philosophy; he studied under Schleiermacher and Hegel, and gained familiarity with the ideas of Goethe. He came to think in terms of the post-Kantian romantic transcendentalists. When he returned to the United States, in 1822, he served briefly as tutor in Greek at Harvard and then became, for eight years, an unsuccessful teacher in the Round Hill School at Northampton, Massachusetts. He left this work in 1831; began in 1834 the publication of his *History of the United States*, and by 1837 he was collector of the port of Boston — the most important patronage-dispensing office in the state of Massachusetts, held by the leader of the Democratic party in that state. Later in his political career, he was briefly Secretary of the Navy in the cabinet of President Polk, and then the ambassador of the United States to Great Britain. At that time, he was also a recognized leader in the inner politics of the Democratic party.

His philosophic position led him to a somewhat different view of "the people" from that held by his fellow-Democrats. He found an "immanent reason," not in individuals alone as did Emerson, but in the entire people; it was by virtue of this quality that the people were able to enforce progress. This doctrine led him to a theory of the competence of the collective mind, a national self-reliance. He did not develop a radically egalitarian position from this doctrine, though he might well have done so. He maintained that immanent reason was diffused through the human species, but not equally developed in all individuals. Thus the "general voice of mankind" proclaims "the dictates of pure reason;" "the people collectively are wiser than the most gifted individual, for all his wisdom constitutes but a part of theirs." How different this from Cooper's readiness, half in fear, to extend the franchise to the populace.

Thus we may see that although it may be said to have been characteristic of the Jacksonians to believe in the people's power to govern themselves, the form of that belief, its occasion, its theoretical foundation, and its outcomes differed from Jacksonian to Jacksonian.

THE ENTERPRISE OF FREEDOM

There are two antithetical elements which must enter into any genuine belief in self-government; the urge for freedom and the need for control. Throughout the history of American political thought these two themes have been considered and their resolution attempted.

The claims of the individual to be free and the necessity for the state to control are counter pressures of vast concern to modern assayers of reconciliation. For the Jacksonians, however, the problem seemed far simpler.

They lived closer than we to an era in which control was vested in but a limited number of institutions; a monarchy and a hierarchy were the most important. Freedom, they thought, must come as the inevitable result of the destruction of monarchy and hierarchy. Control was not so much necessary as traditional. Dispose of tradition and, in particular, of traditional forms, and you have freedom. Whatever limitations must arise will come as the result of self-limitation, self-control. Thus by self-government the Jacksonians meant a resolution of the tension of freedom and authority in which the authority was exercised freely by free men; in which control was not from above, but rather from oneself; in which government was not over the people, but rather "government of the people, by the people," as, before Lincoln, the idea was phrased in the introductory article to the first issue of *The Democratic Review* which is here included.

The American Revolution had destroyed monarchy in their country. Even the brief flurry of excitement of the early years of the Republic, when the Federalists had been accused, in some few cases with reason, of desiring a return to monarchy, had died down. The American nation had lived without a king for half a century; it had proved to the satisfaction of its own people and to the dismay of the royalists of the rest of the world that kings were decorative luxuries rather than necessities.

As for hierarchy, while it presented more of a current threat, it had never really gained a foothold in America. There were too many different religious settlements in colonial America for any one of them to establish itself as dominant over more than a limited area. Even this much of dominance was unusual. Yet the priesthood was regarded as insidious and dangerous; of this the Jacksonians were fully convinced. Their fear of priesthood, added to the ever-present xenophobia on both cultural and economic bases, led to the ready acceptance of "native Americanism" by some fragments of the Jacksonian group.

Monarchy, then, had been eliminated, and the fear of ecclesiastical hierarchies was a shying away from shadows. Yet there was a strong controlling power which the Jacksonians justly feared in politics and another in their economic life; and more than either they dreaded their combination.

The first was a strong central government. Self-government in their opinion had to be local government. Their spokesmen rang the changes on the Jeffersonian theme that the best government is that which governs least. Their major objection to taxation would seem to have been the use of the funds thus collected in governmental activity. "Congress," said Jackson himself, in his farewell to the people he had served, "has no right, under the Constitution, to take money from the people unless it is required to execute some one of the specific powers intrusted to the Government." Jackson, like most of his followers, insisted on the limitation of the government at Washington to "specific" powers. This was the basis of the Jacksonian opposition to the Whig policy, in which Henry Clay was so interested, of government-sponsored internal improvements such as roads and canals.

In 1830, Congress passed a bill authorizing the Federal Government to purchase stock in a private company to build a road from Maysville to Lexington, Kentucky, and thus to give its financial support to an internal improvement. Jackson vetoed this bill, and his reputation for having unduly strengthened the executive branch of the government is largely based upon his resolute stand in this matter, to which he later referred as a "plan of unconstitutional expenditure for the purpose of corrupt influence."

Jackson's heir, Martin Van Buren, carried on the fear of strong government. He went so far as to insist that it was "indispensable" that the general government should have difficulty in raising funds in order to guarantee economical government. "In no other way can extravagance be prevented," he wrote to the Democrats of Indiana who were investigating his fitness as a candidate for the 1844 nomination. "It is the nature of man to spend that heedlessly which he acquires without effort and to think little of that which costs little trouble to gain."

So, too, William Leggett, whose services to the Jacksonian cause in his editorials in the *New York Evening Post* and in the *Plaindealer* were important, wrote of the "True Functions of Government" that they are "restricted to the making of *general laws*, uniform and universal in their operation, for these purposes and for no other." He insisted that government has no power to legislate in such a way that one class gains an advantage over any other, nor "to tamper with individual industry a single hair's breadth beyond what is essential to protect the rights of person and property." In Leggett's writings it is clear that the Jacksonians spoke as a rule for a middle class. He attacks the Federal Government for having assumed authority over the people like that of parents "and with about the same degree of impartiality. One child becomes a favorite because he has made a fortune and another because he has failed in the pursuit of that object; one because of its beauty and another because of its deformity." Thus he censures with an even hand the granting of favors to the wealthy and of relief to the poverty-stricken, an attitude which places the "poor" laborers for whom he claims to talk squarely in the middle.

The other great journalist in the Jacksonian tradition was Walt Whitman, who appeared toward the end, when the pro-slavery forces had all but swamped the democratic elements in the Democratic party. Whitman's editorials were a clarion call to return to the themes of the Jacksonians. Whitman, too, emphasized the principle of freedom from officious and overactive government. "*Men* must be 'masters unto themselves,' and not look to presidents and legislative bodies for aid." He insists that "It is only the novice in political economy who thinks it the duty of government to *make* its citizens happy." Reforms cannot be forced upon men; they must work their way through the minds of individual. Not that legislation is completely useless; "The legislature may, and should, when such things fall in its way, lend its potential weight to the cause of virtue and happiness." It is only that "We generally expect a great deal too much of law," and that there is a tendency to forget that the misuse and intrusions of government have always been effected under the specious pretext of bringing about the increased happiness of the whole community. The only necessary function of government is to prevent any man or group of men "from infringing on the rights of other men."

Whitman described the past of the United States as "our great experiment of how much liberty society will bear." In this he but followed Charles Stewart Daveis, who, nearly a quarter of a century earlier, when the Jacksonian impulse was just arising in Jeffersonian democracy, had said, "We have entered upon a sober experiment how far the simple moral principles of society are competent for their own

.ical preservation." The simple moral principles of society involve .ie self-control of the entire people. Such self-government is certainly the expedient in political life; "the problem is yet to be solved how far the expedient is practicable for reconciling authority with liberty."

Thus the Jacksonians spoke for freedom as they spoke of politics. Like their predecessors, the Jeffersonian democrats of the Age of Reason, they felt the eyes of the world upon them as they carried out the American experiment in democracy. Like the Jeffersonians, too, they thought of this experiment as carrying out the enterprise of freedom.

THE FREEDOM OF ENTERPRISE

This enterprise of freedom the Jacksonians tried to explore on the economic level as well as the political. They took all too seriously the laissez-faire themes of economic liberalism. Here, even more than in their political thinking, they lost sight of the need for control under the spur of the urge to liberty. Their economic thought had sentimental appeal, but was scientifically unsound.

The strong, controlling economic force which they feared was a centralized bank, and it was such a bank which they inherited from their predecessors in political control. Indeed, the Second Bank of the United States was a financial octopus whose stockholders made outrageous profits at the expense of the Government, and therefore at the expense of the citizens. A great deal of the criticism which the Jacksonians levelled at the Bank was justified. The Bank directors were shameless in their purchase of members of Congress; Daniel Webster's relations with the directors are too well known to be worth repeating, and too scandalous to have been repeated as frequently as they have been. The combination of Bank and State, the development of which the Jacksonians feared, was virtually a reality by the time the Bank's charter came up for renewal in 1832. Jackson's veto of the bill rechartering the Bank was one of the most popular acts of his administration.

The Jacksonians, however much they disliked the Bank and distrusted the financial oligarchy which directed its affairs, were at a loss to provide an acceptable substitute. Their principles forbade any attempt at restriction or control of the Bank by the Government. A strong government would have been necessary for that solution to be effective. No more could they advocate that the Government should enter into the banking business, for the same reason. It was characteristic of the Jacksonians that they denied the right of the Government to issue paper money, which they interpreted literally as promissory notes.

The solutions which the Jacksonian theorists proposed had to be based on a policy of decentralization. They favored a decentralized state; they proposed the decentralization of banking. The degree to which they carried such proposals differed. Where more conservative Jacksonians like Jackson himself advocated a system of state banks, extremists like New York's anti-monopolists under the leadership of Theodore Sedgwick, Jr., and Dr. John Vethake, believed that banking should be thrown completely open to the public, that any man who so desired should be allowed to open a bank. Banking, said this group, is an honorific name for the money trade, for the buying and selling of credit, and should be no more restricted than any other business.

Altogether the theme of monopoly loomed large in Jacksonian economic thought. Stated very generally, the position taken was that any corporate charter was a grant of privilege, tantamount to a monopoly. To obviate the problems thus created, either no such charters should be granted or all who applied should be given charters. That is, either no one or everyone should be granted a monopoly. If no one were to be granted a corporate charter, the disadvantages would be great; in partnerships or individual businesses, for example, there is unlimited liability, which may be good from the viewpoint of the creditors but not in the view of the business man. Corporate charters, on the other hand, provided a desirable limitation of liability. The alternative was then to issue corporate charters as a matter of routine to all applicants. Thus every man would be his own monopolist and all would be equal. Had this theory been put into practice, the result would have exceeded the Ruritanian imaginings of W. S. Gilbert.

Yet, with minor individual variations, this was the economic theory which the Jacksonians called "free trade." They carried their theory sometimes to absurd lengths. William Cullen Bryant, well known as a poet, is perhaps less well known as one of the chief editors of the *New York Evening Post* and a leader of the "Locofoco" democrats of

New York. In one of his editorials, which is here reprinted, Bryant declares his objection to usury laws as a form of government interference with free trade. That such laws made it possible for mechanics and small business men to borrow money without getting into the hands of oppressive extortioners did not offset the fact that these laws required the government to intervene between money seller and money buyer. Surely this may well be called consistency carried out to absurd lengths.

On a different tangent, Thomas Skidmore realized that however equal the opportunities for free trading were kept in any one generation, the inheritance of property prevented the members of any one generation from getting off to an equal start. In his book called *The Rights of Man to Property!*, Skidmore worked out an elaborate and detailed, but fantastic, scheme whereby within each generation there might be complete freedom of enterprise, but property could not be handed down from generation to generation. Each new individual got off to a fresh start by being assigned his equal share of the world's property out of the estates of those who died the year the new owners were born.

Although such faddism cannot be completely eliminated in presenting Jacksonian social theory, it must be remembered that every social movement has its lunatic fringe of those who take its slogans seriously as guides to action, rather than lightly as devices for catching votes or support. There were sounder and more moderate economic thinkers among the Jacksonians. William Gouge was one; his *Short History of Paper Money and Banking in the United States* is a careful account based on whatever statistical information was available in his time. It is informed by hostility to banking and to paper money; Gouge was as anxious for data which could be used to attack the Second Bank of the United States as Nicholas Biddle was to collect data in support of his Bank. Gouge's *History* was a platform for the discussion of an economic program which might have been, though it never actually was, tried in practice.

Again, David Henshaw's analysis of the Dartmouth College Case showed a clear grasp of the fundamental socio-economic issues which underlay the purely legal aspects of the decision of the Supreme Court. He realized that, in declaring corporate charters to be perpetual, unbreakable contracts between the state and the corporations,

Justice Marshall and the members of his Court were placing the then-existing corporations outside of the law and thus giving them a status of extraordinary privilege which was dangerous to the well-being of a democratic United States.

To this list of more conservative thinkers on economic themes should certainly be added the names of Stephen Simpson and Gilbert Vale. Both of these men were primarily publicists rather than economists; yet both of them realized that the artisan class for which they spoke could not engage in any considerable political activity without a basic acquaintance with economic theory. Simpson stated specifically his intention to write of political economy from the viewpoint of the American workers. Vale was clearly writing for the same group, though he did not address himself explicitly to it. Vale, in particular, should be recognized as a belated devotee of the Age of Reason. He still wrote without affectation of government as a voluntary compact for mutual protection, of natural rights, and of "the legitimate object of legislators and governors" which is "to *protect* the natural rights of man, and not to take the control of the property of society." Both Simpson and Vale adhered to the theory that value is created by labor. Vale argued against those who would destroy or prohibit the use of machinery that the machine added to the value the laborer could produce and was, therefore, desirable.

Thus on the plane of economics the Jacksonians transformed faith in the enterprise of freedom into belief in the freedom of enterprise. Some were sober in their programs, while others devoted themselves to impossibly Quixotic schemes for the reformation of the social order. In a word, Jacksonian politics was egalitarian, Jacksonian economics libertarian.

A Program for Labor

If this is so, two of the three watchwords of the French Revolution have been accounted for. It is possible to find an expression of the third watchword, fraternity, among the Jacksonians, but always on class lines, never on a national basis. When Theophilus Fisk declared that "capital" and "labor" were in perpetual conflict, he was but making explicit one of the assumptions common among the Jacksonians. To Fisk and the others capital meant an oligarchy of those who lived on the work of others which was united against a disunited class of those who worked themselves.

The obvious solution was that this working class should unite to meet the unity of its opponents. General Trades Unions and Workingmen's parties were the institutions which they thought should be encouraged to strengthen working class unity. From Philadelphia, from Boston, from New York came the call for the mechanics to unite. Langdon Byllesby, a Philadelphian, proposed what might today be called producer's cooperatives as the remedy for existing inequalities. Ely Moore, master printer and later member of Congress from New York, and Frederick Robinson of Boston limited their recommendations to the organization of unions and federations of unions. All alike were hopeful of great achievement through organization. This was their version of fraternity.

CONCLUSION

These introductory remarks and the volume of selections they preface should make it clear to the discerning reader why the Jacksonian movement and the party in which the movement was given partial expression have proved so difficult to interpret. It was a catch-all movement, united in its opposition to the financial and commercial monopolies of the three large cities of Boston, Philadelphia, and New York. The nucleus of the movement everywhere was the same: a relatively well-educated and politically conscious group of lawyers, journalists, and skilled mechanics, whose interests coincided with those of the slave-owning planters of the Southern States. No single statement can cover the variety of positive programs they enunciated. They were agreed on where they did not want the United States to go, but differed sharply on everything else.

Those who have tried to interpret this diversity into unity call to mind the blind men who described an elephant on the basis of partial sensory experience of the animal. To depict a unity of view where a multiplicity of views is evident is a clearer characterization of the observers than of the observed. To deny even the unity of dissent is equally narrow. It is for that reason that the Jacksonians as here presented emerge as a microcosm of the United States, as a diversity in unity.

One final comparison: As one drives out of any large city on a major highway, he is bound to see a large signpost, with arrows pointing him to many possible destinations.   These arrows have but one thing in common; all alike point away from the city he has just left. Let this stand as a symbol of Jacksonians.   Though they pointed to many different possible American futures, all alike pointed away from an America of privilege and monopoly.

PART ONE

The Ideal of Self-Government

1

ANDREW JACKSON

A POLITICAL TESTAMENT[1]

BEING ABOUT to retire finally from public life, I beg leave to offer you my grateful thanks for the many proofs of kindness and confidence which I have received at your hands. It has been my fortune, in the discharge of public duties, civil and military, frequently to have found myself in difficult and trying situations where prompt decision and energetic action were necessary and where the interest of the country required that high responsibilities should be fearlessly encountered; and it is with the deepest emotions of gratitude that I acknowledge the continued and unbroken confidence with which you have sustained me in every trial. My public life has been a long one, and I cannot hope that it has, at all times, been free from errors. But I have the consolation of knowing that, if mistakes have been committed, they have not seriously injured the country I so anxiously endeavored to serve; and, at the moment when I surrender my last public trust, I leave this great people prosperous and happy; in the full enjoyment of liberty and peace; and honored and respected by every nation of the world.

If my humble efforts have, in any degree, contributed to preserve to you these blessings, I have been more than rewarded by the honors you have heaped upon me; and, above all, by the generous confidence with which you have supported me in every peril, and with which you have continued to animate and cheer my path to the closing hour of my political life. The time has now come when advanced age and a broken frame warn me to retire from public concerns; but the recollection of the many favors you have bestowed upon me is engraven upon my heart, and I have felt that I could not part from your service without making this public acknowledgment of the gratitude I owe you. And if I use the occasion to offer to you the counsels of age and experience, you will, I trust, receive them with the same indulgent

---

[1] [From *Farewell Address of Andrew Jackson to the People of the United States: and the Inaugural Address of Martin Van Buren, President of the United States* (Washington, 1837), pp. 3–16 — Text complete.]

kindness which you have so often extended to me; and will, at least, see in them an earnest desire to perpetuate, in this favored land, the blessings of liberty and equal laws.

[THE STATE OF THE NATION]

We have now lived almost fifty years under the Constitution framed by the sages and patriots of the Revolution. The conflicts in which the nations of Europe were engaged during a great part of this period; the spirit in which they waged war against each other; and our intimate commercial connections with every part of the civilized world, rendered it a time of much difficulty for the Government of the United States. We have had our seasons of peace and of war, with all the evils which precede or follow a state of hostility with powerful nations. We encountered these trials with our Constitution yet in its infancy, and under the disadvantages which a new and untried Government must always feel when it is called upon to put forth its whole strength, without the lights of experience to guide it or the weight of precedents to justify its measures. But we have passed triumphantly through all these difficulties. Our Constitution is no longer a doubtful experiment; and, at the end of nearly half a century, we find that it has preserved unimpaired the liberties of the people, secured the rights of property, and that our country has improved and is flourishing beyond any former example in the history of nations.

In our domestic concerns there is everything to encourage us; and if you.are true to yourselves, nothing can impede your march to the highest point of national prosperity. The States which had so long been retarded in their improvement by the Indian tribes residing in the midst of them are at length relieved from the evil; and this unhappy race — the original dwellers in our land — are now placed in a situation where we may well hope that they will share in the blessings of civilization and be saved from that degradation and destruction to which they were rapidly hastening while they remained in the States; and while the safety and comfort of our own citizens have been greatly promoted by their removal, the philanthropist will rejoice that the remnant of that ill-fated race has been at length placed beyond the reach of injury or oppression, and that the paternal care of the General Government will hereafter watch over them and protect them.

If we turn to our relations with foreign powers, we find our condition equally gratifying. Actuated by the sincere desire to do justice to every nation and to preserve the blessings of peace, our intercourse with them has been conducted on the part of this Government in the spirit of frankness, and I take pleasure in saying that it has generally been met in a corresponding temper. Difficulties of old standing have been surmounted by friendly discussion and the mutual desire to be just; and the claims of our citizens, which had been long withheld, have at length been acknowledged and adjusted, and satisfactory arrangements made for their final payment;[2] and with a limited and, I trust, a temporary exception, our relations with every foreign power are now of the most friendly character, our commerce continually expanding, and our flag respected in every quarter of the world.

[THE NEED FOR UNITY IN THE UNION]

These cheering and grateful prospects and these multiplied favors we owe, under Providence, to the adoption of the Federal Constitution. It is no longer a question whether this great country can remain happily united and flourish under our present form of government. Experience, the unerring test of all human undertakings, has shown the wisdom and foresight of those who formed it; and has proved that in the union of these States there is a sure foundation for the brightest hopes of freedom and for the happiness of the people. At every hazard and by every sacrifice, this Union must be preserved.

The necessity of watching with jealous anxiety for the preservation of the Union was earnestly pressed upon his fellow citizens by the Father of his country in his farewell address. He has there told us that "while experience shall not have demonstrated its impracticability, there will always be reason to distrust the patriotism of those who, in any quarter, may endeavor to weaken its bonds"; and he has cautioned us, in the strongest terms, against the formation of parties on geographical discriminations, as one of the means which might disturb our union, and to which designing men would be likely to resort.

The lessons contained in this invaluable legacy of Washington to his countrymen should be cherished in the heart of every citizen to the latest generation; and, perhaps, at no period of time could they

[2] [This refers to the Spoliation Claims against France.]

be more usefully remembered than at the present moment. For when we look upon the scenes that are passing around us, and dwell upon the pages of his parting address, his paternal counsels would seem to be not merely the offspring of wisdom and foresight, but the voice of prophecy foretelling events and warning us of the evil to come. Forty years have passed since this imperishable document was given to his countrymen. The Federal Constitution was then regarded by him as an experiment, and he so speaks of it in his address; but an experiment upon the success of which the best hopes of his country depended, and we all know that he was prepared to lay down his life, if necessary, to secure to it a full and a fair trial. The trial has been made. It has succeeded beyond the proudest hopes of those who framed it. Every quarter of this widely extended nation has felt its blessings and shared in the general prosperity produced by its adoption. But amid this general prosperity and splendid success, the dangers of which he warned us are becoming every day more evident and the signs of evil are sufficiently apparent to awaken the deepest anxiety in the bosom of the patriot. We behold systematic efforts publicly made to sow the seeds of discord between different parts of the United States and to place party divisions directly upon geographical distinctions; to excite the *south* against the *north* and the *north* against the *south;* and to force into the controversy the most delicate and exciting topics, topics upon which it is impossible that a large portion of the Union can ever speak without strong emotion. Appeals, too, are constantly made to sectional interests in order to influence the election of the Chief Magistrate, as if it were desired that he should favor a particular quarter of the country instead of fulfilling the duties of his station with impartial justice to all; and the possible dissolution of the Union has at length become an ordinary and familiar subject of discussion. Has the warning voice of Washington been forgotten? or have designs already been formed to sever the Union? Let it not be supposed that I impute to all of those who have taken an active part in these unwise and unprofitable discussions a want of patriotism or of public virtue. The honorable feeling of State pride and local attachments find a place in the bosoms of the most enlightened and pure. But while such men are conscious of their own integrity and honesty of purpose, they ought never to forget that the citizens of other States are their political brethren;

and that, however mistaken they may be in their views, the great
body of them are equally honest and upright with themselves. Mutual
suspicions and reproaches may in time create mutual hostility, and
artful and designing men will always be found, who are ready to
foment these fatal divisions and to inflame the natural jealousies of
different sections of the country. The history of the world is full of
such examples and especially the history of republics.

What have you to gain by division and dissension? Delude not
yourselves with the belief that a breach once made may be afterwards repaired. If the Union is once severed, the line of separation
will grow wider and wider, and the controversies which are now
debated and settled in the halls of legislation will then be tried in
fields of battle and determined by the sword. Neither should you
deceive yourselves with the hope that the first line of separation would
be the permanent one, and that nothing but harmony and concord
would be found in the new associations formed upon the dissolution
of this Union. Local interests would still be found there, and unchastened ambition. And if the recollection of common dangers in which
the people of these United States stood side by side against the common foe; the memory of victories won by their united valor; the
prosperity and happiness they have enjoyed under the present Constitution; the proud name they bear as citizens of this great republic;
if all these recollections and proofs of common interest are not strong
enough to bind us together as one people, what tie will hold united
the new divisions of empire, when these bonds have been broken and
this Union dissevered? The first line of separation would not last for
a single generation; new fragments would be torn off; new leaders
would spring up; and this great and glorious republic would soon be
broken into a multitude of petty states, without commerce, without
credit; jealous of one another; armed for mutual aggression; loaded
with taxes to pay armies and leaders; seeking aid against each other
from foreign powers; insulted and trampled upon by the nations of
Europe, until, harassed with conflicts and humbled and debased in
spirit, they would be ready to submit to the absolute dominion of
any military adventurer and to surrender their liberty for the sake of
repose. It is impossible to look on the consequences that would
inevitably follow the destruction of this Government and not feel
indignant when we hear cold calculations about the value of the

Union and have so constantly before us a line of conduct so well calculated to weaken its ties.

There is too much at stake to allow pride or passion to influence your decision. Never for a moment believe that the great body of the citizens of any State or States can deliberately intend to do wrong. They may, under the influence of temporary excitement or misguided opinions, commit mistakes; they may be misled for a time by the suggestions of self-interest; but in a community so enlightened and patriotic as the people of the United States, argument will soon make them sensible of their errors; and, when convinced, they will be ready to repair them. If they have no higher or better motives to govern them, they will at least perceive that their own interest requires them to be just to others as they hope to receive justice at their hands.

[NULLIFICATION AND STATES' RIGHTS]

But in order to maintain the Union unimpaired, it is absolutely necessary that the laws passed by the constituted authorities should be faithfully executed in every part of the country, and that every good citizen should, at all times, stand ready to put down, with the combined force of the nation, every attempt at unlawful resistance, under whatever pretext it may be made or whatever shape it may assume. Unconstitutional or oppressive laws may no doubt be passed by Congress, either from erroneous views or the want of due consideration; if they are within the reach of judicial authority, the remedy is easy and peaceful; and if, from the character of the law, it is an abuse of power not within the control of the judiciary, then free discussion and calm appeals to reason and to the justice of the people will not fail to redress the wrong. But until the law shall be declared void by the courts or repealed by Congress, no individual or combination of individuals can be justified in forcibly resisting its execution. It is impossible that any Government can continue to exist upon any other principles. It would cease to be a Government and be unworthy of the name if it had not the power to enforce the execution of its own laws within its own sphere of action.

It is true that cases may be imagined disclosing such a settled purpose of usurpation and oppression on the part of the Government as would justify an appeal to arms. These, however, are extreme cases, which we have no reason to apprehend in a Government where the power is in the hands of a patriotic people; and no citizen who loves his country would in any case whatever resort to forcible resistance, unless he clearly saw that the time had come when a freeman should prefer death to submission; for if such a struggle is once begun and the citizens of one section of the country arrayed in arms against those of another in doubtful conflict, let the battle result as it may, there will be an end of the Union and, with it, an end to the hopes of freedom. The victory of the injured would not secure to them the blessings of liberty; it would avenge their wrongs, but they would themselves share in the common ruin.

But the Constitution cannot be maintained nor the Union preserved in opposition to public feeling by the mere exertion of the coercive powers confided to the General Government. The foundations must be laid in the affections of the people; in the security it gives to life, liberty, character, and property, in every quarter of the country; and in the fraternal attachment which the citizens of the several States bear to one another as members of one political family, mutually contributing to promote the happiness of each other. Hence the citizens of every State should studiously avoid everything calculated to wound the sensibility or offend the just pride of the people of other States; and they should frown upon any proceedings within their own borders likely to disturb the tranquillity of their political brethren in other portions of the Union. In a country so extensive as the United States and with pursuits so varied, the internal regulations of the several States must frequently differ from one another in important particulars; and this difference is unavoidably increased by the varying principles upon which the American colonies were originally planted; principles which had taken deep root in their social relations before the Revolution, and, therefore, of necessity influencing their policy since they became free and independent States. But each State has the unquestionable right to regulate its own internal concerns according to its own pleasure; and while it does not interfere with the rights of the people of other States or the rights of the Union, every State must be the sole judge of the measures proper to secure the safety of its citizens and promote their happiness; and all efforts on the part of people of other States to cast odium upon their institutions, and all measures calculated to disturb their rights of property or to put in jeopardy their peace and internal tranquillity are in direct opposition to the spirit in which the Union was formed, and must endanger its safety. Motives of philanthropy may be assigned for this unwarrantable interference; and weak men may persuade themselves for a moment that they are laboring in the cause of humanity and asserting the rights of the human race; but everyone, upon sober reflection, will see that nothing but mischief can come from these improper assaults upon the feelings and rights of others. Rest assured that the men found busy in this work of discord are not worthy of your confidence and deserve your strongest reprobation.

In the legislation of Congress, also, and in every measure of the General Government, justice to every portion of the United States should be faithfully observed. No free Government can stand without virtue in the people, and a lofty spirit of patriotism; and if the sordid feelings of mere selfishness shall usurp the place which ought to be filled by public spirit, the legislation of Congress will soon be converted into a scramble for personal and sectional advantages. Under our free institutions, the citizens of every quarter of our country are capable of attaining a high degree of prosperity and happiness without seeking to profit themselves at the expense of others; and every such attempt must in the end fail to succeed, for the people in every part of the United States are too enlightened not to understand their own rights and interests and to detect and defeat every effort to gain undue advantages over them; and when such designs are discovered, it naturally provokes resentments which cannot always be easily allayed. Justice, full and ample justice, to every portion of the United States should be the ruling principle of every freeman and should guide the deliberations of every public body, whether it be State or national.

[LIMITS OF FEDERAL POWER]

It is well known that there have always been those amongst us who wish to enlarge the powers of the General Government; and experience would seem to indicate that there is a tendency on the part of this Government to overstep the boundaries marked out for it by the Constitution. Its legitimate authority is abundantly sufficient for all the purposes for which it was created; and its powers being expressly enumerated, there can be no justification for claiming anything beyond them. Every attempt to exercise power beyond these limits should be promptly and firmly opposed. For one evil example will lead to other measures still more mischievous; and if the principle of constructive powers, or supposed advantages, or temporary circumstances, shall ever be permitted to justify the assumption of a power not given by the Constitution, the General Government will before long absorb all the powers of legislation, and you will have, in effect, but one consolidated Government. From the extent of our country, its diversified interests, different pursuits, and different habits, it is too obvious for argument that a single consolidated Government would be wholly inadequate to watch over and protect its interests; and every friend of our free institutions should be always prepared to maintain unimpaired and in full vigor the rights and sovereignty of the States and to confine the action of the General Government strictly to the sphere of its appropriate duties.

There is, perhaps, no one of the powers conferred on the Federal Government so liable to abuse as the taxing power. The most productive and convenient sources of revenue were necessarily given to it, that it might be able to perform the important duties imposed upon it; and the taxes which it lays upon commerce being concealed from the real payer in the price of the article, they do not so readily attract the attention of the people as smaller sums demanded from them directly by the tax gatherer. But the tax imposed on goods enhances by so much the price of the commodity to the consumer; and, as many of these duties are imposed on articles of necessity which are daily used by the great body of the people, the money raised by these imposts is drawn from their pockets. Congress has no right, under the Constitution, to take money from the people unless it is required to execute some one of the specific powers intrusted to the Government; and if they raise more than is necessary for such purposes, it is an abuse of the power of taxation and unjust and oppressive. It may, indeed, happen that the revenue will sometimes exceed the amount anticipated when the taxes were laid. When, however, this is ascertained, it is easy to reduce them; and, in such a case, it is unquestionably the duty of the Government to reduce them, for no circumstances can justify it in assuming a power not given to it by the Constitution nor in taking away the money of the people when it is not needed for the legitimate wants of the Government.

Plain as these principles appear to be, you will yet find that there is a constant effort to induce the General Government to go beyond the limits of its taxing power and to impose unnecessary burdens upon the people. Many powerful interests are continually at work to procure heavy duties on commerce and to swell the revenue beyond the real necessities of the public service; and the country has already felt the injurious effects of their combined influence. They succeeded in obtaining a tariff of duties bearing most oppressively on the agricultural and laboring classes of society and producing a revenue that could not be usefully employed within the range of the powers conferred upon Congress; and, in order to fasten upon the people this unjust and unequal system of taxation, extravagant schemes of internal improvement were got up in various quarters to squander the money and to purchase support. Thus, one unconstitutional measure was intended to be upheld by another, and the abuse of the power of taxation was to be maintained by usurping the power of expending the money in internal improvements. You cannot have forgotten the severe and doubtful struggle through which we passed when the Executive Department of the Government, by its veto, endeavored to arrest this prodigal scheme of injustice, and to bring back the legislation of Congress to the boundaries prescribed by the Constitution.[3] The good sense and practical judgment of the people, when the subject was brought before them, sustained the course of the Executive; and this plan of unconstitutional expenditure for the purpose of corrupt influence is, I trust, finally overthrown.

The result of this decision has been felt in the rapid extinguishment of the public debt and the large accumulation of a surplus in the treasury, notwithstanding the tariff was reduced and is now very far below the amount originally contemplated by its advocates. But, rely upon it, the design to collect an extravagant revenue and to burden you with taxes beyond the economical wants of the Government is not yet abandoned. The various interests which have combined together to impose a heavy tariff and to produce an overflowing treasury are too strong and have too much at stake to surrender the contest. The corporations and wealthy individuals who are engaged

[3] [The reference here is to Jackson's 1830 veto of a bill which authorized the government to purchase stock in a private company to build a road from Maysville to Lexington, Kentucky — the Maysville Road Veto.]

in large manufacturing establishments desire a high tariff to increase their gains. Designing politicians will support it to conciliate their favor and to obtain the means of profuse expenditure for the purpose of purchasing influence in other quarters; and since the people have decided that the Federal Government cannot be permitted to employ its income in internal improvements, efforts will be made to seduce and mislead the citizens of the several States by holding out to them the deceitful prospect of benefits to be derived from a surplus revenue collected by the General Government and annually divided among the States. And if, encouraged by these fallacious hopes, the States should disregard the principles of economy which ought to characterize every republican Government and should indulge in lavish expenditures exceeding their resources, they will, before long, find themselves oppressed with debts which they are unable to pay, and the temptation will become irresistible to support a high tariff in order to obtain a surplus for distribution. Do not allow yourselves, my fellow citizens, to be misled on this subject. The Federal Government cannot collect a surplus for such purposes without violating the principles of the Constitution and assuming powers which have not been granted. It is, moreover, a system of injustice, and, if persisted in, will inevitably lead to corruption and must end in ruin. The surplus revenue will be drawn from the pockets of the people, from the farmer, the mechanic, and the laboring classes of society; but who will receive it when distributed among the States, where it is to be disposed of by leading State politicians who have friends to favor and political partisans to gratify? It will certainly not be returned to those who paid it and who have most need of it and are honestly entitled to it. There is but one safe rule, and that is to confine the General Government rigidly within the sphere of its appropriate duties. It has no power to raise a revenue or impose taxes except for the purposes enumerated in the Constitution; and if its income is found to exceed these wants, it should be forthwith reduced, and the burdens of the people so far lightened.

[Currency and Banking Policy]

In reviewing the conflicts which have taken place between different interests in the United States and the policy pursued since the adoption of our present form of government, we find nothing that has produced such deep-seated evil as the course of legislation in relation to the currency. The Constitution of the United States unquestionably intended to secure to the people a circulating medium of gold and silver. But the establishment of a national bank by Congress with the privilege of issuing paper money receivable in the payment of the public dues, and the unfortunate course of legislation in the several States upon the same subject, drove from general circulation the constitutional currency and substituted one of paper in its place.

It was not easy for men engaged in the ordinary pursuits of business, whose attention had not been particularly drawn to the subject, to foresee all the consequences of a currency exclusively of paper; and we ought not, on that account, to be surprised at the facility with which laws were obtained to carry into effect the paper system. Honest and even enlightened men are sometimes misled by the specious and plausible statements of the designing. But experience has now proved the mischiefs and dangers of a paper currency, and it rests with you to determine whether the proper remedy shall be applied.

The paper system being founded on public confidence and having of itself no intrinsic value, it is liable to great and sudden fluctuations; thereby rendering property insecure and the wages of labor unsteady and uncertain. The corporations which create the paper money cannot be relied upon to keep the circulating medium uniform in amount. In times of prosperity, when confidence is high, they are tempted by the prospect of gain, or by the influence of those who hope to profit by it, to extend their issues of paper beyond the bounds of discretion and the reasonable demands of business. And when these issues have been pushed on from day to day until public confidence is at length shaken, then a reaction takes place, and they immediately withdraw the credits they have given; suddenly curtail their issues; and produce an unexpected and ruinous contraction of the circulating medium which is felt by the whole community. The banks by this means save themselves, and the mischievous consequences of their imprudence or cupidity are visited upon the public. Nor does the evil stop here. These ebbs and flows in the currency and these indiscreet extensions of credit naturally engender a spirit of speculation injurious to the habits and character of the people. We have already seen its effects in the wild spirit of speculation in the public lands and various kinds of stock which, within the last year or two, seized upon such a multitude of our citizens and threatened to pervade all classes of society and to withdraw their attention from the sober pursuits of honest industry. It is not by encouraging this spirit that we shall best preserve public virtue and promote the true interests of our country. But if your currency continues as exclusively paper as it now is, it will foster this eager desire to amass wealth without labor; it will multiply the number of dependents on bank accommodations and bank favors; the temptation to obtain money at any sacrifice will become stronger and stronger, and inevitably lead to corruption which will find its way into your public councils and destroy, at no distant day, the purity of your Government. Some of the evils which arise from this system of paper press with peculiar hardship upon the class of society least able to bear it. A portion of this currency frequently becomes depreciated or worthless, and all of it is easily counterfeited in such a manner as to require peculiar skill and much experience to distinguish the counterfeit from the genuine note. These frauds are most generally perpetrated in the smaller notes, which are used in the daily transactions of ordinary business; and the losses occasioned by them are commonly thrown upon the laboring classes of society whose situation and pursuits put it out of their power to guard themselves from these impositions and whose daily wages are necessary for their subsistence. It is the duty of every Government so to regulate its currency as to protect this numerous class as far as practicable from the impositions of avarice and fraud. It is more especially the duty of the United States where the Government is emphatically the Government of the people, and where this respectable portion of our citizens are so proudly distinguished from the laboring classes of all other nations by their independent spirit, their love of liberty, their intelligence, and their high tone of moral character. Their industry in peace is the source of our wealth; and their bravery in war has covered us with glory; and the Government of the United States will but ill discharge its duties if it leaves them a prey to such dishonest impositions. Yet it is evident that their interests cannot be effectually protected unless silver and gold are restored to circulation.

These views alone of the paper currency are sufficient to call for immediate reform; but there is another consideration which should still more strongly press it upon your attention.

Recent events have proved that the paper money system of this country may be used as an engine to undermine your free institutions; and that those who desire to engross all power in the hands of the few and to govern by corruption or force are aware of its power and prepared to employ it. Your banks now furnish your only circulating medium, and money is plenty or scarce according to the quantity of notes issued by them. While they have capitals not greatly disproportioned to each other, they are competitors in business, and no one of them can exercise dominion over the rest; and although, in the present state of the currency, these banks may and do operate injuriously upon the habits of business, the pecuniary concerns, and the moral tone of society; yet, from their number and dispersed situation, they cannot combine for the purpose of political influence; and whatever may be the dispositions of some of them, their power of mischief must necessarily be confined to a narrow space and felt only in their immediate neighborhoods.

But when the charter for the Bank of the United States was obtained from Congress, it perfected the schemes of the paper system and gave to its advocates the position they have struggled to obtain from the commencement of the Federal Government down to the present hour. The immense capital and peculiar privileges bestowed upon it enabled it to exercise despotic sway over the other banks in every part of the country. From its superior strength it could seriously injure, if not destroy, the business of any one of them which might incur its resentment; and it openly claimed for itself the power of regulating the currency throughout the United States. In other words, it asserted (and it undoubtedly possessed) the power to make money plenty or scarce, at its pleasure, at any time, and in any quarter of the Union, by controlling the issues of other banks and permitting an expansion or compelling a general contraction of the circulating medium according to its own will. The other banking institutions were sensible of its strength, and they soon generally became its obedient instruments, ready, at all times, to execute its mandates; and with the banks necessarily went, also, that numerous class of persons in our commercial cities who depend altogether on bank credits for their solvency and means of business; and who are, therefore, obliged for their own safety to propitiate the favor of the money power by distinguished zeal and devotion in its service. The result of the ill-advised legislation which established this great monopoly was to concentrate the whole moneyed power of the Union, with its boundless means of corruption and its numerous dependents, under the direction and command of one acknowledged head; thus organizing this particular interest as one body and securing to it unity and concert of action throughout the United States and enabling it to bring forward, upon any occasion, its entire and undivided strength to support or defeat any measure of the Government. In the hands of this formidable power, thus perfectly organized, was also placed unlimited dominion over the amount of the circulating medium, giving it the power to regulate the value of property and the fruits of labor in every quarter of the Union and to bestow prosperity or bring ruin upon any city or section of the country as might best comport with its own interest or policy.

We are not left to conjecture how the moneyed power, thus organized and with such a weapon in its hands, would be likely to use it. The distress and alarm which pervaded and agitated the whole country when the Bank of the United States waged war upon the people in order to compel them to submit to its demands cannot yet be forgotten. The ruthless and unsparing temper with which whole cities and communities were oppressed, individuals impoverished and ruined, and a scene of cheerful prosperity suddenly changed into one of gloom and despondency ought to be indelibly impressed on the memory of the people of the United States. If such was its power in a time of peace, what would it not have been in a season of war with an enemy at your doors? No nation but the freemen of the United States could have come out victorious from such a contest; yet, if you had not conquered, the Government would have passed from the hands of the many to the hands of the few; and this organized money power, from its secret conclave, would have dictated the choice of your highest officers and compelled you to make peace or war as best suited their own wishes. The forms of your government might, for a time, have remained; but its living spirit would have departed from it.

The distress and sufferings inflicted on the people by the bank are some of the fruits of that system of policy which is continually striving to enlarge the authority of the Federal Government beyond the limits fixed by the Constitution. The powers enumerated in that instrument do not confer on Congress the right to establish such a

corporation as the Bank of the United States; and the evil consequences which followed may warn us of the danger of departing from
the true rule of construction and of permitting temporary circumstances or the hope of better promoting the public welfare to influence, in any degree, our decisions upon the extent of the authority
of the General Government. Let us abide by the Constitution as it
is written or amend it in the constitutional mode if it is found to be
defective.

The severe lessons of experience will, I doubt not, be sufficient to
prevent Congress from again chartering such a monopoly, even if the
Constitution did not present an insuperable objection to it. But you
must remember, my fellow citizens, that eternal vigilance by the
people is the price of liberty; and that you must pay the price if you
wish to secure the blessing. It behooves you, therefore, to be watchful
in your States as well as in the Federal Government. The power
which the moneyed interest can exercise, when concentrated under a
single head, and with our present system of currency, was sufficiently
demonstrated in the struggle made by the Bank of the United States.
Defeated in the General Government, the same class of intriguers and
politicians will now resort to the States and endeavor to obtain there
the same organization which they failed to perpetuate in the Union;
and with specious and deceitful plans of public advantages and State
interests and State pride they will endeavor to establish, in the different States, one moneyed institution with overgrown capital and
exclusive privileges sufficient to enable it to control the operations of
the other banks. Such an institution will be pregnant with the same
evils produced by the Bank of the United States, although its sphere
of action is more confined; and in the State in which it is chartered
the money power will be able to embody its whole strength and to
move together with undivided force to accomplish any object it may
wish to attain. You have already had abundant evidence of its power
to inflict injury upon the agricultural, mechanical, and laboring classes
of society; and over those whose engagements in trade or speculation
render them dependent on bank facilities, the dominion of the State
monopoly will be absolute, and their obedience unlimited. With
such a bank and a paper currency, the money power would, in a few
years, govern the State and control its measures; and if a sufficient
number of States can be induced to create such establishments, the

time will soon come when it will again take the field against the United States and succeed in perfecting and perpetuating its organization by a charter from Congress.

It is one of the serious evils of our present system of banking that it enables one class of society, and that by no means a numerous one, by its control over the currency to act injuriously upon the interests of all the others and to exercise more than its just proportion of influence in political affairs. The agricultural, the mechanical, and the laboring classes have little or no share in the direction of the great moneyed corporations; and from their habits and the nature of their pursuits, they are incapable of forming extensive combinations to act together with united force. Such concert of action may sometimes be produced in a single city or in a small district of country by means of personal communications with each other; but they have no regular or active correspondence with those who are engaged in similar pursuits in distant places; they have but little patronage to give to the press and exercise but a small share of influence over it; they have no crowd of dependents above them who hope to grow rich without labor by their countenance and favor and who are, therefore, always ready to exercise their wishes. The planter, the farmer, the mechanic, and the laborer all know that their success depends upon their own industry and economy and that they must not expect to become suddenly rich by the fruits of their toil. Yet these classes of society form the great body of the people of the United States; they are the bone and sinew of the country; men who love liberty and desire nothing but equal rights and equal laws and who, moreover, hold the great mass of our national wealth, although it is distributed in moderate amounts among the millions of freemen who possess it. But, with overwhelming numbers and wealth on their side, they are in constant danger of losing their fair influence in the Government and with difficulty maintain their just rights against the incessant efforts daily made to encroach upon them. The mischief springs from the power which the moneyed interest derives from a paper currency which they are able to control; from the multitude of corporations with exclusive privileges which they have succeeded in obtaining in the different States and which are employed altogether for their benefit; and unless you become more watchful in your States and check this spirit of monopoly and thirst for exclusive privileges, you will, in the end, find that the most important powers of Government have been given or bartered away, and the control over your dearest interests has passed into the hands of these corporations.

The paper money system and its natural associates, monopoly and exclusive privileges, have already struck their roots deep in the soil; and it will require all your efforts to check its further growth and to eradicate the evil. The men who profit by the abuses and desire to perpetuate them will continue to besiege the halls of legislation in the General Government as well as in the States and will seek, by every artifice, to mislead and deceive the public servants. It is to yourselves that you must look for safety and the means of guarding and perpetuating your free institutions. In your hands is rightfully placed the sovereignty of the country and to you every one placed in authority is ultimately responsible. It is always in your power to see that the wishes of the people are carried into faithful execution, and their will, when once made known, must sooner or later be obeyed. And while the people remain, as I trust they ever will, uncorrupted and incorruptible and continue watchful and jealous of their rights, the Government is safe, and the cause of freedom will continue to triumph over all its enemies.

But it will require steady and persevering exertions on your part to rid yourselves of the iniquities and mischiefs of the paper system and to check the spirit of monopoly and other abuses which have sprung up with it and of which it is the main support. So many interests are united to resist all reform on this subject that you must not hope the conflict will be a short one nor success easy. My humble efforts have not been spared, during my administration of the Government, to restore the constitutional currency of gold and silver; and something, I trust, has been done towards the accomplishment of this most desirable object. But enough yet remains to require all your energy and perseverance. The power, however, is in your hands, and the remedy must and will be applied, if you determine upon it.

[THOUGHTS ON FOREIGN POLICY AND NATIONAL DEFENSE]

While I am thus endeavoring to press upon your attention the principles which I deem of vital importance in the domestic concerns of the country, I ought not to pass over, without notice, the important considerations which should govern your policy towards foreign powers. It is, unquestionably, our true interest to cultivate the most friendly understanding with every nation and to avoid by every honorable means the calamities of war; and we shall best attain this object by frankness and sincerity in our foreign intercourse, by the prompt and faithful execution of treaties, and by justice and impartiality in our conduct to all. But no nation, however desirous of peace, can hope to escape occasional collisions with other powers; and the soundest dictates of policy require that we should place ourselves in a condition to assert our rights if a resort to force should ever become necessary. Our local situation, our long line of seacoast, indented by numerous bays, with deep rivers opening into the interior, as well as our extended and still increasing commerce, point to the navy as our natural means of defense. It will, in the end, be found to be the cheapest and most effectual; and now is the time, in a season of peace, and with an overflowing revenue, that we can, year after year, add to its strength without increasing the burdens of the people. It is your true policy. For your navy will not only protect your rich and flourishing commerce in distant seas, but will enable you to reach and annoy the enemy and will give to defense its greatest efficiency by meeting danger at a distance from home. It is impossible by any line of fortifications to guard every point from attack against a hostile force advancing from the ocean and selecting its object; but they are indispensable to protect cities from bombardment, dock yards and naval arsenals from destruction; to give shelter to merchant vessels in time of war, and to single ships or weaker squadrons when pressed by superior force. Fortifications of this description cannot be too soon completed and armed and placed in a condition of the most perfect preparation. The abundant means we now possess cannot be applied in any manner more useful to the country; and when this is done and our naval force sufficiently strengthened and our militia armed, we need not fear that any nation will wantonly insult us or needlessly provoke hostilities. We shall more certainly preserve peace when it is well understood that we are prepared for war.

[CONCLUSION]

In presenting to you, my fellow citizens, these parting counsels, I have brought before you the leading principles upon which I endeavored to administer the Government in the high office with which you twice honored me. Knowing that the path of freedom is continually beset by enemies who often assume the disguise of friends, I have devoted the last hours of my public life to warn you of the danger. The progress of the United States under our free and happy institutions has surpassed the most sanguine hopes of the founders of the Republic. Our growth has been rapid beyond all former example, in numbers, in wealth, in knowledge, and all the useful arts which contribute to the comforts and convenience of man; and from the earliest ages of history to the present day, there never have been thirteen millions of people associated together in one political body who enjoyed so much freedom and happiness as the people of these United States. You have no longer any cause to fear danger from abroad; your strength and power are well known throughout the civilized world, as well as the high and gallant bearing of your sons. It is from within, among yourselves, from cupidity, from corruption, from disappointed ambition, and inordinate thirst for power, that factions will be formed and liberty endangered. It is against such designs, whatever disguise the actors may assume, that you have especially to guard yourselves. You have the highest of human trusts committed to your care. Providence has showered on this favored land blessings without number and has chosen you as the guardians of freedom to preserve it for the benefit of the human race. May He who holds in his hands the destinies of nations make you worthy of the favors He has bestowed and enable you, with pure hearts and pure hands and sleepless vigilance, to guard and defend to the end of time the great charge he has committed to your keeping.

My own race is nearly run; advanced age and failing health warn me that before long I must pass beyond the reach of human events and cease to feel the vicissitudes of human affairs. I thank God that my life has been spent in a land of liberty and that He has given me a heart to love my country with the affection of a son. And, filled with gratitude for your constant and unwavering kindness, I bid you a last and affectionate farewell.

2

THE DEMOCRATIC REVIEW

AN INTRODUCTORY STATEMENT
OF THE DEMOCRATIC PRINCIPLE[1]

THE CHARACTER and design of the work of which the first number is here offered to the public are intended to be shadowed forth in its name, the *United States Magazine and Democratic Review*. It has had its origin in a deep conviction of the necessity of such a work, at the present critical stage of our national progress, for the advocacy of that high and holy *democratic principle* which was designed to be the fundamental element of the new social and political system created by the American experiment; for the vindication of that principle from the charges daily brought against it, of responsibility for every evil result growing out, in truth, of adventitious circumstances, and the adverse elements unhappily combined with it in our institutions; for its purification from those corruptions and those hostile influences by which we see its beneficent and glorious tendencies, to no slight extent, perverted and paralyzed; for the illustration of truth, which we see perpetually darkened and confused by the arts of wily error; for the protection of those great interests, not alone of our country, but of humanity, looking forward through countless ages of the future, which we believe to be vitally committed with the cause of American Democracy. This is, in broad terms, the main motive in which this undertaking has had its origin; this is the object towards which, in all its departments, more or less directly, its efforts will tend.

There is a great deal of mutual misunderstanding between our parties; but in truth, there does not exist in the people, with reference to its great masses, that irreconcilable hostility of opinions and leading principles which would be the natural inference from the violence

---

[1] [From the "Introduction" to *The United States Magazine and Democratic Review*, I, No. 1 (October, 1837), pp. 1–15. This statement was probably written by John L. O'Sullivan, part owner and political editor of the *Review*. A few quotations have been deleted; otherwise the text is complete.]

of the party warfare in which we are perpetually engaged. There does exist, it is true, an essential opposition of principles, proceeding from opposite points of departure, between the respective political creeds or systems of our two great parties, the Democratic and the Whig; but we feel well assured that the great body of the latter party, those who supply their leaders and leading interests with their votes, do not rightly understand the questions at issue in their true popular bearings; and that, if these could but be exhibited in their proper lights to their sound minds and honest hearts, they would soon be found ranged, by the hundreds of thousands, under the broad and bright folds of our democratic banner.

[First Principle of Democracy: Self-Government]

So many false ideas have insensibly attached themselves to the term "democracy," as connected with our party politics, that we deem it necessary here, at the outset, to make a full and free profession of the cardinal principles of political faith on which we take our stand; principles to which we are devoted with an unwavering force of conviction and earnestness of enthusiasm which, ever since they were first presented to our minds, have constantly grown and strengthened by contemplation of them and of the incalculable capabilities of social improvement of which they contain the germs.

We believe, then, in the principle of *democratic republicanism,* in its strongest and purest sense. We have an abiding confidence in the virtue, intelligence, and full capacity for self-government, of the great mass of our people, our industrious, honest, manly, intelligent millions of freemen.

We are opposed to all self-styled "wholesome restraints" on the free action of the popular opinion and will, other than those which have for their sole object the prevention of precipitate legislation. This latter object is to be attained by the expedient of the division of power, and by causing all legislation to pass through the ordeal of successive forms; to be sifted through the discussions of coördinate legislative branches with mutual suspensive veto powers. Yet all should be dependent with equal directness and promptness on the influence of public opinion; the popular will should be equally the animating and moving spirit of them all, and ought never to find in any of its own creatures a self-imposed power, capable, when misused either by corrupt ambition or honest error, of resisting itself and defeating its own determined object. We cannot, therefore, look with an eye of favor on any such forms of representation as, by length of tenure of delegated power, tend to weaken that universal and unrelaxing responsibility to the vigilance of public opinion which is the true conservative principle of our institutions.

The great question here occurs, which is of vast importance to this country (Was it not once near dissolving the Union, and plunging it into the abyss of civil war?), of the relative rights of majorities and minorities. Though we go for the republican principle of the supremacy of the will of the majority, we acknowledge, in general, a strong sympathy with minorities and consider that their rights have a high moral claim on the respect and justice of majorities; a claim not always fairly recognized in practice by the latter, in the full sway of power, when flushed with triumph and impelled by strong interests. This has ever been the point of the democratic cause most open to assault and most difficult to defend. This difficulty does not arise from any intrinsic weakness. The democratic theory is perfect and harmonious in all its parts; and if this point is not so self-evidently clear as the rest is generally, in all candid discussion, conceded to be, it is because of certain false principles of government which have, in all practical experiments of the theory, been interwoven with the democratic portions of the system, being borrowed from the example of anti-democratic systems of government. We shall always be willing to meet this question frankly and fairly. The great argument against pure democracy, drawn from this source, is this:

Though the main object with reference to which all social institutions ought to be modelled is undeniably, as stated by the democrat, "the greatest good of the greatest number," yet it by no means follows that the greatest number always rightly understands its own greatest good. Highly pernicious error has often possessed the minds of nearly a whole nation; while the philosopher in his closet, and an enlightened few about him, powerless against the overwhelming current of popular prejudice and excitement, have alone possessed the truth, which the next generation may perhaps recognize and practice, though its author, now sainted, has probably, in his own time, been its martyr. The original adoption of the truth would have saved perhaps oceans of blood and mountains of misery and crime. How much stronger,

then, the case against the absolute supremacy of the opinion and will
of the majority, when its numerical preponderance is, as often happens, comparatively small. And if the larger proportion of the more
wealthy and cultivated classes of the society are found on the side of
the minority, the disinterested observer may well be excused if he
hesitate long before he awards the judgment, in a difficult and complicated question, in favor of the mere numerical argument. Majorities are often as liable to error of opinion, and not always free from a
similar proneness to selfish abuse of power, as minorities; and a vast
amount of injustice may often be perpetrated, and consequent general
social injury be done, before the evil reaches that extreme at which
it rights itself by revolution, moral or physical.

We have here, we believe, correctly stated the anti-democratic side
of the argument on this point. It is not to be denied that it possesses
something more than plausibility. It has certainly been the instrument of more injury to the cause of the democratic principle than all
the bayonets and cannon that have ever been arrayed in support of it
against that principle. The inference from it is that the popular
opinion and will must not be trusted with the supreme and absolute
direction of the general interests; that it must be subjected to the
"conservative checks" of minority interests, and to the regulation of
the "more enlightened wisdom" of the "better classes," and those to
whom the possession of a property "test of merit" gives what they
term "a stake in the community." And here we find ourselves in the
face of the great stronghold of the anti-democratic, or *aristocratic*,
principle.

It is not our purpose, in this place, to carry out the discussion of this
question. The general scope and tendency of the present work are
designed to be directed towards the refutation of this sophistical reasoning and inference. It will be sufficient here to allude to the leading
ideas by which they are met by the advocate of the pure democratic
cause.

In the first place, the greatest number are *more likely*, at least, as a
general rule, to understand and follow their own greatest good, than
is the minority.

In the second, a minority is much more likely to abuse power for
the promotion of its own selfish interests, at the expense of the majority
of numbers, the substantial and producing mass of the nation, than

the latter is to oppress unjustly the former. The social evil is also, in that case, proportionately greater. This is abundantly proved by the history of all aristocratic interests that have existed, in various degrees and modifications, in the world. A majority cannot subsist upon a minority; while the natural, and in fact uniform, tendency of a minority entrusted with governmental authority is to surround itself with wealth, splendor, and power, at the expense of the producing mass, creating and perpetuating those artificial social distinctions which violate the natural equality of rights of the human race and at the same time offend and degrade the true dignity of human nature.

In the third place, there does not naturally exist any such original superiority of a minority class above the great mass of a community in intelligence and competence for the duties of government, even putting out of view its constant tendency to abuse from selfish motives, and the safer honesty of the mass. The general diffusion of education, the facility of access to every species of knowledge important to the great interests of the community, the freedom of the press, whose very licentiousness cannot materially impair its permanent value, in this country at least, make the pretensions of those self-styled "better classes" to the sole possession of the requisite intelligence for the management of public affairs too absurd to be entitled to any other treatment than an honest, manly contempt. As far as superior knowledge and talent confer on their possessor a natural charter of privilege to control his associates and exert an influence on the direction of the general affairs of the community, the free and natural action of that privilege is best secured by a perfectly free democratic system which will abolish all artificial distinctions, and, preventing the accumulation of any social obstacles to advancement, will permit the free development of every germ of talent, wherever it may chance to exist, whether on the proud mountain summit, in the humble valley, or by the wayside of common life.

But the question is not yet satisfactorily answered, how the relation between majorities and minorities, in the frequent case of a collision of sentiments and particular interests, is to be so adjusted as to secure a mutual respect of rights, to preserve harmony and good will, and save society from the *malum extremum discordia*, from being as a house divided against itself, and thus to afford free scope to that competition, discussion, and mutual moral influence which cannot but result, in the end, in the ascendancy of the truth and in "the greatest good of the greatest number." On the one side, it has only been shown that the absolute government of the majority does not always afford a perfect guarantee against the misuse of its numerical power over the weakness of the minority. On the other, it has been shown that this chance of misuse is, as a general rule, far less than in the opposite relation of the ascendancy of a minority; and that the evils attendant upon it are infinitely less, in every point of view, in the one case than the other. But this is not yet a complete or satisfactory solution of the problem. Have we but a choice of evils? Is there, then, such a radical deficiency in the moral elements implanted by its Creator in human society that no other alternative can be devised by which both evils shall be avoided, and a result attained more analogous to the beautiful and glorious harmony of the rest of his creation?

It were scarcely consistent with a true and living faith in the existence and attributes of that Creator, so to believe; and such is not the democratic belief. The reason of the plausibility with which appeal may be made to the experience of so many republics to sustain this argument against democratic institutions is that the true theory of national self-government has been hitherto but imperfectly understood; bad principles have been mixed up with the good; and the republican government has been administered on ideas and in a spirit borrowed from the strong governments of the other forms; and to the corruptions and manifold evils which have never failed, in the course of time, to evolve themselves out of these seeds of destruction is ascribable the eventual failure of those experiments, and the consequent doubt and discredit which have attached themselves to the democratic principles on which they were, in the outset, mainly based.

[STRONG GOVERNMENT A DANGER TO LIBERTY]

It is under the word *government* that the subtle danger lurks. Understood as a central consolidated power, managing and directing the various general interests of the society, all government is evil, and the parent of evil. A strong and active democratic *government*, in the common sense of the term, is an evil, differing only in degree and mode of operation, and not in nature, from a strong despotism. This difference is certainly vast, yet, inasmuch as these strong governmental powers must be wielded by human agents, even as the powers of the despotism, it is, after all, only a difference in degree; and the tendency to demoralization and tyranny is the same, though the development of the evil results is much more gradual and slow in the one case than in the other. Hence the demagogue; hence the faction; hence the mob; hence the violence, licentiousness, and instability; hence the ambitious struggles of parties and their leaders for power; hence the abuses of that power by majorities and their leaders; hence the indirect oppressions of the general by partial interests; hence (fearful symptom) the demoralization of the great men of the nation, and of the nation itself, proceeding, unless checked in time by the more healthy and patriotic portion of the mind of the nation rallying itself to reform the principles and sources of the evil, gradually to that point of maturity at which relief from the tumult of moral and physical confusion is to be found only under the shelter of an energetic armed despotism.

The best government is that which governs least. No human depositories can, with safety, be trusted with the power of legislation upon the general interests of society so as to operate directly or indirectly on the industry and property of the community. Such power must be perpetually liable to the most pernicious abuse, from the natural imperfection, both in wisdom of judgment and purity of purpose, of all human legislation, exposed constantly to the pressure of partial interests; interests which, at the same time that they are essentially selfish and tyrannical, are ever vigilant, persevering, and subtle in all the arts of deception and corruption. In fact, the whole history of human society and government may be safely appealed to, in evidence that the abuse of such power a thousandfold more than overbalances its beneficial use. Legislation has been the fruitful parent of nine-tenths of all the evil, moral and physical, by which mankind has been afflicted since the creation of the world, and by which human nature has been self-degraded, fettered, and oppressed. Government should have as little as possible to do with the general business and interests of the people. If it once undertake these functions as its rightful province of action, it is impossible to say to it "Thus far shalt thou go, and no farther." It will be impossible to confine it to the public interests of the *commonwealth*. It will be perpetually tampering with private interests, and sending forth seeds of corruption which will result in the demoralization of the society. Its domestic action should be confined to the administration of justice, for the protection of the natural equal rights of the citizen and the preservation of social order.

[The Principle of Freedom]

In all other respects, the *voluntary principle*, the principle of *freedom*, suggested to us by the analogy of the divine government of the Creator, and already recognized by us with perfect success in the great social interest of religion, affords the true "golden rule" which is alone abundantly competent to work out the best possible general result of order and happiness from that chaos of characters, ideas, motives, and interests: human society. Afford but the single nucleus of a system of administration of justice between man and man, and, under the sure operation of this principle, the floating atoms will distribute and combine themselves, as we see in the beautiful natural process of crystallization, into a far more perfect and harmonious result than if government, with its "fostering hand," undertake to disturb, under the plea of directing, the process. The natural laws which will establish themselves and find their own level are the best laws. The same hand was the Author of the moral, as of the physical world; and we feel clear and strong in the assurance that we cannot err in trusting, in the former, to the same fundamental principles of spontaneous action and self-regulation which produce the beautiful order of the latter.

This is then, we consider, the true theory of government, the one simple result towards which the political science of the world is gradually tending, after all the long and varied experience by which it will have dearly earned the great secret, the elixir of political life. This is the fundamental principle of the philosophy of democracy, to furnish a system of administration of justice, and then leave all the business and interests of society to themselves, to free competition and association; in a word, to the *voluntary principle;* . . . .

It is borrowed from the example of the perfect self-government of the physical universe, being written in letters of light on every page of the great bible of Nature. It contains the idea of full and fearless faith in the providence of the Creator. It is essentially involved in Christianity, of which it has been well said that its pervading spirit of democratic equality among men is its highest fact and one of its most radiant internal evidences of the divinity of its origin. It is the essence and the one general result of the science of political economy. And this principle alone, we will add, affords a satisfactory and perfect solution of the great problem, otherwise unsolved, of the relative rights of majorities and minorities.

This principle, therefore, constitutes our point of departure. It has never yet received any other than a very partial and imperfect application to practice among men, all human society having been hitherto perpetually chained down to the ground by myriads of lilliputian fetters of artificial government and prescription. Nor are we yet prepared for its full adoption in this country. Far, very far indeed, from it; yet is our gradual tendency toward it clear and sure. How many generations may yet be required before our theory and practice of government shall be sifted and analyzed down to the lowest point of simplicity consistent with the preservation of some degree of national organization, no one can presume to prophesy. But that we are on the path toward that great result, to which mankind is to be guided down the long vista of future years by the democratic principle, walking hand in hand with the sister spirit of Christianity, we feel a faith as implicit as that with which we believe in any other great moral truth.

This is all generalization, and therefore, though necessary, probably dull. We have endeavored to state the theory of the Jeffersonian democracy, to which we profess allegiance, in its abstract essence, however unpopular it appears to be, in these latter days, to "theorize." These are the original ideas of American democracy; and we would not give much for that "practical knowledge" which is ignorant of, and affects to disregard, the essential and abstract principles which really constitute the animating soul of what were else lifeless and naught. The application of these ideas to practice in our political affairs is obvious and simple. Penetrated with a perfect faith in their eternal truth, we can never hesitate as to the direction to which, in every practical case arising, they must point with the certainty of the magnetized needle; and we have no desire to shrink from the responsibility, at the outset, of a frank avowal of them in the broadest general language.

[EXPERIMENTALISM NOT RADICALISM]

But having done so, we will not be further misunderstood, and we hope not misrepresented, as to immediate practical views. We deem it scarcely necessary to say that we are opposed to all precipitate radical changes in social institutions. Adopting Nature as the best guide, we cannot disregard the lesson which she teaches when she accomplishes her most mighty results of the good and beautiful by the silent and slow operation of great principles, without the convulsions of too rapid action. *Festina lente* is an invaluable precept, if it be not abused. On the other hand, that specious sophistry ought to be no less watchfully guarded against, by which old evils always struggle to perpetuate themselves by appealing to our veneration for the wisdom of our fathers, to our inert love of present tranquillity, and our natural apprehension of possible danger from the untried and unknown. . . . .

We are not afraid of that much dreaded phrase, "untried experiment," which looms so fearfully before the eyes of some of our most worthy and valued friends. The whole history of the progress hitherto made by humanity, in every respect of social amelioration, records but a series of *experiments*. The American Revolution was the greatest of experiments, and one of which it is not easy at this day to appreciate the gigantic boldness. Every step in the onward march of improvement by the human race is an experiment; and the present is most emphatically an age of experiments. The eye of man looks naturally *forward;* and as he is carried onward by the progress of time and truth, he is far more likely to stumble and stray if he turn his face backward, and keep his looks fixed on the thoughts and things of the past. We feel safe under the banner of the democratic principle, which is borne onward by an unseen hand of Providence, to lead our race toward the high destinies of which every human soul contains the God-implanted germ; and of the advent of which—certain, however distant—a dim prophetic presentiment has existed, in one form or another, among all nations in all ages. We are willing to make every reform in our institutions that may be commanded by the test of the democratic principle, to *democratize* them, but only so rapidly as shall appear, to the most cautious wisdom, consistent with a due regard to the existing development of public opinion and to the permanence of the progress made. Every instance in which the action of *government* can be simplified, and one of the hundred giant arms curtailed, with which it now stretches around its fatal protecting grasp over almost all the various interests of society, to substitute the truly healthful action of the free voluntary principle, every instance in which the operation of the public opinion and will, fairly signified, can be brought to bear more directly upon the action of delegated powers, we would regard as so much gained for the true interest of the society and of mankind at large. In this path we cannot go wrong; it is only necessary to be cautious not to go too fast.

Such is, then, our democracy. It of course places us in the school of the strictest construction of the Constitution; and in that appears to be involved a full committal of opinion on all the great political questions which now agitate the public mind, and to which we deem it unnecessary here to advert in detail. One necessary inference from the views expressed above is that we consider the preservation of the present ascendancy of the Democratic party as of great, if not vital, importance to the future destinies of this holy cause. Most of its leading members we know to possess all the qualifications that should entitle men to the confidence and attachment of their country; and the arduous functions of the executive department of the Government are administered with an efficiency, and a strictness and purity of principle, which, considering their nature, extent, and complexity, are indeed remarkable. And even without a particular knowledge of the men, the principle alone would still of necessity attach us to that party. The acquisition of the vast influence of the executive department by the present opposition principles, we could not look upon but as a staggering blow to the cause of democracy, and all the high interests committed with it; from which it would take a long and indefinite period of years to recover, even if the loss of time in national progress would not, in that event, have to be reckoned by generations! We shall therefore, while devoting ourselves to preserve and improve the purity of our democratic institutions, labor to sustain the present Democratic administration, by fair appeal to argument, with all the earnestness due to the gravity of the principles and interests involved.

[THOUGHTS ON AMERICAN LITERATURE]

We are admonished by the prescribed limits of this introductory article, to curtail various topics of interest to which we had intended to allude in it. The important subject of national literature cannot, however, be passed without a slight notice.

What is the cause, is sometimes asked among the disciples of the democratic school of political philosophy, of that extensive anti-democratic corruption of sentiment in some portions of our people, especially in the young mind of the nation, which is certainly so just a subject of surprise and alarm? It has lately been a topic of newspaper remark that nineteen-twentieths of the youth of one of the colleges of Virginia were opposed to the democratic principles. The very exaggeration is good evidence of the lamentable truth; and it is well known that a very large proportion of the young men who annually leave our colleges carry with them a decided anti-popular bias, to swell the ranks of that large majority of the "better classes" already ranged on that side, and to exercise the influence of their cultivated talents in a cause at variance with the genius of our country, the spirit of the age, the best interests and true dignity of humanity, and the highest truths of the science of political morals.

And yet the democratic cause is one which not only ought to engage the whole mind of the American nation, without any serious division of its energies, to carry forward the noble mission entrusted to her of going before the nations of the world as the representative of the democratic principle and as the constant living exemplar of its results, but which ought peculiarly to commend itself to the generosity of youth, its ardent aspirations after the good and beautiful, its liberal and unselfish freedom from narrow prejudices of interest.

For Democracy is the cause of Humanity. It has faith in human nature. It believes in its essential equality and fundamental goodness. It respects, with a solemn reverence to which the proudest artificial institutions and distinctions of society have no claim, the human soul. It is the cause of philanthropy. Its object is to emancipate the mind of the mass of men from the degrading and disheartening fetters of social distinctions and advantages; to bid it walk abroad through the free creation in its own majesty; to war against all fraud, oppression, and violence; by striking at their root, to reform all the infinitely varied human misery which has grown out of the old and false ideas by which the world has been so long misgoverned; to dismiss the hireling soldier; to spike the cannon, and bury the bayonet; to burn the gibbet, and open the debtor's dungeon; to substitute harmony and mutual respect for the jealousies and discord now subsisting between different classes of society, as the consequence of their artificial classification. It is the cause of Christianity, to which a slight allusion has been already made, to be more fully developed hereafter. And that portion of the peculiar friends and ministers of religion who now, we regret to say, cast the weight of their social influence against the cause of democracy, under the false prejudice of an affinity between it and infidelity (No longer, in this century, the case, and which, in the last, was but a consequence of the overgrown abuses of religion found, by the reforming spirit that then awakened in Europe, in league with despotism), understand but little either its true spirit, or that of their own faith. It is, moreover, a cheerful creed, a creed of high hope and universal love, noble and ennobling; while all others, which imply a distrust of mankind, and of the natural moral principles infused into it by its Creator, for its own self-development and self-regulation, are as gloomy and selfish, in the tone of the moral sentiment which pervades them, as they are degrading in their practical tendency, and absurd in theory, when examined by the light of original principles.

Then whence this remarkable phenomenon of the young mind of our country so deeply tainted with anti-democratic sentiment, a state of things lamentable in itself, and portentous of incalculable future evil?

Various partial causes may be enumerated in explanation of it; among which we may refer to the following: In the first place, the possession of the executive power, as it exists in our system, is, in one point of view, a great disadvantage to the principles of that ascendant party. The Administration occupies a position of defense; the Opposition, of attack. The former is by far the more arduous task. The lines of fortification to be maintained against the never relaxing onsets from every direction, are so extensive and exposed, that a perpetual vigilance and devotion to duty barely suffice to keep the enemy at bay. The attacking cause, ardent, restless, ingenious, is far more attractive to the imagination of youth than that of the defense. It is, moreover, difficult, if not impossible, to preserve a perfect purity from abuse and corruption throughout all the countless ramifications of the action of such an executive system as ours, however stern may be the integrity and high the patriotism of the presiding spirit which, from its head, animates the whole. Local abuses in the management of party affairs are the necessary consequence of the long possession of the ascendancy. The vast official patronage of the executive department is a weight and clog under which it is not easy to bear up. This must lay any administration open to perpetual assault at great disadvantage; and especially if the great party campaign present at any time such a phase as may render it necessary to put forth, to the full limits of constitutional right, the energies of the executive department, to resist the accumulated pressure of attack, bearing along in its train evils, to avert which almost any means would seem justifiable. This we have seen, in a remarkable manner, the case during the two terms of the late administration. Our natural jealousy of power affords a string to which, when played upon by the bold and skilful hands that are never found wanting, the very spirit of democratic freedom never fails to respond; and many are confused by sophistry and clamor, and carried away by the power of eloquence, divine, even though misused, to array themselves against their own best and most honest friends, under leaders, in truth, the worst enemies of the American principles for which they believe themselves contending.

In the second place, we may refer to a cause which we look upon with deep pain as one of the worst fruits of the evil principles to which allusion has already been made above as existing in our system: the demoralization of many of the great men of the nation. How many of these master-spirits of their day, to whom their country had long been accustomed to look with generous affection as her hope and pride, have we not seen seduced from the path of their early promise by the intrigues of party and the allurements of ambition, in the pursuit of that too dazzling prize, and too corrupting both in the prospect and the possession, the presidential office!

. . . .

The influence of such men, especially on the minds of the young, commanding by their intellectual power, misleading by their eloquence, and fascinating by the natural sympathy which attaches itself to greatness still proud in its "fallen estate," produces certainly a powerful effect in our party contests.

We might also refer to the fact that the anti-democratic cause possesses at least two-thirds of the press of the country, and that portion of it which is best supported by talent and the resources of capital, under the commercial patronage of our cities. To the strong influence that cities, where wealth accumulates, where luxury gradually unfolds its corrupting tendencies, where aristocratic habits and social classifications form and strengthen themselves, where the congregation of men stimulates and exaggerates all ideas, — to the influence that cities exert upon the country, no inconsiderable effect is to be ascribed. From the influence of the mercantile classes, too, extensively anti-democratic, on the young men of the professions, especially that of the law, creating an insensible bias, from the dependence of the latter mainly on the patronage of the former, these young men becoming again each the center of a small sphere of social influence; from that of the religious ministry, silently and insensibly exerted, from the false prejudice slightly touched upon above; from these and some other minor influences, on which we cannot here pause, a vast and active power on public opinion is perpetually in operation. And it is only astonishing that the Democratic party should be able to bear up against them all so successfully as we in fact witness. This is to be ascribed, under that Providence whose unseen hand we recognize in all human affairs, only to the sterling honesty and good sense of the great industrious mass of our people, its instinctive perception of, and yearning after, the democratic truth, and the unwavering generosity of its support of those public servants whom it has once tried well and long, and with whom it has once acknowledged the genuine sympathy of common sentiments and a common cause. Yet still the democratic principle can do little more than hold its own. The moral energies of the national mind are, to a great extent, paralyzed by division; and instead of bearing forward the ark of democratic truth, entrusted to us as a chosen people, towards the glorious destiny of its future, we must fain be content, if we can but stem with it the perpetual tide of attack which would bear it backward towards the ideas and habits of past dark ages.

But a more potent influence than any yet noticed is that of our national literature. Or rather we have no national literature. We depend almost wholly on Europe, and particularly England, to think and write for us, or at least to furnish materials and models after which we shall mold our own humble attempts. We have a considerable number of writers; but not in that consists a national literature. The vital principle of an American national literature must be democracy. Our mind is enslaved to the past and present literature of England. Rich and glorious as is that vast collection of intellectual treasure, it would have been far better for us had we been separated from it by the ocean of a difference of language, as we are from the country itself by our sublime Atlantic. Our mind would then have been compelled to think for itself and to express itself, and its animating spirit would have been our democracy. As it now is, we are cowed by the mind of England. We follow feebly and afar in the splendid track of a literature molded on the whole, notwithstanding a number of noble exceptions, by the ideas and feelings of an utterly anti-democratic social system. We give back but a dim reflection, a faint echo of the expression of the English mind. No one will misunderstand us as disparaging the literature of our mother language; far from it. We appreciate it with a profound veneration and gratitude, and would use it, without abusing it by utterly submitting our own minds to it; but we look upon it, as we do upon the political system of the country, as a something magnificent, venerable, splendid, and powerful, and containing a considerable infusion of the true principle; yet the one no more suitable to be adopted as our own, or as a model for slavish imitation, than the other. In the spirit of her literature we can never hope to rival England. She is immeasurably in advance of us, and is rich with ever active energies, and resources of literary habits and capital, so to speak, which mock our humble attempts at imitation. But we should not follow in her wake; a radiant path invites us forward in another direction. We have a principle, an informing soul, of our own, our democracy, though we allow it to languish uncultivated; this must be the animating spirit of our literature, if, indeed, we would have a national American literature. There is an immense field open to us, if we would but enter it boldly and cultivate it as our own. All history has to be rewritten; political science and the whole scope of all moral truth have to be considered and illustrated in the light of the democratic principle. All old subjects of thought and all new questions arising, connected more or less directly with human existence, have to be taken up again and reexamined in this point of view. We *ought* to exert a powerful moral influence on Europe, and yet we are entirely unfelt; and as it is only by its literature that one nation can utter itself and make itself known to the rest of the world, we are really entirely unknown. In the present general fermentation of popular ideas in Europe, turning the public thoughts naturally to the great democracy across the Atlantic, the voice of America might be made to produce a powerful and beneficial effect on the development of truth; but as it is, American writings are never translated, because they almost always prove to be a diluted and tardy second edition of English thought.

The anti-democratic character of our literature, then, is a main cause of the evil of which we complain; and this is both a mutual cause and effect, constantly acting and reacting. Our "better educated classes" drink in an anti-democratic habit of feeling and thinking from the copious, and it must be confessed delicious, fountain of the literature of England; they give the same spirit to our own, in which we have little or nothing that is truly democratic and American. Hence this tone of sentiment of our literary institutions and of our learned professions, poisoning at the spring the young mind of our people.

If the *United States Magazine and Democratic Review* shall be able, by the influence of example and *the most liberal* encouragement, to contribute in any degree towards the remedy of this evil, as of the other evils in our institutions which may need reform, by vindicating the true glory and greatness of the democratic principle, by infusing it into our literature, and by rallying the mind of the nation from the state of torpor and even of demoralization in which so large a proportion of it is sunk, one of the main objects of its establishment will have been achieved.

3

CHARLES STEWART DAVEIS

POPULAR GOVERNMENT[1]

THE IDEA of some fair-spread region of this description, far over the sea, presented itself in dreams by day to the philanthropist of the old world, to console him for the darkness of ages that had clouded down upon the auspicious dawn of Christianity: where law should be level with liberty, and authority tempered with equity, and government administered with purity, simplicity, and economy!

These were problems for which no satisfactory solution had been found. Society had suffered from too much regulation. Nature had not been trusted enough to her own sagacity. Education had not been raised to its proper height nor expanded to its true power. The principles of natural and universal law were pressed down by feudal and ecclesiastical institutions. These were enigmas which Europe could not explain. The rights of mankind had there been defrauded. The hopes of humanity had there been frustrated. No fruition had been found for the finest aspirations of philanthropy, no consummation of the fairest results of philosophy. Nothing was comparatively realized from the long teachings of example and experience. No permanent progress appeared to have been made in the general career of social improvement. No effectual barrier seemed to be raised against the calamitous recurrence of another furious inroad from a barbarian cast of population, distinguished by no complexional variety, such as the teeming north was ever ready to pour down upon the spreading bounds of civilization, like trade-winds towards a region continually rarefied by the sun, from a source of which the elements are never exhausted, overwhelming the establishments of society like a tornado, burying the monuments of art and genius and blackening the horizon with smoke and ashes, like some terrific eruption of a volcano such as has covered cities under the crust of ages, alternately tormenting

[1] [From Charles Stewart Daveis, *An Address Delivered on the Commemoration at Fryeburg, May 19, 1825* (Portland, Me., 1825), pp. 34–64 — Abridged.]

the world with a vain desire to recover the past and irritating the pride of science by the astonishing revelation of what was before supposed to be new.

[THE AMERICAN EXPERIMENT]

If there was no sure defense from assault and invasion without, neither was there any security against corruption of the principles of society within. In government, it is very true, there was little to be corrupted; and when a combined movement was made to establish in England what Hampden and Pym were about embarking to enjoy, with Cromwell, in America, its promoters could neither find competent security for their own virtue, nor set up any adequate bar against the reaction of arbitrary power. The proper time therefore appeared to have arrived for making a new experiment; the most interesting and important, unquestionably, in all its circumstances and relations, that the world ever witnessed. A new scion was to be sent forth and inoculated into a strange stock. Fresh blood was to be taken from some of the purest arteries in Europe and poured into the veins of a young society, begotten, as it may be said, in the old age of the world. "I like," says Bacon, "a plantation in a pure soil; that is, where people are not displanted, to the end to plant in others; else it is rather an extirpation, than a plantation." In this new process a favored race may appear to have been selected; like that which was chosen in the second stage of the world to restore its primary condition, this to be the repository of the true principles of liberty, as *that* was of the pure elements of religion, and before which the native population was destined to recede and give space, by the operation of natural causes, without precipitate results, and without inspiring any apprehension of its reappearance to embarrass the execution of the project.

The geography of America has been pronounced by one who has investigated the philosophical connection between natural and political causes favorable to freedom. But it cannot be said that the continent was discovered or colonization commenced in any deliberate design to establish its principles. The great magnetic point did not so soon acquire its true polarity. An ulterior object of the voyage gave to the first discovery the name of West Indies. The colonies were bred and treated like silkworms, whose industry is not for themselves.

They were sent to cultivate the sugar cane and tobacco leaf and in due time doomed to prepare the cotton plant for the market of their taskmasters. America was held as an appurtenance to Europe, and her arrangements were all projected on the same model of colonial monopoly as the East-India, Hudson Bay, and North-West Companies. But, by some interesting filiation, "there's a Divinity, that shapes our ends."

The colonial condition is now acknowledged to be the chrysalis of independence. The only El Dorado is to be discovered in the simplest form of government. To the visionary pursuit of gold the world may be indebted for the science of liberty as well as chemistry, and free institutions may be said to have been found in following the fur trade and the fisheries.

The free and glorious spirit that has gone abroad throughout the country may well invite to a refreshing memorial of all the causes to which we owe this national feeling. The true genius of our institutions invites, at all seasons, a constant recurrence to their first principles. To judge of the progress which these principles have made we need only cast our eyes back a century or two, to contemplate those abuses of them from which our ancestors fled, and contrast them against the first results of those free institutions which they founded.

It is true that a natural solicitude concerning the great experiment weighed upon the first founders of our free government, and its lively cornerstones were not laid without many prayers and supplications. The experience of the period subsequent to the revolution, when the pressure of peril was relieved and the danger of subjugation determined, did not leave an entirely satisfactory impression on their minds. The *dii minorum gentium*, the gods of the smaller states, were averse to a predominating power to be exercised over local pride and ambition on behalf of the whole people of the union, and the apprehension of disorder to result from the imperfection of its bond arose coeval with the first form in which it was organized. The portentous fact, moreover, was presented to them by the faithful hand of history, that pure democracy had always failed, in some degree, of sufficient virtue to preserve its principles from corruption. Hence the morning, noon, and evening song of 1788 was anarchy — the danger of anarchy, rather than despotism.

[THE CONSTITUTION]

That there may not have been, in advance, an absolute confidence accorded to the essential principles of republican government, demanded upon so broad a scale, that there might have been some doubt concerning their efficacy for self-preservation, that some scepticism may have been originally entertained relating to the combination of sufficient virtue with the intelligence of the community to secure its own political existence and vindicate at once its liberty and justice may not be deemed altogether incredible. It is not unnatural to suppose that apprehensions of this kind should have forced or infused themselves into some of the fairest minds and purest spirits in the country. If they fastened themselves, for a while, upon a portion of the virtuous and patriotic, if they seized upon the vigorous authors of our constitutional commentary, let the remembrance rise before the nation of the sacrifice that was offered to redeem its faith and discharge the debt of the Revolution, of the zeal that was devoted to rear the fabric of the Federation, and the labors that were exhausted to organize the resources of the Union, and how they were straitened until it was accomplished, and let the prayer come up before the country that was uttered over the hearse of him, the earliest, the only one of that illustrious number whom it mourns, "pardon that single error in a life devoted to your service!"

. . . .

The original apprehension inspired concerning the Constitution undoubtedly was not that it was not strong enough for the purpose of power, but that it was not powerful enough for the purpose of liberty. Time at least was wanting to establish its principles. Hence, meanwhile, its friends inclined to take bonds of fate. But it is vain to seek in the positive structure of society for those securities which must depend in the main upon its spirit. Who shall take care of the keepers? What shall we do with the fire when it seizes the extinguishers? Where shall the powers of art be applied when the springs of nature cease to play? The spirit of a people cannot be perfectly enshrined in the specific form of a constitution. The success of any system must depend forever upon the healthy action of its natural principles.

In a great country which enjoys a freedom like our own, it is plain that the simplest institutions for concentrating the ideas and exerting the energies of the whole community are the most suitable. The principles of society themselves, in the first place, lie at the foundation, and give efficacy to the operative principles of government. There is much truth, if not originality, in the reflection of a fine and liberal mind that what we are accustomed to regard as political order is in a great measure the result of the passions and wants of man combined with the circumstances of his condition; or what is in other words the wisdom of nature; all acting in such beautiful subserviency to her suggestions as to raise the idea of original arrangement. The natural tendency that exists in every society which in consequence of the general spirit of its government enjoys the blessings of tranquillity and liberty is so strong as to overcome many powerful obstacles which the imperfection of human institutions opposes to its progress. The greater portion of political disorders do not proceed from the want of foresight in the framers of political constitutions, rendering their prospective provisions too general, so much as from not paying sufficient regard to the operations of those simple institutions which nature and justice recommend. The superiority of political wisdom consists not in encumbering the machine of government with new contrivances to obviate partial and accidental inconveniences, but in gradually and silently removing the obstacles which disturb the order of nature, and, according to the expression of Addison, "ingrafting upon her institutions." There is, moreover, an intrinsic principle of health, a *vis medicatrix*, in the social system, and especially in the political, like the human, when the general constitution is sound; the virtue of which we may be apt to ascribe to artificial causes when it frequently serves to disguise and correct their ill effects. To these just and liberal considerations may be added reflections arising from the character of our Federal system,—namely, the powerful influence of a gravitating principle to bind and preserve its members in their spheres; and the silent, sublime, celestial mechanism which serves to remedy any irregularity of their planetary motions.

[THE RECONCILIATION OF AUTHORITY AND LIBERTY]

We have entered upon a sober experiment how far the simple moral principles of society are competent for their own political preservation; and the problem is yet to be solved how far the expedient is practicable for reconciling authority with liberty. The extraordinary idea that a whole people is not competent to the office of self-government goes to the root of our system. Popular power is the basis of all our institutions; and the general weal is managed by a simple organization of the sense and reason of the community, manifesting its general will. The notion that a people has not the faculty of self-control is a solecism. It would argue a defect in the moral constitution of mankind, if it did not amount to an impeachment of the wisdom of Providence. It would seem to show that man was unfit to be the subject of moral government, and serve to show the absurdity of all government. It would be matter of singular reflection upon the state of political society if the wisdom of the whole should prove less competent to its management than the wisdom of part.

By giving to public opinion an absolute and audible representation and by placing a more responsible and emphatic reliance upon the presiding sense of the community, by giving that scope and activity to its instincts and operations which are derived from free institutions alone, by bringing home to the business and bosoms of society the immediate consequences of its determinations or causing them to be felt in their remotest bearings, that sense is quickened, corrected, cultivated, disciplined, caution and prudence are inspired, and all its faculties summoned in vindication of its principles. No system possesses such self-repairing resources; none is so little liable to explosion, as one where the safety-valves are always open.

As a fact, in the first instance, that nothing can resist the real power of the people, as the faith of the whole community that nothing ought to be above it, as a point settled equally in the theory and history of our system, it is the part of wisdom to improve and of patriotism to vindicate the principle. Such a circumstance in our condition is not merely to be tolerated as an unavoidable evil. It is to be cherished as a positive good; and the absolute irregularity of its action is entitled to be treated as "the progress of a generous and powerful principle to perfection."

The prevalence of an opposite idea, at whatever period or under whatever circumstances it may predominate, is simply sapping the foundation of our free system which rests on public sentiment solely. Its perdition can, in any event, only come from the abandonment of its principles; and the destruction of the popular faith in them is but an ill omen of their justification. Patriotism is never allowed to despair of the commonwealth. To redeem the true principle of self-government, therefore, from misapprehension and perversion, to rescue it from corruption and reproach, to drag up its drowning honor at any extremity and restore it to its central position, like the heart of the human, or the grand refulgent orb of the solar system, these are ends which it can be no inconsistency to compass, no imputation to imagine. It is worthy of the highest and the purest patriotism to break the spell which may bind such a belief, to dispel the phantom and chase it like a cloud from the mind, and dissipate a delusion so ominous and prejudicial to the public welfare. The purity of testimony given to such a truth there can be no cause to question. The tribute cannot be too ample and unequivocal, and whatever triumph attend it we may hail without regret. For whatever objections may lie against our system, who would ever abandon it? With all its evils, who would discard it for any other form of human authority founded on the admission of any principle at war with the equal rights and liberty of mankind?

[POPULAR GOVERNMENT AND PUBLIC OPINION]

While the theory of popular government undoubtedly presumes the prevailing rectitude of public sentiment, it makes no presumption of which the force is not now universally acknowledged, either in the general reference to its authority or the direct appeal to its arbitrament. It moreover makes no requisition other than what is founded on confidence in the principle and faith in the progress of reason and only demands that those whose voice must be heard on every measure should have a hand in its control. It does not assume that papal infallibility from which its protestant principle has revolted. It challenges no implicit faith, for it exposes everything to examination. It does not imply that the will of any proportion of the community, however transcendent, is paramount to that invariable restriction which principle imposes on power. It does not, of course, confound every light and transient shadow that flies over the landscape, the mere ephemeral indications of passing events, with the solid rocks that have been placed from eternity and the permanent landmarks that have been established by experience. Means are provided for rectifying its results and poising the passions in order to suspend the judgment of the public. The sense of the community must have time to settle; and mankind may repose upon its own judgment after some period has elapsed. The united wisdom of one age, in this respect, bears some ratio to the collected wisdom of several. Neither does the supposition require the sacrifice of independence in regard to any subject on which public opinion is yet to be formed or is capable of being improved or even changed. It requires no compromise of belief, except upon the ground of conviction; for no man has a right to renounce any point of which he is honestly persuaded. The right of appeal is always open, and the public ear is also. The idea requires no impracticable harmony of discordant elements, produces no restraint upon the most wholesome freedom of difference and opposition. It is a principle that disturbs no manly breast. It need work no abatement of an honest zeal to guide and influence public opinion upon important subjects. On the contrary, there is an encouragement and a consolation of the highest description at once afforded by the reliance which may be placed upon its polarity, and the highest inducement is thus held out to aim to improve a standard to the test of which all things must be brought and all subjects submitted. The result of this experiment upon its largest scale, thus far, warrants no just ground of concern respecting the prevalence of truth. It need inspire no fear for honest fame, nor reasonable apprehension in respect to correct estimate of patriotic service. The experience of this whole society does not yet create any painful solicitude in regard to the pursuit and discovery of a more practicable and unerring sanction.

Experience has certainly shown no sufficient reason to question the general aptitude of the People for self-government. When we observe the capacity discovered by the members of society in all their concerns, sagacity entering into all subjects, extending to all relations, and equal to all occasions, carried also into duties of administering its authority; and when we observe them indiscriminately executing or aiding in all its departments, civil and judicial, as jurors, magistrates, legislators, governors, acting as trustees of all the interests of the community for the benefit of the public and as guardians of all those rights for which law was designed as security, taken continually from all classes and returning to the general mass by the perpetual elective process, can we any longer doubt the efficacy of this great principle which is thus receiving constant refreshment and vigor from its original fountains?

[THE EDUCATION OF THE SOVEREIGN PEOPLE]

But popular power, it is to be remembered, is moral power; and it is of the utmost consequence that its intellectual principle should be well informed. The safety of a state was represented by a sensible scholar of the 16th century to depend mainly on three things: upon the proper education of the Prince, upon public teachers, and on schoolmasters. The prime object in any government is undoubtedly the education of the sovereign. In England, it was not long since an object of general concern to provide for the education of a young princess. In proportion as the power vested in the sovereign becomes absolute, the pursuit acquires importance.

With a view to improve the principles of self-government in a state of society that subjects everything to its sense, in a country where the whole sovereignty is lodged in the people and all authority is exercised upon the strictest responsibility to the end of its universal welfare, *the education of the whole becomes the first interest of all.* The diffusion of knowledge becomes, therefore, the distribution of power. Where authority is appropriated for other purposes than the general good under any partial organization, a part is studiously educated for the government of the rest, who are deliberately left in ignorance to support the fundamental principles of the government. The proper system of republican education should *combine* the regular course of useful elementary instruction with that species of education which naturally "results from the political order of society." In this manner the moral education of *the prince*, if I may use the expression, becomes of the first importance, and it is a happy circumstance that there is always a generation of young and fair minds springing up among the people, free from any false impressions, in proper season to assume the real reins of power and exemplify the true principles and influence of education.

It must be obvious that to urge the general interest of education can be influenced by no narrow motive. It can have no insidious purpose. It pleads the cause of no party, it advocates no profession, is propitious to no predominance. It urges one of the most important interests of society. It argues on behalf of its order and comfort, its present and future good; and opens the most ample field to its fairest claims and prospects. Its cause involves the purest objects of benevolence; its concern affects the highest aspirations of virtue and piety;

and its interest touches some of the noblest and tenderest springs of our nature: the affection of the parent for his children; the zeal of the patriot for his country; the ardor of the philanthropist for his kind. With its success is identified almost every rational hope of the future welfare of our race, extending to the suppression of the most fruitful causes of vice and misery, and embracing the widest spread of peace and happiness beneath the cope of heaven.

. . . .

[POLITICAL PARTIES AND REPUBLICAN JUSTICE]

Moral power rests upon the only sure and solid basis of right and justice. Under a political dispensation where the responsibility falls, without relief, upon the people, if the dictates of eternal justice are violated, the consequences of retributive justice may be assured to follow. Justice is one of the first duties of a republic; it is the corner stone of the Temple of Liberty; and it is a virtue, not among the least, exposed to violation. Aristides was banished by a republic, from jealousy of the very name; and its ancient policy was undoubtedly apt to nourish a spirit pernicious to the principle.

Party may unquestionably be salutary, if its end be public and its spirit patriotic; since more may be accomplished by combined, systematic exertions, than can be effected by irregular and distracted efforts. But the greatest good, it is equally obvious, can only be attained by the united and hearty exertion of the whole mass of the community. Party, in such a point of view, may be regarded as a simple expedient for mutilating the state of a measure of its force; for paralyzing one side of its power, depriving the country of a portion of its effective strength for the promotion of its great objects. There were always, it is said, two parties in Carthage, one for peace and the other for war; the consequence was that Carthage never enjoyed the full advantage of peace or war. Certain prejudices are represented to prevail in more early periods of society which are supposed to be beneficial to its welfare, but which gradually lose their influence and would probably disappear entirely if it were not found convenient to prolong their existence as a source of authority over the multitude. The virtue of the people is undoubtedly proved in supporting parties so long as they are salutary and in suppressing them whenever they are nuisances, in cherishing them while they are founded and conducted on principle, and in ceasing to sustain them when their differences are extinguished, or their forms are only preserved for selfish or factious purposes. The Constitution, it is evident, was not designed to systematize a perpetual organization of parties.

It is true that the history of parties in this country is coeval with the origin and connected with the progress of our political institutions. And while they have even left their footprints upon the foundations and impressed their relief upon the strong features of the Federal structure, they have at the same time been mild in their type and complexion beyond all recorded example. Ancient or modern history affords no comparison. They are stained by no marks of blood or violence; they revive the memory of no proscriptions nor massacres; nor can they be deliberately accused of using their predominance with positive cruelty or oppression. The moral character of our population has moderated the natural consequences of civil dissension. If parties may not be permitted to make pretension to generosity, they may properly be allowed to appeal to the unquestionable proofs of their purity; and while they point to the lofty and durable monuments of their patriotism, justly plead the influence of extraordinary causes in vindication against any erroneous imputations. By the theory of our government long ago pronounced, the people themselves are of no party. And it is quite true that some of our most national institutions are the work of "joint counsels and confederate patriotism."

The most eloquent spirit of the age is justice. That spirit is strongly opposed to all political orders, privileges, and dominations. It is distinguished by an aversion to despotism under every form and to monopoly in every shape, from the most simple and obvious example of those systems in Europe, to a virtual establishment under any popular designation in America. An open persuasion prevails abroad of the impolicy of seeking to secure any measure of public good apart from the whole of the people, of raising any exclusive advantage upon the depression of any general concern of the community, or even pushing a legitimate interest at disproportionate expense or sacrifice. An invincible repugnance exists in the breast of the nation against cherishing any project incompatible with the designs of the compact or any sentiment inconsistent with the principles of the Union. All the true interests of society stand on the same footing, in perfect consistency with each other, and in uinson with the greatest product of general prosperity. Hence an augmented appreciation of the value of our common patrimony, and an increasing opinion of the essential injury of suffering the inheritance to be engrossed or of permitting any portion of society to make use of its forms against its spirit. Hence the deliberate judgment of the community against any unwarrantable appropriation of the blessings of social order, or of setting apart any portion from the general mass of honor and happiness belonging to the community, instead of opening the career of public service to an useful and generous strife of competition and emulation and spreading out the highest and most animating inducements. Let there be added a deep reprobation of the gross injustice of all odious political imputation, repugnant to the innate principles of moral rectitude and revolting to the most virtuous feelings of mankind. *Think you those, upon whom the Tower of Siloam fell, — or those, whose blood Pilate mingled in their sacrifices — were sinners above all the Galileans?* Again add a stern, indignant rebuke of all attempts to affect the fame of national benefactors, disturbing the heaps which affection has raised over their remains or defacing the monuments which gratitude has erected to their memory; opening the wounds which the hand of time has gently healed, desecrating the virtues it has cherished, or violating its benevolent amnesty and oblivion. In opposition to all such unhallowed purposes and passions, a different spirit, tolerant, liberal, catholic, has prevailed. Our republican system might indeed be deemed to have failed most ominously in the outset if it had proved incapable of subduing the morbid remains of a malignant spirit. And this triumphant vindication of its moral sense is reviving to a rational confidence in its fundamental principles.

[PUBLIC OPINION AND PEACEFUL CHANGE]

We are warranted to repose upon the wholesome operation of public opinion. Its progressive influence appears like vegetation upon the surface after it has been working and striking its shoots deep into the soil. Its seeds exist in the ground long before its productions are sent forth. It commences in the primary and internal principles of society, proceeding silently, ascending steadily up, invigorating the stock and entering with life into the branches. A change of this description exists in fact before it is announced. Its light advances like the day which first begins to illumine the highest tops until it warms and fertilizes the earth and calls forth all its powers and luxuriance. Its influence is disseminated through the great mass of public sentiment until it thoroughly pervades the whole body of the community. Its changes often anticipate the sagacity of political wisdom; they grow out of each other, in some manner, like the seasons; and when we cannot divine their sources, we may still distinguish their sounds. Too mighty to be attributed to the mere prophetic chants by which they may be preluded, their auguries may be discerned in the most angry aspect of the elements; the bow is bent in the clouds, and the pause, the peace, that follow have all the serene and potent influence of a charm.

Within the experience of this nation, three revolutions have already occurred: the first political, the second civil, and the third moral, the last embracing whatever was salutary and valuable in the two former. The evidence of this last auspicious change, which has been proclaimed by the most distinguished organs of the community, is fresh in the abatement of political strife and the improvement of public feeling, and in the universal direction of public spirit to public objects. It is proclaimed in popular assemblies, in public bodies, in the national legislature, where no addresses are regarded except those which concern the interest of the community, in its general determination against the importance of any other securities than those that are required for the public good, or of maintaining any political ascendancy paramount to the supreme constitutional law. It is proclaimed in the broad appeal, on the recent national occasion, to general considerations — in the harmonious and patriotic character of the result. It is proclaimed in the tone of society, in the peace and the order of the community, in the prosperity of the nation.

[THE MISSION OF AMERICA]

America is always alive to the obligations of justice. Its feeling has been freshly redeemed towards a foreigner.[2] It has been fulfilled in relation to the father of his country. Shall it not be vindicated against every reproach? . . . .

While we felicitate ourselves on the faculty of self-government and on the power which the country possesses to do justice to its bene-factors, let the country likewise be just to itself. There is no power

[2] [Lafayette]

to which a people is not competent that is really requisite for its welfare. There is at least no faculty which a nation does not possess to promote its own prosperity consistent with the principles of public law and eternal justice. There is no form which so fully develops the dignity of human nature as the democratic. There is no system which so soon brings home its sanctions, none which requires so complete a prostration of all partial objects, so entire a devotion to its radical principles in order to bring out its essential perfections.

In the posture that we are placed as the mother republic, in the circumstances under which we are placed in the present condition of mankind, in the circumstances under which we are placed in relation to ourselves, a duty is demanded of us, demanding all our efforts to accomplish, and which can only be discharged by the most rigid and faithful regard to the fundamental principles of our association. Be it ours then to send a searching spirit into these circumstances and consult those lively oracles of nature which accord us at the same time the most profound suggestions of political wisdom. We have great interests to be consulted with which those of the world as it now stands and of generations to arise are linked. We have connections with Europe, where we have long carried on an advantageous commerce, sending out our staples and principles and importing their fabrics and letters. We have relation to all times; and as we proceed to manipulate our own intellectual and economical products, we have an increasing character to sustain and a higher cast, not to be forfeited.

We are all pursuing the same great ends, and intellect is darting its vivifying rays into every subject. We are commanded well and wisely to consider our own situation, to consider our condition as its own greatest innovator, to keep a steady eye to the true ends of our political existence, and while we accompany antiquity to extend the spirit of improvement also to the foot of the very altar. We are to hold nothing as sacred but the true interests of society and those institutions the usefulness of which has been established to human happiness or attested by the consecrating sanctions of religion, and resort to the sacred repository of religion itself not for the dark and portentous arcana of state policy but for those transcendent sanctions which it supplies to establish those obligations which form the basis of all order. As it regards the rest, let the rule, and the only rule, be how to attain the highest possible good and obviate the utmost avoidable evil. Over the porch by which we enter the temple of our national liberty, over the avenues which lead to all its spacious apartments, over the ever open hall of legislation as well as the adjacent chambers of juris- prudence, let the fearless inscription meet the eye:

> Be bold! Be bold! And everywhere, BE BOLD!
> BE NOT TOO BOLD!

Let it become an important object to raise the tone of public senti- ment and elevate the dignity of democratic institutions, improve the rule of social duty and exalt the scale of national excellence. Let us clear the great streams of national prosperity. Let no faculty be denied to the government which is granted by the Constitution; let it be left to be used with discretion, regulated by responsibility. Let it likewise be felt that some inference arises in favor of a power which is attested by an important public benefit. While it will not be for- gotten that, in order to guard their own rights against infraction, the people have invested their public agents with only limited faculties to promote the great ends of government, a conclusion resulting from their long and universal approbation of an actual authority should not be unregarded. And again, if a great national concern which has been generally provided for in our constitutional scheme acquires a new importance in the progress of public economy, or a new region itself arise beneath the broad canopy of the Union with interests for which it had no original opportunity to stipulate, are we at liberty to attribute a prophetic spirit to those general provisions which respect the public welfare and to regard the system itself as expanding with the exigencies of the Union? Shall an austere rule rebuke the true spirit of patriotic policy, uncontrolled by a commanding obligation to supply any chasm which was not contemplated in the Constitution? Shall we still "rock the grown man in the cradle of the infant?"

. . . .

We profess not to have arrived at maturity. To test the truth of *our* principles, *we are obliged* to go forward, to anticipate the progress of time and the operation of their causes on futurity. To test the truth of our principles, *let us go forward!* Let us advance the space of a single century, when, if we are true to our principles and those that shall come after us shall prove true to our examples, we shall have redeemed ourselves from the reproach of living in and for posterity!

Let us be just then to our posterity as well as to ourselves. . . . Let us array before us, or rather array ourselves before, those who shall come after us. Come then, ye future ages of America! spirits that are yet to be, those that may occupy this spot when this period returns! Sit in judgment on the present generation; call us to account for our privileges and demand of us to discharge our trust! And let the voice of those that have gone before us and led the forlorn hope of our national existence rise in our ears and press on our hearts. By the blood shed for our deliverance, by the tears with which our freedom was baptized, by the agony of patriotism in the strife for independence, by the glorious and imperishable cause in which we are all concerned, be just to yourselves, be true to your principles, be faithful to posterity!

4

JAMES FENIMORE COOPER

ON REPRESENTATION[1]

AFTER QUITTING the poll, we familiarly discussed the merits
and demerits of this system of popular elections. In order
to extract the opinions of my friend, several of the more
obvious and ordinary objections were started with a freedom that
induced him to speak with some seriousness.

"You see a thousand dangers in universal suffrage," he said, "merely
because you have been taught to think so, without ever having seen
the experiment tried. The Austrian would be very apt to say, under
the influence of mere speculation too, that it would be fatal to government to have any representation at all; and a vizier of the Grand Turk
might find the mild exercise of the laws, which is certainly practised
in Austria proper, altogether fatal to good order. Now we know, not
from the practice of fifty years only, but from the practice of two
centuries, that it is very possible to have both order and prosperity
under a form of government which admits of the utmost extension of
the suffrage. It is a never-failing argument on these subjects that
American order is owing to the morality of a simple condition of life,
and that our prosperity is incidental to our particular geographical
situation. There are many good men, and in other respects wise men,
even among ourselves, who retain so much of the political theory
which pervades the literature of our language as to believe the same
thing. For myself I cannot see the truth of either of these positions.
Our prosperity is owing to our intelligence, and our intelligence to
our institutions. Every discreet man in America is deeply impressed
with the importance of diffusing instruction among our people, just
as many very well-meaning persons in your hemisphere honestly
enough entertain a singular horror of the danger of school books.
Thus it is our natural means of safety to do the very thing which
must, of necessity, have the greatest possible influence on the happiness,
civilization, and power of a nation.

[1] [*Notions of the Americans Picked Up by a Traveling Bachelor* (Philadelphia, 1828),
I, 263-71 — Text complete.]

"There can be no doubt that, under a bald theory, a representation would be all the better if the most ignorant, profligate, and vagabond part of the community were excluded from the right of voting. It is just as true that if all the rogues and corrupt politicians, even including those who read Latin and have well-lined pockets, could be refused the right of voting, honest men would fare all the better. But as it is very well known that the latter are not, nor cannot well be excluded from the right of suffrage anywhere except in a despotism, we have come to the conclusion that it is scarcely worth while to do so much violence to natural justice, without sufficient reason, as to disfranchise a man merely because he is poor. Though a trifling *qualification* of property may sometimes be useful in particular conditions of society, there can be no greater fallacy than its *representation*. The most vehement declaimers in favor of the justice of the representation of property overlook two or three very important points of the argument. A man may be a voluntary associate in a joint-stock company and justly have a right to a participation in its management in proportion to his pecuniary interest, but life is not a chartered institution. Men are born with all their wants and passions, their means of enjoyment, and their sources of misery, without any agency of their own, and frequently to their great discomfort. Now, though government is, beyond a doubt, a sort of compact, it would seem that those who prescribe its conditions are under a natural obligation to consult the rights of the whole. If men, when a little better than common, were anything like perfect, we might hope to see power lodged with safety in the hands of a reasonable portion of the enlightened without any danger of its abuse. But the experience of the world goes to prove that there is a tendency to monopoly wherever power is reposed in the hands of a minority. Nothing is more likely to be true than that twenty wise men will unite in opinions in opposition to a hundred fools; but nothing is more certain than that, if placed in situations to control all the interests of their less gifted neighbors, the chance is that fifteen or sixteen of them would pervert their philosophy to selfishness. This was at least our political creed, and we therefore admitted a vast majority of the community to a right of voting. Since the hour of the Revolution, the habits, opinions, laws, and I may say principles of the Americans are getting daily to be more democratic. We are perfectly aware that, while the votes of a few thousand scattered individuals can make no great or lasting impression on the prosperity or policy of the country, their disaffection at being excluded might give a great deal of trouble. I do not mean to say that the suffrage may not, in most countries, be extended too far. I only wish to show you that it is not here.

"The theory of representation of property says that the man who has little shall not dispose of the money of him who has more. Now, what say experience and common sense? It is the man who has *much* that is prodigal of the public purse. A sum that is trifling in his account may constitute the substance of one who is poorer. Beyond all doubt the government of the world which is most reckless of the public money is that in which power is the exclusive property of the very rich; and beyond all doubt the government of the world which, compared with its means, is infinitely the most sparing of its resources is that in which they who enact the laws are compelled to consult the wishes of those who have the least to bestow. It is idle to say that an enlarged and liberal policy governs the measures of the one and that the other is renowned for a narrowness which has lessened its influence and circumscribed its prosperity. I know not, nor care not, what men who are dazzled with the glitter of things may choose to say, but I am thoroughly convinced, from observation, that, if the advice of those who were influenced by what is called a liberal policy had been followed in our country, we should have been a poorer and consequently a less important and less happy people than at present. The relations between political liberality and what is called political prodigality are wonderfully intimate.

"We find that our government is cheaper and even stronger for being popular. There is no doubt that the jealousy of those who have little often induces a false economy, and that money might frequently be saved by bidding higher for talent. We lay no claims to perfection, but we do say that more good is attained in this manner than in any other which is practised elsewhere. We look at the aggregate of advantage, and neither our calculations nor our hopes have as yet been greatly deceived.

"As to the forms of our elections, you see that they are beyond example simple and orderly. After an experience of near forty years, I can say that I have never seen a blow struck nor any other violent proceeding at a poll. These things certainly do happen but, in comparison with the opportunities, at remarkably long intervals. So far from the frequency of elections tending to disturb society, they produce an exactly different effect. A contest which is so soon to be repeated loses half its interest by familiarity. Vast numbers of electors are content to be lookers-on, rarely approaching a poll except to vote on some question of peculiar concern. The struggle is generally whether A or B shall enjoy the temporary honor or the trifling emolument in dispute, the community seldom being much the better or the worse for the choice. People talk of the fluctuations which are necessarily the consequences of a popular government. They do not understand what they say. Every other enlightened nation of the earth is at this moment divided between great opposing principles; whereas here, if we except the trifling collisions of pecuniary interests, everybody is of the same mind except as to the ordinary immaterial question of a choice between men. We have settled all the formidable points of policy by conceding everything that any reasonable man can ask. The only danger which exists to the duration of our confederacy (and that is not a question of a form of government, but one of mere policy) proceeds from the little that is aristocratical in our Union. The concentrated power of a State may become, like the overgrown power of an individual, dangerous to our harmony; though we think, and with very good reason, that, on the whole, even this peculiarity adds to the durability of the Union.

"It is unnecessary to say that so far as mere convenience goes this method of election can be practised by a hundred millions of people as easily as by twelve. As to corruption, comparatively speaking, it cannot exist. No man can buy a state, a county, or even a town. In a hotly contested election it is certainly sometimes practicable to influence votes enough to turn the scale; but, unless the question involve the peculiar interests of the less fortunate class of society, it is clear both parties can bribe alike, and then the evil corrects itself. If the question be one likely to unite the interests and the prejudices of the humbler classes, nine times in ten it is both more humane and wiser that they should prevail. That sort of splendid and treacherous policy which gives a fallacious luster to a nation by oppressing those who have the most need of support is manifestly as unwise as it is unjust. It violates the very principles of the compact, since governments are not formed to achieve but to protect. After a sufficient force has been obtained to effect the first great objects of the association, the governed, and not the governors, are the true agents in every act of national prosperity. Look at America. What people or what monarch, if you will, has done half so much as we have done, compared to our means, in the last half century, and precisely for the reason that the government is obliged to content itself with protection or, at the most, with that assistance which, in the nature of things, strictly requires a concentrated action.

"It is of far less importance, according to our notions, what the executive of a nation is called, than that all classes should have a direct influence on its policy. We have no king, it is true, for the word carries with it, to our ears, an idea of expenditure; but we have a head who, for the time being, has a very reasonable portion of power. We are not jealous of him, for we have taken good care he shall do no harm.

"Though we are glad to find that principles which we have practised and under which we have prospered so long are coming more in fashion in Europe, I think you must do us the justice to say that we are not a nation much addicted to the desire of proselyting. For ourselves we have no fears, and as for other people, if they make some faint imitations of our system and then felicitate themselves on their progress, we are well content they should have all the merit of inventors. That is a miserable rivalry which would make a monopoly of happiness. I think, as a people, we rather admire you most when we see you advancing with moderation to your object, than when we hear of the adoption of sudden and violent means. We have ever been reformers rather than revolutionists. Our own struggle for independence was not in its aspect a revolution. We contrived to give it all the dignity of a war from the first blow. Although our generals and soldiers might not have been so well trained as those they fought against, they were far more humane, considerate, and, in the end, successful than their adversaries. Our own progress has been gradual. It is not long since a trifling restriction existed on the suffrage of this very State. Experience proved that it excluded quite as many discreet men as its removal would admit of vagabonds. Now it is the distinguishing feature of our policy that we consider man a reasonable being, and that we rather court than avoid the struggle between ignorance and intelligence. We find that this policy rarely fails to assure the victory of the latter while it keeps down its baneful monopolies. We extended the suffrage to include everybody, and, while complaint is removed, we find no difference in the representation. As yet it is rather an improvement. Should it become an evil, however, we shall find easy and moderate means to change it, since we are certain that a majority will be sufficiently sagacious to know their own interests. You have only to convince us that it is the best government, and we will become an absolute monarchy tomorrow. It is wonderful how prone we are to adopt that which expectation induces us to think will be expedient and to reject that which experience teaches us is bad. It must be confessed that, so far, all our experiments have been in favor of democracy. I very well know that you in Europe prophesy that our career will end in monarchy. To be candid, your prophecies excite but little feeling here, since we have taken up the opinion you don't very well understand the subject. But should it prove true, *a la bonne heure;* when we find that form of government best, depend on it, we shall not hesitate to adopt it. You are at perfect liberty, if you will, to establish a journal in favor of despotism under the windows of the Capitol. I will not promise you much patronage at first, neither do I think you will be troubled with much serious opposition. At all events there is nothing in the law to molest the speculation. Now look behind you at the 'poll' we have just left; reflect on this fact, and then draw your conclusions of our own opinion of the stability of our institutions. We may deceive ourselves, but you of Europe must exhibit a far more accurate knowledge of the state of our country before we shall rely on your crude prognostics rather than on our own experience."

I could scarcely assure myself that Cadwallader was not laughing at me during a good deal of the time he was speaking, but, after all, it must be confessed there is some common sense in what he said. There were three or four other passengers in the stage, men of decent and sober exterior, among whom I detected certain interchanges of queer glances, though none of them appeared to think the subject of any very engrossing interest. Provoked at their unreasonable indifference to a theme so delightful as liberty, I asked one of them "If he did not apprehend there would be an end to the republic should General Jackson become the next President?" "I rather think not," was his deliberate, and somewhat laconic answer. "Why not? he is a soldier, and a man of ambition." My unmoved yeoman did not care to dispute either of these qualities, but he still persevered in thinking there was not much danger, since "he did not know anyone in his neighborhood who was much disposed to help a man in such an undertaking."

It is provoking to find a whole nation dwelling in this species of alarming security, for no other reason than that their vulgar and everyday practices teach them to rely on themselves instead of trusting to the rational inferences of philanthropic theorists, who have so long been racking their ingenuity to demonstrate that a condition of society which has delusively endured for nearly two hundred years, has been in existence all that time in direct opposition to the legitimate deductions of the science of government.

5

WILLIAM EMMONS

DEMOCRATIC REPUBLICANISM[1]

[LIBERTY AND LUXURY INCOMPATIBLE]

Let us avoid luxury as the greatest bane to liberty. Look back to such men as Cincinnatus, Hancock, Putnam, Adams, Jefferson, Madison, Monroe, Jackson, and that great champion of equal rights, Johnson, the hero and patriot of the west, whose whole life has been devoted to the cause of civil liberty. Come, then, fellow citizens, animate the strong and encourage the weak to march boldly on until their efforts are crowned with triumphant success. Recollect the times are sadly out of joint. Man has departed too far from his primitive state. . . . .

If ever a time existed in this country demanding the immediate action of the people, that time is the present. Oh, then, I conjure you by the love of liberty! by the value of true national glory! by the holy ashes of your fathers! by the love you bear toward the partners of your holy love! by the filial affection you owe your children, whose duty, yours it is, to point them to true happiness and Independence, to remember like causes produce like effects.

[NAVAL STRENGTH AND NATIONAL REPUTATION]

Fellow citizens, as it respects our foreign relations, our government is as much, if not more in repute, than at any former period in our history. Our flag is respected on every sea; the condition of our navy is superior to any other time since we were a nation; our improvements in shipbuilding are greater than any other nation; besides a powerful armament afloat, we have many noble ships of the line on the stocks that could, if occasion called, in a short time be placed on the bosom of the ocean to hurl their thunders on any power that dare cast a stain on our Star-spangled Banner; our naval officers generally are worthy

[1] [From *An Oration, commemorative of the Declaration of Independence, delivered Fourth of July, 1834, on Boston Common* (Boston, 1834) — Abridged.]

of the Government and entitled to the fullest confidence of the American people.   As to our seamen, no nation on earth can boast of such noble, generous souls as we can furnish, ever ready to pour forth their blood in defense of their country's honor. . . . .

. . . .

Yes, fellow citizens, it was reserved to Perry to display a brilliant superiority of American seamanship over our then haughty foe; after the conquest of Barckley, such was the ardor of Perry and his Yankee Tars that they formed themselves into a battalion and tendered their services to Col. Johnson at the ever memorable Battle of the Thames, which followed in proud succession, thus terminating in brilliancy our western campaign, covering with unfading laurels the names of Perry, Johnson, and McDonough, not forgetting the renowned mounted regiment of Kentucky Riflemen, and the brave tars who had the honor to receive *eight hundred stands of arms belonging to the British Army under General Proctor, who made his own escape by flight!*

[COLONEL RICHARD MENTOR JOHNSON, POPULAR HERO]

When we contemplate the fearful odds of forces in the memorable Battle of the Thames, on the 5th of October, 1813, the decided victory achieved by the mounted regiment, under the command of that statesman and warrior Colonel Johnson, over nearly three times his own number of well disciplined British regulars and Indian warriors, under the command of General Proctor and the celebrated Indian Chief Tecumseh, whose band alone consisted of more than one thousand five hundred; (this body of Indians were concealed in a swamp extending from the River Thames to the road). In order to bring on the battle without exposing the whole to the first fire of the Indians, the Colonel addressed his regiment as follows: Fellow soldiers, the hour has arrived to test our strength. I must draw the first fire from the enemy. Are there twenty that are willing to die for their country? if so, let them advance. At that moment the regiment, as one man, came forward. The Colonel applauded their ardor! As twenty was all he wanted, he selected Major Suggett and nineteen others and moved on to encounter Tecumseh and his band. As they advanced they received the fire of the savages, and nineteen of the twenty fell dead on the spot, leaving but one man and the Colonel to pursue the charge. At this moment the whole regiment followed their brave leader who had already received two balls in his person; but nothing daunted, he pressed on in the thickest of the battle, dealing death to all around, till he came in contact with the mighty chief Tecumseh who, at a distance of a few yards, raised his rifle and gave the Colonel another wound, the severest received during the battle. Tecumseh then moved on to dispatch him, with his tomahawk raised; when within a few feet, Colonel Johnson raised a pistol which he had kept concealed and discharged its contents, a ball and three buck shot, into his breast and laid him dead on the spot. Thus fell the greatest chief America ever had to contend with. His enmity was like Hannibal to the Romans; but before the unconquerable spirit of a Johnson he fell and with him fled the terror of the fight. Johnson was taken from the field bleeding and almost lifeless, in the arms of Perry, assisted by the present Secretary of War, the then General Cass, attended by Major Barry and other brave men from Kentucky, while his brother, Lt. Colonel James Johnson, continued the charge until victory was complete, leaving the field covered with dead and dying.

In due time Colonel Johnson was restored, although covered with scars received defending his country, and has for near thirty years served the people in the national councils, and for many years he combatted, *alone*, against fearful odds, on the importance of abolishing imprisonment for debt, until he carried his bill in triumph through the Senate! His efforts have been responded to in this, my native State, by a [Frederick] Robinson and other true sons of liberty, until the foul stain has been removed which so long continued at the expense of violating the chartered rights of man, and giving you additional cause, this day, to rejoice!

The next inroad on the people's liberties he found to attack was the unholy design formed by a party, under the name of Religion, for stopping the mail's running on a Sunday. The memorial was received by a committee raised, and Colonel Johnson was appointed Chairman, whose report on that occasion has not only been printed in *golden letters* but is also engraven on the hearts of his countrymen.[2] If we can judge from the signs of the times, a grateful people are about to reward him by the first office in their gift, thus giving another evidence that the American people are not *ungrateful*. We need not despair while such men as Woodbury, Benton, Cass, Johnson, Stevenson, and

[2][For the text of this justly praised report, see pages 274-281.]

a Forsayth are to be found to rally around our institutions and guard them against *constructive powers*. Well indeed, it is for us as a people that among all the various parties each can furnish talent of the first order, whose aim should be to watch and ferret out abuses in order to advance the general prosperity of the nation.

[TRIBUTE TO PRESIDENT JACKSON]

Fellow citizens, unless I turn traitor to the honest conviction of my own mind, I must publicly declare, even if I stand alone, *that I believe the President of the United States to be a persecuted man; at the same time acknowledge that he has rendered this nation more real benefit than any of his predecessors since the days of Washington.* Yes, and the glory and renown that will be awarded him in after-time — yea, and by those who now revile him — will endure and increase in splendor even when theirs will be as dust forgot. "Yea, like the baseless fabric of a vision, and leave not a wreck behind."

I have recently discovered a new coin which meets with a rapid sale in various parts of the city, inscribed "my experiment," of near one cent value, which brings from two to three cents each. The vendors of this coin may well boast of General Jackson's experiment, and well may they "go the whole hog!" and cry "down with the Bank." I have no doubt it is the reverence due the General for his *noble experiment* that has induced them to engrave his likeness on brass, which enhances the value of their coin. As to credit, honest men can obtain, and none others are entitled to receive it. Respecting commerce, look to the receipts of customs, or cast your eye on the ocean, and behold it whitened with canvas; displayed at their masts is the Stars and Stripes proudly unfurled to the breeze! Look, then, fellow citizens, to your *own* resources and you will find them abundant. Guard your own altars; call up the noble spirit of defense; look to your bulwark in the hour of danger. Remember that a well-regulated militia is the only sure panoply of defense in times of peril. See to it, then; let it fire your souls with the glorious spirit of your ancestors; awake the dormant, *suppressed opinions of your countrymen*, and organize anew the bulwark of your nation's glory and defense. Let it be so kept up as that *all classes* shall bear *equally* its burdens. We cannot expect to enjoy our republican institutions if we, as a people, divest ourselves of the means to perpetuate them.

If time permitted, I would point out the dark work that is now going on in Europe and satisfy all thinking and reasonable men that our own land is swarming with their emissaries, acting under the mandates of their imperial masters. Look, then, to your country; *teach your children for that country alone to live — for its defense to die!*

6

WILLIAM LEGGETT

DEMOCRATIC EDITORIALS

THE DIVISION OF PARTIES[1]

SINCE THE ORGANIZATION of the Government of the United States the people of this country have been divided into two great parties. One of these parties has undergone various changes of name; the other has continued steadfast alike to its appellation and to its principles and is now, as it was at first, the *Democracy*. Both parties have ever contended for the same opposite ends which originally caused the division, whatever may have been, at different times, the particular means which furnished the immediate subject of dispute. The great object of the struggles of the Democracy has been to confine the action of the General Government within the limits marked out in the Constitution; the great object of the party opposed to the Democracy has ever been to overleap those boundaries and give to the General Government greater powers and a wider field for their exercise. The doctrine of the one party is that all power not expressly and clearly delegated to the General Government remains with the States and with the people; the doctrine of the other party is that the vigor and efficacy of the General Government should be strengthened by a free construction of its powers. The one party sees danger from the encroachments of the General Government; the other affects to see danger from the encroachments of the States.

This original line of separation between the two great political parties of the Republic, though it existed under the old Confederation and was distinctly marked in the controversy which preceded the formation and adoption of the present Constitution, was greatly widened and strengthened by the project of a National Bank, brought forward in 1791. This was the first great question which occurred under the new Constitution to test whether the provisions of that instrument were to be interpreted according to their strict and literal

---

[1] [*New York Evening Post*, November 4, 1834 — Text complete.]

meaning; or whether they might be stretched to include objects and powers which had never been delegated to the General Government and which consequently still resided with the States as separate sovereignties.

The proposition of the Bank was recommended by the Secretary of the Treasury on the ground that such an institution would be "of primary importance to the prosperous administration of the finances, and of the greatest utility in the operations connected with the support of public credit." This scheme, then, as now, was opposed on various grounds; but the constitutional objection constituted then, as it does at the present day, the main reason of the uncompromising and invincible hostility of the Democracy to the measure. They considered it as the exercise of a very important power which had never been given by the States or the people to the General Government and which the General Government could not therefore exercise without being guilty of usurpation. Those who contended that the Government possessed the power effected their immediate object; but the controversy still exists. And it is of no consequence to tell the Democracy that it is now established by various precedents and by decisions of the Supreme Court that this power is fairly incidental to certain other powers expressly granted; for this is only telling them that the advocates of free construction have, at times, had the ascendancy in the Executive and Legislative and, at all times, in the Judiciary Department of the Government. The Bank question stands now on precisely the same footing that it originally did; it is now, as it was at first, a matter of controversy between the two great parties of this country, between parties as opposite as day and night, between parties which contend, one for the consolidation and enlargement of the powers of the General Government, and the other for strictly limiting that Government to the objects for which it was instituted and to the exercise of the means with which it was entrusted. The one party is for a popular government; the other for an aristocracy. The one party is composed, in a great measure, of the farmers, mechanics, laborers, and other producers of the middling and lower classes, according to the common gradation by the scale of wealth, and the other of the consumers, the rich, the proud, the privileged, of those who, if our Government were converted into an aristocracy, would become our dukes, lords, marquises, and baronets. The question is still disputed between these two parties; it is ever a new question; and whether the democracy or the aristocracy shall succeed in the present struggle, the fight will be renewed whenever the defeated party shall be again able to muster strength enough to take the field. The privilege of self-government is one which the people will never be permitted to enjoy unmolested. Power and wealth are continually stealing from the many to the few. There is a class continually gaining ground in the community who desire to monopolize the advantage of the Government, to hedge themselves round with exclusive privileges and elevate themselves at the expense of the great body of the people. These, in our society, are emphatically the aristocracy; and these, with all such as their means of persuasion or corruption or intimidation can move to act with them, constitute the party which are now struggling against the democracy for the perpetuation of an odious and dangerous moneyed institution.

Putting out of view, for the present, all other objections to the United States Bank, — that it is a monopoly, that it possesses enormous and overshadowing power, that it has been most corruptly managed, and that it is identified with political leaders to whom the people of the United States must ever be strongly opposed — the constitutional objection alone is an insurmountable objection to it.

The Government of the United States is a limited sovereignty. The powers which it may exercise are expressly enumerated in the Constitution. None not thus stated, or that are not "necessary and proper" to carry those which are stated into effect, can be allowed to be exercised by it. The power to establish a bank is not expressly given; neither is it incidental; since it cannot be shown to be "necessary" to carry the powers which are given, or any of them, into effect. That power cannot therefore be exercised without transcending the constitutional limits.

This is the *democratic* argument stated in its briefest form. The *aristocratic* argument in favor of the power is founded on the dangerous heresy that the Constitution says one thing and means another. That "necessary" does not mean *necessary* but simply *convenient*. By a mode of reasoning not looser than this it would be easy to prove that our Government ought to be changed into a monarchy, Henry Clay crowned king, and the opposition members of the Senate made peers of the realm; and power, place, and perquisites given to them and their heirs forever.

RICH AND POOR[2]

The rich perceive, acknowledge, and act upon a common interest, and why not the poor? Yet the moment the latter are called upon to combine for the preservation of their rights, forsooth the community is in danger. Property is no longer secure and life in jeopardy. This cant has descended to us from those times when the poor and laboring classes had no stake in the community and no rights except such as they could acquire by force. But the times have changed though the cant remains the same. The scrip nobility of this Republic have adopted towards the free people of this Republic the same language which the feudal barons and the despot who contested with them the power of oppressing the people used towards their serfs and villains, as they were opprobriously called.

These would-be lordlings of the Paper Dynasty cannot or will not perceive that there is some difference in the situation and feelings of the people of the United States and those of the despotic governments of Europe. They forget that at this moment our people — we mean emphatically the class which labors with its own hands — is in possession of a greater portion of the property and intelligence of this country, ay, ten times over, than all the creatures of the "paper credit system" put together. This property is indeed more widely and equally distributed among the people than among the phantoms of the paper system, and so much the better. And as to their intelligence, let any man talk with them, and if he does not learn something it is his own fault. They are as well acquainted with the rights of person and property and have as just a regard for them as the most illustrious lordling of the scrip nobility. And why should they not? Who and what are the great majority of the wealthy people of this city, we may say of this country? Are they not — we say it not in disparagement, but in high commendation — are they not men who began the world comparatively poor with ordinary education and ordinary means? And what should make them so much wiser than their neighbors? Is it because they live in better style, ride in carriages, and have more money or at least more credit than their poorer neighbors? Does a man become wiser, stronger, or more virtuous and patriotic because he has a fine house over his head? Does he love his country the

[2] [*Ibid.*, December 6, 1834—Text complete.]

better because he has a French cook and a box at the opera? Or does he grow more learned, logical, and profound by intense study of the daybook, ledger, bills of exchange, bank promises, and notes of hand?

Of all the countries on the face of the earth or that ever existed on the face of the earth, this is the one where the claims of wealth and aristocracy are the most unfounded, absurd, and ridiculous. With no claim to hereditary distinctions, with no exclusive rights except what they derive from monopolies, and no power of perpetuating their estates in their posterity, the assumption of aristocratic airs and claims is supremely ridiculous. Tomorrow they themselves may be beggars for aught they know, or at all events their children may become so. Their posterity in the second generation will have to begin the world again and work for a living as did their forefathers. And yet the moment a man becomes rich among us, he sets up for wisdom; he despises the poor and ignorant; he sets up for patriotism; he is your only man who has a stake in the community and therefore the only one who ought to have a voice in the state. What folly is this? And how contemptible his presumption? He is not a whit wiser, better, or more patriotic than when he commenced the world, a wagon driver. Nay, not half so patriotic, for he would see his country disgraced a thousand times rather than see one fall of the stocks, unless perhaps he had been speculating on such a contingency. To him a victory is only of consequence as it raises, and a defeat only to be lamented as it depresses a loan. His soul is wrapped up in a certificate of scrip or a bank note. Witness the conduct of these pure patriots during the late war, when they, at least a large proportion of them, not only withheld all their support from the Government but used all their influence to prevent others from giving their assistance. Yet these are the people who alone have a stake in the community and, of course, exclusively monopolize patriotism.

But let us ask what and where is the danger of a combination of the laboring classes in vindication of their political principles or in defense of their menaced rights? Have they not the right to act in concert when their opponents act in concert? Nay, is it not their bounden duty to combine against the only enemy they have to fear as yet in this free country: monopoly and a great paper system that grinds them to the dust? Truly, this is strange republican doctrine, and this is a strange republican country, where men cannot unite in one common effort, in one common cause, without rousing the cry of danger to the rights of person and property. Is not this a government of the people, founded on the rights of the people, and instituted for the express object of guarding them against the encroachments and usurpations of power? And if they are not permitted the possession of common interest, the exercise of a common feeling, if they cannot combine to resist by constitutional means these encroachments, to what purpose were they declared free to exercise the right of suffrage in the choice of rulers and the making of laws?

And what, we ask, is the power against which the people not only of this country but of almost all Europe are called upon to array themselves, and the encroachment on their rights they are summoned to resist? Is it not emphatically the power of monopoly and the encroachments of corporate privileges of every kind which the cupidity of the rich engenders to the injury of the poor?

It was to guard against the encroachments of power, the insatiate ambition of wealth, that this government was instituted by the people themselves. But the objects which call for the peculiar jealousy and watchfulness of the people are not now what they once were. The cautions of the early writers in favor of the liberties of mankind have in some measure become obsolete and inapplicable. We are menaced by our old enemies, avarice and ambition, under a new name and form. The tyrant is changed from a steel-clad feudal baron or a minor despot, at the head of thousands of ruffian followers, to a mighty civil gentleman who comes mincing and bowing to the people with a quill behind his ear, at the head of countless millions of magnificent *promises*. He promises to make everybody rich; he promises to pave cities with gold; and he promises to pay. In short he is made up of promises. He will do wonders such as never were seen or heard of, provided the people will only allow him to make his promises equal to silver and gold and human labor, and grant him the exclusive benefits of all the great blessings he intends to confer on them. He is the sly, selfish, grasping, and insatiable tyrant the people are now to guard against. A *concentrated money power;* a usurper in the disguise of a benefactor; an agent exercising privileges which his principal never possessed; an impostor who, while he affects to wear chains, is placed above those who are free; a chartered libertine that pretends to be manacled only that he may the more safely pick our pockets and lord it over our rights. This is the enemy we are now to encounter and overcome before we can expect to enjoy the substantial realities of freedom.

OBJECTS OF THE EVENING POST[3]

Those who only read the declamations of the opponents of the *equal rights* of the people may be induced to believe that this paper advocates principles at war with the very existence of social rights and social order. But what have we asked in the name of the people that such an interested clamor should be raised against them and us? What have we done or said that we should be denounced as incendiaries, striking at the very roots of society and tearing down the edifice of property? It may be useful to recapitulate what we have already done, in order that those who please may judge whether or not we deserve these reproaches from any but the enemies of the equal rights of person and property.

In the first place, in designating the true functions of a good government, we placed the protection of property among its first and principal duties. We referred to it as one of the great objects for the attainment of which all governments were originally instituted. Does this savor of hostility to the rights of property?

In the second place, we maintained that all grants of monopolies, or exclusive or partial privileges to any man or body of men, impaired the equal rights of the people and was in direct violation of the first principle of a free government. Does it savor of hostility to the rights of property to maintain that all property has equal rights and that exclusive privileges granted to one class of men or one species of property impair the equal rights of all the others?

As a deduction from these principles, we draw the conclusion that charters conferring partial or exclusive monopolies on small fractions of society are infringements on the general rights of society and therefore that the system ought to be abandoned as soon as possible as utterly at war with the rights of the people at large. It is here that the shoe pinches, and here the clamor against us will be found to originate. Thousands and tens of thousands of influential individuals, at the bar, on the bench, in our legislative bodies, and everywhere, are deeply interested in the continuance of these abuses. Lawmakers, law expounders, and law executors have invested either their money

[3] [*Ibid.*, January 3, 1835 — Text complete.]

or their credit in corporations of every kind, and it is not to be wondered at that they should cry out against the abandonment of a system from whence they derive such exorbitant gains.

We are accused of violating vested rights when we ask, in the name of the people, that no more be created and that all those possessing the means and the inclination may be admitted, under general regulations, to a participation in the privileges which hitherto have been only enjoyed through the caprice, the favor, the policy, or the corruption of legislative bodies. We never even hinted at touching those vested rights until the period to which they had been extended by law had expired and till it could be done without a violation of legislative faith. We defy any man to point out in any of our arguments on this subject a single idea or sentence that will sustain the charge of hostility to actually vested rights. Our opposition was prospective, not retroactive; it was not to present, but to future vested rights.

In attacking a course of policy in the future, do we make war on the past? In pointing out what we believe errors in former legislation and recommending their abandonment in future, do we violate any right of property or recommend any breach of public faith? Or, in advocating the equal rights of all, do we impair the constitutional rights of any? It might be well for the clamorous few who assail our principles and our motives with opprobrious epithets, which, though they do not understand their purport themselves, they mean should convey the most dishonorable imputations — it might be well for them to answer these questions before they resort to railing.

One of the greatest supports of an erroneous system of legislation is the very evil it produces. When it is proposed to remedy the mischief by adopting a new system, every abuse which has been the result of the old one becomes an obstacle to reformations. Every political change, however salutary, must be injurious to the interests of some, and it will be found that those who profit by abuses are always more clamorous for their continuance than those who are only opposing them from motives of justice or patriotism are for their abandonment. Such is precisely the state of the question of monopoly at this moment.

Under the abuses of the right to grant exclusive privileges to the few, which is a constructive if not a usurped power, a vast and concentrated interest and influence has grown up among us which will undoubtedly be seriously affected in its monopoly of gain from that source by the discontinuance of their chartered privileges when they shall expire by their own limitation. The admission of all others having the means and the inclination to associate for similar purposes, by destroying the monopoly at one blow, will in all probability diminish the prospect of future gains; and these will be still further curtailed by at first restricting banks in their issues of small notes and in the amount of notes they are permitted to put into circulation, and finally by repealing the restraining law and throwing banking open to the free competition of the whole community. These may prove serious evils to the parties concerned; but it is a poor argument to say that a bad system should be persevered in lest a small minority of the community should suffer some future inconvenience. The magnitude of the evils produced by an erroneous system of legislation, far from being a circumstance in favor of its continuance or increase, is the strongest argument in the world for its being abandoned as soon as possible. Every reformation may in this way be arrested under the pretense that the evils it will cause are greater than those it will cure. On the same principle the drawing of a tooth might be opposed on the ground that the pain is worse than that of the toothache, keeping out of sight the fact that the one is a lasting and increasing, the other a momentary evil.

It is the nature of political abuses to be always on the increase unless arrested by the virtue, intelligence, and firmness of the people. If not corrected in time, they grow up into a gigantic vigor and notoriety which at length enables them to wrestle successfully with the people and overthrow them and their rights. The possessors of monopolies and exclusive privileges, which form the essence of every bad government, pervert a long perseverance in the wrong into a political right; abuses grow venerable by time; usurpation matures into proscription; distinctions become hereditary; and what cannot be defended by reason is maintained on the ground that a long continuance of wrongs and a long possession of rights are equally sacred.

TRUE FUNCTIONS OF GOVERNMENT[4]

"There are no necessary evils in Government. Its evils exist only in its abuses. If it would confine itself to *equal protection*, and, as

[4] [*Ibid.*, November 21, 1834 — Text complete.]

heaven does its rains, shower its favors alike on the high and the low, the rich and the poor, it would be an unqualified blessing."

This is the language of our venerated President, and the passage deserves to be written in letters of gold, for neither in truth of sentiment or beauty of expression can it be surpassed. We choose it as our text for a few remarks on the true functions of government.

The fundamental principle of all governments is the protection of person and property from domestic and foreign enemies; in other words, to defend the weak against the strong. By establishing the social feeling in a community, it was intended to counteract that selfish feeling which, in its proper exercise, is the parent of all worldly good and, in its excesses, the root of all evil. The functions of government, when confined to their proper sphere of action, are therefore restricted to the making of *general laws*, uniform and universal in their operation, for these purposes and for no other.

Governments have no right to interfere with the pursuits of individuals, as guaranteed by those general laws, by offering encouragements and granting privileges to any particular class of industry or any select bodies of men, inasmuch as all classes of industry and all men are equally important to the general welfare and equally entitled to protection.

Whenever a government assumes the power of discriminating between the different classes of the community, it becomes, in effect, the arbiter of their prosperity and exercises a power not contemplated by an intelligent people in delegating their sovereignty to their rulers. It then becomes the great regulator of the profits of every species of industry and reduces men from a dependence on their own exertions to a dependence on the caprices of their government. Governments possess no delegated right to tamper with individual industry a single hair's breadth beyond what is essential to protect the rights of person and property.

In the exercise of this power of intermeddling with the private pursuits and individual occupations of the citizen, a government may at pleasure elevate one class and depress another; it may one day legislate exclusively for the farmer, the next for the mechanic, and the third for the manufacturer, who all thus become the mere puppets of legislative cobbling and tinkering instead of independent citizens relying on their own resources for their prosperity. It assumes the functions which belong alone to an overruling Providence and affects to become the universal dispenser of good and evil.

This power of regulating, of increasing or diminishing the profits of labor and the value of property of all kinds and degrees by direct legislation, in a great measure destroys the essential object of all civil compacts which, as we said before, is to make the social a counterpoise to the selfish feeling. By thus operating directly on the latter, by offering one class a bounty and another a discouragement, they involve the selfish feeling in every struggle of party for the ascendancy and give to the force of political rivalry all the bitterest excitement of personal interests conflicting with each other. Why is it that parties now exhibit excitement aggravated to a degree dangerous to the existence of the Union and to the peace of society? Is it not that by frequent exercises of partial legislation almost every man's personal interests have become deeply involved in the result of the contest? In common times the strife of parties is the mere struggle of ambitious leaders for power; now they are deadly contests of the whole mass of the people whose pecuniary interests are implicated in the event because the Government has usurped and exercised the power of legislating on their private affairs. The selfish feeling has been so strongly called into action by this abuse of authority as almost to overpower the social feeling which it should be the object of a good government to foster by every means in its power.

No nation, knowingly and voluntarily, with its eyes open, ever delegated to its government this enormous power, which places at its disposal the property, the industry, and the fruits of the industry of the whole people. As a general rule, the prosperity of rational men depends on themselves. Their talents and their virtues shape their fortunes. They are therefore the best judges of their own affairs and should be permitted to seek their own happiness in their own way, untrammeled by the capricious interference of legislative bungling, so long as they do not violate the equal rights of others nor transgress the general laws for the security of person and property.

But modern refinements have introduced new principles in the science of government. Our own Government, most especially, has assumed and exercised an authority over the people not unlike that of weak and vacillating parents over their children and with about the same degree of impartiality. One child becomes a favorite because he has made a fortune and another because he has failed in the pursuit of that object; one because of its beauty and another because of its deformity. Our Government has thus exercised the right of dispensing favors to one or another class of citizens at will; of directing its patronage first here and then there; of bestowing one day and taking back the next; of giving to the few and denying to the many; of investing wealth with new and exclusive privileges and distributing, as it were at random and with a capricious policy, in unequal portions, what it ought not to bestow or what, if given away, should be equally the portion of all.

A government administered on such a system of policy may be called a government of equal rights, but it is in its nature and essence a disguised despotism. It is the capricious dispenser of good and evil, without any restraint except its own sovereign will. It holds in its hand the distribution of the goods of this world and is consequently the uncontrolled master of the people.

Such was not the object of the Government of the United States, nor such the powers delegated to it by the people. The object was beyond doubt to protect the weak against the strong by giving them an equal voice and equal rights in the state; not to make one portion stronger, the other weaker, at pleasure, by crippling one or more classes of the community, or making them tributary to one alone. This is too great a power to entrust to government. It was never given away by the people and is not a right but a usurpation.

Experience will show that this power has always been exercised under the influence and for the exclusive benefit of wealth. It was never wielded in behalf of the community. Whenever an exception is made to the general law of the land, founded on the principle of equal rights, it will always be found to be in favor of wealth. These immunities are never bestowed on the poor. They have no claim to a dispensation of exclusive benefits, and their only business is to *"take care of the rich that the rich may take care of the poor."*

Thus it will be seen that the sole reliance of the laboring classes, who constitute a vast majority of every people on the earth, is the great principle of *equal rights;* that their only safeguard against oppression is a system of legislation which leaves all to the free exercise of their talents and industry within the limits of the general law and which, on no pretense of public good, bestows on any particular class of industry or any particular body of men rights or privileges not equally enjoyed by the great aggregate of the body politic.

Time will remedy the departures which have already been made from this sound republican system, if the people but jealously watch and indignantly frown on any future attempts to invade their equal rights or appropriate to the few what belongs to all alike. To quote, in conclusion, the language of the great man, with whose admirable sentiment we commenced these remarks, "it is time to pause in our career — if we cannot at once, in justice to the interests vested under improvident legislation, make our government what it ought to be, we can at least take a stand against all new grants of monopolies and exclusive privileges and against any prostitution of our Government to the advancement of the few at the expense of the many."

THANKSGIVING DAY[5]

... In framing our political institutions, the great men to whom that important trust was confided, taught by the example of other countries the evils which result from mingling civil and ecclesiastical affairs, were particularly careful to keep them entirely distinct. Thus the Constitution of the United States mentions the subject of religion at all only to declare that "no religious test shall ever be required as a qualification to any office or public trust in the United States." The Constitution of our own state specifies that "the free exercise and enjoyment of religious professions and worship, without discrimination or preference, shall forever be allowed in this State to all mankind;" and so fearful were the framers of that instrument of the dangers to be apprehended from a union of political and religious concerns that they inserted a clause of positive interdiction against ministers of the gospel, declaring them forever ineligible to any civil or military office or place within the state. In this last step we think the jealousy of religious interference proceeded too far. We see no good reason why preachers of the gospel should be partially disfranchised, any more than preachers against it or any more than men devoted to any other profession or pursuit. This curious proscriptive article of our Constitution presents the startling anomaly that, while an infidel who delivers stated Sunday lectures in a tavern against all

[5] [*Plaindealer*, December 3, 1836 — Abridged.]

religion may be elected to the highest executive or legislative trust, the most liberal and enlightened divine is excluded. In our view of the subject neither of them should be proscribed. They should both be left to stand on the broad basis of equal political rights, and the intelligence and virtue of the people should be trusted to make a selection from an unbounded field. This is the true democratic theory; but this is a subject apart from that which it is our present purpose to consider.

No one can pay the most cursory attention to the state of religion in the United States without being satisfied that its true interests have been greatly promoted by divorcing it from all connection with political affairs. In no other country of the world are the institutions of religion so generally respected, and in no other is so large a proportion of the population included among the communicants of the different Christian churches. The number of Christian churches or congregations in the United States is estimated, in a carefully prepared article of religious statistics in the *American Almanac* of the present year, at upwards of sixteen thousand and the number of communicants at nearly two millions or one-tenth of the entire population. In this city alone the number of churches is one hundred and fifty, and their aggregate capacity is nearly equal to the accommodation of the whole number of inhabitants. It is impossible to conjecture, from any data within our reach, the amount of the sum annually paid by the American people, of their own free will, for the support of the ministry and the various expenses of their religious institutions; but it will readily be admitted that it must be enormous. These, then, are the auspicious results of *perfect free trade in religion* — of leaving it to manage its own concerns in its own way, without government protection, regulation, or interference of any kind or degree whatever.

The only instance of intermeddling on the part of the civil authorities with matters which, being of a religious character, properly belong to the religious guides of the people is the proclamation which it is the custom for the Governor of each State annually to issue, appointing a day of general thanksgiving or a day of general fasting and prayer. We regret that even this single exception should exist to that rule of entire separation of the affairs of state from those of the church, the observance of which in all other respects has been followed by the happiest results. It is to the source of the proclamation, not to its

purpose, that we chiefly object. The recommending a day of thanksgiving is not properly any part of the duty of a political Chief Magistrate; it belongs, in its nature, to the heads of the church, not to the
head of the State.

It may very well happen, and, indeed, it has happened in more
instances than one that the chief executive officer of a State has been
a person who, if not absolutely an infidel or sceptic in religious matters,
has at least in his private sentiments and conduct been notoriously
disregardful of religion. What mockery for such a person to call
upon the people to set apart a day for returning acknowledgments to
Almighty God for the bounties and blessings bestowed upon them!
But even when the contrary is the case and it is well known that the
Governor is a strictly religious man, he departs very widely from the
duties of his office in proclaiming, in his gubernatorial capacity and
under the seal of the State, that he has appointed a particular day as
a day of general thanksgiving. This is no part of his official business,
as prescribed in the Constitution. It is not one of the purposes for
which he was elected. If it were a new question, and a Governor
should take upon himself to issue such a proclamation for the first
time, the proceeding could scarcely fail to arouse the most sturdy
opposition from the people. Religious and irreligious would unite in
condemning it; the latter as a gross departure from the specified duties
for the discharge of which alone the Governor was chosen; and the
former as an unwarrantable interference of the civil authority with
ecclesiastical affairs and a usurpation of the functions of their own
duly appointed ministers and church officers. We recollect very distinctly what an excitement arose in this community a few years ago
when our Common Council, following the example of the Governor,
undertook to interfere in a matter which belonged wholly to the
clerical functionaries and passed a resolution recommending to the
various ministers of the gospel the subject of their next Sunday discourse. The Governor's proclamation would itself provoke equal
opposition if men's eyes had not been sealed by custom to its inherent
impropriety.

If such a proceeding would be wrong, instituted now for the first
time, can it be right because it has existed for a long period? Does
age change the nature of principles and give sanctity to error? Are
truth and falsehood of such mutable and shifting qualities that though,

in their original characters, as opposite as the poles, the lapse of a little time may reduce them to a perfect similitude and render them entirely convertible? If age has in it such power as to render venerable what is not so in its intrinsic nature, then is paganism more venerable than Christianity, since it has existed from a much more remote antiquity. But what is wrong in principle must continue to be wrong to the end of time, however sanctioned by custom. It is in this light we consider the gubernatorial recommendation of a day of thanksgiving; and because it is wrong in principle and not because of any particular harm which the custom has yet been the means of introducing, we should be pleased to see it abrogated. We think it can hardly be doubted that, if the duty of setting apart a day for a general expression of thankfulness for the blessings enjoyed by the community were submitted wholly to the proper representatives of the different religious sects, they would find no difficulty in uniting on the subject and acting in concert in such a manner as should give greater solemnity and weight to their proceeding than can ever attach to the proclamation of a political governor, stepping out of the sphere of his constitutional duties and taking upon himself to direct the religious exercises of the people. We cannot too jealously confine our political functionaries within the limits of their prescribed duties. We cannot be too careful to keep entirely separate the things which belong to government from those which belong to religion. The political and the religious interests of the people will both flourish the more prosperously for being wholly distinct. The condition of religious affairs in this country fully proves the truth of the position; and we are satisfied it would receive still further corroboration if the practice to which we object were reformed.

ASSOCIATED EFFORT[6]

Some days ago, we observed in one of the newspapers a paragraph stating that a meeting of mechanics and laborers was about to be held in this city for the purpose of adopting measures of concerted or combined action against the practice, which we have reason to believe exists to a very great extent, of paying them in the uncurrent notes of distant or suspected banks. No such meeting, however, as far as

[6] [*Ibid.*, December 10, 1836 — Text complete.]

we can learn, has yet been held. We hope it soon will be; for the object is a good one, and there is no other way of resisting the rapacious and extortionate custom of employers paying their journeymen and laborers in depreciated paper half so effectual as combination.

There are some journalists who affect to entertain great horror of combinations, considering them as utterly adverse to the principles of free trade; and it is frequently recommended to make them penal by law. Our notions of free trade were acquired in a different school and dispose us to leave men entirely at liberty to effect a proper object either by concerted or individual action. The character of combinations, in our view, depends entirely upon the intrinsic character of the end which is aimed at. In this subject under consideration, the end proposed is good beyond all possibility of question. There is high warrant for saying that the *laborer is worthy of his hire;* but the employer who takes advantage of his necessities and defenselessness to pay him in a depreciated substitute for money does not give him his hire; he does not perform his engagement with him; he filches from the poor man a part of his hard-earned wages and is guilty of a miserable fraud. Who shall say that this sneaking species of extortion ought not to be prevented? Who will say that separate individual action is adequate to that end? There is no one who will make so rash an assertion.

The only effectual mode of doing away the evil is by attacking it with the great instrument of the rights of the poor — associated effort. There is but one bulwark behind which mechanics and laborers may safely rally to oppose a common enemy, who, if they ventured singly into the field against him, would cut them to pieces; that bulwark is the *principle of combination.* We would advise them to take refuge behind it only in extreme cases, because in their collisions with their employers, as in those between nations, the manifold evils of a siege are experienced, more or less, by both parties and are therefore to be incurred only in extreme emergencies. But the evil of being habitually paid in a depreciated substitute for money, of being daily cheated out of a portion of the just fruits of honest toil, of having a slice continually clipped from the hard-earned crust, is one of great moment and is worthy of such an effort as we propose.

LEADING PUBLIC OPINION[7]

There are several public journals in this country which, owing to circumstances of position, deserve and receive a good deal of attention from the newspaper press generally, to which very little respect would be due on account of any intrinsic qualities they possess.

What is leading public opinion? Public opinion we take to be composed of the opinions of individuals. When the sentiments of a majority of the thinking men of a community concur on any given subject, their opinions are the public opinion. Any person who, whether by the mere influence of his character or by argument, seeks to change to any extent the prevailing opinion or the views of any individual of the prevailing number may be said in a certain sense to assume the character of a leader of public opinion. Every man's example is, in a greater or less degree, a leading influence; and it is not merely the undoubted right but it is the imperative duty of a good citizen to do all within the compass of his opportunities to lead the public opinion aright; to lead it in the direction which he conceives will most effectually promote general prosperity and social order and happiness.

If this is the duty of a private individual, it becomes in a much stronger point of view that of the conductor of a newspaper press. His vocation is emphatically that of a public leader. Its obligations are very imperfectly and impotently discharged if he confines himself to the mere drudgery of chronicling events. It requires him to maintain principles, investigate measures, expose the evil motives and effects of erroneous public conduct, tear off the veil in which sophistry conceals its object, and assist the cause of truth with every argument that reason can furnish and every embellishment that fancy affords. To discharge fully the duties of a public journalist would be to elevate the vocation to the loftiest summit of human dignity and usefulness. A public journalist, animated with a due sense of the obligations of his responsible trust and gifted with the faculties, intellectual and physical, for their adequate performance, would well deserve to be a public leader in a more extended signification of the phrase than that in which we desire it should be understood. He should have a head cool, clear, and sagacious; a heart warm and benevolent; a nice sense of justice; an inflexible regard for truth; honesty that no temptation

[7] [*Ibid.*, January 21, 1837 — Abridged.]

could corrupt; intrepidity that no danger could intimidate; and independence superior to every consideration of mere interest, enmity, or friendship. He should possess the power of diligent application and be capable of enduring great fatigue. He should have a temperament so happily mingled that while he easily kindled at public error or injustice his indignation should never transgress the bounds of judgment but, in its strongest expression, show that smoothness and amenity which the language of choler always lacks. He should, in short, be such a man as a contemporary writer described that sturdy democrat, old Andrew Fletcher, of Saltoun — "a gentleman steady in his principles; of nice honor, abundance of learning; brave as the sword he wears, and bold as a lion; a sure friend, and irreconcilable enemy; who would lose his life readily to serve his country, and would not do a base thing to save it." This is the *beau ideal* of the character of a conductor of a political newspaper. . . . .

The reader may be disposed to interrupt us here and tell us that we are drawing an outline of an editor which no human being can fill. It is nevertheless the model which all who undertake the vocation should propose to themselves, and according to the degree in which their emulation succeeds is the approbation they deserve. . . . .

The charge of arrogance is misapplied when aimed at those who, like ourselves, have neither the natural nor acquired talents necessary to the most perfect discharge of editorial functions. Circumstances thrust one man into one vocation, and another into another; and all that can justly be required of him is that he should exercise with diligence and fidelity such talents and skill as he has to promote the interests of truth and of his fellow-man. Every physician cannot be a Boerhaave or a Rush; every lawyer a Coke or a Hamilton; nor every newspaper editor an Ames or a Bryant. But it is in the power of every one to be an honest man and to exert his powers with constant assiduity and integrity for the promotion of sound principles of public government or, in other words, to lead the public opinion aright. The conductor of the humblest newspaper occupies the centre of a circle of larger influence than more commanding intellects, if shut out from access to the press; and the duty to obey punctually *but censure freely*, which Jeremy Bentham sets down as a maxim for the government of every good citizen, should be considered especially incumbent upon him.

THE MORALS OF POLITICS[8]

Public moralists have long noticed with regret that the political contests of this country are conducted with intemperance wholly unsuited to conflicts of reason and decided, in a great measure, by the efforts of the worst class of people. We apply this phrase not to those whom the aristocracy designate as the "lower orders;" but to those only, whether well or ill dressed, and whether rich or poor, who enter into the struggle without regard for the inherent dignity of politics and without reference to the permanent interests of their country and of mankind, but animated by selfish objects, by personal preferences or prejudices, the desire of office, or the hope of accomplishing private ends through the influence of party. Elections are commonly looked upon as a mere game, on which depends the division of party spoils, the distribution of chartered privileges, and the allotments of pecuniary rewards. The antagonist principles of government, which should constitute the sole ground of controversy, are lost sight of in the eagerness of sordid motives; and the struggle, which should be one of pure reason with no aim but the achievement of political truth and the promotion of the greatest good of the greatest number, sinks into a mere brawl, in which passion, avarice, and profligacy are the prominent actors.

If the questions of government could be submitted to the people in the naked dignity of abstract propositions, men would reason upon them calmly and frame their opinions according to the preponderance of truth. There is nothing in the intrinsic nature of politics that appeals to the passions of the multitude. It is an important branch of morals, and its principles, like those of private ethics, address themselves to the sober judgment of men. A strange spectacle would be presented should we see mathematicians kindle into wrath in the discussion of a problem and call on their hearers, in the angry terms of demagogues, to decide on the relative merits of opposite modes of demonstration. The same temperance and moderation which characterize the investigation of truth in the exact sciences belong not less to the inherent nature of politics when confined within the proper field.

The object of all politicians, in the strict sense of the expression, is happiness, the happiness of a state, the greatest possible sum of

[8] [*Ibid.*, June 3, 1837. — Abridged.]

happiness of which the social condition admits to those individuals who live together under the same political organization. It may be asserted as an undeniable proposition that it is the duty of every intelligent man to be a politician. This is particularly true of a country the institutions of which admit every man to the exercise of equal suffrage. All the duties of life are embraced under the three heads of religion, politics, and morals. The aim of religion is to regulate the conduct of man with reference to happiness in a future state of being; of politics, to regulate his conduct with reference to the happiness of communities; and of morals, to regulate his conduct with reference to individual happiness.

Happiness, then, is the end and aim of these three great and comprehensive branches of duty; and no man perfectly discharges the obligations imposed by either who neglects those which the others enjoin. The right ordering of a state affects, for weal or woe, the interests of multitudes of human beings; and every individual of those multitudes has a direct interest, therefore, in its being ordered aright.

. . . .

The sole legitimate object of politics, then, is the happiness of communities. They who call themselves politicians, having other objects, are not politicians but demagogues. But is it in the nature of things that the sincere and single desire to promote such a system of government as would most effectually secure the greatest amount of general happiness can draw into action such violent passions, prompt such fierce declamation, authorize such angry criminations, and occasion such strong appeals to the worst motives of the venal and base, as we constantly see and hear in every conflict of the antagonist parties of our country? Or does not this effect arise from causes improperly mixed with politics and with which they have no intrinsic affinity? Does it not arise from the fact that government, instead of seeking to promote the greatest happiness of the community by confining itself rigidly within its true field of action, has extended itself to embrace a thousand objects which should be left to the regulation of social morals and unrestrained competition, one man with another, without political assistance or check? Are our elections, in truth, a means of deciding mere questions of government, or does not the decision of numerous questions, affecting private interests, schemes of selfishness, rapacity, and cunning, depend upon them, even more than cardinal principles of politics?

It is to this fact, we are persuaded, that the immorality and licentiousness of party contests are to be ascribed. If government were restricted to the few and simple objects contemplated in the democratic creed, the mere protection of person, life, and property, if its functions were limited to the mere guardianship of the equal rights of men, and its action in all cases were influenced not by the paltry suggestions of present expediency but the eternal principles of justice, we should find reason to congratulate ourselves on the change in the improved tone of public morals as well as in the increased prosperity of trade.

The religious man, then, as well as the political and social moralist should exert his influence to bring about the auspicious reformation. Nothing can be more self-evident than the demoralizing influence of special legislation. It degrades politics into a mere scramble for rewards obtained by a violation of the equal rights of the people; it perverts the holy sentiment of patriotism; induces a feverish avidity for sudden wealth; fosters a spirit of wild and dishonest speculation; withdraws industry from its accustomed channels of useful occupation; confounds the established distinctions between virtue and vice, honor and shame, respectability and degradation; pampers luxury; and leads to intemperance, dissipation, and profligacy, in a thousand forms.

The remedy is easy. It is to confine government within the narrowest limits of necessary duties. It is to disconnect bank and state. It is to give freedom to trade and leave enterprise, competition, and a just public sense of right to accomplish by their natural energies what the artificial system of legislative checks and balances has so signally failed in accomplishing. The Federal Government has nothing to do but to hold itself entirely aloof from banking, having no more connection with it than if banks did not exist. It should receive its revenues in nothing not recognized as money by the Constitution and pay nothing else to those employed in its service. The state governments should repeal their laws imposing restraints on the free exercise of capital and credit. They should avoid, for the future, all legislation not in the fullest accordance with the letter and spirit of that glorious maxim of democratic doctrine which acknowledges the equality of man's political rights. These are the easy steps by which we might arrive at the consummation devoutly to be wished.

The steps are easy but passion, ignorance, and selfishness are gathered round them and oppose our ascent. Agrarian, leveller, and visionary are the epithets, more powerful than arguments, with which they resist us. Shall we yield, discouraged, and submit to be always governed by the worst passions of the worst portions of mankind; or, by one bold effort, shall we regenerate our institutions and make government, indeed, not the dispenser of privileges to a few for their efforts in subverting the rights of the many but the beneficent promoter of the equal happiness of all? The monopolists are prostrated by the explosion of their overcharged system; they are wrecked by the regurgitation of their own flood of mischief; they are buried beneath the ruins of the baseless fabric they had presumptuously reared to such a towering height.

Now is the time for the friends of freedom to bestir themselves. Let us accept the invitation of this glorious opportunity to establish on an enduring foundation the true principles of political and economic freedom.

7

MARTIN VAN BUREN

POLITICAL OPINIONS[1]

[A NATIONAL BANK]

I AM OPPOSED to the establishment of a National Bank in any
form or under any disguise, both on constitutional grounds and
grounds of expediency. The power to create such an institution
has not been given to Congress by the Constitution, neither is it necessary to the exercise of any of the powers which are granted; and if
exercised, would be, as it always has been, highly injurious to the
public welfare. These opinions, alike adverse to the constitutionality
and expediency of a National Bank, have been frequently and extensively laid before the people, and sometimes on occasions of deep
interest. . . . .

I might rest here, content with this explicit avowal, and proceed to
reply to your other interrogatories, were it not that this appears to
me a proper occasion to advert to the deplorable calamities inflicted
on the people by the conduct and final catastrophe of the late Bank,
through the perversion of its means and the abuse of its power. It is
true that this institution is now no more. It has sunk under the
weight of its own enormities and has left nothing behind but the
wrecks of its career. But the interests, pecuniary and political, the
parents who first gave it birth, and the nurses by whom it was fostered
still survive, with the same means of producing another offspring,
and the same disposition to employ them whenever a favorable opportunity presents itself. The question of a National Bank is still before
the people, and will continue to be, so long as avarice and ambition
see in it the means of gratifying the love of money and the love of
power. It is one of the greatest leading measures of a party which
will never be extinct in this country. It is essential to the acquisition

[1] [From *Opinions of Mr. Van Buren, on the subject of a National Bank, Distribution
of the Proceeds of the Public Lands, an Exchequer or Government Fiscal Agent, a
Tariff, the Veto Power, and a National Convention*. Mr. Van Buren's Reply to the
Democratic State Convention of Indiana, 1843 — Abridged.]

as well as preservation of its power, and will never be relinquished while there exists a hope of its attachment. The only security against its revival is in the public opinion, and even that has more than once been found to be an insufficient barrier. For this reason, I conceive it proper that every occasion should be taken to recall to the public recollection, by way of a warning example, what otherwise it might be better for the honor of our country to bury in oblivion.

. . . .

My views on the subject of exchanges, and of the propriety, necessity, or expediency of any interference of government in their regulation, were communicated to Congress in 1837. To repeat them here would lengthen this communication, which from a desire to answer your questions fully, frankly, and explicitly will, I fear, be extended to the verge of tediousness. I must, therefore, respectfully refer to that document. You will there see a clear, broad distinction between that species of exchanges aptly denominated "kiting," which was little better than an instrument of fraud, and bills drawn for the transfer of actual funds from one place to another. I endeavored also to satisfy Congress of what is now so apparent, that the exchanges would here, as they do in other countries, regulate themselves, if Congress would but leave them as they are left elsewhere to the management of private enterprise. It is doubtless within your recollection what a tempest of denunciation I received from those who thought proper to overlook those considerations. The opinions then advanced would, it is quite certain, be received with more favor now; and I have only to add that they have undergone no other change than that of additional conviction arising from additional experience of their truth.

The tremendous power of a bank for evil, when impelled by avarice and ambition, self-preservation or vengeance, has been seen. It is a maxim in every government constituted on free principles to withhold all power from rulers which is not indispensable to the preservation and defense of the rights of person and property. And this maxim is founded on the experience of mankind, which has taught them by a long series of suffering that not only is power much more liable to abuse than to beneficial exercise, but that with the purest intentions it can do far less good than it can perpetrate mischief when perverted to evil. The people of the United States have repudiated despotic or discretionary power, in all their political institutions, because of its propensity to abuse. Yet they have been, and mark my words, will be again and again called upon to create a despotic irresponsible moneyed power, stronger than their government, because it is expected to do what that government cannot of itself perform. I hope and trust that such appeals will never again be successful and that the good people of the United States will always bear in mind that an institution which can do what its advocates affirm this can, must, if subservient to the government, give it a vast accession of power dangerous to the rights of the States, and which, if from any cause it should become hostile, can either subject that government to its will or, like the defunct institution of which I have spoken, involve the country in confusion and difficulty, its government in perpetual struggles, and its people in an interminable series of panic and dismay. Nothing but an ever watchful vigilance on the part of the people will prevent a recurrence of these evils. The enemy is not dead, nor doth he sleep. The schism in the ranks of the opponents of the democracy turns almost exclusively on the question of a National Bank, and the complete triumph of federalism will be the precursor of such an institution.

In expressing my opposition to all the schemes which have been submitted to the Congress at its last session for managing the fiscal concerns of the country, involving, as they all do, a union of bank and state, I do but speak the sentiments of a vast majority of my fellow citizens, as evinced in the votes of their representatives, and in the almost universal condemnation they have apparently received at the hands of the people themselves.

The manufacture of paper money has been attempted in every form; it has been tried by individuals, been transferred to corporations by the States, then to corporations by Congress, engaged in by the States themselves, and has signally failed in all. It has in general proved not the handmaid of honest industry and well regulated enterprise, but the pampered menial of speculation, idleness, and fraud. It has corrupted men of the highest standing, almost destroyed the confidence of mankind in each other, and darkened our criminal calendar with names that might otherwise have conferred honor and benefit on the country. There is strong ground for believing that such a system must have some innate incurable defect of which no legislation can divest it, and against which no human wisdom can guard or human integrity sustain itself.

The history of the past, however, leaves little room for doubt that paper money in some form will, notwithstanding, continue to constitute part of the circulating medium of the country. But my most sincere and ardent wish is that its issue by the Federal Government may in all future time be prevented. The lights of experience have in vain been diffused, the lessons of repeated and widespread ruin have been unavailing, if there be any who yet can bring themselves to believe that the Government of the United States, which possesses nothing but what it receives from the people, can bestow on them anything other than what it has thus received. If it contracts loans, the people must pay them; and if it issues paper money, it must be redeemed by the people. How then can relief to the people be derived from incurring obligations which they themselves must redeem?

But in addition to this deception, I might almost say fraud, on the people, there is a decisive objection to the issue of paper currency by governments, upon whatever principle it may be founded. The experience of all nations where this expedient has been adopted demonstrates that this is a prerogative which will always be abused. It gives almost unlimited facilities for raising money and has everywhere led to extravagant expenditures, public debt, and heavy burdens, always increasing and never diminished. Where extravagant appropriations can be met by a mere vote of Congress and without an immediate resort to the pockets of the people, there will be found no sufficient check to boundless prodigality, except when the government finally loses its credit by pushing it to excess. It is then that it reacts upon the people; for this great resource being exhausted, the whole superstructure of credit falls on their hands and they must bear it as best they can.

. . . .

To insure economy in public expenditures, it is indispensable that those by whom they are authorized should have some difficulty and even serious responsibility in obtaining the means of defraying them. In no other way can extravagance be prevented, since it is the nature of man to spend that heedlessly which he acquires without effort and to think little of that which costs little trouble to gain.

I have dwelt more at length on that part of your inquiry which relates to a National Bank than I might otherwise have done, from a belief that you look upon it as one of the most vital consequence to the public welfare. In this I entirely coincide with you. Such being the case, it seems due to you as well as to myself to say that in referring to the public declarations I have heretofore made on this subject, I have been in no degree influenced by any feeling of dissatisfaction at the repetition of these inquiries on the present occasion. So far from this, I most highly applaud the enlightened patriotism of the democracy of Indiana in seizing an occasion so appropriate as that of an approaching Presidential election to require new securities that the principles they themselves cherish should be carried out to their fullest extent, and more especially on this all important question.

.   .   .   .

[Proceeds of Sale of Public Lands]

The tenacity with which our opponents adhere to the distribution of the proceeds of the public lands among the states, in the present condition of the Treasury, is a political anomaly which it is not a little difficult to explain, or to reconcile with a fair understanding of or a proper regard for the true interests of the country. If any apology for it can be made, it is to be traced to that unwillingness to abandon, in the face of their opponents, a position which has been assumed with confidence and supported with earnestness — an indisposition from which but few political associations are altogether exempt. Whatever may have been expected from the measure by its authors, or however plausibly deceptive its theory may have been at a period when the country was threatened with the evils incident to an overflowing treasury, subsequent experience in regard to the working of our political and financial systems ought long since to have satisfied every reflecting mind as well of its utter inutility as a means of relief to the States, as of its destructive tendency to the stability and welfare of the Union. As the matter now stands, and has for years stood, it presents in the former aspect the simple question whether the people of the States can possibly be benefited by receiving into the state treasury a certain sum of money annually, to be immediately re-collected from themselves in the shape of taxes upon what they eat, drink, and wear, with the addition of the expenses of collection. Every attempt to give the measure any other tenable aspect has proved utterly unavailing. It is certainly paying but a poor compliment to the capacity of the people to suppose for a moment that they could be brought, by any pretext however plausible, to stultify themselves so far as to adopt a proposition so preposterous. Can any intelligent mind hesitate in giving to it a prompt negative? And can any patriotic one fail to regret that the character of our people for intelligence and sagacity, in the estimation of mankind, should be exposed to hazard by the grave and continued agitation of such a question before them?

It can, after this, and after what I have heretofore said upon the subject, be scarcely necessary to repeat that I am opposed to the distribution of the proceeds of the public lands among the states. The best evidence I can give you of my present opinion, in regard to the proper disposition of the public lands, is to refer you to those which are avowed and acted upon by me while in office and which were very fully stated in my first annual message to Congress, in December, 1837.

[PROTECTIVE TARIFFS]

My views in relation to the Protective System were also called for by the Shocco Springs meeting in 1832, and freely given. A conviction that the establishment of commercial regulations with a view to the encouragement of domestic interests is within the constitutional power of Congress was on that occasion distinctly avowed. But, holding this opinion, I at the same time denied the propriety of exercising this power in a manner calculated to oppress any portion of my fellow citizens, or to advance the interests of one section of the Union at the expense of another. I, on the contrary, affirmed it to be the duty of those who are entrusted with the administration of the Federal Government to direct its operations in the manner best calculated to distribute as equally as possible its burdens and blessings among the several States and the people thereof. In addition to the declaration of these general views, I suggested more specific rules for the action of the Government in this particular, by the observance of which I believed those views would be most likely to be carried into fair effect.

.   .   .   .

Adequate revenue for the support of all governments must be derived from some source. It has nowhere been found an easy task to preserve equality in raising it and at the same time to overcome the general repugnance to the payment of taxes in any shape, a repugnance arising more from an apprehension that their avails will not be wisely applied than from an unwillingness on the part of the people to sustain their government by the necessary contributions. All must agree that taxes should be imposed with a fair and full reference to the advantage derived from the existence of good government by those who pay them. Those advantages may in general terms be justly described as resulting from ample security in the enjoyment of our personal rights and rights of property, with adequate safeguards against internal commotion and foreign aggression. In respect to the immunities of the person and civil and religious freedom, the interest as well as the immediate advantages of all are equal. Not so with the other privileges secured to us by our free government. The unavoidable disparity in the pecuniary condition of our citizens makes the degree of benefit they respectively derive from the maintenance of an efficient government over property and the rights of property essentially different. The modes of raising revenue allowed to and adopted by the State governments are generally graduated by this disparity. If the results are not always equitable, the fault, it is believed, will in most cases be found in their action upon the principle rather than in the principle itself. The right to raise revenue for its support by the imposition of duties in lieu of direct taxation is, by the Constitution, subjected to the exclusive control of the Federal Government. This right, subject to the limitations imposed by the grant, was given to it for that purpose and has been freely exerted by it since its establishment. It would afford me much pleasure to be able to say that the exercise of this power has borne as equally upon all classes of the people, however unequal their pecuniary conditions, as the taxes imposed by the State governments. But this cannot with truth be said. Nor is the inequality unavoidably resulting from the Federal mode of collecting taxes a new discovery. It was foreseen and objected to when the power was conferred, as an evil inherent in the system, which could not fail to show itself in its operation, and the injustice of which no form of legislation, however it might be made to mitigate, could ever be able to remove. The advocates of the system were notwithstanding reconciled to it by a belief, no doubt sincerely entertained, that the inequalities which it was feared would result from the collection of duties upon imported articles would be prevented by the

fact that the consumption would be in proportion to the means of
the consumer. It was upon this ground that the principle was defeated.
That this expectation has not been realized is undeniably true. There
are but few if any who cannot, in their immediate vicinity, point out
numerous instances in which poor men with large families are actually
obliged to pay more for the support of the Federal Government than
others who are in affluent circumstances but are either without, or
have smaller families; and few if any countervailing examples are to
be found. At the same time the great body of wealth invested in
incorporated or associated companies and in bonds and notes entirely
escape Federal taxation. The mass of the people seem, nevertheless,
to prefer this mode of collecting the revenue. Paying their taxes in
the form of an increased price upon the commodities they buy, their
contribution loses, in their estimation, much of the odium that would
be attached to it if severed from the price of the article and converted
into a tax by name as it is in fact. It also wears the appearance of a
voluntary contribution, although its payment is for the most part as
unavoidable as a compulsory imposition would be. It is supported
too by the odium which was attached to the imposition of direct taxes
many years since for purposes which were not approved by the people,
and by the fact that in most of the States the taxes are direct; rendering it for that reason desirable to substitute some other mode of raising
revenue for the Federal Government. These and other considerations
have given to the impost a preference in the public mind which would
render the imposition of direct taxes in time of peace exceedingly
odious and have produced as great a degree of unanimity in favor of
a tariff for revenue as can ever be expected upon a public question.
Of the great mass of opponents to a protective tariff, there is not, so
far as I know, a single State or even district that has taken ground
against a revenue tariff.

. . . .

[The Veto Power]

I am satisfied with the veto power as it exists by the Constitution
and opposed to any modification which shall materially change the
principle upon which it rests.

. . . .

[PATRONAGE AND THE SPOILS SYSTEM]

The control of the President over the dispensation of Federal patronage presents a subject far more deserving of the watchful vigilance of the people. Charged by the Constitution with the execution of the laws, it was altogether proper to confer upon him an important share in the selection of the agents through whose instrumentality that great duty is to be performed. The power which he possesses in this respect is also wisely restricted by the checks upon it which are placed in other branches of the government, viz., in the Senate, by an absolute veto upon the most important of his selections, and in each branch of the legislature, by an equally absolute negative upon the appropriations necessary to their compensation. It is nevertheless true that this control over the distribution of public patronage is, in its tendency, adverse to a pure administration of the important trusts which the people have committed to their agents. Experience has shown that there is a temptation in the possession of this power to its abuse which cannot be effectually guarded against by human laws, and against the influence of which even honest and patriotic men not unfrequently find it difficult to guard themselves. With all the restraints imposed upon its exercise, it may still be wielded by the Executive to influence widely the action of his associates in the public service, to secure and perpetuate his own authority, for the aggrandizement of his personal adherents, and to depress those who, though they may possess the strongest claims upon the public confidence, have not the good fortune to stand in that relation to the appointing power. It would be honorable to human nature if we could flatter ourselves with the belief that such have not been, or the hope that such will not in future be, the results of its exercise. But experience unfortunately teaches us a different lesson; and from the fallible nature of man, we are scarcely allowed to hope that it will ever be otherwise. To encourage an honest observance of sound political principles by the dispensation of patronage is, I fear, an advantage seldom if ever realized under any government. Its tendencies, there is too much reason to apprehend, have been in general far otherwise. For this evil, and a grave one it is, there is but one effectual remedy. When we cannot dispense with the offices, we must distribute as widely as possible the power of appointing them. To make this remedy more effectual, it is always wise to reserve the selections of public officers, as far as is practicable and convenient, to the people themselves. It is not an easy matter to keep individual action in public affairs wholly free from the influence, in some form, of personal interests. That of the mass of the people is, on the contrary, almost invariably disinterested and seldom if ever fails to come right in the end. As much power over appointments as is deemed really necessary to enable the Executive to perform his responsible duties should be left to him. Of all beyond that and which can be as well exercised by the people themselves or otherwise, he should by constitutional means be divested. The possession of the excess is decidedly adverse to the healthful action of the department. No rightminded man, occupying the Presidential chair after he has had an opportunity to judge by experience of its effects, will desire to possess it. From this prolific source proceed most of the temptations which draw the ambitious politician from his duty to his constituents. While the veto is generally applied to questions exclusively of public concern and is exercised under a personal responsibility which will not be incurred except with great reluctance, and in cases in which there is a strong reliance upon the public judgment for support, this power is peculiarly adapted to the sinister purpose of ambitious and selfish aspirants. It is therefore by diminishing this executive power and not that of the veto, which is least liable to abuse and has been thus far uniformly exercised for the public advantage, that our statesmen can render the most essential and, I doubt not, the most acceptable service to the cause of the people. To accomplish this great and salutary object presents a proper field for the patriotic exertions of all who think it wise, as I do, to keep a jealous eye upon executive authority and particularly upon its administration of the public patronage. Placed at the head of the committee upon appointments in the convention for the amendment of the constitution of my own State, I took an active, and I hope not an ineffectual part, to carry out this principle as far as with the lights which experience had then afforded I thought we could safely go. As those lights multiplied, I united in giving it a still wider range, and I am well satisfied that a periodical review of the subject by the legislature and people, with views to its still greater extension, would be eminently useful, as well in the administration of the Federal as of the State Governments.

[A NATIONAL NOMINATING CONVENTION]

To your last interrogatory I unhesitatingly answer, Yes. The democracy of the Union will not fail, as I am sure they ought not, to adopt every proper precaution to secure, through the instrumentality of the convention they propose to hold, an honest and full expression of the wishes and opinions of a majority of their political associates. Bearing in mind the disreputable scenes of 1840, conscious of the effects which those scenes necessarily had in shaking the confidence of mankind in the fitness of the American people for free institutions, and actuated by a patriotic zeal to wipe off, now and forever, every injurious impression which was thus made upon the character of either, they will not, I am certain, permit their noble efforts in so good a cause to be stained by a single act of indirection or unfairness. So believing, I hold it to be impossible that a selection can proceed from such a source which I could not cheerfully support, or a nominee be selected in whose hands the interests of the country would not be entirely safe.

My name and pretensions, however subordinate in importance, shall never be at the disposal of any persons whatever for the purpose of creating distraction or division in the Democratic Party. Every attempt to use them for such a purpose, whenever and wherever made, shall be arrested by an interference on my part, alike prompt and decisive. I regard the Presidency as the highest and most honorable of political distinctions, yet it is only as the undoubted and free-will offering of the democracy of the Nation that I could accept it, because it is in that aspect only that I could hope to render the discharge of its high duties either useful to the country or honorable to myself.

8

BENJAMIN F. HALLETT

THE SOVEREIGNTY OF THE PEOPLE[1]

THE FIRST of these causes comes before this Court by writ of error to the Circuit Court of the United States for the District of Rhode Island, upon a judgment pro forma against the plaintiff in error.

The second is sent up from the same Court upon a certificate of division of opinion between the two Judges.

Both causes involve similar questions and principles and therefore may with great propriety be argued together, the distinction between them being that in the first the distinct issue raised is the validity of the People's Constitution, which the plaintiff claims was in force in Rhode Island; and in the second the question is definitely raised as to the force and validity of Martial Law, under which the defendants justify their acts of trespass.

If the new constitution, and laws under it, were in force in Rhode Island, and the old Charter Government rightfully superseded thereby, then the justification of the defendants fails in both cases. If, on the other hand, that constitution was not in force, but the Charter Legislature was in fact the law-making power, yet, if they had not the power to declare Martial Law in the manner they did, or if the act itself, and the proceedings under it, were illegal or defective, or if the defendants have failed to show their authority as subordinates, then also the defense in both cases, but especially in the latter, fails.

The first is an action for trespass to the property of the plaintiff, Martin Luther; the second is an action for trespass to the person of the plaintiff, Rachael Luther.

The facts which appear upon the record and are to be taken as fully proved are these: —

In June, 1842, Martin Luther was living in the town of Warren, in

[1] [From *The Right of the People to Establish Forms of Government. Mr. Hallett's Argument before the Supreme Court of the United States, January, 1848* (Boston, 1848) — Abridged.]

the State of Rhode Island, in his own house (which was also occupied by his mother, Rachael Luther) and had lived there for nearly forty years. On the 29th of June, in the night time, the defendants, Luther M. Borden, Stephen Johnson, William L. Brown, John H. Munroe, William B. Snell, James Gardner, and John Kelly, are charged with breaking into the plaintiff's dwelling house, they being armed with muskets and other dangerous weapons, and in a menacing manner breaking and tearing down the doors, glasses, windows, and furniture, and otherwise defacing and injuring the house.

They are also charged, in the second suit, with a personal trespass upon the plaintiff, Mrs. Luther, an elderly lady of some eighty years of age, by forcibly, in the night time, breaking into her chamber, in which she was sleeping with her maid servant, driving them from their beds in their night clothes, and with bayonets pointed to the breast and body of the plaintiff and her servant, menacing and threatening to stab and kill them if they did not disclose where Martin Luther was, and detaining them in their night dress and not permitting them to dress for more than an hour to their great terror and alarm.

These trespasses are obviously of a highly aggravated character: a midnight invasion of the rights of domicile, and an outrage upon personal security, under circumstances that would call for the highest exemplary damages. The parties in both suits, by these violent proceedings of armed men against them, were compelled to leave the State, in which they could find no protection from law, and became citizens of the State of Massachusetts. It was vain for them to have sought redress in the State Courts of Rhode Island. Hence this was precisely the case for a resort to the Courts of the United States, contemplated by the framers of the Constitution, in order to lift the questions that might arise between citizens of different States above the partial influences of the local tribunals.

. . . .

They[2] became citizens of Massachusetts and as such commenced suits against the defendants in the Circuit Court for the District of Rhode Island.

Thus was the history of persecution between Massachusetts and Rhode Island reversed. Two hundred years before, Roger Williams had fled from Massachusetts to find protection against the persecution

2 [That is, Martin and Rachael Luther.]

of *Church* Law; and now Rhode Island drove her citizens back to Massachusetts to seek redress for outrages committed under the guise of *Martial* Law.

In the Circuit Court below, the defendants set up *a plea in justification*. They admitted that they had committed the trespasses complained of, doing no more damage than they affirm was necessary; but they say they were justified in law because they were enrolled in a company of infantry, in the town of Warren, under the command of John T. Child, duly appointed and legally qualified to act in that capacity; and that, by order of said military commander, they broke and entered the said dwelling house of the plaintiff in error in order to arrest and take the said plaintiff, which they aver it was lawful for them to do.

And further the defendants say that at the time of the alleged trespass large numbers of men assembled in arms in different parts of said State made and levied war upon said State and were attempting the overthrow of the government of said State by military force. That the Legislature of said State, duly and legally chosen and constituted according to the provisions of the charter or fundamental law and the ancient and long established usages of said State, and in the exercise of the legislative powers conferred on them by said charter and usages, did enact and establish Martial Law over said State; and that under such authority and by order of a military commander duly appointed by such authority, the defendants committed the alleged trespass.

To the several pleas of the defendants the plaintiff replied *de sua injuria*, thus denying the truth of the defendants' plea, which issue was joined, and upon this issue came up the question of the validity of the Charter Government and the acts thereof, under which the defendants justified, and of the new constitution and frame of government adopted by the people of Rhode Island, called the People's Constitution, and the acts and doings of the Legislature under the same.

Thus far the pleadings in both cases are alike; but at this point, with the permission of the Court, I shall leave for future consideration the subject of Martial Law and proceed to the argument upon the record in the case of Martin Luther.

In reply to the justification which the defendants set up, under the authority of the Charter Governor and Legislature, the plaintiff contended that the old charter form of government and the acts of the Legislature under which the defendants justified were, at the time of such trespass, superseded and abolished by a new form of government and invalid so far as repugnant to the same; which new form of government was then in force as the fundamental law of the State; and that the Legislature chosen by the people and acting under the said new form of government, and the military and other officers appointed by law under such legislative power, constituted the actual government of said State; and that acts done under any assumed authority, in opposition to said constitution and laws so established, were unlawful and void.

The question, therefore, was directly between two forms of government, both claiming to be in force at the same time; and upon the construction of law as to which of these forms of government was in legal existence at the time depended the issue whether the defendants had acted under law, or against all law.

Both parties agreed that, up to May, 1842, the old Charter Government of Rhode Island was rightfully in existence. But the plaintiff maintained that it was then superseded by the new government then organized under the People's Constitution, which had been adopted Jan. 12, 1842, to take full effect in the following May.

It followed that, if the Charter Government then ceased, neither the Martial Law, under which the defendants justify the attempt to break into his house and seize Mr. Luther, nor the military commission and the military orders of their commander, were of any avail.

Plainly, then, the rights of the parties in this cause can only be decided by deciding that issue *distinctly* and *directly;* and in the judgment of the plaintiffs' counsel, and I may add of the learned Judge since deceased who framed the instructions upon the record, that issue was intended to be brought and is brought before this Court in such form that it must be met, and must be passed upon in the indispensable exercise of the ordinary judicial functions of this high tribunal.

I do not say this, may it please your Honors, as if there were or could be any doubt that this is the issue here, or that this elevated tribunal will meet it as decidedly and calmly as if it involved the simple question of title to a piece of land, instead of the people's title to their great right of self-government. . . . .

Upon this statement of the issue, therefore, we contend that it will become indispensable (as it seems to us) for this Court, in order to determine this case, to decide, incidentally to the merits, whether the People's Constitution was in force in Rhode Island as the fundamental law of the State; and hence the importance of this cause, as presenting, in fact, a judicial test, before the highest tribunal in the land, whether the theory of American free government for the States of this Union is available to the people in practice; in short, whether the basis of popular sovereignty is a living principle, or a theory, always restrained in practice by the will of the law-making power and therefore subject and not sovereign.

In this view of the aspect of this cause, it becomes necessary to go back to fundamental principles to determine which was the existing form of government, which was the Legislature, and what were the laws in force at the time of the trespass. This is apparent from the fact that by the pleadings the defendants admit they have committed a trespass, but justify their acts under the authority derived from the Charter Assembly and the commissions and orders of military commanders, deriving their sole power from that source.

.   .   .   .

[CAN THE PEOPLE CHANGE THEIR GOVERNMENT?]

I then submit the preliminary proposition that upon the pleadings and the record of this case the Court cannot determine the issue, whether a trespass was or was not committed, without first deciding what were the constitution and frame of government in force in Rhode Island at the time.

And with this view, and under the permission of the Court, I shall proceed to open this cause upon the broad basis of this argument, in its full force and extent, covering the whole ground of *rightful changes of government by the people of the States of this Union.*

These preliminary suggestions embrace within the issue three general propositions:

1. That the assumed authority, legislative and military, and the acts and orders under which defendants justify, are invalid and insufficient.

2. That the issue was properly before the Court below, and it is necessary for this Court to pass upon it in order to determine the rights of the parties on the record in this cause.

3. That it is a judicial power and not a political power which the Court is called upon to exercise in applying the rule of decision that is to govern this case.

The burden of proof is on the defendants to show their justification, but the plaintiff, doubtless, must show, at least, so far as to set aside the authority of the defendant's plea, that the new government had superseded the old form.

I propose, therefore, to maintain, in the argument, the following points, which were ruled against the plaintiff, merely formally, in the Court below:

1. That the People's Constitution was in force in Rhode Island in June, 1842.

2. That the Legislature chosen under it was the law-making power.

3. That consequently the pre-existing Charter Government was superseded; and

4. That the plaintiff need show such change of government only so far as the justification the defendants set up, under the first, is concerned.

In order to sustain these propositions, we must first establish the great basis upon which alone they can rest in the American system of government, viz.:

1. That the majority of the people, or of the legal voters of a State, have a right to establish a written constitution.

2. That this is pre-eminently their right, in the absence of any provision in the existing frame of government for its amendment.

3. That this right is independent of the will or sanction of the Legislature, and can be exercised by the right of eminent sovereignty in the people, without the form of a precedent statute law. . . .

.   .   .   .

Having traced the History of Government in Rhode Island, and the proceedings in framing, adopting, and establishing the People's Constitution, in 1841–42, what are the inferences to be drawn applicable to the issue between the parties in this cause as to the respective rights they claim, and the respective authorities under which they assume to have acted?

First, I will consider it with reference to the local history and institutions of Rhode Island herself, and then upon the broad basis of American sovereignty.

We have seen that the old charter of Rhode Island, in 1663, was entirely free and democratic. The community consisted of landed proprietors, and it was, in effect, a landed company in which all were partners and participants. As society progressed and the number of inhabitants increased who did not own land, in the changes and progress of business, the inequality became more apparent.

The people then looked back to the old guarantees of liberty. Efforts at reform began and were continued without success. The minority, holding the Legislature in their control, denied all extension of suffrage, and without it the majority could not act within the form of law. Their only resource was to go out of it. The reluctance to take such a step or to change existing institutions was one cause of the continuance of the old form. We have seen that during the Revolution a committee on suffrage and reform was appointed, which shows the first impulse of public opinion, on the adoption of the Declaration of Independence, but the state of the times prevented action. The patriotism of the people submitted to unequal government rather than to disturb it at the risk of weakening the aid necessary to carry on the war of independence.

After the Revolution, Rhode Island was involved in debt and difficulties and became embarrassed in her wretched paper money system. For a long time her Legislature, representing the landholding minority, held her back from the Union and refused to adopt the United States Constitution. . . .

In this state of things and having a charter tolerably free, she did not adopt a written constitution, as did all the other States, except Connecticut for a like cause. The majority did not break out, but for the time acquiesced. But there were no principles or practice of government in Rhode Island which denied the right of the people, with or without the consent of the existing government, to make a constitution when and how they pleased.

On the contrary, Rhode Island, which had been foremost in religious freedom, had, by her great founder, Roger Williams, equally pledged herself to civil liberty. . . .

.   .   .   .

We have seen how the Rhode Island Assembly departed from the doctrines of religious freedom in 1663. They have still more flagrantly repudiated the principles of their illustrious founder touching civil liberty. It is therefore no proof of a prescriptive right in her Assembly, in 1842, to deny self-government to the people, because that Assembly had always refused to extend suffrage or permit the majority to participate in government by framing a written constitution.

The conclusion is that both precedent and principle fairly construed, up to the Revolution, affirm or at least favor the right of the *people* of Rhode Island (not merely the landholders) to alter and establish government. At the Revolution this principle was authoritatively recognized. The Convention that adopted the United States Constitution, in 1790, went further, and all power was resolved into the hands of the people.

What then became of the Charter Government, and what powers can a legislature under it have to control the organic law for a longer time than the people, consenting and agreeing, shall betrust them with. . . .

. . . .

What was there of *paramount* organic law in Rhode Island? Not the charter. It had no element of change or modification. The laws under it, passed by the Assembly, were repealable at pleasure. The Legislature had no power, either from the charter or the people, or inherent, to change the organic law, or to make one. If the *people* could not act, the Legislature could not, the voters could not; who could? Hence —

The American doctrine of a paramount written constitution, binding the legislature and subject only to the people, was lost in Rhode Island, if it did not exist in the whole people.

Admitting the right of the people to make a constitution and overthrow the British colonial government to have been acquired or confirmed by the Revolution, how did they lose it? When regrant it? If never, how can this right be denied to the people of Rhode Island, in setting aside their Charter Government, and adopting a written constitution to control their legislature and officers? Then, if the right existed, how was it to be exercised? The subsisting government had no power or right to make a constitution. All their declarations of rights in the Digests of Laws were only repealable legislative acts, without guarantee.

Our opponents, doubtless, will concede a *right* of revolution, but say we must take it by *physical force!* The value of that sort of right to a State of this Union I will consider presently, but the right of revolu-

tion being admitted, does it follow that it must be by force? If the
people have a right, they must also have a right to exercise it peaceably. If they do so without attacking the existing government and
peaceably set up a government of organic law, defined in a written
constitution, and if after this is done, the old government, which is
virtually superseded, attacks the new, then to defend the latter is not
revolution, but *law and order*, and the old disbanded government is the
aggressor.

*This is the distinction between rebellion and the change of organic laws
by adopting a written constitution where none exists.*

Shays' Rebellion, the Whisky Insurrection, and the Anti-Rent Riots
in New York, illustrate this; and this was the relation of government
and people before the Revolution. Under the colonial government,
the people, if they adhered to it, had no legal right to change it. The
sovereignty of the King and Parliament precluded any such right.
Revolution, therefore, and if revolution was resisted, war upon the
existing government, were, at that period, the only resource — there
was no lawful mode of changing a form of government. If the Charter
Government of Rhode Island had sided with Great Britain, the people
would have put them down. By siding with the people, the Charter
Government gave no legitimate sanction to the Revolution. It was
the same rebellion under the existing form of government. It had no
foundation of right, except in the right of the majority to change
government.

[The Right of Peaceable Revolution]

*But we claim a new principle in government: The right peaceably to
change government.* The limit is that it shall be done by a majority.
Not by first attacking the existing government or overturning the
laws, and then making a constitution, as in the revolution of '76, but
by first adopting peaceably a new organic law, establishing the fundamental principles on which the government shall be conducted, the
officers chosen, and the laws enacted. In order to do this, the concurrence of the old government is convenient and desirable, but not
indispensable.

The right to begin this work rests in the right of the people to assemble.
Who has the right to interfere with them? Up to the point of adoption
of the People's Constitution in Rhode Island, where was the right to

interfere with them or put them down by force? No matter how the constitution was begun or put together. It was peacefully made, peacefully put to the people, and peacefully adopted by the majority. It then became the organic law. It went into effect by its own force, and organization and legislation took effect under it. It has all the efficacy of a government *de jure* and *de facto*. At this point the men of the old government attacked the new and attempted to suppress it by military force.

Not an act was done by the people, but in pursuance of the new organic law. If the majority had a right to make a constitution, then it was made and became the supreme law. Therefore, to deny that the People's Constitution was the supreme law, when they assembled under it and chose officers, and their Legislature met to carry it out, all of which was done without revolution or violence or attack, is to deny the right of the people, under any circumstances, to *frame government except by the consent of their rulers;* and to this point our opponents must come, or yield the whole argument.

This would make the Revolution of '76 the shame instead of the glory of the nation. In some of the old thirteen colonies new forms of government were adopted against the consent of a portion of the legislative and all of the executive power. In Virginia, for instance. When attacked by the old government, ought they to have yielded to it? Why, then, should the people yield in Rhode Island, after they had peacefully adopted their constitution, chosen officers under it, and put the new frame of government in full operation? What had the majority done that constituted rebellion, insurrection, treason, or domestic violence?

They stood on better grounds as to RIGHT *than even the grounds of the Revolution.* They had the great civil right recognized as the cornerstone of American institutions — the peaceful right which the Revolution had established to frame government, and when duly adopted, then all the rights, civil and military, attached to sustain it.

There were no votes taken by the masses, or in conventions, in the Revolution of '76, to change the government. It was a resort to natural right, to be enforced, if resisted, by war, and in no other form. The first step to dissolve government or to deny the supremacy of the Crown was rebellion and treason, under all the then recognized legitimate doctrines of government. The colonial governments existed only by the sovereign grace and mere motion of the King. They had no inherent principle of reform or change.

The Revolution, being successful, established this new fundamental principle of government, and in Rhode Island it was distinctly recognized — "that the powers of government may be reassumed by the people whensoever it shall become necessary to their happiness."

This the people did, and no more. They made no attack on existing institutions. They changed no organic relations of the people to the government. They violated no allegiance, they dissolved no community, they changed no relation of the State to the Union. The identity and integrity of the State remained the same. It was no more a change of identity, of relations of people and rulers, of the government and the governed, or of the federal relations to the Union, than a change in the codes of legislation.

The fundamental law was changed by peaceful, popular process. If the right to do so was with the people, the form was legal, and even legitimate, for it was sanctioned by the fundamental rule of government, lying at the foundation of all government. If they had this right, they exercised it as peacefully and legally as the legislature could exercise their right in revising the code of State laws.

The theory of the opposite side assumes that the people of the States of this Union have acquired no rights in regard to government by the Revolution that the people under old governments did not possess. That is physical right, natural right. The *right* of *might*, which is no right, but mere physical power to do wrong or right. But there was no such thing as a peaceful change of government under old systems, and consequently no change of government without the consent of government. On the other hand —

American institutions recognize three great principles:

1. The elective power, to change rulers.

2. The representative power, substituting agency from the people for irresponsibility to the people.

3. And behind all this, the power and right of the majority of the community to change at pleasure the organic law of the State, and prescribe forms of constitution as the supreme law.

This makes the distinction in principle and fact; the distinction between attacking an existing government with lawless violence, and the peaceful organization of a new frame of the same government, and then, after it is so established, sustaining it under the forms of law. This is the Rhode Island case, and this is shown by the history of the proceedings up to the first attempts of the Chartists to resist the operations of the People's Constitution.

.   .   .   .

If the principles on which the adoption of the People's Constitution are placed in the foregoing argument are sound, then the facts in the record being to be taken as proved, the conclusion follows that the acts done according to the law, under the new constitution, were valid, and all other acts contrary thereto were invalid.

What title to perpetual government can the charter party set up? Was it the right of possession? Was it prescription? The defendants say that the charter and form of government under it continued to be the fundamental law until the adoption of the present constitution, in 1843. We contend that the People's Constitution and acts under it intervened from May, 1842, until the adoption of the present constitution of 1843. All the pleadings and offers of evidence on both sides resolve themselves into this single issue, of previous consent of the Legislature as the indispensable antecedent of a constitution! The old Assembly made this the whole issue. They said to the people of Rhode Island, "you have assumed to make and establish a constitution, without our consent, and therefore it is void."

Whether it was a constitution of *right* depends solely upon the *first step* in making it, viz., whether the action of the legislature, and that merely a *request*, was indispensable.

It all comes back to this: Is a constitution void and inoperative, unless the legislature *request* the people to make it?

Must the legislature alone *permit*, and cannot the people go behind such permission? Can the legislature refuse to act for half a century, and then *punish* the people for acting?

If of right, without such beginning, it takes effect *proprio vigore*. The obstinacy of the General Assembly caused the whole difficulty. If they had done in 1841 what they did in June, 1842, all dissension would have ceased. The result shows that they were only contending for dogmatism, for they have done, in the last constitution, just what they charge us with rebellion and treason for doing. The surrender of land suffrage, as the only means of saving the collision that would have shattered the old dynasty, shows the necessity of the change demanded by the people; and the whole point of law and order is that the Assembly would not do, in answer to the wishes of the people, what they afterward did do and thereby admit they ought to have done at first.

The judges of the Rhode Island Court, after sentencing Governor Dorr for sustaining the People's Constitution, should have changed places and sentenced themselves for making a like constitution, which was equal treason to the old charter.

And yet they exhibited the singular spectacle of judges sitting under a new constitution, which, by the charter, the old assembly had no right to make, and trying a distinguished citizen for treason to a departed government, which they themselves had helped to exterminate!

And the whole pith and point of this modern treason was that the Assembly *requested* the landholders to put down the old government, but refused to request the people to do it!

We are now prepared, in the argument, to apply the foregoing facts in the Rhode Island case to the broad and general proposition, which embraces all free American States, of *the Right of the People to Change Government, and to judge of the Occasion.*

Did this right vest in the people of the colonies by the operation of the Declaration of Independence? This has already been demonstrated, and will hardly be denied from any quarter.

Then, have American institutions, in the States or in the Union, changed, modified, limited, or restricted this right, as it originally was declared to exist, "inherent and unalienable" in the people? In short, is the sovereignty in the people, and how may they exercise it?

It may safely be assumed that no man or set of men, in a government where suffrage is in the hands of the masses, will venture to deny, in so many words, that the people are sovereign. Doubtless this will be conceded, gracefully if not graciously, by the distinguished counsel on the other side. But how conceded, is the question. I apprehend, from the tenor of the defendants' abstract of points, that while this same sovereignty may *seem* to be yielded to the people in terms, it will be qualified away and in effect denied and abrogated in detail and in all efficient operation. By their limitations and constructions, the people will turn out to be very great sovereigns, with very great powers, but without any possible *right* to exercise that sovereign power short of *rebellion* against the governments of their own creation! That is the question we are to try; whether this virtue of sovereignty has gone out of the people, by some sort of prescription, grant, acquiescence or submission, and become vested in the government, so that the people can never have the free use of it again without some process of license or re-grant from the legislature.

We are not discussing revolutions by mere physical force, but a fundamental principle of right; and to test this, we must first see what the right is, and then whether it is a mere abstraction or active and operative. When they talk of sovereignty, what is the sovereignty they mean? That which we rest our argument upon is the sovereignty defined by the enlightened advocates of liberty in the old world, and its founders and expounders in the new. Here I leave all speculation and abide by the highest sanction of precedents. If dry in detail, it is vital in principle. Then *what is the Sovereignty of the People, as defined by the American principles of Government?*

The theory of the other side, and the only theory they can stand on to invalidate a constitution framed by a clear majority, through the peaceful forms of conventions, is that the people are sovereign not in themselves but through the forms of law emanating from the legislature. In short, that the sovereignty has no power to make *fundamental* law except through the permissive agency of *statute* law. We maintain that there is not a precedent, from the time of Algernon Sydney to the time of Thomas W. Dorr, that gives a colorable sanction to such a theory of American liberties.

.   .   .   .

I will close these judicial references by an authority that will surely be respected here, and which, with what has preceded it, must be conclusive, viz., Chief Justice Marshall, in 1803, speaking for the whole Court, in the case of Marbury vs. Madison, (1 Cranch, 176, cited 3, Story's Commen., 431):

"The question, whether an act repugnant to the constitution can become the law of the land, is a question deeply interesting to the United States; but, happily, not of an intricacy proportioned to its interest. It seems only necessary to recognize certain principles, supposed to have been long well established, to decide it.

"That the people have an original right to establish, for their future government, such principles as, in their opinion, shall most conduce to their own happiness, is the basis on *which the whole American fabric has been erected*. The exercise of this original right *is a very great exertion;* nor can it, nor ought it to be very frequently repeated. The principles, therefore, so established, are deemed fundamental. And as the *authority* from which they proceed is *supreme*, and can seldom act, they are designed to be *permanent*."

In McCulloch vs. State of Maryland, in 1819, 4th Wheaton, 404, the same high authority treats this as not an open question before the Court:

"It has been said, that the people have already surrendered all their powers to the State sovereignties, and had nothing more to give. *But, surely, the question whether they may resume and modify the powers granted to government, does not remain to be settled in this country*."

And yet, may it please your Honors, Governor Dorr and his friends have been charged with treason for acting upon this solemn dictum of the whole Supreme Court as if it were true! Now take this emphatic expression of the opinion of the Supreme Court, through Chief Justice Marshall, and test it by the Rhode Island Bill of Rights, adopted by her *Convention* in 1790, viz., "that the powers of government may be *reassumed* by the people," and we have the entire doctrine contended for by the plaintiff here, judicially established by the Supreme Court of the United States as unquestionable, and almost in the very words of that Bill of Rights, viz., "the people may resume the powers granted to government."

"Granted TO government," is the phrase, not granted *by* government. Not granted subject to the condition that the power shall be resumed only by the consent and in the form of statute law prescribed by the grantee, the legislature! This "does not remain to be settled in this country!" and if so, how then stand these defendants here on their plea of justification by a denial of the sovereignty of the people?

May it please your Honors, with this array of authorities and unbroken precedents against them, the counsel for the defendants, whatever may have been their original purpose, will be constrained to say that they concede the sovereignty to the people. What else have they to say? But I could not trust to that concession, as they may be pleased to call it, followed as it must be, unless they surrender the whole cause, with restrictions and limitations; and therefore, the sovereignty which we mean, as defined by those who best understood and appreciated it, has been thus broadly spread out upon the argument. Well, then, if we have this sovereignty, how and when and by what process may it act? Does it really exist in practice or only in abstraction? And this brings us to the practical operation of this sovereignty in framing constitutions of government.

[THE METHOD OF CONSTITUTIONAL CHANGE]

Then, if the People have the right, how may they exercise it? Who shall begin, the People or the Government, Conventions or Legislatures? We say the former. The proposition on the other side is, you must have a statute law to call your convention and count your votes, and say who shall vote and how, or you cannot take a step to make or alter the frame of government.

It is not so, unless this boasted sovereignty is but a mockery, a delusion, and a snare. Will this Court say to the people of each State in this Union that true it is they are the source of all political power, but if they presume to exercise their sovereignty in establishing or changing constitutions of government without consent of the legislature, they shall be followed with pains and penalties, enforced by the lawless despotism of Martial Law, and backed by the whole military power of the United States, called out by the President to suppress insurrection and domestic violence! Whenever this tribunal shall proclaim this to be the law, it will have decreed that, in contemplation of law, the people here, as in Great Britain, do not exist. Such is not the law of this land, here, nor elsewhere. On the contrary, all American precedents and practice of government demonstrate that the assumption that the first step in reforms and changes of government must emanate from the established government and not from the people is the dogma of *despotism!*

To this point all the foregoing authorities directly tend. It is the incident that follows the principle, for it were as absurd to concede entire freedom to the individual and deny his right to move a hand without the leave of a master as to affirm a sovereignty of the people incapable of taking the first step to make or remodel their frame of government. This is our main point of difference.

We shall agree on the right to abolish, but divide on the *mode.* They make the mode an inseparable barrier to the exercise of the right, the form superior to the substance — dependent on another tribunal than the people and one of their own creation!

True, it is said that the people, though sovereign, may limit themselves, as well as their governments, by their constitutions. Doubtless
they do so, through representation, as to the making and enforcing of
statute law, which they leave to the subsisting organization. And so
they prescribe the modes of amending constitutions. But who do
they *limit* in this power of making and amending constitutions! The
legislature and not *themselves!*

I pray this may be marked because the practical exercise of the
sovereignty depends upon it. Constitutions are made to control the
legislature and to control majorities as to all exercise of rights under
the constitution. While it subsists, all are governed by its limitations,
and so far the majority as well as the minority have limited themselves.
Now comes the question of change in the constitution. Who are
limited by it in making that change? The *legislature.* They can
move only by proposing amendments to be sent out to the people who
are voters under the existing constitution, or to call conventions, if
the constitution so provides. They cannot move a step outside of
the constitution. But are the *people* who made this constitution
limited in their power of amendment, because they have restricted
the legislature? Will the learned counsel on the other side show a
provision in the twenty-nine constitutions of these States which says
that "We the people hereby agree never to amend this constitution,
or to make another, in any other way except that which is prescribed
herein, through the legislature!"

There is no such thing in existence, nor anything like it. All the
power of amendment given in all the constitutions *limits* the legislatures. *They* shall not touch the constitution except in the way the
sovereign power permits them to act. But behind this stands the
sovereign who made, and who has the like power to unmake. The
sovereign, if he had power to make, has not granted away that power.
The power given to the legislature is *permissive* and exhausts no part
of the reserved powers of the grantor. Even the present constitution
of Rhode Island says "that the General Assembly *may* propose amendments to be submitted to the electors, and if *three-fifths* of the electors
approve, such amendments shall become a part of the constitution."

It follows, then, that the legislature cannot propose or adopt any
amendment of the constitution in any other way; but the people have
not tied themselves down to a three-fifth rule; they have tied the

legislature, but behind all this is the sovereignty acting by and through majorities, and if they ever had a right to act through conventions to establish a frame of government, they have nowhere granted or ceded it away. True, the State constitutions require more than a majority of the legislature to propose amendments, but this only limits the legislature and does not touch the majority principle in the people.

Now let us go back to the first step in free government, and having the source of power in the people, trace its practical operation in making constitutions.

The position may seem plausible and eminently conservative that it will not do to trust the mass of community with the power to assemble together and ascertain the will of the majority in any other form except by a statute, prescribing who shall vote, and when, and where, and how! But this is not an American principle.

The serious objection to this position is that it resolves sovereignty into the government and takes it from the people. This is plain, because he who *alone* can take the first step is the sovereign. At his will all progress stands still.

Another objection is that this theory founds sovereignty in *suffrage* and not in the *people*. The argument resolves itself into the proposition that suffrage limits sovereignty, and, when suffrage is once prescribed, whether to a minority or a majority of community, these are the eternal limits of sovereignty. Everything outside of suffrage is excluded from participation in sovereignty and of consequence in government.

In other words, the legal voters once established, few or many, are, through their representation in the law-making power, the sovereign and ultimate power in a State, and they may forever exclude all others from government.

But who made the legal voters? In a limited monarchy they are made by the grant of the King, or act of Parliament, both acting as the sovereign power in the State. In governments of a more popular form they are made by the constitution; or, as in Rhode Island, by the Legislature without a constitution.

True, then, the legal voters are the ultimate power under the constitution; but that is the act of the sovereignty, the rule prescribed by it, and not the sovereignty itself, which is higher and beyond the organic form of its own creation.

While that constitution subsists, or while the law-making power, which says who shall vote, is supreme in power, the people consent to limit the exercise of government within these bounds, and so far the right to elect and be elected to office is limited and prescribed for the time being. But it is not perpetual, and if in the hands of a minority, it is not past all remedy without the consent of that minority, unless the majority resort to violence, revolution, and civil war.

This is the theory of the old world, which American liberties have exploded. The theory may stand very well when the whole people can act through organization. But when the legal voters refuse to act through organization, or in its absence, we must go outside of organization to look for the sovereignty, or we have a *despotism;* and whether it be a despotism of the divine right of kings which is their law, or of a legislature restricting suffrage to a minority which is their law, it is the same in its effect upon all who are excluded thereby from participation in government. And if these are a majority, as in France, in England, and in Rhode Island, then there can be a state wherein the sovereignty is rightfully held by a minority, and the majority of the people are *not* sovereign!

.   .   .   .

And now, may it please your Honors, with the utmost deference, permit me to ask, how could this Honorable Court — nay, how can any *American* maintain, in the face of these authorities and of the sovereignty of the people, to which all at least *pretend* to bow that, in contemplation of law, and in the cognizance of this Court, there can be no *legitimate* change in the constitutions and forms of government, unless the permission to make the change, and the form in which the people shall proceed, is *first* prescribed by an act of the subsisting legislature?

What a discouragement to the oppressed millions of the old world would it be for the "model republic" of America to send forth, as her solemn judicial judgment, a decree in this cause in favor of unchangeable despotism. What a repudiation of the doctrines and the practice of our fathers, and what a reproach upon their memories. Whatever may be your decision, or no decision in this case, no such result can be apprehended. The theory that government cannot be rightfully changed except by force of the formal consent of the law-making power, whether in a king or a legislature, we maintain is wholly anti-American, and is nothing but a dogma of despotism; and I will now proceed to prove it.

[CONSTITUTIONAL CHANGE IS THE AMERICAN WAY]

The fundamental distinction between the American principle of POPULAR *government and the European principle of* LEGITIMATE *government is this:*

1. In the former *the people are the ultimate source of power and can change government without a law permitting them to do so.*

2. In the latter *the reigning dynasty, or at best the parliament,* is the sovereign power in the state, and the people can make no change in government whatever; they can only take what is granted and submit to what is decreed.

The great distinction is the power of *originating and framing,* as well as of accepting. There can be no sovereignty, no direction, no control, without the first. A constitution in Russia depends upon the free will of the Emperor to grant it. Now, if in Rhode Island, or any State of this Union, the forming or changing of a constitution depends upon the *grant* of the legislature, through a previous permissive law to hold a convention, where is the difference between the "legitimate" king and the republican assembly? The people are equally tied down in both cases. They cannot move without somebody's consent, and if anybody, then he who holds that power of consent in his hands is the sovereign.

The people of Rhode Island could no more change their King, the Assembly, than the Russians can theirs, because the Assembly were landholders chosen by landholders and refusing suffrage to the great majority. What matters it whether the Assembly makes or amends a constitution and asks the people to take it, with the sole power to say yea or nay, and nothing more, or whether a king or a parliament grants the people a constitution and compels them to take it or nothing, as is the European custom, when the people demand their rights by a threat of revolution?

Let the people of this country, whatever else they may yield, *never yield by remotest implication the great right to originate, frame, remodel and amend government!*

The moment they descend to become mere acceptors or rejectors of amendments emanating from any other source, they are *slaves of government* and no longer sovereign. For this is the vital distinction between the American principle of free institutions and the European principle of *legitimate* government.

. . . .

How then can the validity of a constitution depend upon the fact whether the legislature did or did not act first by allowing the people to meet in convention? On the contrary, we maintain that *government is subjected to the sovereignty of the nation, the people — and not the people or nation made subject to the Government.*

. . . .

Now we find the majority of the people of Rhode Island adopting a constitution. Must it not be treated as an act of the sovereign power? They answer no, because the Assembly refused to request the convention to meet. Then *the basis of the defendants' proposition is this:*

1. That when any commonwealth or state exists under an organic law and has created a legislature, no convention, with a view to a change of the organic law by the whole people, can be rightfully held, without the previous consent of the legislature, however constituted, and whether chosen by a minority or majority of the whole people.

2. That if held without such previous consent, it is revolutionary, and its acts, though ratified by the whole people, invalid, unauthorized and insurrectionary.

In short, that the fundamental law depends upon the legislature and not upon the people. *The inference from this theory is unavoidable, viz.:*

1. That the legislature is sovereign, and that however oppressed the majority may be under a system of minority suffrage, no change can take place unless the people conquer it in battle by force, or unless the legislature grants them leave to assemble in convention to make a constitution!

2. That if the majority of the people (or if all except a quorum of the legislature and the executive) should attempt by force to put down the government, or to change it at all without legislative consent, this constitutes a case of "domestic violence," which the whole naval and military forces of the Union may be called out to suppress!

3. That there are no inherent liberties in the people, and the entire substance must yield to the mere shadow of form.

Such is not the American theory of government. On the contrary, the preliminary forms in making a constitution are nothing to the substance. "They are but the scaffolding of the building, which is of no further use after the edifice is completed and occupied."

It may be suggested that the People's Constitution is not proved. It is proved by the facts in the record. But how prove a constitution? How does the present constitution of Rhode Island or of any State exist, and how could it be proved? Would it depend upon no one objecting to the present constitution in Rhode Island? It received not 7000 votes; much less than a majority of the whole legal voters under it. The people's party might have objected or may now object. The seal of the State might be abstracted. This is no test of authenticity. The people's officers had their seal. The record shows no seal on either side. In fact the only distinction between the present constitution and the People's, as to authenticity, for the time they were in force or to be in force, is the act of the assembly calling the convention, and that was a mere *request*.

Then we must fall back on the system of paramount right. Where is it? Where is *the power behind* all, *beyond* all constitutions? What is outside of the frame of government?

Can a constitution be altered only by its own terms, and in its own forms? Even if this were conceded, it cannot apply to Rhode Island. But if only this were true, then we have made at least *one* step beyond the doctrines of the Laybach Circular. We have made one step in getting constitutions that authorize change.

The doctrine then would be, "All changes in government must emanate from those whom the *constitution* has intrusted with the power to recommend such change." But if it also applies to the case of Rhode Island, then we have not advanced a step beyond the divine right of kings — only to the divine right of the king's charter.

They will contend that the American practice has been to make all changes through the organized government. Such is not the fact. It may be convenient, desirable; but it is not the ultimatum, neither is it a rule. It is, at most, a question of concurrence between the people and the government. Where the voters are the great majority, this might be in practical operation sufficient. But suppose they do not concur? Suppose the government gets into the hands of a minority and won't yield? This provision for concurrence does not take away the reserved right of the people to act. *They* give all the validity, and not the act calling the convention. The form prescribed is mere direction to the agents, not a bar to the people. If the necessity arises, the people may act. It did arise in Rhode Island, and the people acted. The preliminary call, had it emanated from the Assembly, could give no validity or precedent authority until the people voted on it and confirmed it. The confirmation made it the act of the people. But it would have been just as much their act had they originated the call without the unauthorized *request* of the Assembly.

Where, then, was the sovereignty to institute the preliminary steps in Rhode Island? The Legislature had no power. They could give no power to the people. They had no priority of recommendation. They in fact only *requested.* Hence *the absurdity of defendants' hypothesis is manifest.* They say that the people had no power to move as a body. We show that the Legislature had no power. That the landholders, the legal voters, were the creatures of the Legislature, and they had no power as such to give to the Legislature. Hence it follows that if neither the people nor the legal voters had power to move only by consent of the Legislature, and the Legislature had no power to grant, then the power was lost, or must be exercised merely as recommendatory and not as binding, and this involves the absurdity of reasoning in a circle.

The whole force of the argument that a previous act of the assembly is indispensable, is to affirm, in the name of the Legislature, as did the Holy Allies in their own, "you shall not have a constitution unless it emanates from our sovereign will and pleasure."

.   .   .   .

[The Whole People Sovereign]

If the foregoing positions are well founded, they prove that the *people* in their aggregate capacity, as a political community, are sovereign as to government and have a right to exercise that sovereignty and to judge of the occasion.

But who constitute the people who hold this sovereignty? Is it the legal voters, the whole body of adult males, or all the human beings in a State? Standing by itself, each community, being independent, may establish its own rules as to qualifications of voters. The question, so circumscribed, would be one of convenience and acquiescence. It could conclude no right of the majority. With this qualification, the States being independent by the Revolution, each might establish the limitations and exceptions it chose to as to the rule which they all laid down that the sovereignty resided in the people. When they formed the Union and conceded some of the attributes of sovereignty, they yielded nothing on this point, except that the United States were to guarantee to each State a republican form of government. The power to frame their own government, subject only to this limitation, was unrestricted. Each State might adopt its own construction as to the organic law and the rights of voting. It left each State as an independent community, and the question who were the people in that community was to be determined by the community, but subject always to the right of the majority to change the organic law. And however this maxim was restricted in practice, its force was not destroyed whenever the rightful majority chose to act.

Now from what source does the rightful majority spring? Who are the people? To answer this, what was the doctrine promulgated by the American Revolution? There can be but one reply: "That the sovereignty in all the free States was placed in the whole body of the adult male population, with exceptions, and in the other States in the whole body of the free white adult males." There is no case of exclusion of citizens who demanded a voice. The exceptions to the rule in all these States were *those persons not competent to form a contract.* In one class of States, this excluded children under twenty-one years, idiots and insane, strangers and women. In another class of States, slaves are to be added. The reasons of these exclusions it is unnecessary to discuss, because all our governments were formed without any innovation on this common consent of mankind in all governments. *But if a doubt were raised here, it is no argument in favor of limiting the sovereignty to a less number* than all the adult males. If that argument is good, it is the strongest against their theory. So slaves are excluded for the same reason that minors and incompetent persons are, because by the laws of the community in which they are found they are incapable of making contracts. They are not citizens, and by no qualifications placed within their reach can become such.

The case, as applied to Rhode Island, or any State where the minority held the right of suffrage and the political power, would be parallel only in case the non-voters were not only excluded for want of qualification, *but could never become qualified!*

The attempt to alarm the South on this point is absurd. It is not necessary, in order to sustain the relation of slavery in the States where it exists, to limit the rights of a majority of a free people and make them the subjects of a minority. If it were, it would be the strongest possible argument against slavery! Admit it, and it gives no security to the voters. The physical force of the slave to rise upon his master remains the same in either case, and the recognition of the right of the majority of the whole citizens to form government recognizes no more right in the slave to act as a citizen in that organization than does the opposite doctrine.

Then, having established the position that the majority have the right to change the form of government, what is the quality of this political right?

Clearly it is to be distinguished from mere physical force, or superiority of military skill or strength; for political power is political right. Power and right are convertible terms when the law authorizes the doing of an act which shall be final and for which the agent is not responsible.

The right to exercise a power is a consequence of the possession of the power. But mere physical or military power is not necessarily either political right or moral right. The distinction is clear between a mere right of revolution resting on physical force, and a right of a majority to change government in the exercise of that political sovereignty which the majority of community embodies. . . . .

In their capacity as the community composing a State, the people have conceded nothing which is not expressly delegated. This is a conservative principle in all popular government and is a necessary check upon government in order to preserve republican forms.

To avoid the force of this reasoning, those who have opposed the People's Constitution in Rhode Island have usually conceded what they call the "sacred right of revolution," as if by that concession they gave the people all the rights it would do to trust them with. And having conceded this much, they make the right of revolution depend upon success, and thus resolve the whole right into physical force.

This may be a correct view as applied to recognitions between independent governments, but how will it apply to our congress of nations, called the United States? Before the confederation, this right, or rather power, (for if its quality depends upon *success* or *defeat*, it is no right,) existed, as it now does in Russia or France; but *what is the right of Revolution as applied to a State of this Union?*

Even if the right of revolution is conceded, in what practical form does it exist under our institutions?

If by revolution is meant overthrowing the existing government and setting up another by military force, this is no political right. In this form, the same right exists to revolutionize for monarchy as for republicanism. It can only be a natural and physical right, the right of minorities as well as majorities. It exists in every despotic or monarchical government.

It was proclaimed in the Declaration — looking, however, to a new source of sovereignty in the people. A revolution in government, not like that of 1688, which was only a revolution in men and dynasties. But in the American system, in opposition to the European, the *moral* was first combined with the physical and natural right to resist oppression. It became a voting as well as a fighting right. "It is the right of the people to alter or to abolish government, and to institute new government."

The Confederation of 1777 left the right of revolution in each State, except so far as limited by the pledge of perpetual union, and prohibiting each State from engaging in war without the consent of Congress. The Constitution of the United States went farther. It explained and reduced to practice the right of change of government recognized in the Declaration. It secured the right of the people peaceably to assemble and to keep and bear arms. It left to them all rights not conceded. It gave to Congress the power of calling forth the militia to execute the laws of the Union, suppress insurrection and repel invasion, and to declare war; but no State to engage in war unless invaded. It required the United States to guarantee to every State in this Union a republican form of government and protect each of them against invasion, and — on application of the legislature, etc. — against *domestic violence.*

And here we are met with the objection that the revolution in Rhode Island, though perfected by voting and legislating, yet not having been sustained by military force against the old government and the threats of the President, it became rebellion, insurrection, and domestic violence. So that, the moment they give us the right of revolution, they send the President, at the head of all the troops of the United States, to suppress it.

This phrase "domestic violence" becomes most important in the construction of this highest of all State rights, the right to model and remodel its own local institutions. We contend it can only mean resistance to the statute or common law of a State, and hence there was no case of domestic violence in Rhode Island except on the part of the men of the old government against the new. It was no case of domestic violence, because

1. The whole people there had a right to participate in government. It was not a question between slaves and masters, subjects and sovereigns, but between the majority of the citizens who possessed every civil right except that of voting, unless they could buy land of the landholders, and the minority who held the land and restricted suffrage.

2. In point of fact there was no violence and no act done against existing laws of the old government until the new constitution was adopted.

3. In point of fact the new constitution was adopted by a majority of the legal voters in Rhode Island.

This fact renders it unnecessary to consider the question of domestic violence as applied to the body of non-voters in a State forming a new government, aside from the action of the voters. We do not admit that the people could have been restrained by laws forbidding their meeting, but this is another question, and we need not consider its effect. It is enough that all their acts were within existing laws until the new government went into effect. Then it was too late to interfere.

Now if "revolution" in a State of this Union necessarily involves a case of "domestic violence," this right of revolution is held by the whole people of a State, subject to the arbitrary will of the governor, or the quorum of a legislature of a State, and the President of the United States. This would make all State institutions subservient, in effect, to the military power of the President. If the legislature are to determine, in the first instance, whether a movement of the people is revolution or "domestic violence," then the right of revolution is made to depend upon the legislature. This brings back the sovereign power in subserviency to the legislature, for "the legislature will always make the power it wishes to exercise."

Thus if the governor or the legislature construe a case of revolution to be an act of "domestic violence," then it rests with the president to call out the whole military power of the Union to suppress revolution in a single State.

.   .   .   .

The order of the President to call out the militia might protect the militia; but the order must issue from the President, in conformity to law, and must be executed by officers duly commissioned, through all the forms of law, or it would be no justification. And if an unreasonable interference with State rights, it would never be submitted to by the rest of the Union to crush a single State.

This discretionary power of the President can be rightly or safely construed only as applying to resistance to State or United States laws: plain insurrection and rebellion. At best, it is a dangerous power and the most alarming Executive prerogative in our institutions, and public opinion would go far to restrain it.

But it need not be considered in reference to the Rhode Island question. However dangerous the power, the President did not exercise it in any form to give effect to his constitutional right of decision as to the existing cause; and in any event, his acting with either of the two Legislatures would decide nothing as to their constitutional or legal right and conclude nothing. The threat of interference and of military demonstration may have compelled the people to abandon the further support of their government, but the President did nothing under the provisions or sanction of the Constitution. All his acts were private and never consummated. . . . .

.   .   .   .

This view has been followed out to test the practical value of what is called the right of revolution in the people of a State of this Union. It fails, and we fall back upon the great conservative right of the people: the American doctrine of popular government, viz., that peaceful changes of government are provided as the substitute of violence and bloodshed, "for the people possess over our constitutions control in *act* as well as in right."

The right is left to the people in each State peacefully to reassume the powers of government whenever it shall become necessary to their happiness — "and to institute new government, laying its foundation in such principles and organizing its power in such form as shall to them seem most likely to effect their safety and happiness." This right the people have never surrendered, but if they have only the right of the strongest, nothing is gained over old forms of government.

They may *begin* government better, but if there is a mistake and the power gets into the hands of the minority there is no remedy. It is not so. The people have the right to progress as well as to begin. The pyramid does not stand upon the apex, but the base.

. . . .

This we hold is the true doctrine of American liberties. We deny, emphatically, that in changes of government the people of the States, in this Union, hold the "sacred right of revolution," subject to be hanged for treason if they fail! This is the right of serfs and slaves. American citizens claim a higher right, unalienable and practical as a great political right. Not a mere physical right of revolution by force, which whenever resorted to must be at the risk of all the penalties attached to an unsuccessful resistance to established authority.

If then, the people of a State are practically denied a change by revolution and can get no change without the previous consent of the legislature, the *legislature* and *not* the people are sovereign in government; and in practice, whatever may be our theory, we are not a free people. Such a conclusion proves that the premises from which it follows cannot be well founded.[3]

. . . .

[3][The opinion of the Supreme Court, delivered by Chief Justice Roger B. Taney, sustained the decision of the Circuit Court in the case of Martin Luther vs. Borden, *et al.*, and remanded the case of Rachael Luther vs. Borden, *et al.* to the Circuit Court. The opinion was based upon the contention that Hallett's argument was political, not judicial. In the case of Rachael Luther, Associate Justice Levi Woodbury prepared a dissenting opinion. See 48 *U. S. Reports*, 1 ff., for the report and opinions.]

9

WALT WHITMAN

REFLECTIONS ON DEMOCRACY[1]

[THE WORKINGS OF DEMOCRACY][2]

IT IS THE FASHION of a certain set to assume to despise "politics" and the "corruption of parties" and the unmanageableness of the masses; they look at the fierce struggle and at the battle of principles and candidates, and their weak nerves retreat dismayed from the neighborhood of such scenes of convulsion. But to our view the spectacle is always a grand one, full of the most august and sublime attributes. When we think how many ages rolled away while political action, which rightly belongs to every man whom God sends on earth with a soul and a rational mind, was confined to a few great and petty tyrants, the ten thousandth of the whole, when we see what cankerous evils gradually accumulated and how their effect still poisons society, is it too much to feel this joy that among *us* the *whole surface* of the body politic is expanded to the sun and air, and each man feels his rights and *acts* them? Nor ought any member of our Republic to complain as long as the aggregate result of such action is what the world sees it is. Do we not behold evolving into birth, from it, the most wondrous nation, the most free from those evils which bad government causes, the really widest extending, possessing the truest riches of people and moral worth and freedom from want ever yet seen aneath the broad heavens? . . . We know, well enough, that the workings of democracy are not always justifiable in every trivial point. But the great winds that purify the air and without which nature would flag into ruin — are they to be condemned because a tree is prostrated here and there in their course?

---

[1] [Selected from editorials written by Whitman as editor of the Brooklyn *Daily Eagle*, as published in C. Rodgers and J. Black, eds., *The Gathering of the Forces* (New York, 1920).]

[2] April 20, 1847.

[THE STRENGTH OF THE DEMOCRATIC PARTY][3]

The democracy of this country never can be overthrown. The true democratic spirit is endued with immortal life and strength. Our star glitters far above; clouds may now and then pass under it, but there it shines undimmed and untouched, and there it will shine when the factions who decry it, with all that belongs to them, shall be remembered as the creatures of a day and the offspring of corruption. Nor can the Democratic Party become essentially corrupt, either. For true democracy has within itself a perpetual spring of health and purity. In its very nature it is at war with all selfishness and wickedness. It tempts no man or body of men with sinecures or swelling salaries. On the contrary, its defenders often have to bear odium and reproach; they are the marks at which wealthy insolence and supercilious pride level many an arrow. The leading spirits of the democratic faith are always in advance of the age; and they have, therefore, to fight against old prejudices. The contest they engage in does not call for brute courage but moral courage — courage that can stand unappalled and without giving up the hate of enemies, the lukewarmness of friends, the ridicule and malice of many a flippant popinjay who thinks himself of better clay than ordinary men. Why, what had Jefferson, the Columbus of our political faith, to encounter? If we are to believe the chronicles of the past, he underwent, during what was called the "reign of terror," the most provoking indignities both personal and political. Leading Republicans were at that time taunted and hooted at in the streets. No one, we have the authority of Jefferson himself for saying, can realize the afflicting persecutions and insults they had to brook amid that gloomy period, the administration of the older Adams. But resting on their own stanch, manly hearts and defended by the breastplate of a righteous cause, they faltered not. Throwing to the winds all fear, they came out before the people, incessantly teaching and expounding their doctrine and openly proclaiming the falseness and injustice of their opponents' creed. For *their* opponents had a creed. The result was that they triumphed. And *we* shall triumph. We stand here the inheritors of their principles and opposed to the same foe — the foe of equal rights. Democracy must conquer again as it did then — and more certainly than it did

[3] November 7, 1846.

then. We think so from two simple facts. One is that the great body of workingmen are more powerful and more enlightened now than they were in those days. The other is that there is a mighty and restless energy throughout the length and breadth of this nation for going onward to the very verge with our experiment of popular freedom.

[DEMOCRATIC SUCCESS][4]

From the days of Washington, the course of the Democratic Party has been a course of success and triumph. We do not mean that our party has succeeded in every *election*, because there are very many minor contests, and some of vast importance, in which the Conservatives — under their various names — carried the day. But we mean to say that our *principles* have advanced with a steady and sure progress. Every year has added something to our political or commercial knowledge and decreased, thus, the hopes of the more illiberal among us, by whom we mean the citizens, many of them as candid and well-wishing as any others, who think that everything is to be *regulated by law.* . . . And it is in this progress and this invariable addition to the good and diminution of the bad that we find the auguries of the future. The Democracy must still succeed. Even the intelligent Whigs will probably acknowledge this and, with all their distrust of the "common people" and of the integrity and intelligence of the masses, will hardly so degrade their own judgment as to deny the likelihood of those masses and the party they attach to wielding political sway in the aggregate. Such thoughts as these are well to dwell upon; the lover of his fellows and of the serene principles of political truth will always find joy and encouragement in them.

["THE BEST GOVERNMENT IS THAT WHICH GOVERNS LEAST"][5]

In plain truth, "the people expect too much of the government." Under a proper organization, and even to a great extent as things are, the wealth and happiness of the citizens could hardly be touched by the government, could neither be retarded nor advanced, Men must be "masters unto themselves," and not look to presidents and legislative bodies for aid. In this wide and naturally rich country, the best government indeed is "that which governs least."

[4] May 3, 1847.
[5] July 26, 1847.

One point, however, must not be forgotten — ought to be put before the eyes of the people every day; and that is, although government can do little *positive* good to the people, it may do an *immense deal of harm*. And here is where the beauty of the Democratic principle comes in. Democracy would prevent all this harm. It would have no man's benefit achieved at the expense of his neighbors. It would have no one's rights infringed upon and that, after all, is pretty much the sum and substance of the prerogatives of government. How beautiful and harmonious a system! How it transcends all other codes, as the golden rule, in its brevity, transcends the ponderous tomes of philosophic lore! While mere politicians, in their narrow minds, are sweating and fuming with their complicated statutes, this one single rule, rationally construed and applied, is enough to form the starting point of all that is necessary in government; *to make no more laws than those useful for preventing a man or body of men from infringing on the rights of other men.*

[GOVERNMENT NO MEDDLER][6]

It is only the novice in political economy who thinks it the duty of government to *make* its citizens happy. Government has no such office. To protect the weak and the minority from the impositions of the strong and the majority, to prevent any one from positively working to render the people unhappy (if we may so express it), to do the labor not of an officious intermeddler in the affairs of men but of a prudent watchman who prevents outrage — these are rather the proper duties of a government.

Under the specious pretext of effecting "the happiness of the whole community," nearly all the wrongs and intrusions of government have been carried through. The legislature may, and should, when such things fall in its way, lend its potential weight to the cause of virtue and happiness, but to legislate in direct behalf of those objects is never available and rarely effects any even temporary benefit. Indeed, sensible men have long seen that "the best government is that which governs least." And we are surprised that the spirit of this maxim is not oftener and closer to the hearts of our domestic leaders.

[6] April 4, 1846.

[THE METHOD OF REFORM][7]

It is amazing, in this age of the world, with the past and all its causes and effects like beacon lights behind us, that men show such ignorance not only of the province of law but of the true way to achieve any great reform. Why, we wouldn't give a snap for the aid of the legislature in forwarding a purely moral revolution! It must work its way through individual minds. It must spread from its own beauty and melt into the hearts of men, not be forced upon them at the point of the sword or by the stave of the officer.

[THE PROVINCE OF LAW][8]

We generally expect a great deal too much of law. After all, government does not exercise anything like the influence for good or for evil over us that we are apt to imagine. We have grown in the way of resting on it to do many things which ought to be done by individuals, and of making it answer for much that society alone (for government and society are distinct) is in truth the responsible author of. Ah, no man can be readier than we to unite in behalf of a true measure to prevent crime or to reform it where it has once been allowed to get headway! But we would hunt immorality in its recesses in the individual heart, and grapple with it there, *but not by law*. We would direct our blows at the substance not the shadow.

[ON COMPULSION IN GOVERNMENT][9]

There is not a greater fallacy on earth than the doctrine of *force* as applied in government. We of course allude to the physical, not moral, force — to compulsion, as it may be called, though it very seldom compels the effect it desires. Everybody knows the old paradox that "a little is greater than much." So it frequently is in laws. Multiply laws, confuse the people ruled by a legion of entangled statutes, and there is not near as much harmony (the aim of all good government), as though laws were few, simple, and general!

[7] March 18, 1846.

[8] March 27, 1846.

[9] November 13, 1846.

[THE TRUE OFFICE OF GOVERNMENT][10]

One of the favorite doctrine of leading Whigs teaches the intricacy and profundity of the science of government. According to them, the most elaborate study and education are required in any one who would comprehend the deep mysteries, the hidden wonders, of the ruling of a nation and the controlling of a people. Nor is this doctrine confined altogether to the Whigs; many in our own ranks acknowledge its truth and infer from its premises. We have Democrats, and not obscure ones either, who hesitate not to act (whatever they may say) in a manner acknowledging assent to the same views. Really, however, the principles that lie at the root of true government are not hard of comprehension. The error lies in the desire after *management*, the great curse of our legislation; everything is to be regulated and made straight by force of statute. And all this while evils are accumulating in very consequence of excessive management. The true office of government is simply to preserve the rights of each citizen from spoliation; when it attempts to go beyond this, it is intrusive and does more harm than good.

[AMERICA'S FUTURE GLORY][11]

Thirty years from this date, America will be confessed the *first nation* on the earth. We of course mean that her power, wealth, and the happiness and virtue of her citizens will then obtain a pitch which other nations cannot favorably compare with. Her immense territory is filling up with a rapidity which few eyes among us have realized. And back of what can possibly be filled up in fifty years, lay enormous untravelled plains and forests, fat of their own riches, and capable of sustaining nations like the greatest in Europe. The mind is lost in contemplating such incalculable acres; and the lover of his race, whose fellowship is not bound by an open or dividing line, yearns that the degrading, starving, and ignorant ones of the Old World, whatever and whosoever they are, should be transplanted thither where their cramped natures may expand and they do honor to the great humanity they so long have been a blot upon.

[10] January 2, 1847.
[11] November 24, 1846.

[THE OLD WORLD AND THE NEW][12]

Let us not think because we are ahead of the tyrannical system of the Old World, that *we* of the New have no advance to make. Every season, indeed, witnesses a great onward movement, even now. Some twenty years since, and the doctrine of universal suffrage was a bold and dangerous doctrine in the eyes of many who thought they yielded to none in their democracy. In Leggett's time, he was persecuted and "read out" for daring to question the infallibility of banks and high tariff. Yet what has the progress of a few circling suns done toward opening the minds of men to receive these heresies! In less than twenty years from this time, we venture to predict with every assurance of safety, the nation will find, boldly promulgated in its midst and supported by numerous and powerful advocates, notions of law, government, and social custom as different from the present day as Leggett's and Jefferson's to those of past ages. We must be constantly pressing onward, every year throwing the doors wider and wider and carrying our experiment of democratic freedom to the very verge of the limit.

The old and moth-eaten systems of Europe have had their day, and that evening of their existence which is nigh at hand will be the token of a glorious dawn for the down-trodden people. *Here* we have planted the standard of freedom, and here we will test the capacities of men for self-government. We will see whether the law of happiness and preservation upon each individual, acting directly upon himself, be not a safer dependence than musty charters and time-worn prerogatives of tyrants. Doctrines that even now are scarcely breathed, innovations which the most fearless hardly dare propose openly, systems of policy that men would speak of at the present day in the low tones of fear for very danger lest they might be scouted as worse than Robespierrian revolutionists—that hackneyed bug-bear theme which has never been presented in its fairness to the people of this Republic—will, in course of time, see the light here and meet the sanction of popular favor and go into practical play. Nor let us fear that this may result in harm. All that we enjoy of freedom was in the beginning but an experiment. We have been long enough frightened by the phantom of the *past;* let us dare to know that we are out of leading strings.

[12] July 28, 1846.

[WORLD DEMOCRACY][13]

Rain is not drunk in more eagerly by the parched earth than the ears of men, for the past fifty years, have listened to those doctrines that would increase their political rights and that teach improvement in governing. The progress of this democratic yearning for a better state bids fair to place the American people, twenty years hence—by elevating humanity itself, and disregarding mere wealth and circumstances, by a wholesome pruning of too much and too meddlesome laws — as far beyond what they now are as what they now are is beyond what they were seventy years ago. There must be continual additions to our great experiment of how much liberty society will bear. . . . And not only here, on our own beloved soil, is this democratic feeling infusing itself and becoming more and more powerful. The lover of his race, he whose good-will is not bounded by a shore or a division line, looks across the Atlantic and exults to see on the shores of Europe a restless dissatisfaction spreading wider and wider every day. Long enough have priestcraft and kingcraft stalked over those lands, clothed in robes of darkness and wielding the instruments of subjection. The age of iron rule is passing away. A few divine spirits there are who dared royalty even in its own stronghold; and the Pen shows itself mightier than the Scepter. The moth-eaten and age-decayed fabric of kingly government has been and now is attacked on all sides and by the ablest champions. It is a strong caste, a structure of the feudal times, yet its enemies are stronger. Long did it resist all encroachments; firmly did it defy every besieger; loudly from its battlements came the shrill laugh of defiance and scorn; insolently flaunted its banners in the breeze. But the time is arrived when it can no longer withstand the united force of truth and might. Tower after tower falls. The gates have been broken in, and the laugh of defiance is changed to a disturbed look of apprehension. The citadel itself even now yields to a hundred lusty blows — and the period will ere many years be here when every vestige will be swept away!

[13] October 8, 1846.

PART TWO

Economic Themes

10

STEPHEN SIMPSON

POLITICAL ECONOMY AND THE WORKERS [1]

A NEW THEORY of political economy, at the present day, and from the pen of an American, may by some be considered as a bold and hazardous undertaking. Adventure and peril, however, are the characteristics of our country. Its physical features are stamped with an energy and grandeur that invite to imitation. Its moral history and its political career are equally distinguished for peril of achievement and novelty of execution. We are confessed to have achieved, as a nation, what no other people would ever have attempted. The career of intellect, of science, and of arts lies in broad characters before us, and it may surely be permitted to the most humble aspirant to add to the common stock of knowledge and of happiness.

It has been left to the people of the United States to present to the world for the first time a self-formed government, whose basis was established in the equal rights of man, civil equality, and common privileges, and whose end was the general prosperity, virtue, and happiness of the people. The Declaration of American Independence was the first formal annunciation to the world that all men were born equally free, with equal claims to the pursuit of happiness, and with unalienable rights to self-government. This truth, once proclaimed, flashed conviction on every mind. It became an obvious and self-evident axiom the moment it was uttered; it was received by all, disputed by none; and now constitutes a maxim in government, as well as philosophy, which every people pant to reduce to practice, as the only road to liberty, reason, affluence, and felicity.

Nothing more was required than such a basis of government to develop the full power and cultivate to the utmost perfection the human intellect. There was a grandeur, a noble exaltation in the very idea, that gave to every man his full altitude and dimensions.

[1] [From *The Working Man's Manual: a New Theory of Political Economy, on the Principle of Production the Source of Wealth* (Philadelphia, 1831), "Preliminary Dissertation," pp. 5–50 — Abridged.]

The mind expanded to unlimited conceptions, under the consciousness of a truth which removed all barriers to the progress of genius, talent, industry, and science. In theory, at least, all distinction was annihilated, except that which arose from *merit;* and the public mind assumed a corresponding tone and took a congenial spring in the path of bold investigation and untried research. The action of self-government infused activity, energy, and decision into our character, while the theory of civil equality inspired a daring of ambition mixed with virtue that aspired to reach every perfection both of knowledge and of arms and pluck from the faded escutcheon of feudal Europe the brightest gems that glittered in her wreath of martial glory or adorned her temples of science with the spoils of fame.

With such a Declaration of Independence, with such constitutions, formed on principles purely identical, and theoretically imparting to the heart the fondest dreams of perfect liberty, blessed with a fertile soil, a frugal government, and a disposition to cultivate happiness or bow down into content, it is not surprising that a long period should elapse ere the inconsistencies and discrepancies between our theoretical constitutions and feudal laws and customs should be discovered, exposed, and resisted. The mere acquisition of independence, the novelty of an untried condition, the glow of fervid patriotism and the heats of party conflicts would long engross attention and keep it from too close a scrutiny into the actual condition of the great mass of the community. It was natural that joy and satisfaction should be inspired, upon having escaped some of the intense oppressions of European systems, without feeling a restless curiosity to ascertain whether the abstract doctrines of government had actually been reduced to practice so as to secure the *happiness of the many instead of ministering to the benefit of the few!* All advantages and situations are comparative, all advances to knowledge are progressive, and all changes leave the mind in tranquillity and repose long after their occurrence. But acquisitions soon grow familiar and, when enjoyed, speedily satiate. We desire to go forward in the race of human destiny and realize the full conception of happiness that we deem attainable to our nature; but this desire can only arise after the flush of conquest and liberty has passed over the heart, leaving it cooled, composed, and refreshed by the breezes of reflection and philosophy.

.   .   .   .

[NATURE PROVIDES PLENTIFULLY]

The slightest observation will satisfy the most prejudiced and sceptical mind that nature has superabundantly supplied the industry of man with the means of universal comfort. We behold a demonstration of the fact in every form of luxury, every object of magnificence, every refinement of pleasure, every waste of riot and sensuality, every monument of pride, every display of vanity, every gorgeous decoration of wealth, power, and ambition. We behold the proof in the lord of ten thousand acres, tortured on his sick couch by the agonies of repletion, whilst the laborer famishes at his gate; we behold it in the luxurious capitalist, swelling with the overweening pride of overpampered opulence, whilst the hearts that *labored* to produce his wealth shiver and faint with misery and want or drag out a protracted life of endless toil, blasting existence by the despair even of a bare competence. But unfortunately for the human family, this abundance of nature and this industry of man are alike unavailing to his happiness. What God has spread before us as the reward and the property of him whose *labor* shall bring it into use, government, unjust, despotic, proud, all-grasping government, has ordained shall belong to those who never labor, and for whose exclusive benefit the laborer shall toil for ever. Thus do human institutions, founded on tyranny, or perverted from their original principles of justice, destroy and circumvent the beneficence of heaven; or, where those institutions are congenial to equity, customs and usages devolved from a prior age and a different government wrest the fruit of industry from the mouth of labor and heap it in the overflowing storehouse of the patron or land proprietary of the monarch whose royal charter superseded the decrees of justice and the laws of nature.

. . . .

[SOURCES OF INEQUALITY]

From one extremity to the other of this vast Union, the origin, or the conquest, emanated from England. The royal charters of the British monarchs form the first title to most of the soil of the United States. . . . . Here we discover at one view the entire origin of those *unequal* landed estates which, even in this country, have reduced the industrious agriculturalist to the degradation of a mere vassal to some super-affluent and idle patroon, and which, in the best effects they

produce, are so pernicious to the population of the country by retard-
ing its settlement and so injurious to those whose labor gives them
all the real value they possess. Chiefly, however, are they to be
deplored because they create wealth independent of merit or industry
and so far tend to unhinge government from its only true and substantial foundation, by creating an aristocracy whose origin is the
royal patent for lands they never saw and can never till. When we
know that the inequality of wealth is the cause of misery to thousands,
this *identity* of condition, on our part, to that of England must at
once lead to reflections that inspire as much of degradation as they
tend to stimulate to reform.

It must ever form a subject of amazement and regret to succeeding
generations that at the era of the Declaration of Independence or at
that of the adoption of the Federal Constitution the common law of
England and the royal grants and titles to land were not instantly
and totally abolished as of no force and virtue under the new government. Such a measure, more than all others now in the power of the
people, would have established society on the true basis of merit and
labor in the citizen, and tended, by its own weight, to equalize property on a scale of equity and comfort and to adjust the wages of labor
in a manner conducive to the general happiness.

Next in magnitude, as one of the parents of that unequal distribution
of property and that unjust principle of distribution which now prevail, was the establishment of the *funding system*, another fungus of
the corrupt institutions of a kingdom from which we had declared a
nominal independence at the same time that we retained with obstinate
infatuation all her moral, civil, and political cancers, under the false
impression that descent, propinquity, a common origin, and a common language, ought to excite a sympathy and an emulation that
would blind us to their vices, and so consecrate their errors as to make
it the duty of a kind of filial affection to adopt them without examination, resting satisfied with the uncontested fact that their *English
character* alone fully entitled them to our implicit approbation. Whilst
I feel no disposition to deprecate or detract from a proper feeling of
amity towards a foreign kingdom, once the fountain of the blood that
circles and plays in our own veins, yet that feeling ought never to
sanction English error or lead us to adopt English corruptions. The
duty imposed on us now is that of *self-happiness* as well as self-govern-

ment, terms that ought to be synonymous, duties that ought to mix and blend into one, ends that only are attained when both are accomplished; and to carry them into fruition no pseudo-partiality ought to be permitted to interfere. Unhappily, and to our eternal detriment, it was permitted at the very commencement of the government. Our great statesman, Jefferson, has boldly avowed, that it was for the purpose of assimilating our institutions to those of that monarchy and erecting a throne on the ruins of our republic; but I should rather refer this abuse to blind admiration than to deliberate treason, to unappeasable cupidity in a penurious aristocracy rather than to the frenzied designs of insatiable ambition.

In itself or its consequences, the *funding system*, of all the perversions of this equitable government, is especially oppressive to the children of labor. If it did not create a fiscal necessity, it at least afforded a plausible pretext for the *banking system*, that fruitful mother of unutterable affliction to the sons of industry, which brought us, at one fatal step, into the vortex of English aristocracy, overgrown fortunes and hopeless poverty, taxation through all the elements of existence, and speculation to the utter grinding down of the *producer* to pamper the fortunes of the rich and swell the hoard of the speculator. The *banking system* and the *funds* are, in the fiscal world, precisely what the royal grants were in the landed interest. They created even a greater inequality of fortune, by means more nefarious as well as more pernicious; for they levied a tax directly upon every commodity produced by labor, which tax became immediately absorbed into the pocket of the *capitalist*. So that what England did through her royal charters and grants antecedent to the Revolution, our own aristocracy deliberately committed through the *funding* and *banking* systems, whose results upon the happiness and comfort of an industrious and free people must be estimated fully as calamitous in respect to labor as the consequences that would attend the subjugation of the country by a foreign king who should partition the property of the conquered people among his chiefs and followers in large and princely domains, thus creating a monopoly of land and capital which would extort labor upon their own terms of bare subsistence.

Thus far, then, we perceive our constitution of *equal rights* to be the merest untenanted skeleton of liberty that the imagination of man can conceive; which, by its *operation*, creates aristocracy, privileges, extortion, monopoly, and overgrown fortunes, and which, by its *letter*, declares that equality of rights shall be guaranteed to all and the pursuit of happiness be a common boon secured to industry by the equity of her principles and the simplicity of her laws.

Such are the defects of organic law, practical government, and property, which are thrown as obstacles into the path of the working-man. In themselves these are formidable enough to intimidate the most intrepid champion of reform. But when are superadded to these the obstacles of opinion, prejudice, the long descended prejudice of antiquity, flinging the odium of servility upon the head of labor, it extorts a doubt of success even in the very moment it excites the soul to dare all perils in so laudable a task. *Antiquity!* The word excites the most pleasing and sublime association, but on this subject it gives rise to the most humiliating and degrading thoughts. Happily Aristotle knew little of the true principles of political economy, and we may pardon the ignorance of a people on that score, whose occupation was war and whose recreation was pleasure, who spent their hours in alternate devotion to the muses or sacrifices to their gods!

[RIGHTS OF PRODUCERS]

From the earliest epochs of civilized society, after its maturity from the pastoral to the commercial state, the *producers* of wealth have, with few exceptions and little variation, been degraded to the condition of slaves, serfs, vassals, or servants, and this degradation has even extended up to the present age. In Greece the mechanics and artisans, with the exceptions of those branches intimately connected with literature and science, such as sculpture and painting, were mostly slaves. The same degrading custom was also peculiar to Rome, in her first ages, until the practice of *manumission* and the rewards and honors decreed to valor in the field gradually wore out some of the stain and ignominy attempted to be put upon those whose lives were devoted to *useful* labor in the state. All barbarous nations or those just emerging from the dark era to the twilight of civilization have been remarkable for the same confinement of labor to the class that was held in bondage. The Germans, the Gauls, and the Britons had their *serfs* to whom were confined the duties of all servile labor, from the drudgery of the workshop to the more blightsome toils and cares of agriculture.

To be a gentleman and to work were utterly as incompatible as to aspire to rank and possess the faculty of *writing*, an ignorance of which in the middle ages was generally confounded with servile labor. Idleness, the pleasures of the chase, and the havoc of war, or the perils of personal combat were then as now considered as the peculiar occupation of the nobles and gentry. To be useful was to be degraded and when we consider that even *writing* was considered a disgrace because it required labor, we may conceive upon what whims of opinion and customs of tyranny rested the whole system of ranks, titles, and distinctions. Writing was then confined to the lower order of monks, who were termed *clerks*, a term which is even yet considered derogatory, as associating ideas of meanness and servility; but now writing, however, when separated from the last mentioned degradation, is considered not only creditable, but is boasted of as a mark of distinction and honor, which shows upon what frivolous grounds the whole system of *rank* rests. To labor for another, even among us of the nineteenth century, is held as disreputable; whilst to labor for ourselves wipes away the stigma of reproach. In this distinction we behold the cause and origin of that ignominy and depression which has been cast upon the working classes. In all countries except this, they are the slaves, serfs, or servants, or the descendants of that class, stamped with the features of hard toil and hard usage, mental ignorance, brutal passion, and stinted nourishment; their *occupation* is associated with the idea of their condition, and because bondage degrades, cramps, and degenerates man, labor shares in the same disgrace because it is a part of the slave. Even in Russia and other countries of the present day, our own (*in the Southern States*) not excepted, labor is chiefly confined to the slaves and few toil unless scourged to the task by their masters. The condition of the working classes of Great Britain is little better than that of the American slaves or the Russian serfs, of which class they are the descendants, bearing about them all the hereditary hardships, toil, famine, and ignorance which habit and tradition reconcile them to endure, or which a military government compels them to submit to.

As it appears indubitably to be owing to the existence of slavery combined with labor, from the earliest to the latest ages of the world, that industry and toil have become associated with baseness and degradation, it would seem that nothing more was necessary to reverse the character of the productive classes in public estimation, than to confine labor to a community of freemen and abolish every vestige of bondage and servitude. This, it must be acknowledged, is an indispensable prerequisite to divesting labor of disgrace and investing it with ideas of honor and merit; but it cannot be deemed entirely efficient in itself. Other causes must combine to produce this salutary revolution; previous to considering which, however, let us return to that auspicious feature in our Constitution to which I alluded at the commencement of this essay.

This is the only free government whose organic laws are sustained by the mixture of slavery and labor. Here, for the first time, we behold a country whose mechanics, laborers, farmers, and operatives are all eligible to the highest posts of power where they may claim equality with kings and emperors and for a time be equally as absolute and mighty in wielding the engines of human destiny. Labor brings neither disqualification nor stigma upon the citizen of the United States, in a political capacity. His rights are confessed, recorded, and practised; honor may be his if genius seconds his efforts; and fame may be won by him without restriction of law.

On the part of political right, then, the *producer* suffers no disparagement from our free constitutions, whose efficiency is allowed to be complete both in theory and practice.

Another question, however, arises. Did the Constitution intend to provide for nothing beyond *mere political right?* Does not the political embrace, necessarily, the *moral equality?* Does it not declare that equality is the basis of the whole social compact, and that all laws and regulations, customs and usages, shall bear equally upon all the members of the community? Hence, the remarks of a celebrated writer upon the principles of our Constitution: "The idle, who seek for wealth by chartering laws, are wiser than their equalising brethren. Law has never been able to produce an equality of property, where industry exists, but it can produce its monopoly. Our policy rejects its application to both objects, and our constitutions unequivocally disclose an opinion, that civil liberty depends *upon leaving the distribution of property to Industry; hence, laws for this end are as unconstitutional as those for re-establishing king, lords, and commons. Legal wealth and hereditary power, are twin principles.* These frauds beget all the parties or factions of civil society, such as patrician and plebeian, military, civil, stock, and landed. The enmity and contrast in all these cases, arise from a *legal difference* of interest, and the active and passive members of this fraudulent system, are distinctly designated by the *wealth* and *poverty* it diffuses. In England, every seventh person draws support from the parish, at some period of his life, exclusive of those who submit to misery, in preference to the humiliation of asking charity."[2]

Independent, however, of this conclusive authority upon the subject, it is obvious on the very face of our organic laws that it was never designed by the people who framed this government to grant the power that *Law* should regulate the distribution of wealth instead of industry. I use the term Law as a generic word, embracing all the details that affect the distribution of wealth, such as moneyed corporations, chartered monopolies, and that endless chain of levers which move industry to empty her gains into the lap of *capital*, and which effectually frustrate and defeat the grand object of rational self-government on the basis of individual freedom and personal merit.

The distinctive features of the *feudal* systems of Europe, which we have in form and in fact essentially repudiated, are those of *entails*, *nobility*, *hierarchy*, *monopolies*, which are synonymous to the distribution of wealth by Law, instead of its distribution by the same power which is alone active in its production, *industry and labor*. Having shaken off, renounced, and branded those systems of antiquated barbarism and monkish superstition, by all the great leading documents of our national existence, we are bound by the highest and most sacred ties of moral, religious, and political obligation to bring the condition of the people, in respect to the wages of labor and the enjoyment of competence, to a level with their abstract political rights, which rights imply necessarily the possession of the property they may produce, on principles of equity congenial to the equal rights guaranteed by the organic law. To substitute Law for the distribution of labor is to introduce the chief feature of the feudal systems of Europe into the free, self-formed, and equitable republic of this country, and amounts to a virtual repeal of the very first principle of the Declaration of Independence and the Constitutions of the Union and the States.

Happily, however, for the integrity of these institutions and the

[2][John Taylor, *An Inquiry into the Principles and Policy of the Government of the United States* (Fredericksburg, Va., 1814), p. 634.]

perpetuity of the great doctrines upon which they are based, we possess a redeeming trait in our government, which opens wide the channels through which the people may enter to produce a conformity of practice to principle. Legislative abuses are never beyond the corrective control of a people whose suffrages properly directed, by a judicious concentration, can periodically annul, remove, and recreate the power that is above the laws, and mold the popular sovereignty to its own will and pleasure. Let the producers of labor but once fully comprehend their injuries and fully appreciate their strength at the polls, and the present oppressive system will vanish like the mists of the morning before the rising sun. The power to remedy the evil is unquestionable; it resides in the *producers* of wealth, who constitute so overwhelming a majority of the people, when not carried away by the infatuation of faction, the delusion of personal allegiance, and the vain pursuit of phantoms of liberty, which are no sooner touched than they melt into air, leaving the wretched follower to bewail his disappointment and execrate his fatuity.

[Defects of Party System]

Nothing of a public nature, at the present era, is so worthy of the attention of the people as the fallacious structure and pernicious tendency of the parties now in vogue, whose foundations are as futile as their results are nugatory to the great body of the people, neither advancing the good of the nation nor the prosperity of her citizens, but blindly ministering to the avarice, ambition, or pride of some temporary idol, who is worshipped one day and immolated on the next. A party grafted purely *on principle* has never yet engrossed the ardent people of this excited country; that of 1798 approximated nearer to such a party than any other, but its principles were so soon perverted, its object so soon merged into mere personal views, and the honest people were so soon duped by unprincipled leaders that it could scarcely lay a claim to purity of feeling or soar to patriotism of purpose. Since that era faction has rapidly generated faction, of grovelling views and unholy ends, so as to cause political collisions to fester into mere cancers upon the body politic, eating into their vitality and spreading disease and death over the whole face of our institutions. Yet have the people been enticed into their support by plausible professions of leaders and the wheedling arts of insincere demagogues to the detriment of their best interests, the sacrifice of their time, and the loss of their character. Lured on by the cant of party, the slang of affected patriotism, and the hollow promise of patronage, men have closed their eyes as well as their understandings to the deception of the game, which made use of them and their interests for the sheer and exclusive benefit of an aspiring demagogue, who, when his purpose was obtained, cast the squeezed orange from him with undissembled contempt. It is to be hoped this epoch of delusion is rapidly passing into the waste of oblivion, never to be recalled; and that the producers of wealth will now be reinforced by the former deluded followers of faction, to second their reforms and aid them in their labors. A little reflection and inquiry cannot fail to produce this highly desirable result. Let us progress a little further in this investigation.

Personal parties are at all times and under all circumstances highly dangerous, and often prove fatal to the liberties of a free people. They are founded on selfishness and terminate in usurpation and abuses. They first lead to the obscurity of principles, and gradually produce a total obliteration of all the great landmarks which are founded on the fundamental differences of government and engraven on the inalienable rights of man. After confounding, in this manner, all distinctions between right and wrong, justice and oppression, freedom and bondage, they soon tend to beget in the popular mind a total apathy or indifference to whatever relates to political affairs. What is radically erroneous or pernicious is often glossed over as right and adopted by affection or reverence for a *name;* what is nefarious in principle and even frightful in its consequences is often welcomed, cherished, and promoted, without reflection or inquiry, because a voice gilded with popularity has suggested its performance. Men of conflicting views, irreconcilable principles, and incompetent minds are huddled together in personal parties for a moment until some shock of interest severs them wider than ever, with embittered animosity and aggravated feelings; or, if they cohere after the first collision, it is at the increased expense of all that is worthy of esteem and admiration in the human character. Honesty is sacrificed to expediency, truth to self-interest, patriotism to ambition, and public virtue to private aggrandizement. Honor and right can never tolerate such heterogeneous associations. The most callous and adroit knaves, in such parties, smile at the hypocrisy of one another. Mutual distrust, suspicion, and contempt sit upon the face of every thinking man of the ill-assorted group. Yet nothing discomposes the complacency of these venal spirits, and acquiescence in the ruin of their country is purchased by a bribe, a commission, or a promise of patronage, hid in the mists of the indefinite future. The *mere animals* disport with their wonted glee under the shadow of any power however corrupt, as there are some birds that can live even upon the gum and berries of the upas tree. A wise, prudent, and virtuous people, therefore, in order to continue free, will never lose sight of *principle;* and as parties never can be wholly demolished in a country where government is founded on *equality of rights*, it well deserves its attention whether that party ought not to be embraced and cherished which is built upon the grand fundamental doctrines of *industry, merit, general happiness*, the *distribution of property on the principle of the worth of labor,* and the intelligence, virtue, and comfort of the whole people.

Parties of interest, however, though some of them are not much better in principle, are less noxious because one party may be brought to check or control another, as the party of stockholders and capitalists may be met and counteracted by the *party of the producers*, which is a real party of *general interest*, whose ascendency could not fail to shed a genial and prosperous beam upon the whole society. Such a party would merely exhibit the *interest of society*, concentrating for the true fulfilment of the original terms of the social compact the happiness and comfort of the whole. This we now behold in those parties of the workingmen, who, resisting the seductions of fanatics on the one hand, and demagogues on the other, steadily follow in the path of science and justice, under the banner of *labor the source of wealth* and *industry* the arbiter of its distribution.

It must be accounted a most calamitous circumstance for the sons of labor that, at the period of their emancipation from the rigors of feudal servitude, in all countries there should have arisen at the same time, to distract their attention and entice them from their rights and their happiness, the turmoil, tumult, and collision of political excitement, to lead them still in manacles at the heels of ambitious demagogues and as effectually blast their hopes of competence as the old system from which they had just emerged. This untoward event, however, is rather to be ascribed to their former ignorance of their rights than to a wilful neglect of them. The specious colors with which capital invests her extortions, the appearance of justice, when protected by law, in which she envelops her oppressions, all tend to blind the uninformed multitude and even perplex the intelligent and scientific. But that era of darkness has happily passed away, and regenerated man is slowly progressing to the recovery of his violated rights, in defiance of all the formidable obstructions of pride, prejudice, wealth, rank, and intellect.

[EDUCATION]

The physician, to cure a disease, must be free and candid with his patient, and his patient must exhibit neither reserve nor petulance; the wound must be probed to the bottom, all gangrene cut away, or labor and skill are both spent in vain. It cannot be concealed, it would be unwise to dissemble the fact that the most formidable obstruction to the attainment of justice in the distribution of labor, and the consequent opinion of honor and merit attaching to industry, instead of disgrace, is to be found in the pride and lofty bearing of the literary, erudite, intellectual, and scientific classes. The *educated* are generally the rich; and, where the exception prevails, necessity, or accident, as in the case of labor, soon brings the object under the influence and within the patronage of the affluent. No habit of mind is so decided and obstinate as the contempt of learning for ignorance, or of genius for stolidity. In addition to this, the *feudal* forms of all colleges and universities place an insuperable barrier between the unlettered mechanic and the classical dignitary. In all situations and under all circumstances, charters create a virtual *nobility*. The Doctor of Laws, the Master of Arts, and other similar unmeaning titles betray the aristocracy of the revival of learning, under popes, kings, emperors, and princes, and express the determination of wealth to protect its privileges by golden barriers as well as legal restraints and intimidations. Literature and education, thus affianced to opulence, naturally feel a strong repugnance to share their intellectual dominion with the mass of society or to look upon ignorance with a feeling of complacency or even of tolerance. The prejudice is by this means confirmed that the occupations of labor not only do not require the lights of science and the polish of letters, but that the successful prosecution of trade, mechanics, and other modes of toil are entirely incompatible with that celestial light which education sheds upon the mind. Thus it is that after the shackles of feudal tyranny have been stricken from us, and our equality solemnly proclaimed and acknowledged by the *voice of nations*, the very light which should beam upon our path to lead us to the temple of truth and justice, is transformed to a thunderbolt, to shatter and destroy. Even this obstacle, however, will prove unavailing and must yield to the force of opinion whilst the press remains unshackled and the ballot boxes free.

It is admitted on all hands by the philanthropists of the age that the condition of society demands amelioration. They affect to sympathize with the misery, and exhort to reform the depravity of man. They call upon the laboring mass to cease their crime and to study frugality, yet refuse them education to give them a knowledge of virtue, and deny them that justice which would rescue them from beggary. The problem lies in the *insincerity* of their concern and is solved by the pertinacity of their injustice. By imposing the compulsion to labor for a meager subsistence, they have degraded the minds and obliterated the principles of those upon whom they make a requisition for qualities which can only belong to intelligence and competence. If those who labor are already despised, they have little motive for virtue. If they are oppressed by the extortion of capital within the narrow confines of "keeping soul and body together," they have as little motive as they have room for economy. It is, therefore, a mere pretense to affect regard for the happiness of society, and at the same time deny the means by which alone it can be happy. It is worse than pretense to say our children cannot meet you in *common schools*, but we will give you for yourselves a *"charity school"*; we cannot consent to receive and pay for your labor on principles of equity; but we will provide you a *poorhouse* to die in; we cannot agree to treat you as equals and furnish you education to meet us on equal terms, but we will build *penitentiaries*, in which to incarcerate you when you commit crime. This is the *philanthropy of the age;* it is worse than the tyranny of the twelfth century.

[Social Position of Labor]

Nor yet is it the best possible physical condition of man that can make him virtuous and happy. His *moral* state controls his destiny. As he is treated by society, so will he rise or fall in the scale of human excellence and infirmity. Contemned, despised, degraded, he sinks to the lowest level of the brute. Respected, cherished, honored, he becomes ambitious of esteem and aspires to excel in all that confers reputation or extorts applause. By the one, he becomes happy himself and the source of happiness to others; by the other, he is driven to degradation and misery and becomes the cause of degradation and misery to others.

The *virtual* distinctions of rank, which too frequently extend into forms and titles, and which have for their basis injustice and extortion, which are the adjuncts of wealth, and which draw the line of exclusion where labor commences, are the cause of all that moral depravity over which the pampered man of opulence affects to shed tears of compassion and projects systems of amelioration. When the children of toil are as much shunned in society as if they were leprous convicts just emerged from loathsome cells, the most powerful obstacle is erected between them and all that can make them estimable and happy. The family tie of the race is snapped asunder; and man thus degraded and oppressed would be less than man, if he did not feel enmity towards his oppressor and view with resentment an order of things so contrary to the dictates of justice and humanity, so broadly in contradiction to his political rights, and so basely in violation of his equal attributes as a man. Here is the fountain, the sacred fountain of all revolutions; this is the point at which nature revolts; this is the point to which the productive classes have been depressed, and at which they now rebel, claiming their rights and resolving to attain them, not by violence and bloodshed, but through the constitutional channels of action: the press, the ballot boxes, and the power of legislation.

[Aims of Labor]

It is a perversion of the aims of the enlightened advocates of labor to represent that they are contending for an *equality of wealth* or a community of property. Our object is as remote from that as the existing system of extortion is from justice. Aware that there exists in nature no equality of industry, skill, strength, talent, wit, or any of the attributes which are essential to production, we could not advocate an equality of possessions without committing an infraction of the rights of others and being guilty of that very injustice of which we now accuse *capital*. Equality of rights to what we produce is not equality of possession, for some will produce more than others. As this is one of the great perversions of our enemies to bring odium and opposition upon our cause, it is necessary here to mark a distinction which I shall note more at large in the succeeding pages.

If ever a party set out upon scientific principles grounded on mathematical precision, it is surely that of the working men. They are a philosophical, political, economical party. They have gone to the fountain-head of first principles and dragged forth justice from the waters of time. They have analyzed the elements of national wealth and individual happiness; they have detected the errors of established systems and exposed the injustice of privileged orders, vested with exclusive rights, to accumulate wealth at the sacrifice of those who produce it. Constituting in fact, though not under the banner of an organized party, a large majority of society, they have at length discovered that they have heretofore been voting for representatives to make laws and for governors to suggest and ratify them on principles directly inimical to their industry, prosperity, and interest, instead of supporting men for those high trusts who will be true to the grand fundamental doctrines of constitutional equity. Forming the bulwark of the nation in time of war, as well as the source of its opulence at all times, they have found themselves oppressed in a period of profound peace by a militia system as onerous, as degrading, and as futile, as immoral, a system which never reaches to the idle drove of society and which it smiles on with contempt. Finding their want of education an impediment to the correction of the abuses practised on them, they have claimed *public instruction* for their children and have been answered by the sneer of derision on the one hand and the cry of revolution on the other. It is even pronounced dangerous to let them know, what no art can now conceal from them, and no sophistry induce them to disbelieve, that they produce all the wealth of society without sharing a thousandth part of it; that they do all the work, elect all the public functionaries, fight all our battles, gain all our victories, cause all our enjoyments to flow upon us, generation after generation and age after age, and still remain destitute of the frugal store of competence which ought to be the reward of industry. If there is danger in the announcement of this monstrous system of injustice, let wrong be removed, and the danger will cease; but the danger ought to exist whilst such an oppressive result flows with mathematical precision from the present perverted organization of government.

It is a common and sound objection to all pre-existing parties that they are mercenary, personal, and selfish, hingeing entirely upon the exchange of places by successful over defeated politicians, not only without regard to merit in men, or truth and justice in principles, but most frequently in utter defiance of all the usual causes of rational preference of men and public tests of benefit to the commonwealth. What a splendid contrast does the party of the Working Men present to such grovelling and besotted factions! It must be matter of astonishment to a mind divested of the yoke and harness of party that even one solitary workingman should be found among those who drag the car of faction for the exclusive benefit of a few interested leaders and inane demagogues, patricians in spirit, if not in fortune, and to their own detriment, their own disadvantage, their own oppression; it is indeed marvelous, and not less lamentable than marvelous.

The inequality of property in this country has chiefly arisen from two causes: first, the *monopoly of land;* second, the monopoly of stock, or *public funded debt!* Let us examine into these sources of fortune!

By what title founded in justice did William Penn and the other original proprietors of land in the United States obtain possession of princely dominions? By the gift of the British king, by royal grants and imperial charters! What right had he to give that which the God of nature had bestowed upon another? Was the land untenanted, was it without proprietors, and did it not furnish nourishment, shelter, and home to thousands of great nature's unsophisticated children? The land thus given was the property of another; the gift, therefore, was null and void, as was subsequently confessed by the proprietary again becoming *a purchaser* from him who held it in possession, the hapless, deluded, and defrauded Indian.

But even the second purchase from the ignorant savage was still less valid and binding; and while it strikingly illustrates the extortion and guile of one party, it shows in strong colors the unhallowed means which cupidity adopts to impose on ignorance and make that very ignorance the foundation of a title which it presumes to style just. For is it within the scope of human reason and the instincts and principles of our nature that a few tinsel beads and burnished trinkets should form a just purchase money for the state of Pennsylvania?

But even that frail tenure was nominal until the acquisition had been sealed by the blood of those proprietors, the hapless Indians, whose tenure was the gift of God, consecrated by the fiat, the sacred fiat, and the bleeding necessities of nature. Nation after nation of defenseless Indians must be immolated before even the gift of the king was worth a groat. Yet this is the foundation of most of our inequality of fortune; this, and the public funded debt.

Of a character even more unjust is the funded debt of this perverted country and its abused institutions. The funding of the poor soldier's pay, earned during the horrible trials of our Revolution, could scarcely have been expected to contribute to the detriment of labor, and erect customs, privileges, and classes, subversive of liberty. Yet so it proved. Did it go to the poor veteran, his helpless widow, his shivering orphans? No! It was diverted from its pure channel by the patrician officers and greedy capitalists and hungry speculators of the army and of the government. It was adopted with a full knowledge that it never could reach the soldier but must immediately go to form a moneyed aristocracy; and the funded debt was created by those immediately interested in its creation, by those who had bought up the soldier's certificates for a song! Here, then, we behold the origin of the landed and funded wealth of this country, of what we denominate capital! What labor or industry could ever come in competition with such enemies? The land in fee simple to those who never, perhaps, saw it; and the funded debt to those who never paid for it, in sums too enormous for industry to equal, and too tempting either for the practice of virtue, the observance of justice, or even the abstinence from oppression. Here we have a double burden upon industry: a ground rent to the proprietor forever, by the laborer; and a tax, or duty, to pay the stockholder his interest, paid by every workingman, from the time of the Revolution to the present day. And yet we are told, and gravely told, that capital is the best friend of industry; and that capitalists, merchants, stockholders, gentlemen and lottery brokers, produce their portion of the wealth of the nation, always giving a due share of credit to those highly meritorious characters, beggars and misers! And yet these latter characters are made by the operation of the corrective principle of vicissitudes, by the spending of the prodigals and the economy of the beggars. This system of social economy, I must confess, appears to me not less a strange one than

it is utterly inconsistent with the spirit of the age and repugnant to
the dictates of a liberal and unaffected philanthropy. . . . .

.   .   .   .

[AIMS OF THE AMERICAN REVOLUTION]

As soon, therefore, as the first generation that had emigrated had
passed away, and with them the shackles and prejudices of education
had fallen off, the *American Revolution* commenced; not immediately
in acts of oppugnation or deeds of violence and bloodshed; but in the
more rational and dignified investigation of the tenure of royal power
and the injustice of coercive government without the ingredients of
voluntary compact or express representation. Having established
this equality of rights and necessity of representation, the war of the
Revolution commenced; and finally eventuated in the recognition of
the principles contended for; that all have *equal rights*, and that the
delegated mass of those rights, by compact, forms the only just and
free government.

The object gained was sublime and magnificent in the highest degree.
But it is the weakness of human reason to relax its vigor the moment
it has acquired a conquest. The very hour we established the principle
of *equality* and the fact of *nominal political independence*, we submitted
to all the forms, usages, and trappings of the old gothic monarchies,
whose deformity we detested and whose oppressions we had cast off.
The contradiction, however astonishing it may appear to us, did not
seem to be perceived by the worthies of 1776, whose attention was
entirely engrossed by magnanimous ideas of augmented friendship
with those nations whose notions of government and claims of power
we had just exploded in the best blood of our bravest sons. Thus,
what we gained in *principle*, we lost in *practice*, and opened our arms
wide to receive the *laws, customs, manners, fashions, morals, literature,
arts, science, and manufactures* of our defeated enemy. In doing this,
we voluntarily became *dependent* in fact, while we proclaimed ourselves
to be independent in theory; and in virtue of the theory, we became
reconciled to every custom that could possibly operate against its
realization. Reason and the genius of our institutions directed us to
follow an opposite course. Governments, to be sustained and perpetuated, must be followed up by manners, fashions, customs, and laws
congenial to their *peculiar principles*, or they become degenerated,

perverted, and turned from their *original* end and spirit. The manners of a people under a monarchy ought to be the reverse of those under a republic, and vice versa. But we were willing to adopt a democracy, and at the same time cherish all the appendages peculiar to a monarchy; and the consequence now is that while the government is republican, society in its general features is as *regal* as it is in England. The tendency of so unnatural a state of things is twofold: either the government must tend to reform the people to simplicity; or the vices of the people must result in deteriorating the government. It is like a watch constructed partly of *jewels* and partly of *metal;* the attrition wears out the latter because it is the softer substance, and a general derangement of the whole machine is the consequence.

The Revolution of 1776, therefore, is, I contend, not yet fully accomplished; and all that part which relates to a moral change remains to be effectuated; that of 1776, merely being a *political* one: a separation of governments, without such a separation of manners as is necessary to give the former permanence and full effect. . . . .

[CULTURAL INDEPENDENCE]

The importance of having the habits and manners of a people correspond to their government has never been duly appreciated by American statesmen; for it extends even to that *system of manufactures* which receives the name of *American,* as a sign of pre-eminence. Our manners and habits should all conduce to happiness, simplicity, and independence! TITLES should be totally abolished and personal distinctions reduced so as to admit of easy access to all. Forms, pomp, grandeur, luxury, and expense, on a magnificent scale, ought to be discouraged. What is called "good society" is a *regal* fungus upon our social system, engendered by a desire to imitate foreign luxuries. In this regard we have not yet commenced our *American revolution.* The whole field lies widespread before us. Let it not be imagined that I am inimical to good breeding, refinement, literature, taste, all that ease and polish which renders social intercourse the charm of life. I am only inimical to the exclusive assumption of "good society" by the rich and the vain, the stockholders and the idle. It should be the aim of a genuine philanthropy to impart the benefits of good breeding to all the members of the human family, if practicable. This may be done by diffusing the blessings of education, by qualifying the working classes to mix with and converse with the more cultivated, polished, and refined. If ignorance and rudeness are made the pretext for a separation of classes and a distinction of ranks, remove the causes and let the barriers of separation be broken down by the omnipotent lever of intellect, at least so far as congenial knowledge spreads her influence over the mind of the community and assimilates in a bond of brotherhood those now repellent prejudices which sunder man from man, as if an animal of another species, whose approach was incompatible with honor, safety, happiness, and even existence.

The prejudice of occupation cannot long endure after the influence of education has approximated closer the extremes of society. Merit will always attach to industry and labor, when blended with the social and intellectual virtues, in despite of pride, wealth, and vanity; and contempt will as invariably follow *personal uselessness* and *mental impotence*, however gilded with the external trappings of fortune. Instinctive admiration pays the spontaneous homage of applause to all who overcome the obstacles of life by vigor, industry, energy, and intellect. "A brave man struggling with the storms of fate" presents a spectacle of the sublime which kindles universal applause! Whilst enervated grandeur, on its throne of state or bed of roses, excites little other emotion than pity and contempt. As it is mind that makes the man, we have but to combine intellect with labor, and the task of equal happiness is completed; teach those who toil how to think, and toil will no longer be degrading, however humble or however poor.

To some, this consummation of a civilized age may appear visionary. But let it be remembered that at one period all the improvements which subsequently arose were adjudged impossible. Time and mind are the creators of human destiny, which accomplish more than miracles and produce revolutions that only fail to astonish because they enlighten.

It is only under the dark and hush policy of silence that abuses can expect to continue, extortion to thrive, capital to luxuriate, and monopoly to expand. With the Bible locked up in a dead language and science mystified into a being of the upper skies, as unapproachable to the people, aristocracy and priestcraft would rule the world with a scepter of iron, and yoke the souls as well as bodies of the people in eternal servitude. The effort of capital and power is always on the side of ignorance in the people and injustice in the principles

and laws of the government. Inquiry, discussion, argument, are esteemed deadly enemies to aristocracy, extortion, fraud, and oppression of all kinds, that denude the people and fatten the few of the
high privileged classes. It is the attitude of capital to intimidate,
repress, silence! But if the people will speak, it is then made a point
to cover them with ridicule, to treat them with contempt, to tell them
they are not initiated and speak too much upon subjects they know
nothing of. To all this I stand opposed, and against it I shall never
fail to array the little strength that nature has given me.

Before the Revolution, it was esteemed absurd to question the
right of the king to tax the colonies. Before the reign of English
King John, it was ridiculous to doubt the divine right of the monarch.
There was a time when it was judged the height of folly to declare
that the earth moved; and it was punished as impiety to say that the
other planets also had their revolutions! The application of steam,
as now used, would in ancient times have been termed *madness*. The
doctrine of the sovereignty of the people has only been rational since
it has been reduced to practice; in despotic countries, it is still thought
to be silly and absurd. When the working people gain their just
rights, to controvert the doctrine of extortion will no longer be deemed
illogical, dangerous, unscientific, and absurd. That time must arrive,
and if I can do aught that will tend to accelerate it, I shall esteem it
the most happy, honorable, and fortunate effort of my existence.

Yet it is not, after all, a party object merely for which we are
struggling. It extends to higher and nobler aims; it reaches to the
expansion of our national resources, the consolidation of the national
strength, the increase of our moral, as well as physical energies.

Congenial to all her principles, customs, and habitudes of mind was
the manner in which the gothic ages enveloped science in mystery,
or mistook mystery for learning. The refuge which literature found
in the cells of the Christian monasteries necessarily associated her in
habits of such intimacy with religion as reciprocally to impart to one
another their peculiar properties; so that when science at last emerged
from her retirement, she appeared babbling the cant of superstition
and covered with the rags of fanaticism and the mummery of priestcraft. So inveterate is habit, so deep the sense of reverence for antiquity, that even the present age has not yet wholly shaken off the
trammels of mystification that encumbered science in the darkness of

the cloister. It is still held as heresy that a man who labors shall dare to think, and that he who thinks shall venture to write, unless under the license of a *diploma* or the authority of a literary title. To obstruct the passage of the populace to the temple of knowledge as much as possible, the impediments of an obsolete language and a hieroglyphic character were industriously thrown in their way. The union of church and state presented powerful motives to withhold from the multitude those beams of intellectual light which would expose their oppressions and reveal their rights. The safety of a system based upon *wrong* depended upon darkness. As mankind, however, gradually tore the veil from their eyes, they partially redressed their wrongs; but as the light has never been full and effulgent, the wrong has never been entirely removed. Progressive developments have been made in defiance of the systematic opposition of the combined power of government and aristocracy. Further advances are still obstinately resisted by the same powerful influences. Every inch of ground is disputed; and every fresh conquest of reason, truth, and justice only tends to add vigilance to capital, power to monopoly, and rancor to aristocracy.

When we reflect, therefore, that the first discovery and true doctrine of the rights of man and the title to property are not more than a century old from their first glimmerings of pale uncertainty, we need not express astonishment that they have advanced no farther and still retain the rude proportions of an imperfect structure, partaking more of the heterogeneous gothic style than of the fair and just proportions of science and taste. But the mind, although slow in its march, is yet sure in its progression. Every day adds new truths to science and divests knowledge of its monkish garments of mysticism. Every day gathers fresh crowds of votaries to the shrine of scientific inquiry and research and sends forth thousands to disseminate truth, invoke justice, and denounce fraud and oppression.

[CONCLUSION]

In the following pages, I have endeavored to strike out some new truths, establish some disputed rights, and elucidate the operations of labor, capital, monopoly, credit, and commerce, in their natural and unsophisticated features. The principal object was to divest science of the mummery of its pomp, the mystery of its trappings, and the cant of its phraseology, as well as to exhibit the real attitude and importance of the producers of labor to the wealth, happiness, and independence of a nation. According to Lord Bacon's rule of philosophizing, I have drawn my theory from facts, and not deduced facts to suit my theory; resting upon the great fundamental doctrines of human happiness and freedom, however deficient they may prove in ingenuity, their origin and tendency will never fail to afford solace and consolation to the author, for the omissions of ignorance or the blunders of precipitancy, so long as he can escape the imputation of being inimical to the rights or indifferent to the happiness of mankind. Proceeding on this plan, I have rather labored to elucidate and break down antiquated forms than to systematize and digest with scholastic precision. Truth is often "curtailed of her fair proportions" by a too rigid classification on scientific principles. A general division of political economy, however, may not be amiss when founded on its chief fundamental principles, such, for instance, as the production, distribution and consumption of industry.

It has not, however, been so much owing to an ignorance of this science as to the misapplication of its principles and the great perversions and misrepresentations of the champions of capital and the stock interest that the people have hitherto derived no practical benefit from its labors. Thus far, science has only toiled to show to the idle *few* the means by which they acquired the industry of the *many;* and the facility with which imbecile minds, backed by wealth, could rule millions who were debased by eternal labor and degenerated by penury, famine, and low diet. At the same time that these feudal ministers of mercy, in the shape of abstinence and death, have the assurance to proclaim to the people that the beneficence and wisdom of government have made them comfortable, affluent, and happy. By confounding the wealth of the higher orders with the *unity of the nation,* the gross amount of industry in a country has been represented as so much stock of comfort to the *whole people;* a fallacy which sagacity could not overlook, and which nothing but conscious fraud, intent upon deception, could have devised. But such a cloak was necessary to cover oppressions which no people, however debased, could perceive and yet endure. Among the foremost of these apologists of tyranny and deceivers of the populace stands Adam Smith, who, so late as in the last century, thus ventured to assure the *English mechanic* that justice entered into the system which stripped him of his earnings to pamper the *three orders*, whose only title to respect was idleness and sensuality. . . . .

. . . .

Similar deceptions mark the course of every writer on political economy, in a greater or less degree. They are very exact in tracing the manner in which *capital* extorts from industry, and very scientific in their distinctions and classifications of the elements of society; but they studiously avoid any application of the natural principles of justice to the comfort of those whose labor creates wealth by insisting on a system consonant to a more equal distribution of industry.

Where shall we look for the triumphs of science but in the improved happiness of man? Of what utility are all our recondite researches and intellectual investigations, if they tend not to exalt the race and better the condition of the human family? Surely an enlightened age cannot rest satisfied with the measurement of its wealth; content to behold it measured, and indifferent to its appropriation? What opinion should we form of an architect, who resided in an old gothic tower, destitute of commodious apartments and without beauty or convenience, who should satisfy himself by measuring its ill-assorted proportions, instead of building up a new one, on the true principles of beauty, convenience, and comfort? We should, without hesitation, compassionate the unfortunate state of his mind and exclaim: What infatuation! What folly! Similar to this is the conduct of the political economists of Europe, who look up to their gothic tower with sensations of reverence approaching to adoration so that passion blinds them to its deformities, while interest tells them, without it, their despotism and aristocracy must soon crumble to atoms, and capital and monopoly roll in the dust, together with the heads of kings and the mummeries of hierarchies!

. . . .

It is a singular infatuation prevailing among all modern writers on economy that the scarcity of food among the laboring people is attributable to excess of population, whilst the palpable fact was staring them in the face that the excess of bloated accumulation in the rich demonstrated the falsity of the hypothesis.

There is some apology, however, for the economists of Europe, in the fact of the genius of their institutions presenting an insuperable barrier to the effectuation of the principles of justice in the distribution of labor; inasmuch that the people do not there enjoy universal suffrage. This reform of society must be accomplished in the halls of legislation, through the action of suffrage in the choice of the representatives of the people. Like the abolishment of the laws of primogeniture and entails, we must commence with laws establishing the true principle of the distribution of wealth. To do this, the producers of wealth must coöperate through the usual means of commanding a majority of voters and of representatives, by *parties*, by combinations among the *wronged* never to vote for men who will favor the principles that oppress them; by exhortations to the mass of the people to remain faithful to themselves; by public expositions of their grievances, public appeals to support their rights, and an inflexible determination to abide by the principles of our Declaration of Independence, and our national charter; until they shall become practical and real blessings, instead of nominal and visionary honors. Such are the means by which "the industrious classes of our countrymen shall be enabled better to obtain and secure the fruits of their industry," and with those fruits the blessings of education and knowledge, without which liberty is a burden and competence a curse.

.   .   .   .

The *working man of the United States*, placed by nature in a moral and physical attitude which conspire to carry to perfection all the attributes that ennoble his mind and procure happiness to his being, presents to the world the imposing spectacle of Liberty and Reason combining to consummate Justice. For the first time since the origin of government, he presents the instance of the sovereign power residing in the producer of labor, to be exercised at his pleasure and discretion. *Holding this weapon of self-defense, he cannot be oppressed but through the concurrence and action of those touched with his own condition.*

11

DAVID HENSHAW

THE DARTMOUTH COLLEGE CASE[1]

[VALUES AND PRIVILEGES OF BUSINESS CORPORATIONS]

Business corporations, excluding banks and all large corporations for trading in money, when judiciously granted and suitably regulated, seem to me generally beneficial and the natural offspring of our social condition. But if they are to be placed beyond legislative control and are thus to become monopolies and perpetuities, they assume an aspect the reverse of this and become alarming excrescences upon the body politic. We may assume this axiom as perfectly sound: that *Corporations can hold their rights upon no firmer basis nor different tenure than individuals hold theirs.* The legislature exercises the undisputed right to regulate the business of individuals and to define their rights to property. It has first prohibited, then licensed, and then made penal, the selling of lottery tickets. It prohibits the selling of certain articles without a license therefor from designated officers. It forbids the selling of goods at auction without a license and the payment of a tax. It forbids the selling of other articles, except in certain quantities, and with certain brands put upon them by public officers — unwise and vexatious regulations, I grant, but still who disputes the legality of the inspection laws? It requires, in other cases, that the name of the vender or packer be branded on the article sold. It prohibits people from doing business on certain days and on particular hours, as in the case of the laws respecting the observance of the Lord's day, and selling goods by auction after sunset. It prohibits certain amusements, and has even affixed a fine to a particular exercise of the liberty of speech, as may be seen in the laws against gaming and profane swearing. It regulates the rights of inheritance, prescribes the rules for the transfer of property from individuals to individuals, and their rights and remedies in matters of private contract; and all these rules are changed at

[1] [From *Remarks upon the Rights and Powers of Corporations, and of the Rights, Powers, and Duties of the Legislature Toward Them.* By a citizen of Boston (Boston, 1837) — Abridged.]

the will of the legislature. What particular quality, then, is there, in a law, in the form of a charter, or limited copartnership to a number of individuals, that places it beyond the power that created it, the legislative power, and gives to it the character of a contract in perpetuity? From the very nature of the case, the legislature must have the same right to repeal as to grant a charter. It has the same right, inherently, to repeal a special law or charter creating a bank, insurance company, manufactory, or any other business corporation that it has to repeal the general law of limited copartnerships. But this right to repeal the charters gives it no right to the private property of the corporation, any more than the right to repeal the general law of limited copartnerships gives it the right to the property of the partners.

In this state, the legislature transcends its constitutional power if it attempt to farm out the rights of the community and of succeeding generations by means of corporate perpetuities to individual or associated grantees. Our institutions abhor private perpetuities and monopolies as much as nature abhors a vacuum. The constitution of Massachusetts says: "No man, nor corporation, or association of men, have any other title to obtain advantages or *particular* or exclusive privileges, distinct from those of the community, than what arises from considerations of services rendered to the public." It also says, "that government is instituted for the *common good;* for the protection, safety, prosperity and happiness of the *people*, and *not* for the profit, honor, or private interest of any one man, family or class of men: Therefore, the people alone have an incontestable, unalienable, and indefeasible right to institute government, to reform, alter or totally change the same, when their protection, safety, prosperity and happiness require it." Again it says, "that the legislature ought frequently to assemble for the redress of grievances, for *correcting*, strengthening and confirming the laws, and for making new laws, as the *common good* requires."

The constitution of this state, though it allows and supposes that "particular and exclusive privileges, distinct from those of the community" may be granted by the legislature "to individuals, corporations and associations of men," allows them to be granted only for services rendered. They must be considered by the legislature to be generally beneficial; they must conduce to the common good, or it has no constitutional power to grant them. The framers of the constitution well knew that corporations and associations of men possessing "particular" privileges adapted to the nature and purposes of their pursuits were necessary in this community; that the charter for a college would not answer for the business of a church; that a charter to a glass manufactory would not answer for a bank; and they hence clothed the legislature with power to make these grants, limited, however, by the consideration that they are in consequence of the benefit they will confer on the public, that they will conduce to the *common good*. They were, from their constitutional origin, to be considered public laws, for public purposes; and whenever they should cease to minister to the purposes of their creation, the *common good*, the legislature, for the time being, not only has a right, but is in duty bound by the same constitution, to "correct" them, either by making new laws respecting them, or amending the old ones. There is no more propriety in saying that these institutions can only be controlled by general laws than in assuming that they can only be created by general laws; or than there would be in saying that the legislature cannot regulate the affairs of a single town or city by a particular or special law. Indeed, if these acts of incorporation or charters are not to be considered laws of the land, great wrong has been committed under them in so considering them for some purposes. The legislature has no constitutional right, by a special act, to permit my neighbor to take my land for his own use against my consent. But it has a right to take my land or other property for public purposes, paying me therefor a just equivalent. If railroad, turnpike, canal, and the like corporations are mere private associations, existing for the benefit of the corporations and not for the *common good*, I would ask, What right have they to occupy my land against my consent? All these corporations then exist by the law of the land and, like all other laws, are liable to modification at the legislative will. Such, in effect, has been the decision of the Supreme Court of the United States in regard to the Bank of the United States, in the cases of Maryland and Ohio, which states taxed that bank. The court decided that the Bank of the United States was a *public institution*. Such, too, was the opinion of the legislature of Massachusetts in revising the laws of the state. In the third section of the second chapter of the revised code, it is declared that "all acts of incorporation shall be deemed public acts."

There is more sound than substance in the term "vested rights," as applied to acts of incorporation. Every right any citizen holds is a vested right until he is divested of it; and the remark applies with equal truth to corporations as to individuals. But it by no means follows that, because they have a "vested right," they may not be legally divested of it. Last year our farmers had a vested right to screw their hay into bundles and sell it as they pleased; this year the legislature has divested them of that right, unless they put the name of the packer on the bundle. This year a bank has a vested right, vested for the common good, to loan its credit; next year the legislature may, if it choose, divest it of that right, if it will more conduce to the common good to divest it. And this, too, inherently, and without any special reservation in the charter to that effect. Numerous instances, in this and other States, might be cited, where this power has been exercised upon banks, and other charters of incorporation; but I omit them, preferring the question should be decided in the mind of the reader upon its own merits to relying upon precedents. Mere precedents have little binding force upon my mind.

The safety of the public and of corporations themselves depends on the establishing of these principles. Corporate charters would not be repealed, admitting this right to exist, as all experience teaches us, unless they had become a public grievance in the opinion of the legislature; in which case their "particular" privileges ought to be taken from them. They were originally granted to promote the common good; and whenever they cease to accomplish the purposes of their creation, an end should be put to their existence.

[CHARITABLE CORPORATIONS]

It being conceded by all that municipal corporations are public institutions, always controllable by the legislative will, there is no need now to examine their rights. I will therefore proceed to examine the remaining great class of American corporations, eleemosynary corporations. It is admitted in the previous remarks that the legislature, in changing or abrogating the charters of business corporations, acquired thereby no right to the property of the corporation. The franchises of such corporations, only, and not the property, belong to the public. It is not, however, certain that such are the rights of eleemosynary corporations.

It is the prevalent opinion and sanctioned, it is believed, by judicial decision, which, by the way, is not always good authority, that the property held by such institutions is private property, as much so as the property held by business corporations; that donations made to them must be always applied to the purposes prescribed by the donors; that if the trustees or directors are unfaithful to their trusts, their duties can be enforced by a court of chancery; that money thus given cannot be diverted from the original object of the donation by any legislative enactment; that if money be so diverted or the corporation cease to exist, it reverts, of right, to the donor or his heirs. These principles, it is believed, are more in conformity with the English than the American law. The powers, rights, and duties of these corporations, like those of every other social and political institution among us, depend upon our own, and not upon the foreign law. And these powers, rights, and duties, like the laws of inheritance and dower, are subject to legislative changes and control. The right to give, receive, and, for the time being, to manage eleemosynary corporate funds, here, depends not upon the common law of Great Britain but upon our own statutes, and the particular charters of such institutions, which are themselves but special statutes, laws of the land, public acts, subject to the general principles that limit and control all statutes. The foundation of these rights is in the colonial law of 1641.

. . . .

In this country we may say that all endowments are public, given under our laws, originally, for *public* uses.

Upon the principle before stated, and which applies as much to this class of corporations as to business corporations, that corporations can hold their rights on no different tenure, the laws of the land, than that on which individuals hold theirs, the legislature has a right to direct anew, by law, the application of these corporation funds. It constantly exercises a similar power over individual property. Until the act of the colony of 1641, no inhabitant had a right to give his property to a corporation to be applied to the uses he might designate; and no corporation had a right to receive it; that act gave him and them the right. He has also, under other laws of this state, the right to bequeath his property to his relatives or to others. This is "a vested right," as much so as the right of a corporation to receive the bequest; but who would deny the power to the legislature to change the law in regard to wills and inheritances, to enact that no man shall give his property to these institutions; that it shall all, or any given portion of it, go to his kindred or his connections, or that a certain portion of it shall go to the public treasury? It is common, in some states, to take specified portions of the estates of deceased persons for public uses. It has been objected, that if a law were made to change the use of funds already given, it would be *ex post facto* and hence unconstitutional. Such, however, is not the case. The Supreme Court of the United States, in the case of Calder against Bull, in the 3d Dallas, 386, decided that the prohibition in the Federal Constitution of *ex post facto* laws extends only to penal statutes and does not extend to cases affecting only the civil rights of individuals. The whole current of adjudicated cases has been in conformity to this view of the Constitution.

With respect to the rights of wives, a married woman, now, has a right, and of course a vested right, to the use of certain portions of her husband's real estate, if she survive him, of which her husband cannot divest her without her consent; but the legislature can change the law, and divest her of this right, and this, too, though she has no voice in choosing the representatives.

Under existing laws the personal property of the wife becomes the property of the husband on marriage, but not her real estate. The legislature could change the law, and vest in the husband the real as well as the personal estate. Can corporations, then, *the mere creatures of the law, created not for themselves, but for the common good*, claim rights superior to those of individuals, and above the reach of the legislative power? ! ! In maintaining the legislative authority to alter, amend, or totally to abolish all charters, I am far from advocating any general, indiscriminate, or wanton exercise of that power. The legislature, composed as it is of the representatives of the whole people, chosen annually, could have no motive to legislate upon this subject, unless necessity and the common good required it, nor unless the people sanctioned it. When any institution of this kind, in any of its branches, from age or other causes, has ceased to answer the design of its creation, the common good, there should be a power in the legislature, and it ought to be exercised, to put an end to such institution. Who shall judge of the wants of the existing generation, the living or the dead? Who shall control the property of this world and prescribe its application, the dead, who once owned it in part, or the living, who own it entire? The conservatives cling to the dead; I am for the living. This right is inherent and exists in all communities, from the very nature of civil society; and, in this country, the principle is recognized in our written and fundamental law. The constitution gives to the legislature, for the time being, authority to pass laws creating and regulating these institutions for the *common good;* but one legislature has no constitutional competency to bind its successor, who is coequal in power, both holding their authority from the same constitution, and not the one from the other. Hence, happily, one legislature cannot bind another, and thus farm out, irrevocably, the rights of succeeding generations.

[CRITIQUE OF DARTMOUTH COLLEGE CASE]

Where lies the difficulty in applying these principles to practice by amending or repealing all such acts of incorporation as may be found objectionable? The difficulty arises from the assumption of authority on the part of the Supreme Court of the United States, which, if submitted to, prostrates the power of the states to the footstool of that bench, that acts of incorporation are contracts between the state granting them and the corporators; and cannot be annulled except with the consent of the corporators, because the Constitution of the United States, the paramount law of the land, says that no state shall pass any laws impairing the obligation of contracts. This principle was maintained, if not established, in the case of the Dartmouth College, tried before the Supreme Court at Washington, in 1819. It may be necessary therefore to a right understanding of this subject and to a just appreciation of the principles laid down by the court and of their effect upon the rights and interests of the states, to take a view of the facts in this case and of the course of reasoning which brought the court to such an extraordinary result.

In the year 1769, a charter was granted in the name of the King of Great Britain, George the 3d, through his governor of the then province of New Hampshire, John Wentworth, by and with the advice of the council of the province, to Eleazer Wheelock and others for a college, authorizing them by voluntary endowments to support suitable teachers and other officers therein named. The object of the charter is recited in the preamble, and is to further the exertions of Dr. Wheelock in spreading the truths of the Gospel and the lights of civilization among the Indians and in giving the best means of education to the people of New Hampshire, for their own benefit.

. . . .

This grant, it will be recollected, was made under the colonial law, though, like processes in law, it ran in the name of the king, and was given by the colonial authority, subject to all its limitations, and liable at any time to be modified at the legislative will, with or without the consent of the grantees. It was an institution, not for private emolument, but to promote the public good, the civilization and Christianizing the Indians, and for the education of the people of New Hampshire. By the Revolution the people of New Hampshire succeeded to all the rights of sovereignty held before by the crown, the parliament of Great Britain, and by the colony of New Hampshire. Every kind of civil and political power, before held, jointly or severally, by the different or collective branches of the government of the mother country and of the province of New Hampshire, devolved upon the state of New Hampshire at the time of the revolution. The powers thus acquired still remain to be exercised by the legislature, except so far as they may have been restricted by their own state constitution or that of the United States. In the year 1816, the legislature of New Hampshire, for the purpose of making the college more useful to the people of New Hampshire, the Indians, for whose benefit it was originally, in part, founded, having become extinct, and the funds being no longer applied or applicable to their use, passed an act enlarging and changing the government of the college. The trustees, disliking to lose their power and the profits of office, as they were likely to do by this act, resisted, on the ground that the charter vested in them rights of which the legislature had no authority to divest them; that the charter was a "contract" within the meaning of the Constitution of the United States; and that the act aforesaid impaired its obligation, contrary to the Constitution. They brought a suit in the state courts, contesting the validity of the law, which was decided against them. The trustees then carried it by appeal to the Supreme Court of the United States; and that tribunal decided in their favor. Chief Justice Marshall, who presided at the trial, *assumed* the whole question, as settled, as follows: "It can require *no argument* to prove that the circumstances of this case constitute a contract. An application is made to the *crown* for a charter to incorporate a religious and literary institution. In the application, it is stated, that large contributions have been made in England for the object, which will be conferred on the corporation as soon as it shall be created.

"The charter is granted, and on its faith the property is conveyed. Surely, in this transaction, every ingredient of a complete contract is to be found." That may be true, but is it such a contract as was intended by the framers of the Federal Constitution and the people who adopted it should come within the reach of the inhibitory clause in that instrument? The institution of government is a contract between the whole body of citizens and each citizen; but does it hence follow that we cannot impair that contract, that we cannot change the constitution without the unanimous assent of the citizens? Every civil institution is in some sense a contract; but does it follow that, hence, we cannot change those institutions? This charter was a contract of this kind, given by the provincial executive, containing express and implied conditions, the former limited, qualified, and controlled by the latter. The trustees were declared to be a corporation, with power to hold forever certain gifts, grants, and other property for certain purposes, subject, however, to the fundamental laws of the colony, liable to taxation, and to such laws as subsequent legislatures might deem proper to enact, within their legislative competency; and their powers, at the time, over local grants, were plenary. If the grant had emanated directly from the king, which it did not, it must have been limited by these well-known, though implied conditions. The king himself was legally incompetent to make any grant other than thus limited. The Chief Justice, apparently conscious of the sophistical position he had assumed, comes, subsequently, more to the point, and asks:

First, "Is this a contract protected by the Constitution of the United States?"

Second, "Is it impaired by the acts under which the defendant holds?"

The last question it is unnecessary to consider, for, notwithstanding the finely-spun arguments of the state counsel to show that the law did not impair the charter, even if it were a contract, that to change and enlarge the charter was not to impair the contract, I am free to admit that there is more ingenuity than candor in it, and that the law of New Hampshire did abridge and impair the rights of the trustees under the charter. Judge Marshall says the general correctness of these observations cannot be controverted, viz., "That the framers of the Constitution did not intend to restrain the states in the regulation of their civil institutions adopted for internal government, and that the instrument they have given us is not to be so construed, may be admitted. This provision of the Constitution never has been understood to embrace other contracts than those which respect some object of value, and confer rights which may be asserted in a court of justice." Does not this embrace every possible case or transaction in society, particularly if it come before a judge avowing the vicious principle on which most English and some Anglo-American judges act, that "the first duty of a good judge is to extend his jurisdiction?"

It has extended to officers appointed by the executive who have demanded a compulsory process to procure a commission made out for an officer, but subsequently withheld by order of the President. The office was an object of value, though not a "freehold," and the appointment and commission conferred rights which were asserted in a court of justice; and hence the case comes within that clause of the Federal Constitution respecting contracts, as expounded and defined above by Judge Marshall. If the appointment of men to office be a contract, charters of incorporation contracts, and marriage be a contract, as Judge Marshall pretty plainly, and Judge Story unequivocally, intimates, coming within the scope of the before-cited inhibitory clause of the Federal Constitution, it would seem to follow that every other transaction of civil society may be engulfed in this vortex and whirled under the jurisdiction of the Supreme Court; and that the people of the states, instead of having governments adapted to their wants, liable to be modified, altered, repealed, or totally changed, as was supposed to be their inherent and unalienable right, have, in fact, myriads of little perpetuities beyond the control of state and national legislation, and subject only to the will of their directors or of the lord patrons.

Judge Marshall says, respecting the contract of marriage, "When any state legislature shall pass an act annulling all marriage contracts (and if they can annul one they can many), or allowing either party to annul it without the consent of the other, it will be time enough to inquire whether such an act be constitutional."

Judge Story, in the same case, was much more explicit, and develops the doctrine of the court on the subject of contracts more boldly than Judge Marshall. He says, "As to the case of the contract of marriage, which the argument supposes not to be within the reach of the prohibitory clause, because it is a matter of civil institution, *I profess I do not feel the weight of the reason assigned for the exception.* In a legal sense, *all contracts* recognized as valid in any country, may be properly said to be *matters* of *civil institution*, since they obtain their obligation and construction *jure loci contractus.*".

(And the judge would perhaps hold the converse of this doctrine as a legitimate deduction from his premises, that all *civil institutions* are "contracts," the changing of which institutions or contracts would impair their obligation, and come within the clause of the Constitution before cited.)

"But," continues the judge, "if the argument means to assert that the legislature has power to dissolve such contracts without any breach on either side, against the wishes of the parties, and without *judicial* inquiry to ascertain the breach, I certainly am not prepared to admit such a power, or that its execution would not intrench upon the prohibition of the Constitution." .... "A man has just as good a right to his *wife*, as he has to the *property* acquired under a marriage contract. He has a legal right to her *society*, and her *fortune;* and to divest such right without his default, and against *his will*, would be as flagrant a violation of the principles of justice as the confiscation of his own estate."

Judge Marshall says, "According to the theory of the British constitution, their parliament is omnipotent. To annul corporate rights, might give a shock to public opinion which that government has chosen to avoid; but the power is not questioned." (Here the judge mistakes, for Great Britain has exercised this power in many cases in that of church funds, as I have before shown.) "By the Revolution," continues Judge Marshall, "the duties as well as the powers of government devolved on the people of New Hampshire. It is admitted, that among the latter was comprehended the transcendent power of parliament, as well as of the executive. ... Religion, charity, and education, are, in the law of England, legatees or donees, capable of receiving bequests or donations in this form." (But they are not under our laws, and the fact of their capability in England, to say the least, is irrelevant.)

"This," continues the judge, "is plainly a contract, to which the donors, the trustees, and the crown, to whose rights and obligations New Hampshire succeeds, were the original parties. It is a contract made for a valuable consideration. It is a contract for the security and disposition of property. It is a contract, on the faith of which real and personal estate has been conveyed to the corporation. It is then a contract within the letter of the Constitution; and within its spirit also, unless the fact that property is invested by the donors in trustees for the promotion of religion and education, for the benefit of persons who are perpetually changing, though the objects remain the same, shall create a particular exception, taking this case out of the prohibition contained in the Constitution.

"It is *more than possible*, that the preservation of rights of this description was *not* particularly in view of the framers of the Constitution, when the clause under consideration was introduced into that instrument. It is *probable* that interferences of more frequent recurrence, (tender laws and stop laws,) to which the temptation was stronger, and of which the mischief was more extensive, *constituted the great motive for imposing this restriction on state legislatures.*" . . . . "It is not enough to say that this particular case (or class of cases) was not in the mind of the convention when the article was framed, nor of the American people when it was adopted. It is necessary to go further, and to say that, had this particular case been suggested, the language would have been so varied as to exclude it, or it would have been made a special exception" ! ! Can there be anywhere found upon record a more unsound and dangerous stretch of judicial law? What can more directly shake the public confidence in the judgment of the court than these admissions? Judge Marshall admits, what everybody knows, that the prohibitory clause in the Constitution was *not* intended by the convention who framed, nor the people who adopted that instrument, to extend to cases of this kind. It had reference only to money contracts, and was intended to restrict the states from cancelling those obligations by bankrupt laws, stop laws, and tender laws.

This construction, too, violates well-settled principles of law and of common sense, long and often recognized by the Supreme Court itself. Every man knows that the *intention* of the parties in making laws is to be the rule of construction. Their intentions are to be gathered from the words of the law, and if they be ambiguous, from any other credible source.

. . . .

Whatever was granted in the Constitution was meant to be a well-defined grant. It was never intended by those who framed, and the people who adopted the Constitution, that its powers should be enlarged by construction. So jealous and careful were the people upon this point, that they adopted an amendment to guard against the apprehended evil. It is the 10th article of amendment in the Constitution, as follows: "The powers not delegated to the United States by the Constitution, nor prohibited by it to the states, are reserved to the states respectively, or to the people." The framers intended a specific thing in the clause, inhibiting the states from passing laws impairing the obligations of contracts; they made use of the word *contracts* in its ordinary meaning, as it was then well understood. It was to remedy the then well-known evil of tender laws, stop laws, and absolving laws. It was never designed to apply to the civil institutions of the states, but was confined in its application to contracts for the buying and selling of things. If there were any doubt as to this fact — but there appears to be none even on the mind of the Chief Justice — the testimony of Luther Martin, a member of the convention from Maryland, in his letter or report to the legislature of his state, would remove it. It was meant, he says, only to secure the rights of debtor and creditor from the operations of state tender laws, stop laws, and bankrupt laws. Mr. Madison, another member of the convention, in the *Federalist*, written about the period the Constitution was adopted, bears his testimony corroborative of the same fact.

The principle assumed by Judge Marshall and sanctioned by all the court except Judge Duval in effect annihilates the Federal Constitution, or makes it a plastic mass in the hands of the Supreme Court to mean anything or nothing. It can mold the state institutions to suit the will of the court.

The Chief Justice admits that this kind of contract was not in view when the convention adopted and the people approved the inhibitory clause. But that, he says, is not enough; you must go further; you must show that if this case had been presented to them at the time, they would have rejected it; *and of this probability the court assume the sole right to judge.* The counsel for the state show that the convention had not this class of contracts in view when they framed the clause; their object and design were confined to property contracts and private rights; and all history bears testimony that the states never would have surrendered the very object for which they had contended before the Revolution and encountered its miseries and perils to attain, the right to regulate their own internal civil institutions. "Very true," say the court, "but this particular class of cases did not occur to them at the time, and if it had, would they have excluded it? We decide that they would not; and consequently it is embraced within the meaning of the clause."

Thus the authority to regulate some of the most important civil institutions, and particularly that of education in the higher branches of literature and the sciences, the control over those seminaries where the citizens are educated who are destined to fill what are termed the liberal professions and, as ministers, lawyers, physicians, and men of letters, are to enter every city, town, hamlet, and family in the state and directly to influence the condition of society, is wrested from the states and confided to irresponsible perpetuities, thus made independent within the limits of the state. With such latitudinous and far-fetched constructions, the Federal Constitution is whatever the Federal judiciary may please to make it; and the states are in fact in possession of little more power than the bailiffs who officiate in the Federal courts.

The case, from beginning to end, was tried and decided, in all its cardinal points, upon an assumption of facts and principles that have no real existence here. It is an English, not an American decision; made by a court who are English in all their legal learning and principles. The rights, powers, privileges, and duties of the corporation are gathered, not from the *laws* of New Hampshire, where alone we should look for them, but from British "authorities," that is, from the opinions of English judges, in what the court assume to be analogous cases, and English law writers, who have figured on the British bench, in British "reports," and British law books, for the last five hundred or a thousand years. The industrious research into the musty precedents of English judges and the misty opinions of English jurists so quaintly displayed by some members of the court in deciding this cause might have been very praiseworthy and perhaps useful if they had been sitting on the king's bench in Westminster; but they appear sadly grotesque from the supreme bench at Washington.

The court assume that the grant was made by the king and is to be defined by the British law; when, upon the face of the charter, though, like the precepts of the courts, running in the name of the king, it appears to have been granted by the executive of New Hampshire, by the advice of the council of New Hampshire, attested by the seal of the province; and upon every principle of law and common sense, it is to be defined, limited, and controlled, by the local laws of New Hampshire, and by the nature of her political institutions.

The theory of colonial government maintained by the Americans before the Revolution and enforced by the Revolution was that the king is the supreme head, officiating as the executive personally in the realm of England, and by viceroys and governors in the colonies and his other dominions, that each branch thus constituted was a perfect state, having power to make laws binding within its jurisdiction.

.   .   .   .

New Hampshire, on her first organization as a separate province in 1680, asserted her right to exclusive legislation within her own limits by enacting in her first General Court that "no act, imposition, law or ordinance should be made or imposed upon them, but such as should be made by the assembly and approved by the president and council."

New Hampshire, while a part of Massachusetts, was governed by her laws, among which was the act of 1641, respecting grants to colleges and schools, showing that they were deemed *public institutions;* and those laws continued to be the laws of New Hampshire until they were repealed; and this act never was repealed; and hence, when the charter of Dartmouth College was granted, it was under all the restrictions, limitations, and conditions to which this early and fundamental law subjected like institutions. It is to be judged by the colonial and not the English law; and by the colonial law it is a *public institution,* controllable by statute law, and *not* a private grant in the nature of a contract. The charter of Dartmouth College, upon the face, also purports to be granted for public purposes, to enlighten the savage and to educate the citizen of New Hampshire. Though Dr. Wheelock was declared nominally to be the founder, it is well known that he gave comparatively little towards its funds. It was endowed with forty-four thousand acres of land; one whole township of which was given by the state; five hundred acres in the town of Hanover, a public reservation, were bestowed upon it by Gov. Wentworth; and besides these, about seventeen hundred dollars were subscribed by citizens of New Hampshire, to be paid in labor, provisions, and building materials. From its very origin, it was deemed in New Hampshire to be a public institution, erected and endowed for public purposes. The legislature very early conferred upon it a civil jurisdiction of three miles square, and made the president of the college, *ex officio*, a magistrate to keep order. This is as much a franchise, in English law, as the charter itself; but who would deny the rights of the state legislature to repeal *this* law?

I have shown that all institutions of this nature, in Great Britain, are within the entire and absolute control of the parliament. Judge Marshall says, "By the Revolution, the duties as well as the powers of government, devolved on the people of New Hampshire. It is admitted that among the latter was comprehended the transcendent power of parliament, as well as that of the executive department." I have shown that institutions of this kind, as early as 1641, were considered here as public institutions; that they depend upon local and not British law for their existence, their rights, powers, and duties; that, being public institutions, founded by virtue of colonial statute law, they were subject to the modifications which the local, legislative authority chose to impose; and that it is admitted by the Supreme Court, even if they hold under the British law, the people of New Hampshire, at the termination of the Revolution, had an unlimited control over the institution. This control can have been abridged only in two ways: first, by the constitution of New Hampshire, and secondly, by the Constitution of the general government. The constitution of New Hampshire, which was adopted before the Constitution of the United States, and since twice, I believe, amended, says, "Government being instituted for the common benefit, protection and security of the whole community, and *not* for the private interest or emolument of any one man, family, or class of men, therefore . . . . the people may, and of right ought to, reform the old or establish a new government."

It further says, "No subsidy, charge, tax, impost, or duty, shall be established, fixed, laid, or levied, under any pretext whatsoever, without the consent of the people, or their representatives in the legislature, or authority derived from that body." And in conformity with the first declaration of the province in 1680, the constitution of New Hampshire says, "Nor are the inhabitants of this state controllable by any other laws than those to which they or their representative body have given their assent."

It further says, "Knowledge and learning, generally diffused through the community, being essential to the preservation of a free government; and spreading the opportunities and advantages of education through the various parts of the country, being highly conducive to promote this end; it shall be the duty of the legislators and magistrates, in all future periods of this government, to cherish the interests of literature, and the sciences, and all seminaries and public schools, etc." Allowing, for argument sake, that this college rested its rights originally upon English "authorities," and that, by the English law, the charter was a contract between the state and the grantees, irrepealable by the state, the state constitution, adopted previous to the Constitution of the United States, modified this grant, and placed the institution within the legislative control. No institution could exist except those instituted for the general benefit, nor could any institution hold rights, whatever they might have previously acquired, after the adoption of the state constitution, which were adverse to the great principles established by that instrument. Whenever any institution had failed to promote the general benefit, the legislature had a right, and were in duty bound to reform it. Again, no tax could be raised or levied but by legislative authority. The income from the funds of the college and the rental of lands within the state are an indirect tax upon the people. The constitution enjoins upon the legislature to cherish seminaries of learning and public schools; this presupposes that it is to have a control over such institutions and that they are matters of great public interest. The people of New Hampshire are controllable by no other laws than those to which they have given their assent. They have never assented to the *independence* of Dartmouth College.

We repeat, if the charter were originally such a contract as to make it a perpetuity, the constitution of New Hampshire, made before the Constitution of the United States, destroyed that quality and placed the institution on the footing of all other public institutions, controllable by the legislative will. The Constitution of the United States could not confer any new rights upon the college. It could at most only preserve what it then possessed; and as the charter, by the state constitution, if it ever possessed the character of a contract, had been deprived of that character, the inhibition of the United States Constitution, subsequently made, was inoperative upon it. But, waiving all these considerations, and take the admission of Judge Marshall before quoted, and it is conclusive that the case was brought within the reach of that clause only by the boldest and most licentious construction, viz., "That it is more than possible the preservation of rights of this description was *not* particularly in the view of the framers of the Constitution when the clause under consideration was introduced into that instrument, ... nor of the American people when they adopted it;" but as Judge Marshall did not know that this view would have been rejected if it had been presented, the court *assume* that the clause does therefore embrace this class of civil institutions and give judgment accordingly. I repeat that admitting, for argument sake, the English definitions of corporations, as laid down by the court, to apply to Dartmouth College charter, and that it held its rights originally from the king in England, and not from the provincial authority, then, from the foregoing admission of the Chief Justice, the case did not come within the inhibitory clause of the Constitution. The conclusions drawn by the court are at war with their own premises.

Let us examine for a moment the actual position in which this decision places the college and New Hampshire.

Judge Story says, "When a private eleemosynary corporation (like Dartmouth College) is thus created by the charter of the crown, it is subject to no other control on the part of the crown, than what is expressly or impliedly reserved by the charter itself. Unless a power be reserved for this purpose, the crown cannot, in virtue of its prerogative, without the consent of the corporation, alter or amend the charter, or divest the corporation of any of its franchises, or add to them, or add to or diminish the number of trustees, or remove any of the members, or change or control the administration of the charity, or compel the corporation to receive a new charter. This is the uniform language of the *authorities*, (that is, English law decisions,) and forms one of the most stubborn and well-settled doctrines of the *common law.*" "But an eleemosynary, like other corporations, is subject to the general law of the land. It may forfeit its corporate franchises by misuser or nonuser of them. It is subject to the controlling authority of its legal visitor, who, unless restrained by the terms of the charter, may amend and repeal its statutes, remove its officers, and generally superintend its trusts."

Before the adoption of the Federal Constitution, this college, it is admitted by the court, was liable to the control of the people of New Hampshire, who, by the Revolution, succeeded to the transcendent power of parliament and all the rights of the crown, within which is embraced the right to abolish or modify this charter. By the adoption of the United States Constitution, according to this decision, the college *acquired new rights*, became independent, and New Hampshire subordinate to it. This corporation is subject to the controlling authority of its legal visitor, and none else, who may amend or repeal its statutes and remove its officers. Dr. Wheelock, in "contemplation of law," and of the Supreme Court, "is recognized as the founder of the college, and the charter is granted upon his application, and the trustees are named by him." .... "The law therefore has provided that there shall somewhere exist a power to visit, inquire into, and correct all irregularities and abuses in such corporations." .... "And of common right, by the donation, the founder and his heirs are the legal visitors, unless the founder has appointed and assigned another person to be visitor." .... "As founder, too, Dr. Wheelock and his heirs would have been completely clothed with the visitorial power; but the whole government and control over, as well of the officers as of the revenues of the college, being, with his assent, assigned to the trustees in their corporate character, the visitorial power, which is included in this authority, rightfully devolved on the trustees." So says Judge Story.

Here then we have the government of the college, which, by a "fiction of law," is said to have been granted by the king, and founded by Dr. Wheelock, when in fact it was established by the public authority of the province of New Hampshire and principally endowed by the state for the benefit of the people of New Hampshire, put by him under the government of trustees, who can amend or repeal the laws of the institution, remove its officers, diminish or increase their number, augment or lessen their salaries, raise the revenues of the institution by indirect taxation from the people of New Hampshire, and then laugh at the constitution and laws of the state within whose borders it exists; and this character of perpetuity and independence, according to the decision and admission of the court, the college *acquired* by the adoption of the Federal Constitution. The national government pretends to no *further* control over it, and this decision nullifies the power of the state over it. Can a decision producing such results inspire the public confidence in the tribunal that made it? Can we reconcile it to American law or find in it a trace of sound common sense? Sure I am that the evils incident to corporate perpetuities may be remedied by legislative enactment if this decision be reversed; and that they *never will be* until it and all its kindred principles are reversed and repudiated. Sure I am that, if the American people acquiesce in the principles laid down in this case, the Supreme Court will have effected what the whole power of the British Empire, after eight years of bloody conflicts, failed to achieve against our fathers; they will have subjected us to ancient British law, without giving us the benefit of its modern improvements. But this decision will be reversed; the erroneous doctrines of this Anglo-American bench will be overthrown; the true principles of our institutions will be reinstated in their pristine force and vigor; they will be recognized again in our courts of judicature; and we shall yet again reap the rich fruit of that precious and bloody sacrifice offered by our fathers upon the altar of patriotism, the right of being governed by our own written legislative law.

12

WILLIAM M. GOUGE

PRINCIPLES AND EFFECTS
OF THE BANKING SYSTEM[1]

O UR VIEW of the extent to which paper-money banking affects our social condition will be very imperfect if we confine it to the *direct* operations of the system. These are, as it were, but the first links of a long extended chain. Each effect becomes in its turn a cause and the remote consequences are of more importance than the immediate. To prove this, a few plain truths will suffice.

[THE REMOTE CONSEQUENCES OF THE SYSTEM]

If two men start in life at the same time, and the one gets at the commencement but a small advantage over the other and retains the advantage for twenty or thirty years, their fortunes will, at the end of that period be very unequal.

If a man at the age of twenty-one years is deprived of one hundred dollars which he had honestly earned and honestly saved, the injury done to this man must be estimated by the advantage he would have derived from the use of his little property during the rest of his life. The want of it may prevent his turning his faculties to the best account. The loss may dispirit his future exertion.

If a man is at any period of his life deprived of a property, large or small, accumulated for him by the honest industries and economy of his ancestors, the wrong done to him is of the same character as that which he sustains when he is unjustly deprived of property which was the fruits of his own industry. It is the dictate of nature that parents shall leave their wealth to their children, and the law of the land, in this case, only confirms the dictate of nature.

[1] [From *A Short History of Paper Money and Banking in the United States, including an account of provincial and continental paper money, to which is prefixed an inquiry into the principles of the system, with considerations of its effects on Morals and Happiness. The whole intended as a plain exposition of the way in which paper money and money corporations, affect the interests of different portions of the community* (Philadelphia, 1833), Part One, pp. 90–101 — Abridged.]

It is not easy to set bounds to the effects of a single act of injustice. If you deprive a man of his property, you may thereby deprive him of the means of properly educating his children and thus affect the moral and intellectual character of his descendants for several generations.

Such being the consequences of single acts, we may learn from them to estimate the effects of those political and commercial institutions which operate unequally. They lay the foundation of an *artificial* inequality of wealth; and, whenever this is done, the wealth of the few goes on increasing in the ratio of compound interest, while the reflex operations of the very causes to which they owe their wealth, keep the rest of the community in poverty.

Where the distribution of wealth is left to natural and just laws, and the natural connection of cause and effect is not violated, the tendency of "money to beget money," or rather of wealth to produce wealth, is not an evil. A man has as strong a natural right to the profits which are yielded by the capital which was formed by his labor as he had to the immediate product of his labor. To deny this would be to deny him a right to the whole product of his labor. The claims of the honest capitalist and of the honest laborer are equally sacred and rest, in fact, on the same foundation. Nor is it the law of nature that the idle and improvident shall suffer temporary inconvenience only. By neglecting to form a capital for themselves, they render their future labor less productive than it otherwise might be; and finally make themselves dependent on others for the means of both subsistence and employment.

But unequal political and commercial institutions *invert* the operation of the natural and just causes of wealth and poverty, take much of the capital of a country from those whose industry produced it and whose economy saved it, and give it to those who neither work nor save. The natural reward of industry then goes to the idle, and the natural punishment of idleness falls on the industrious.

Inasmuch as personal, political, commercial, and accidental causes operate sometimes in conjunction and sometimes in opposition, it is difficult to say, in individual cases, in how great degree wealth or poverty is owing to one cause or to another. Harsh judgments of rich and poor, taking them individually, are to be avoided. But it is notorious that as regards different *classes* in different countries wealth and poverty are the consequences of the positive institutions of those countries. Peculiar political privileges are commonly the ground of the distinction; but peculiar commercial privileges have the same effect and when the foundation of the artificial inequality of fortune is once laid (it matters not whether it be by feudal institutions or money corporations), all the subsequent operations of society tend to increase the difference in the condition of different classes of the community.

One consequence of unequal institutions is increasing the demand for luxuries and diminishing the effective demand for necessaries and comforts. Many being qualified to be producers of necessaries and few to be producers of luxuries, the reward of the many is reduced and that of the few raised to an enormous height. The inventor of some new means of gratification for the rich is sure to receive his recompense, though thousands of able-bodied men may be starving around him.

.   .   .   .

Through all the operations of business the effects of an unequal distribution of wealth may be distinctly traced. The rich have the means of rewarding most liberally the professional characters whom they employ and the tradesmen with whom they deal. An aristocracy in one department of society introduces an aristocracy into all.

These effects are, it is true, most obvious in countries where the causes of an artificial inequality of wealth are of a permanent character and connected with political organization; but they can be discovered in our own country. The inequality of reward our lawyers and physicians receive is caused but in part by inequality of talent. It is owing in part to the inequality of the means of those who employ them and to the disposition the many have to prefer the lawyer or the physician who is patronized by the rich and fashionable. They feel that their own education disqualifies them for forming a proper estimate of professional talent and take the judgment of those they suppose must, from their superior wealth, have better means of information.

It is, however, among the hard-working members of society that the ultimate effects of such causes are most observable.

The condition of a multitude of poor women in our large cities has lately attracted the attention of the benevolent. It appears from the statements that have been published, that they can, by working ten or twelve hours every day, earn no more than from seventy-five cents to a dollar a week. Half of this sum goes for house rent and fuel, leaving them from thirty-seven and a half cents to fifty cents a week for food and clothing for themselves and children. Some thousands are said to be in this situation in Philadelphia alone.

Various proposals have been made to better their conditions, some futile, others absolutely pernicious. The laws of supply and demand are too powerful to yield to sermons and essays. The low rate of the wages of these poor women is the effect of general causes; causes which affect, in one way or another, every branch of business. In the great game we have been playing, much of the wealth of the country has passed into a few hands. Many men dying have left nothing to their widows and children; and others, who still live, cannot support their families except by the additional industry of their wives. The work of a seamstress can be done by a woman in her own house in the intervals she can spare from attention to her children. In this way, the number of seamstresses has been increased.

On the other hand, many families who would gladly employ these poor women are compelled by their own straitened circumstances to do this kind of work themselves. In this way the demand for seamstresses is diminished.

Private benevolence may improve the condition of individuals of this class; but the class itself can be benefited by such causes only as will diminish the number of seamstresses or increase the demand for their labor. The cause that will improve the condition of one of the industrious classes of society will improve the conditions of all. When an end shall be put to unfair speculation, then, and not till then, will honest industry have its just reward.

[Effects on Moral Character]

The practices of trade seem, in most countries, to fix the standard of commercial honesty. In the Hanse towns and Holland, while they were rising to wealth, this standard was very high. Soldiers were not more careful to preserve their honor without stain than merchants were to maintain their credit without blemish.

The practices of trade in the United States have debased the standard of commercial honesty. Without clearly distinguishing the causes that have made commerce a game of haphazard, men have come to perceive clearly the nature of the effect. They see wealth passing continually out of the hands of those whose labor produced it or whose economy saved it into the hands of those who neither work nor save. They do not clearly perceive *how* the transfer takes place, but they are certain of the fact. In the general scramble, they think themselves entitled to some portion of the spoil and, if they cannot obtain it by fair means, they take it by foul.

Hence we find men without scruple incurring debts which they have no prospect of paying.

Hence we find them, when on the very verge of bankruptcy, embarrassing their friends by prevailing on them to indorse notes and sign custom-house bonds.

Instances not unfrequently occur of men who have failed once or twice afterwards accumulating great wealth. How few of these honorably discharge their old debts by paying twenty shillings in the pound.

How many evade the just demands of their creditors by privately transferring their property.

It is impossible in the present condition of society to pass laws which will punish dishonest insolvents and not oppress the honest and unfortunate.

Neither can public opinion distinguish between them. The dishonest share the sympathy which should be given exclusively to their unfortunate neighbors; and the honest are forced to bear a part of the indignation which should fall entirely on the fraudulent.

The standard of commercial honesty can never be raised very high while trade is conducted on present principles. "It is hard," says Dr. Franklin, "for an empty bag to stand upright." The straits to which many men are reduced cause them to be guilty of actions which they would regard with as much horror as their neighbors if they were as prosperous as their neighbors.

We may be very severe in our censure of such men, but what else ought we to expect when the laws and circumstances give to some men so great advantages in the great game in which the fortunes of the whole community are at issue; what else ought we to expect but that those to whom the law gives no such advantage should exert to the utmost such faculties as remain to them in the struggle for riches, and not be very particular whether the means they use are such as the law sanctions or the law condemns.

Let those who are in possession of property which has been acquired according to the strict letter of the law be thankful that they have not been led into such temptations as those on whom the positive institutions of society have had an unfavorable influence.

But banking has a more extensive effect on the moral character of the community, through that distribution of wealth which is the result of its various direct and remote operations. Moralists in all ages have inveighed against luxury. To it they attribute the corruption of morals and the downfall of nations. The word luxury is equivocal. What is regarded as a luxury in one stage of society is in another considered as a comfort, and in a still more advanced stage as a necessary. The desire of enjoyment is the great stimulus to social improvement. If men were content with bare necessaries, no people would in the arts and sciences and in whatever else renders life desirable be in advance of the lowest caste of the Hindoos or the unhappy peasantry of the most unhappy country of Europe.

But whatever moralists have said against luxury is true when applied to that *artificial* inequality of fortune which is produced by *positive* institutions of an unjust character. Its necessary effect is to corrupt one part of the community and debase the other.

The bare prospect of inheriting great wealth damps the energies of a young man. It is well if this is the only evil it produces. "An idle man's brain," says John Bunyan, "is the devil's workshop." Few men can have much leisure and not be injured by it. To get rid of the *ennui* of existence young men of wealth resort to the gambling table, the race ground, and other haunts of dissipation. They cannot have these low means of gratification without debasing those less favored by fortune.

The children of the poor suffer as much in one way as the children of the rich suffer in another. The whole energies of the father and mother are exhausted in providing bread for themselves and their family. They cannot attend properly to the formation of the moral character of their offspring, the most important branch of education. They can ill spare the means to pay for suitable intellectual instruction. Their necessities compel them to put their children to employments unsuited to their age and strength. The foundation is thus laid of diseases which shorten and embitter life.

Instances occur of men by the force of their innate powers overcoming the advantages of excess or defect of wealth; but it is true, as a general maxim, that in early life and in every period of life too much or too little wealth is injurious to the character of the individual, and when it extends through a community, it is injurious to the character of the community.

In the general intercourse of society this artificial inequality of wealth produces baneful effects. In the United States the pride of wealth has more force than in any other country because there is here no other pride to divide the human heart. Some of our good Republicans do, indeed, boast of a descent from the European nobility; but when they produce their coats of arms and their genealogical trees they are laughed at. The question is propounded if their noble ancestors left them any *money*. Genius confers on its possessor a very doubtful advantage. Virtue with us, as in the days of the Roman poet, is viler than seaweed unless it has a splendid retinue. Talent is estimated only as a means of increasing riches. Wealth alone can give permanent distinction, for he who is at the top of the political ladder today may be at the bottom tomorrow.

One mischief this state of things produces is that men are brought to consider wealth as the *only* means of happiness. Hence they sacrifice honor, conscience, health, friends, everything to obtain it.

The other effects of artificial inequality of wealth have been treated of at large by moralists from Solomon and Socrates downwards. To their works and to the modern treatises on crime and pauperism we refer the reader. The last mentioned treatises are for the most part only illustrations of the ultimate effects of positive institutions which operate unequally on different members of the community.

[EFFECTS ON HAPPINESS]

The inferences the intelligent reader must have drawn from what has already been stated preclude the necessity of much detail in this part of our inquiry.

Wealth is, if independently considered, but one among fifty of the causes of happiness; and poverty viewed in the same light is but one among fifty of the causes of misery. The poorest young man having health of body and peace of mind and enjoying the play of the social sympathies in the affections of wife, children, and friends is happier than the richest old man, bowed down with sickness, oppressed with anxiety for the future, or by remorse for the past, having nobody to love, and beloved by nobody.

But though we may by mental abstraction consider wealth independently, or poverty independently, neither the one or the other is absolutely independent in its operation. There is no cause in either the physical or the moral world but which works in conjunction with other causes. Health of body and peace of mind, with the just play of the social affections, may give happiness, independently of wealth; but in extreme poverty it is difficult to preserve either health of body or peace of mind, and the play of the social affections becomes then a source of misery.

Some little wealth, at least enough for daily subsistence, is necessary for the enjoyment of life and the pursuit of happiness; and hence it is that the right to property is as important as the right to life and the right to liberty. "You take my life when you do take the means by which I live."

The majority of men are of such temperament that something more than the means of subsistence for the bare twenty-four hours is necessary for their happiness. They must also have a prospect of enjoying the like means of subsistence in future days. But this is a prospect which, with the reflecting part of the poor, is frequently overcast with clouds and gloom. Few journeymen mechanics are able to make adequate provision for sickness and old age. The wages of a laborer will support him and his family while he enjoys health and while employment is steady; but in case of long continued sickness he must look for relief from the hand of public or of private charity. If he casts his eyes on his wife and children, his dying hours are embittered with thoughts of the misery which may be their portion. Corroding care is the inmate of the poor man's breast. It is so heart-withering that it may be made a question if the condition of some slaves in the Southern States is much worse than that of many citizens of the other States. The want of liberty is a great drawback on happiness; but the slave is free from care. He knows that when he grows old or becomes infirm his master is bound to provide for his wants.

There would be less objection to that artificial inequality of wealth which is the result of unjust positive institutions if it increased the happiness of one class of society in the same proportion that it diminishes the happiness of another class. But increase of wealth beyond what is necessary to gratify the rational desires of a man does not increase his happiness. If it gives birth to irrational desires, the gratification of them must produce misery. Even when inordinate wealth does not give birth to irrational desires, it is attended with an increase of care, and this is a foe to happiness.

With some men, the love of wealth seems to be a blind passion. The magpie in hiding silver spoons in its nest appears to act with as much reflection as they do in piling money-bag on money-bag. They have no object in view beyond accumulation. But with most men the desire of great wealth appears subordinate to the love of great power and distinction. This is the end, that the means. They love fine houses, splendid equipage, and large possessions less for any physical gratification they impart than for the distinction they confer and the power they bestow. It is with some as much an object of ambition to be ranked with the richest men as it is with others to be ranked with the greatest warriors, poets, or philosophers.

The love of that kind of distinction which mere wealth confers is not a feeling to be highly commended; but it is hardly to be reprobated when it is constitutional and when it is under the government of proper moral principle. In this case it is a simple stimulus to vigorous industry and watchful economy. With some men the love of ease is the ruling passion, with others the love of pleasure, and with others the love of science. If the love of riches was not with many men stronger than any of the other loves we have mentioned, there might not be enough wealth accumulated to serve the general purposes of society. They may claim the liberty of gratifying their particular passion in a reasonable way; but it is a passion which derives less gratification from the actual possession of a large store, than from the constant increase of a small one. The man whose wealth increases gradually from one hundred dollars to one thousand, thence to five thousand, thence to ten thousand, and thence to fifty thousand, has more satisfaction in the process than he who suddenly becomes possessed of one hundred thousand dollars. As to the distinction which mere wealth confers. it would be obtained in a state of society in which the distribution of wealth was left to natural laws as certainly as in a state in which positive institutions operate to the advantage of the few and to the disadvantage of the many. If the riches of men were made to depend entirely on their industry, economy, enterprise, and prudence, the possession of one hundred thousand dollars would confer as much distinction as the possession of five hundred thousand dollars confers at present. Those worth "a plum," would then rank among the "first men" on change; those who are worth "five plums" can rank no higher now.

But the system has not a merely negative effect on the happiness of the rich. Such is the uncertainty of fortune in the United States that even the most wealthy are not exempt from painful solicitude for the future. Who can be sure that he will be able to navigate his own bark in safety to the end of the voyage when he sees the shore strewed with wrecks? If a man leaves an estate to his children, he knows not how long they will keep possession of it. If he extends his views to his grandchildren, the probability will appear strong that some of them will be reduced to abject poverty.

Such is the present custom of trade, that a man who has a considerable capital of his own not unfrequently gives credit to four or five times the amount of that capital. He is a rich man, but even if the debts due to him are perfectly secure, the perplexity which is created by a long train of credit operations, the failure of but one of which may prove his ruin, must leave him little ground for solid satisfaction; and the necessity he is under in times of embarrassment of courting the good-will of bank directors, goes far towards destroying his personal independence. "The servile dependence on banks, in which many of our citizens pass their lives," was observed by Mr. Carey as long ago as the year 1811.

There is one other evil resulting from the super-extended system of credit which has its origin in banking, and with a few observations on this, we shall close our remarks on this head of the subject. We allude to the *misery* suffered by an honest man who is involved in debts. We have known cases in which none of the common rules of prudence had been transgressed in incurring the debts, in which the creditors were perfectly convinced of the honesty of the debtor, and neither pressed for payment nor reflected on his disability to comply with his engagements, in which the debtor was sensible that his failure would not subject his creditors to any serious inconvenience; and yet a gloom would overspread the mind of the debtor, and remain there for years.

SUMMARY[2]

To place the subject fairly before the reader, we shall bring together the principal propositions that have been supported in this essay and leave the decision to his candid judgment.

We have maintained:

1. That real money is that valuable by reference to which the value of other articles is estimated, and by the instrumentality of which they are circulated. It is a *commodity*, done up in a particular form to serve a particular use, and does not differ *essentially* from other items of wealth.

2. That silver, owing to its different physical properties, the universal and incessant demand for it, and the small proportion the annual supply bears to the stock on hand, is as good a practical standard of value as can reasonably be desired. It has no variations except such as *necessarily* arise from the nature of value.

3. That real money diffuses itself through different countries and through different parts of a country in proportion to the demands of commerce. No prohibitions can prevent its departing from countries where wealth and trade are declining; and no obstacle except spurious money can prevent its flowing into countries where wealth and trade are increasing.

4. That money is the tool of all trades and is, as such, one of the most useful of productive instruments and one of the most valuable of labor saving machines.

5. That bills of exchange and promissory notes are a *mere commercial medium* and are, as *auxiliaries* of gold and silver money, very useful; but they differ from metallic money in having no inherent value and in being evidences of debt. The expressions of value in bills of exchange and promissory notes are according to the article which law or custom has made the standard; and the failure to pay bills of exchange and promissory notes does not affect the value of the currency or the standard by which all contracts are regulated.

6. That bank notes are *mere evidences of debt* due by the banks and in this respect differ not from the promissory notes of the merchants; but, being received in full of all demands, they become to all intents and purposes the money of the country.

2 [*Ibid.*, pp. 135–140 — Text complete.]

7. That banks owe their credit to their charters; for, if these were taken away, not even their own stockholders would trust them.

8. That the circulating quality of bank notes is in part owing to their being receivable in payment of dues to government, in part to the interest which the debtors to banks and bank stockholders have in keeping them in circulation, and in part to the difficulty, when the system is firmly established, of obtaining metallic money.

9. That so long as specie payments are maintained, there is a limit on bank issues; but this is not sufficient to prevent successive "expansions" and "contractions" which produce ruinous fluctuations of prices; while the means by which bank medium is kept "convertible" inflict great evils on the community.

10. That no restriction which can be imposed on banks and no discretion on the part of the directors can prevent these fluctuations; for bank credit, as a branch of commercial credit, is affected by all the causes, natural and political, that affect trade, or that affect the confidence man has in man.

11. That the "flexibility" or "elasticity" of bank medium is not an excellence, but a defect, and that "expansions" and "contractions" are not made to suit the wants of the community but from a simple regard to the profits and safety of the banks.

12. That the uncertainty of trade produced by these successive "expansions" and "contractions" is but *one* of the evils of the present system. That the banks cause credit dealings to be carried to an extent that is highly pernicious; that they cause credit to be given to men who are not entitled to it, and deprive others of credit to whom it would be useful.

13. That the granting of exclusive privileges to companies or the exempting of companies from liabilities to which individuals are subject is repugnant to the fundamental principles of American government; and that the banks, inasmuch as they have exclusive privileges and exemptions and have the entire control of credit and currency, are the most pernicious of money corporations.

14. That a nominal responsibility may be imposed on such corporations but that it is impossible to impose on them an effective responsibility. They respect the laws and public opinion so far only as is necessary to promote their own interest.

15. That on the supposition most favorable to the friends of the banking system, the whole amount gained by the substitution of bank medium for gold and silver coin is equal only to about 40 cents per annum for each individual in the country; but that it will be found that nothing is in reality gained *by the nation*, if due allowance be made for the expense of supporting three or four hundred banks, and for the fact that bank medium is a machine which performs its work badly.

16. That some hundreds of thousands of dollars are annually extracted from the people of Pennsylvania and some millions from the people of the United States for the support of the banks, insomuch as through banking the natural order of things is reversed and interest paid to the banks on evidences of debt due by them, instead of interest being paid to those who part with commodities in exchange for bank notes.

17. That into the formation of the bank capital of the country very little substantial wealth has ever entered, that capital having been formed principally out of the promissory notes of the original subscribers, or by other means which the operations of the banks themselves have facilitated. They who have bought the script of the banks at second hand may have honestly paid cent. per cent. for it; but what they have paid has gone to those from whom they bought the script and does not form any part of the capital of the banks.

18. That if it was the wish of the Legislature to promote usurious dealings, it could not well devise more efficient means than incorporating paper money banks. That these banks, moreover, give rise to many kinds of stock-jobbing, by which the simple-minded are injured and the crafty benefited.

19. That many legislators have, in voting for banks, supposed that they were promoting the welfare of their constituents; but the prevalence of false views in legislative bodies in respect to money corporations and paper money is to be attributed chiefly to the desire certain members have to make money for themselves, or to afford their political partisans and personal friends opportunities for speculation.

20. That the banking interest has a pernicious influence on the periodical press, on public elections, and the general course of legislation. This interest is so powerful that the establishment of a system of sound currency and sound credit is impracticable, except one or other

of the political parties into which the nation is divided makes such an object its primary principle of action.

21. That through the various advantages which the system of incorporated paper-money banking has given to some men over others, the foundation has been laid of an *artificial* inequality of wealth, which kind of inequality is, when once laid, increased by all the subsequent operations of society.

22. That this artificial inequality of wealth adds nothing to the substantial happiness of the rich and detracts much from the happiness of the rest of the community. That its tendency is to corrupt one portion of society and debase another.

23. That the sudden dissolution of the banking system without suitable preparation would put an end to the collection of debts, destroy private credit, break up many productive establishments, throw most of the property of the industrious into the hands of speculators, and deprive laboring people of employment.

24. That the system can be got rid of, without difficulty, by prohibiting, after a certain day, the issue of small notes and proceeding gradually to those of the highest denomination.

25. That the feasibility of getting rid of the system is further proved by the fact that the whole amount of bank notes and bank credits is, according to Mr. Gallatin's calculation, only about one hundred and nine million dollars. By paying ten or eleven millions a year, the whole can be liquidated in the term of ten years. If, however, twenty or thirty years should be required for the operation, the longest of these is but a short period in the lifetime of a nation.

26. That it has not been through the undervaluation of gold at the mint that eagles and half-eagles have disappeared; but from the free use of bank notes. Nevertheless, a new coinage of pieces containing four and eight, or five and ten dollars worth of gold is desirable to save the trouble of calculating fractions. The dollar being the money of contract and account, no possible confusion or injustice can be produced by an adjustment of the gold coinage to the silver standard.

27. That incorporating a paper-money bank is not the "necessary and proper" or "natural and appropriate" way of managing the fiscal concerns of the Union; but that the "necessary and proper" or "natural and appropriate" way is by sub-treasury offices.

28. That incorporating a paper-money bank is not "the necessary and proper" or "natural and appropriate" way of correcting the evils occasioned by the State banks, inasmuch as a national bank, resting on the same principles as the State banks, must produce similar evils.

29. That "convertible" paper prevents the accumulation of such a stock of the precious metals as will enable the country to bear transitions from peace to war and insure the punctual payment of war taxes, and that the "necessary and proper" or "natural and appropriate" way of providing for all public exigencies is by making the Government *a solid money Government* as was intended by the framers of the Constitution.

30. That if Congress should, from excessive caution or some less commendable motive, decline passing the acts necessary to insure the gradual withdrawal of bank notes, they may greatly diminish the evils of the system by declaring that nothing but gold and silver shall be received in payment of duties and by making the operations of the Government entirely distinct from those of the banks.

31. That, on the abolition of incorporated paper-money banks, private bankers will rise up who will receive money on deposit and allow interest on the same, discount promissory notes, and buy and sell bills of exchange. Operating on sufficient funds and being responsible for their engagements in the whole amount of their estates, these private bankers will not by sudden and great "expansions" and "curtailments" derange the whole train of mercantile operations. In each large city an office of deposit and transfer similar to the Bank of Hamburg will be established, and we shall thus secure all the good of the present banking system and avoid all its evils.

32. That, if the present system of banking and paper money shall continue, the wealth and population of the country will increase from natural causes till they shall be equal for each square mile to the wealth and population of Europe. But, with every year, the state of society in the United States will more nearly approximate to the state of society in Great Britain. Crime and pauperism will increase. A few men will be inordinately rich, some comfortable, and a multitude in poverty. This condition of things will naturally lead to the adoption of that policy which proceeds on the principle that a legal remedy is to be found for each social evil, and nothing left for the operations of nature. This kind of legislation will increase the evils it is intended to cure.

33. That there is reason to *hope* that, on the downfall of moneyed corporations and the substitution of gold and silver for bank medium, sound credit will take the place of unsound, and legitimate enterprise the place of wild speculation. That the moral and intellectual character of the people will be sensibly, though gradually, raised, and the causes laid open of a variety of evils under which society is now suffering. That the sources of legislation will to a certain extent be purified, by taking from members of legislative bodies inducements to pass laws for the special benefit of themselves, their personal friends, and political partisans. That the operation of the natural and just causes of wealth and poverty will no longer be inverted, but that each cause will operate in its natural and just order and produce its natural and just effect: wealth becoming the reward of industry, frugality, skill, prudence, and enterprise; and poverty the punishment of few except the indolent and prodigal.

13

THEOPHILUS FISK

CAPITAL AGAINST LABOR[1]

T HE HISTORY of the producers of wealth, of the industrious classes, is that of a continued warfare of *honesty* against *fraud,* *weakness* against *power, justice* against *oppression.* The purchasers of labor have in all ages had the advantage of the sellers and they have rarely failed to use their power to the furtherance of their own interest. Until within a comparatively short period of time, the laboring classes even in England and Scotland were slaves, serfs, bondmen. Colliers in the latter country even down to as late a period as 1776 were slaves in fact as well as in name. Gradually, however, the rust of time weakened their chains of bondage; the period at length arrived when the grievous burdens upon their shoulders were too galling longer to be borne; the collar was slipped from the galled neck, and their aristocratic masters, finding it impossible longer to *ride* in safety, consented with an ill grace to forego a privilege they were no longer able to preserve. But in losing the *name* of slaves, we are not to suppose that the sellers of labor were allowed to assume the place in society that God and nature designed for them. That the laborer had natural, inalienable rights, that they were free and independent members of society and possessed the right, if they sold their labor, to fix their own price upon it would have been scouted at as of all things the most levelling, disorganizing and dangerous. Hence the government, those who purchased labor, were continually passing partial, unequal, unjust laws and paying for it according to the ideas of its value by those who wanted to use it. Then commenced the struggle between the two great dealers in the market of the world, viz., Capital and Labor; and as Capital had always the government with its legion of bayonets to support its claims, the result may easily be imagined.

[1] [From "Capital against Labor. An Address delivered at Julien Hall before the mechanics of Boston on Wednesday evening, May 20, 1835" in the *New York Evening Post*, August 6, 1835, p. 2 — Abridged.]

During the existence of the ancient monopolies, called "guilds or fraternities," capital and labor were identified. These fraternities were composed both of masters and workmen whose interests were one and the same; at length, however, the privileges of these bodies which had originally been conferred upon them for their protection against the violence of the feudal nobility became so odious and oppressive that it became indispensable that they should be abridged. The parties then became opponents; the one endeavoring to raise, the other to depress the prices of labor. Combinations were then formed. As early as 1548, we find a notice in a preamble of an act of Parliament, in these words: "artificers, handicrafts men and laborers have made confederacies and promises and have sworn mutual oaths, not only that they should not meddle with one another's work and perform and finish that another hath begun, but also to constitute and appoint *how much work they shall do in a day and what hours and times* they shall work, contrary to the laws and statutes of this realm, to the great injury and impoverishment of his majesty's subjects." Parliament also passed sundry acts expressly prohibiting combinations for the purpose of raising the prices of labor. In 1824, after long experience had tested the folly and inutility of laws of that nature, that they were partial and unjust, that they raised one class and depressed another, that they were impolitic, unwise, and inexpedient, the system was abandoned and the laws repealed.

By this brief and imperfect outline, it may be seen that those who live without labor are and have been the enemies of the producing classes. Their interests, although naturally, where justice prevails, one and the same, have almost always clashed with each other. We find by glancing at the past that the laboring classes have been struggling for centuries under the iron yoke of despotism, against fraud, tyranny, and injustice. "Upward and onward" has been their watchword until now they are enabled from the proud eminence to which they have attained to look forward and behold the promised land. If they are true to themselves they must inevitably enter in and possess it. Although the Jebusites and Gershashites and Parasites, all the various classes, castes, and tribes of the Canaanites who live by prey and plunder may look fierce and "talk big," the inheritance is ours.

The history of the amelioration, improvement, and elevation of the working classes is but the history of the progress of wealth, civilization, and all that ennobles, dignifies, and exalts humanity. It is the history of all the wonderful improvements in the arts and sciences, in manufactures and commerce.

The record of the past affords the highest encouragement for the present and the future. If the laboring classes have been able with all the stupendous obstacles that have been thrown in their way to fight an uphill battle against the omnipotent power of Capital and to possess themselves of many of the privileges that belong to free citizenship, we can easily determine the question of their ultimate emancipation and triumph. The controversy will never cease, the warfare will never end, until all are placed upon the broad tableland of perfect political equality. The sellers of labor will yet wrest from the unholy grasp of the apostles of Mammon the right to govern themselves, to make their own laws, and to select their own agents to execute them.

Though the power of wealth in the hands of the *few* may for a time keep down the industrious *many*, yet the hazard of experimenting too far with those who have suffered so much and so long had better be taken into the calculation before a system of continued, permanent robbery be determined upon; before they determined to treat the unmanacled workingman as they would a convict in the state prison, they would do well to pause. Beneath their feet an earthquake slumbers. There is a period in the affairs of men when forbearance ceases to be a virtue, when patient endurance becomes criminal. Let the interested beware how they accelerate the sands in Time's hourglass and thereby hasten a season when resistance and not resignation and passive obedience will be the rallying watchword.

The laws by which we are governed were not made by us although said to be —— had they been, they would have been equal, equitable, and impartial —— for the benefit and protection of the masses, the great whole of which society is composed. It is quite impossible for the laboring classes to make laws to rob one another; they cannot steal from themselves by partial legislation. What is for the interest of one is for the interest of all. But let the privileged few make the laws and what is the result? What has been the natural consequence in all past time? Why, that the many have been ground up to feed the nabobs. What has been, will be. Like causes produce like effects under similar circumstances. Pore over the musty folios of the past and the startling truth meets you at every page that all laws made by rich men have been in favor of Capital, never in favor of Labor. And yet our blood-proud and purse-proud nobility talk of *protecting the laborer!* "Such protection as the vulture gives to lambs, covering and devouring them!" Their misnamed laws of *protection* always have made them rich at our expense, have ever added to their already over-flowing coffers by filching the products of industry from the pockets of the poor. The laborer asks no protection, their offers therefore are entirely gratuitous; the laborer can and does both protect himself and the non-producer into the bargain. In case of invasion or insurrection, who talks of protecting them? When the appalling cry of "fire!" falls upon the ear, who protects the scanty property of the laborer, the "palaces of the poor?" Not the men who make the laws. They do not even protect their own gorgeous mansions from the devouring element. No. We ask no protection; we simply desire *to be let alone.*

A great deal of affectionate regard is, and has been, manifested by the aristocracy for the interests of the "dear people." They have clung to them like the poisonous ivy to the monarch of the wood, palsying the faculties, throwing fetters of bondage upon the intellect until at last they perish in the entwining folds of hollow-hearted dis-simulation. All the friendly embraces of those who fatten upon the toil of others are, like the hug of the bear, certain death. Let our motto be, "Take your delicate fingers from our throats; 'white paws,' if you please, gentlemen."

But the monopolists, the professional men, the men of wealth, *they* labor, it is said, as well as the farmer and the mechanic. They do labor to be sure, but *it is laboring to collect that which others have earned.* The lawyer's "may it please your honor" never made the pot boil. The presidents' and cashiers' printed paper rags, covered with false promises to pay, never crowned the hill with ripening sheaf, nor made the valley smile. The lazy drone by sucking a quill behind his ear never yet felled the boundless forest and reared the castle's dome, breaking the repose of ages with the busy tones of hardy enterprise. If our houses could spring up spontaneously like mushrooms, if we could sit in our seats like dried mummies and by single scratch of a pen could construct canals, bridges, and railroads, we might then talk about equality of rights and privileges with some degree of propriety. But no. If houses are to be erected, it is to be done by the hard hand of labor, in sweat, and toil, and fatigue. The legislature grants no charters for the *workingmen* to build houses without labor and to grow rich without being industrious.

We hear at almost every corner of the streets the stereotyped Billingsgate about the "lower classes." "Lower classes" indeed! The time has been when they were as low as the sordid spirit of avarice and the iron heel of bloodsucking ambition could tread them down; thousands living and dying mere cogs in the social machine; dragging out a miserable existence in the squalor of toil, want, and degradation. They have stood still as stocks, quiet as the charnel house, while "lisping infancy" has been foredoomed by the unholy lust of gold to labor 12, 14, 16 hours per day, withering and blasting the bud of youth ere its petals were unfolded to the sun. If they dared to remonstrate, to utter a word of expostulation, the dry, hard, cold lip of unfeeling selfishness would contract with scorn and malignity, and the stony eye of unpitying brutality would "look daggers," while the hand used them. This has been borne; their taskmasters were rich, and could talk Latin.

The natural consequences of laziness, the penalty of idleness, has fallen upon the industrious classes instead of the rich capitalist who lives without labor, those who earn and save have been compelled to toil early and late for a pittance barely sufficient to keep their families from starving that the indolent drones might be clothed in purple and fine linen and fare sumptuously every day. The natural reward of honest industry has been wrested from the laborer by unjust laws and given to those who were never guilty of earning a dollar in their lives, who are too lazy to work, and too proud to beg; but the days of oppression are numbered; God grant they may soon be finished.

The subject which has called us from our homes this evening is vitally important inasmuch as it seems the dawning light of a coming day. It will have this good effect if nothing more: it will teach those who live by plunder that a part of mankind were never born to be hewers of wood and drawers of water to those no better than themselves. It will call upon the public for their strong reasons why the producers of wealth should be kept in ignorance, servility, and bondage; why they must longer be debarred the blessings they have purchased with tears and blood, and lazy men riot upon the miseries of the poor! It calls upon the philanthropist and Christian to advocate and demand the immediate emancipation of the "white slaves of the North," and to declare to the world that the workers "are, and of right ought to be, free and independent citizens of these United States."

The recent movements among our industrious fellow citizens speak a language that can neither be perverted nor misunderstood. The world is told by acts that speak more plainly than volumes of words, that "he who will shun the exertions and sacrifices necessary to qualify him to know his rights, and also to maintain them, deserves to be duped, to groan in perpetual slavery, to wear the inextricable chains the *few* are forging for the *many*."

Knowledge and virtue being the only sure foundation of American Liberty, you have taken the proper steps towards a resumption of your sacred rights. By reducing the number of hours of labor, you give yourselves opportunity to obtain that knowledge which is power. They whose god is gain have long feared that if the laborer should be allowed to take his nose from the grindstone five minutes at a time, he would be learning how to govern and provide for himself, so he must be compelled to toil on like a galley slave at the oar. "Is there not," exclaims an eloquent gentleman in the British Parliament, "something inexpressibly cruel, most disgustingly selfish in thus attempting to ascertain the utmost limits to which labor and fatigue may be carried without their certainly occasioning misery and destruction, the full extent of profitable torture that may be safely inflicted and in appealing to learned and experienced doctors to fix the precise point beyond which it would be murder to proceed?" Eight hours for work, eight hours for sleep, and eight hours for amusement and instruction is the equitable allotment of the twenty-four. But to a great majority of the buyers of labor even the granting of your present just demand that ten hours shall constitute a day's work seems preposterous in the extreme. They think that mankind were not only born to trouble as the sparks fly upward, but according to their creed we were born to labor as the sweat drops downwards. Says *Blackwood's Magazine*, "Are not the poor the 'working classes?' Then let them work — work — work. If they are to have resting hours on weekdays, pray, what is the use of the Sabbath? Work is the chief end and whole duty of man." Nobody thinks of asking what rest does the law of nature require? We are governed by the laws of avarice which, like bigotry, "has no head, and cannot think, no heart and cannot feel." We even seem to forget there ever were laws of natuie, we are groping in such an unnatural state of society. We might almost as well talk of the empire of Chaos as of the empire of mind while it is fettered with chains of midnight.

The proverb "All work, and no play, makes Jack a dull boy" is truth, but not the whole truth. Sir Anthony Carlisle, an English physician of great eminence, says that after 40 years observation and practice, he is satisfied that vigorous health and the ordinary duration of life cannot be generally maintained under the circumstances of twelve hours labor, day by day. Dr. Farre says "Man can do more than he is allowed or permitted to do by nature, and in attempting to transgress the bounds Providence has pointed out to him, he abridges his life in the exact proportion in which he transgresses the laws of nature and the divine command." When will the mass learn that the life is more than meat, the body more than raiment?

Dr. Green, surgeon of St. Thomas' Hospital, draws a most frightful picture of the maladies that are engendered by long continued, unremitting toil. The medical profession in England raise their united voices against a system that demands uniform, unceasing labor. They declare that the average labor of full grown, strong, healthy men ought not to exceed twelve hours, meals included. The vigor of life is well known to depend upon the perfection of the blood. "If the arterial circulation be too much exhausted, an accumulation takes place on the venous side, the blood is deteriorated, and organic diseases are produced which abridge life." So far they regard man as an animal! — over-exertion having the same baneful influence upon both. But man is to be considered as vastly superior to an animal; over-labor has a most debasing influence upon his mind, that faculty alone which renders him more exalted in the scale of being than the animal creation. "The bonds of domestic love become relaxed; and as a consequence, the filial and paternal duties are uncultivated. The over-worked artisan has not time to cherish these feelings by the familiar and grateful arts which are their constant food, and without which nourishment they perish." An apathy benumbs his better sympathies, chills his spirit, and turns the heart to stone. Such is the natural, aye, almost inevitable result of the barbarous system against which you have so nobly taken up arms; should you succeed, of which I do not entertain a shade of doubt, if you are true to yourselves, the blessings of posterity will be showered upon your memories. The cruel system of slavery must be robbed of its sting; the venom must be destroyed.

We demand not mere justice to the animal body, but time to do justice to the heart and mind, time to grow in knowledge, and the practice of equity and virtue. We wish to see the beacon of knowledge lighted up in every hilltop and shedding its hallowed rays across the path of ignorance, shining with a saving light, brighter and brighter even unto the perfect day.

But it is objected that if the "ten hour system" succeeds, the young men, the apprentices, will become wild and unruly. The objection is a base and unfounded libel both upon masters and men. They have one whole day in seven to themselves under the present system; the same moral or physical restraints that operate on that day would upon other days in the week. The master or the guardian would hardly become relaxed in their rules of duty, even if the apprentices did not labor more than four hours in the day.

But they will get less wages because they will produce less. We must have other proof than mere assertion for this before it can be deemed worthy of credence. If a man works better when he is fresh than when he is fatigued then we could hardly suppose he would do less in a twelvemonth upon the system you are contending for than upon the barbarous "all day" bondage. Suppose he does less, and receives less; how much less? Why only one twelfth part at most; and what is one twelfth part of a week's wages compared with the amount of happiness that would be thus increased at the family hearthstone?

If he works less, he will suffer less, and it will cost him less to live. The fees to the doctor, the apothecary, and the nurse will be sensibly diminished. It will also be an immense saving to the nation. The health and strength of the operatives being no longer broken by excessive toil, the workhouse will no longer be thronged. They would not only perform as much labor as at present but would become healthy and wise, if not wealthy.

The efforts you are now making to relieve yourselves of the odious oppressions, which for ages have disgraced humanity, are deserving the warmest approbation of every friend to the right of man throughout the world. . . . .

A mighty spirit is abroad in the earth overthrowing the pillars of despotism and the fetters of bondage. With the friends of freedom throughout the world let us be co-workers. Let the present effort be but the glimmering twilight of a day of unclouded glory. Remember that this is but the lopping off of but one single head of the political monster that feeds on human gore; the other ninety-nine are hissing and sputtering fiercely as ever. So long as you allow capital to make laws for labor, standing out for higher wages or reducing the hours of toil will only be doing the work by halves. There must be a radical reform and this can only be accomplished at the ballot boxes. Allow the capitalists to make a compromise with you, allow them to play the lawgiver, and they will not care a brass farthing how few hours you work or what prices you receive. They will take good care how to strike the balance when they come to pay you for your labor. For every hour you abstract from toil, they will levy an indirect tax upon you that shall treble its value. No. There is not a nabob in Boston that would raise a finger to prevent the "ten hour system," if he thought the great work of reform would stop there; for all that could be remedied in a hundred ways by partial legislation next winter. But the great fear of those who grow rich upon your industry is that if you get time to improve your minds, you will get your eyes open to the monstrous frauds that have been perpetrated upon you by the heathen idolaters, the worshippers of Mammon. Let their worst fears be realized. Shoulder to shoulder, man to man, our fathers fought and triumphed; let their sons profit by their illustrious example. Shrink not, disband not, and fear nothing.

Teach the lawgivers a salutary lesson at the polls; vote for no man who is not pledged to maintain your cause at all risks and at every hazard. If you are united, your strength is well nigh omnipotent. Throw away all party names; *all parties* are, and ever have been, opposed to your interests. Form a party of your own that shall be all-controlling and uncontrollable. Take any name you please, I care not. Call yourselves Whigs, Tories, Democrats, Federalists — it is all one to me, so that you are united. Your opposers will seek to divide you by some party jealousy because they know that divide and ruin is the only policy that will overthrow you. Bind yourselves together by the strongest of all bonds: that of self-interest. You have all one common cause, one common name, one common interest: the interest of Labor, the interest of honest industry. Keep this one single object in view, no longer at elections throw the rope over the roof of the house and pull at each end, but all one way; give one steady "yo yeave yoo" the long, strong and the pull altogether, and the mass of human wrong, inequality, and oppression will be scattered to the four winds of heaven.

14

WILLIAM CULLEN BRYANT

ON USURY LAWS [1]

THE FACT that the usury laws, arbitrary, unjust, and oppressive as they are, and unsupported by a single substantial reason, should have been suffered to exist to the present time can only be accounted for on the ground of the general and singular ignorance which has prevailed as to the true nature and character of money. If men would but learn to look upon the medium of exchange, not as a mere sign of value, but as value itself, as a commodity governed by precisely the same laws which affect other kinds of property, the absurdity and tyranny of legislative interference to regulate the extent of profit which, under any circumstances, may be charged for it would at once become apparent.

The laws do not pretend to dictate to a landlord how much rent he may charge for his house; or to a merchant what price he shall put upon his cloth; or to a mechanic at what rate he shall sell the products of his skill; or to a farmer the maximum he shall demand for his hay or grain. Yet money is but another form into which all these commodities are transmuted, and there is no reason why the owner of it shall be forbidden to ask exactly that rate of profit for the use of it which its abundance or scarcity makes it worth — no reason why the laws of supply and demand, which regulate the value of all other articles, should be suspended by legislative enactment in relation to this, and their place supplied by the clumsy substitute of feudal ignorance and worse than feudal tyranny.

The value of iron and copper and lead consists of exactly the same elements as the value of gold and silver. The labor employed in digging them, the quantity in which they are found, and the extent of their application in the useful arts, or, in other words, the relation of the demand to the supply, are the circumstances which fix their market price. Should some great manufacture be undertaken in which a vast additional amount of iron or copper or lead would be

<hr>

[1] [From the *New York Evening Post*, September 26, 1836 — Text complete.]

used, a sudden and considerable rise of price would be the inevitable consequence. Should this increased demand lead to any valuable improvement in the mining art, or to investigations which should discover new and prolific beds of ore, a corresponding fall of prices would occur. These fluctuations are continually taking place, and an attempt to prevent them by state legislation would be about as effectual as the command of the barbarian king that the ocean should not overpass a certain bound. Silver and gold, though in a less degree, are liable to precisely the same fluctuations of intrinsic value, and to seek to confine them to a fixed point is an attempt marked by equal folly.

If, then, the intrinsic value of money cannot be established by law, the value of its use is no less beyond the proper compass of legislation. Though a certain per centum is established as the rate which may be demanded for the use of money, we find, when the article is relatively abundant, that, notwithstanding the law, a much lower rate is received; and why, on the other hand, when money is scarce, should an attempt be made to prevent it from rising to its natural level?

Such attempts have always been, and always will be, worse than fruitless. They not only do not answer the ostensible object, but they accomplish the reverse. They operate, like all restrictions on trade, to the injury of the very class they are framed to protect; they oppress the borrower for the advantage of the lender; they take from the poor to give to the rich. How is this result produced? Simply by diminishing the amount of capital, which, in the shape of money, would be lent to the community at its fair value, did no restriction exist, and placing what is left in the most extortionate hands. By attaching a stigma and a penalty to the innocent act of asking for money what money is worth, when that value rises above seven per cent, the scrupulous and reputable money lenders are driven from the market and forced to employ their funds in other modes of investment. The supply, the inadequacy of which in the first place caused the increase in the rate of usance, is thus still further diminished, and the rate of usance necessarily rises still higher. The loanable funds, too, are held only by those who do not scruple to tax their loans with another grievous charge as security against the penalty imposed by an unwise law; and thus our Legislature, instead of assisting the poor man, but makes his necessities the occasion of sorely augmenting his burden.

But usury laws operate most hardly in many cases, even when the general rate of money is below their arbitrary standard. There is an intrinsic and obvious difference between borrowers, which not only justifies but absolutely demands, on the part of a prudent man disposed to relieve the wants of applicants, a very different rate of interest. Two persons can hardly present themselves in precisely equal circumstances to solicit a loan. One man is cautious; another is rash. One is a close calculator, sober in his views, and unexcitable in his temperament; another is visionary and enthusiastic. One has tangible security to offer; another nothing but the airy one of a promise. Who shall say that to lend money to these several persons is worth in each case an equal premium?

Should a person come to us with a project which, if successful, will yield an immense return, but, if unsuccessful, leave him wholly destitute, shall we not charge him for the risk we run in advancing his views? The advocates of usury laws may answer that we have it at our option either to take seven per cent or wholly refuse to grant the required aid. True; but suppose the project one which is calculated, if successful, to confer a vast benefit on mankind. Is it wise in the Legislature in such a case to bar the door against ingenuity, except the money lender turns philanthropist and jeopards his property, not for a fair equivalent, but out of mere love to his fellow man?

The community begin to answer these questions aright, and there is ground for hope that they will ere long insist upon their legislative agents repealing the entire code of barbarous laws by which the trade in money has hitherto been fettered.

15

JOHN W. VETHAKE

THE DOCTRINE OF ANTI-MONOPOLY [1]

To prevent misunderstanding and possible misrepresentations, the anti-monopoly Democrats of the City of New York tender to their brethren of the Democratic family the following *address:*
The equal rights of mankind and free competition in all departments of social industry were held by our political fathers to be the primitive element of republican government. Accordingly, these, with all the sub-principles which distinctly flow from them, as, for example, universal suffrage, a liberal code of naturalization laws, liberty of conscience, of speech, and of the press, purity of elections, right of instruction, limited term of official tenures, and careful avoidance of legal favoritism in any possible form, constitute with us, as they did with our ancestors, the essential ingredients of democratic institutions. By these, as by the beaconlights to social happiness, or monumental signals directing to the *greatest good of the greatest number*, do we propose to be always exclusively guided, in full confidence of the inherent justice of the Democratic cause and the ultimately permanent success of our united exertions.

But however proud of our victorious party and confident of our principles, there are in vogue some grievous perversions thereof which it is our leading object to remedy.

It will not be questioned that the sovereignty of the people is, in theory, an indisputable truth; but in its practical bearing, in its direct operation upon systems of law and public policy, it is not in the power even of universal suffrage, unless exercised with a severe and jealous vigilance, to preserve it from gradually sinking into an empty sound. It has been well said that it is the natural tendency of power "to steal from the many to the few." The selfishness of individual character, augmented by the confiding indulgence of the many, is continually encouraging the forwardness of some *spoiled children* in the republican family. It has, therefore, happened that during a just

[1] [From the *New York Evening Post*, October 21, 1835, p. 2 — Abridged.]

now terminated period of deep repose, when, for a long series of years, all the cardinal interests of society were utterly forgotten in a mere money-making mania, the tacit and thoughtless assent of the people to some one exclusive privilege or to the establishment of a monopoly having a specious outside was greedily seized upon by the aforesaid *forward ones* as a pretext for other and much larger favors, until special grants and charters upon charters have come to constitute nearly the whole mass of legislative enactments; while, by a coördinate procedure, the pert few for whose benefit these things are have usurped all the powers and claim even the name itself of "the party" or "the people." The monopoly principle has thus been artfully and corruptly engrafted upon democratic institutions, and its weedy spread has so entirely covered up the Jeffersonian basis of the Constitution that all distinction has vanished between practical democracy and practical toryism. The common good, the interests of the many, have long been entirely neglected in a confused scramble for personal favors; and instead of leaving one business man to cope with another, on the fair and equitable principles which nature and the Constitution sanction, the Legislature, the *democratic* Legislature of the State of New York, by means of chartered privileges, has been all along engaged in *siding* with some to the injury of others and in doing all that is possible to make the *unchartered* multitude "poor indeed."

Special charters for particular objects are rarely applied for unless they will contribute to special and particular gain. This is emphatically true of *moneyed* incorporations which are always sought for with a zeal commensurate with the unfair advantages expected to be derived from them. Under the flimsy disguise of some secondary measure of public utility, which but too often is itself a deception, or even of a winning and popular title such as the name of some revered patriot or mechanic occupation, personal and evidently exorbitant profit is in every case the real object of the application and the real substance of the grant. The price, or *bonus*, as it is insidiously termed, which is sometimes paid for such privileges, the open and the half-developed bribery to which such legislation is eminently subject, the indefatigable labor bestowed by *lobbying* agents in furthering the acquisition of these abominations, and the ravenous grasp very generally made for a portion of them when granted by law, are glaring and resistless proofs of their wholly artificial character, their injustice, and their evil nature. If the public good, as is often and falsely alleged, were the actual motive for the creation of moneyed incorporations, if mercantile or any other convenience really called for such things, they would come into being, as do all *impartial* enactments, by the spontaneous, unbought, and ordinary action of the legislature. It is, therefore, but too plainly evident that gross selfishness, the most mercenary spirit, and mere private considerations are at the basis of this species of legislation.

But it has been repeatedly said, and with effect upon the thoughtless, that banks, insurance companies, ferry grants, etc., however accompanied with objectionable qualities, are indispensable to "the business wants of the community." That there is gross deception in this claim will be briefly shown by the following remarks and accompanying illustrations.

The wealthy of the land are the strong of the *legal* world, as the athletic are of the *natural;* in haughtiness and in oppressive disposition the analogy is perfect between them. Relatively considered, it is now precisely as if all things were in a state of nature; the *strong* tyrannize over the weak; live, as it were, in a continual victory, and glut themselves on incessant plunder. It is as humiliating now to be poor, as in the state of nature to be feeble of body; and although the ordinary difference between the rich and the poor, as between the athletic and the feeble, is clearly unavoidable and doubtless right, just, proper, and expedient, yet that such difference should be enhanced by legal enactments, that the rich or the strong should be artificially legislated into still greater riches or still greater strength, is not only unnecessary, but decidedly improper and even *cruel*. True it is, civilization, in substituting an artificial mode of relative strength for that which is natural, has brought within control an ungovernable quality of varying man; a control, however, which we think has of late been exercised more for general woe than weal. But let us for an instant suppose that human muscularity, as is human wealth, were manageable by law and that it was proposed to *incorporate* — that is, to give *individuality* and in some cases *immortality* to a considerable number of ordinary men, say one hundred, and thus to constitute a giant being, or some fifty of them, for the City of New York — we are confident that the public voice would exclaim against such a project with extraordinary unanimity. It might be said in vain, and uselessly repeated again and again, that such creatures are well calculated to aid in the erection of massive buildings and the extinction of fires, and *might be* extremely useful in case of a sudden insurrection or invasion. Such reasoning would be futile indeed. The huge arms of the proposed monsters, wielded by a multiplied selfishness, and without fear of immediate death, would be anticipated in fancy as but too likely to be used for other purposes than the public good; and a general conviction would possess the whole community that the aggregate of evils to be reasonably apprehended from such incorporations would render all their positive advantage to society an inconsiderable mite. Nay, we risk nothing in saying that if enacted into being all evil power and social influence would soon come into their exclusive possession and their oppressions know no other bounds than as remotely fixed by their own peculiar and mutual interests.

The above picture, fellow Democrats, is but an allegory of the real state of things. There are now in the midst of us many of the peculiar giants of civilized society. All honor be to the energy of democratic freemen and to the firmness and skill of their venerable chief; the Goliath is slain, but there remain vast numbers of his dangerous kind among the Philistines of wealth. Habit, long endurance, and the bias of early education have indeed rendered these beings familiar to us all and blunted our perception of their more abhorrent characteristics. But it needs not demonstration to show that if *moneyed* incorporations, say *fifty* of them for the City of New York, were to be now for the first time suggested, the proposition would be quite as revolting to an unsophisticated community as the supposed case of incorporated athletes. It would be grievous folly to recommend their creation by asserting that a poor man, if rich in friends, might occasionally borrow a small sum of money from them; it would at once be seen that if they did not exist, did not absorb, so to speak, the *loanable* means of society, aided by a friend, he could borrow of individuals. It would be alike useless to argue that they might work wonders on great public emergencies; it would be distinctly perceived that like as by a monster's touch, wholly destitute of gentleness, their benefits, if benefits they can be called, and injuries would be always at unhealthy extremes: at one time effecting mushroom prosperity; at another unreasonable distress; and it would then be most clearly absurd to attribute to such artificial creations, as is now too often done, the multiplication of valuable capital and the production of indispensable facilities for mercantile business. Such qualities belong not to their nature, but are simply impressed upon them by the neglect of other commercial means.

If incorporated banks were at once suppressed, an event by no means desirable, but contemplated only for the argument's sake, not a cent of money would be lost to the business community. The evolutions of capital and of credit, in all abundance, would be conducted by active and intelligent individuals under a measure of competition and a degree of personal responsibility to society which, when compared with incorporated institutions, would be vastly great and vastly advantageous to the humbler circles of business men. The "indispensable utility" of moneyed incorporations is at best but a common and empty prejudice. Were society equally accustomed to immense giant laborers, solely employed, under a *restraining law*, in the construction of buildings, their sudden and total extinction would doubtless convey to the minds of many an impression that building would, in consequence, cease altogether; they would fear that no contrivances of human ingenuity could enable ordinary men to supply the vacant places. We, wise on this one point, full well know that such a calamitous supposition would be grossly absurd, while, at the same time, some of us are ready to yield assent to a similar absurdity in the case of individual banking.

There is, we admit, an extensively prevalent aversion to private banks, arising out of the impositions which have heretofore been practised upon the public by a few of the kind. An analysis, however, of these cases will invariably point out their true cause to belong, not to their *singleness of direction*, but to certain prejudices and customs attached to the existing banking system at large. The magnificence of incorporated banks, the formal ostentation with which they do business, has long since clothed the simple idea of a *bank* with some sort of mystic right to extra respect. Like as to monarchs among the enthralled nations of Europe, there is a species of imposing dignity belonging to institutions consecrated by special law which effectually repels all inquiry into the details of character and forbids a doubt of their immaculate honor. When, therefore, it has happened that some daring individual, with cunning equal to the task, has assumed the outward guise of a *bank*, as practised by the chartered samples, the same attributes of sanctuary and of honor have been readily imputed to his institution.   Taking advantage of this weakness of human nature, or yielding to the temptations involved in the reigning system of business, the vile and mercenary have occasionally robbed the public through facilities *not of their own creation,* but incidental to the general or chartered mode of banking.   If to this cause be added the equally dangerous facility of becoming largely indebted to the public by means of *paper money,* a sort of pictured notes of hand which it has become customary rarely to present for redemption, we have abundant explanation of the evils of private banking while charters and paper money are the principal elements of the banking business. Let but this sort of employment be left free to general competition and paper money be forbidden, private bankers will stand in a very different and much safer relation to the community than they, or even chartered banks have ever stood.   Banking institutions will lose much of that spurious character upon which their undue credit is based, and the public be effectually protected against the most dangerous, because the most insidious of impositions.

For the reasons here assigned, we, as constituent members of an ascendant political party, call for the repeal of the restraining law which forbids private banking, and require that no more moneyed incorporations be henceforth created.   We are satisfied that the repeal of the law alluded to will, by opening a wide, unlimited field for competition, sufficiently disarm the incorporated institutions now in being and, in all probability, cause even their premature death in the ordinary progress of business.   So far from relatively increasing the money monopolies now existing, by refusing to create more, the repeal of the restraining law will at once destroy much that belongs to them of the monopoly character; and even without such repeal, it may be justly said that the profits and influence of incorporated banks are always at the full, in proportion to their capitals, and therefore cannot be enhanced by the diminution of numbers.

And instead of our plan promoting the social and political power of the few individuals who possess actual capital, we are confident that their power would be greatly abbreviated, inasmuch as, under the present system, it is their private *influence at bank,* much more than the loan of their money, that renders them the objects of servile homage and productive of degrading adulation.   The high grandeur of giant incorporations forbids the near approach of but a select few, and through that few all moneyed operations must now be transacted; these are thereby constituted a virtual nobility, not by their own power or wealth, but by the sovereign pleasure of the magisterial monopolies. Again, we desire the repeal of the famous restraining law on the principle of even-handed justice. There is no such protection in existence for the mechanic or producing classes. If solicited, for example, by an association of carpenters, if these were to ask for a restraining law to prevent persons from following their craft unless specially chartered so to do by law, they would be hooted at as presumptuous fools, and thus tacitly informed that *they* are not entitled to so very exclusive a privilege; that such legislative favors belong only to the wealthy and *respectable* among our citizens, and that if such matters were to become general, in accordance with mechanics' ideas of justice, they would cease to be advantageous. The partiality of the obnoxious law constitutes at once its whole value and its gross unfairness.

The above remarks particularly apply to banking institutions, but the principles involved are equally applicable to all species of partial legislation. Charters for objects of mere empty show or fulsome dignity are unworthy of even a passing objection. For the more efficient promotion of literature, science, and the arts, or for the purposes of social benevolence, a law, like that under which libraries may now be instituted without special leave, would meet, we think, with general approbation; for assuredly if any advantages are to be derived to learning or charity from the use of "a corporate seal" with artificial immortality, they ought to be within easy reach of any two or more individuals without selection or favor. And with regard to the subject of internal improvements — ferries, railways, turnpikes, etc. — we hold that like the Great Erie and Champlain Canals they should all be paid for out of the common purse for the common benefit of all. If national in character, these works should be constructed by the general government; if local, by the state, county, or town to which their benefits are more especially confined; for it is as palpably wrong that any partial associations of individuals should possess the privilege of levying and collecting taxes for their own benefit under the specious appellation of tolls, as it is for similar associations to levy the like upon the gross amount of commercial business by means of incorporated banks, or upon the calamities of fire and shipwreck by means of insurance companies, under the equally specious terms of *discounts* and *premiums*.

To save the public from the evils of complicated and excessive legislation, the statute book from ridiculous changeableness, the legislature itself from systematic corruption, ... and above all to redeem the Constitution and its great predominant principle of equal rights from the wretched degradation into which it has long been plunged by *loose construction*, or, in the language of the justly celebrated Veto, "to restore the government to that simple machine which it was originally designed to be," we are, in addition to the great points of public policy urged above, in favor of a general law of partnerships, and opposed to every species of special legislation. A general law by which any two or more individuals may declare themselves in business partnership, as well for wood-sawing, if they choose, as for manufacturing or banking, and regulated by such provisions as careful inquiry and practical experience may point out, would possess nothing of an exclusive or monopoly character. Without some such law, the suspension of special charters would totally prevent the prosecution of every business which requires a heavy capital, inasmuch as ordinary partnerships are constantly liable to be suddenly dissolved by the death or self will of a member. A limited form of permanent succession and a circumscribed right to transfer an interest in such partnerships seems to us to be perfectly reasonable and requisite. We are confident that a wholesome system of general business on this scheme would grow up gradually amongst us, infinitely more favorable than the present to the small capitalist, on account of the plenitude of semi-incorporated partnerships to which it would give rise and its evident tendency to divide, and not, as the present system, to concentrate patronage. We are sure an unprecedented activity on equitable principles would thereby come to pervade all occupations, and, instead of as now, a few becoming rich at the expense of the many, the advances of society would be comparatively uniform and in mass; and, instead of observing as now nought but rapid and destructive fluctuations of prosperity and adversity, with continual commercial alarm, the *money market* would be relatively stable and the public mind settled and serene.

It is scarcely necessary for us to add that we are warmly in favor of the constitutional currency of gold and silver, and therefore opposed to the repeal of the existing law in relation to the smaller bank notes; and in the desired general law of partnerships we believe it will be found expedient to forbid the issue of paper "on demand" except, perhaps, when drawn by one house or firm upon another.

Thus, fellow citizens and fellow members of the Democratic party, we present to you a system of public policy which we confidently believe will stand the test of examination by Jeffersonian principles. The selfish advocates of banks and the armies of abject dependents on the *tender mercies* of moneyed incorporations are endeavoring to deceive you and us into their mercenary purposes; they resort to even the meanest expedients to gain their ends. The laboring and producing classes are scandalously branded as agrarians. You are told that banking is an affair above your feeble comprehension, and a subject that exclusively belongs to the mercantile community — as if you did not know that all social interests, to the minutest ramification, are subject to the baneful control of moneyed power. They indeed predicate much of their plans on the alleged ignorance of the poor, in despite of their professions of democratic principles which, if just, must be based upon the truth of the all-sufficient virtue and intelligence of the people. But, fellow citizens, we entreat you to ponder the subject of monopolies in your minds. Trace, as you easily may, your ill-paid toil and humiliation to unfairness of legislation. Claim your right, your unquestionable right, to equal participation in the one and only justly *chartered company*, viz., the people of the State of New York, and take especial care that those who are elected to the directorship of the general concern deceive you not, but that they, in despite of all self interested motives to the contrary, are in some way obliged to obey your will. Be not deceived by the clamor against *the pledge;* specific instructions of any kind would be precisely the same thing to them and the same thing to us; it is our anti-monopoly principles, our resolute determination to put an end to partial and selfish legislation, that galls them to the quick. The mere *form* of their unwilling obligation to do justice to all is to them, as to us, of little importance. When, therefore, they cry out against the pledge, they covertly cry out against the principles we profess. We beseech you then, fellow citizens, that none but anti-monopoly Democrats obtain your suffrages, and thus doing all in your power to set your house in order, rest confident of that ultimate success which is an attribute of truth.

16

THEODORE SEDGWICK JR.

WHAT IS A MONOPOLY?[1]

[GOVERNMENT BY DISCUSSION]

THE MEASURES of the present administration have had a remarkable tendency to stimulate the national intellect. Its history is one of continual contest. The strife has been of a character to call forth all the resources of the popular intelligence, and to direct them to subjects most worthy of consideration. The excitement of which we have so recently been witnesses and partakers was not caused by foreign war or internal commotion; it did not derive its origin from questions addressing themselves rather to the passions than the judgment; no topic of temporary interest and minor character, no impressment of seamen, no Shays' or whiskey insurrection, aroused the country to the efforts and exertions it has made.

The controversy we have witnessed sprang from the discussion of principles; of those fundamental maxims of the science of government, and of political economy, which it is absolutely essential that a free people should understand. It is in this respect that the tendency of the present administration has been so admirably beneficial. It has urged forward the whole American mind.

At an early period, during the President's first term, the propriety of great national works of internal improvement became a topic of discussion, and the wisdom of leaving all such outlays of capital to the greater economy and more rigid supervision of the separate States or of private individuals, together with the inexpediency of augmenting the patronage of the central power, soon made itself apparent to the mind of the people. The contest with South Carolina brought up the investigation of the fundamental principles of political economy and resulted in the triumph of free trade. The more recent and more exciting measures connected with the Bank have created a no less

[1] [From *What Is a Monopoly? or some Considerations upon the Subject of Corporations and Currency*. By a citizen of New-York (New York, 1835) — Abridged.]

beneficial spirit of inquiry into questions of perpetual and unfluctuating interest.

We have as yet scarcely begun to see the advantageous results that must flow from this last controversy. In the contest between the United States Bank and the people, it was long ago apparent that the former must succumb. But this is only a small portion of the good consequences that are yet to ensue. The mind of the country has been aroused to a consideration of topics that have hitherto been but superficially examined. The same principles that have been established in the general government present themselves to the administration of the several States. The destruction of the greatest chartered Bank in the Union has led the way to a discussion of the whole question of corporations and of the comparative merits of a paper and specie currency, of a restricted and an unrestricted circulating medium.

Of these topics, then, I design in the following pages to treat. Although in no wise necessarily connected with each other, yet with us these subjects cannot be satisfactorily investigated apart, owing to the fact that our entire currency is in the management of corporate bodies, and that it is for this purpose the most important of these institutions are created.

Of charters of incorporation, then, first it is my intention to inquire how far they are monopolies, how far they are beneficial, and how far the advantages they produce can be attained in another and better manner. To many minds even yet this investigation will be new; the Revolution of 1776 gave us a free Government, but did not equally emancipate our opinions; in prejudice many of us are still colonists. We received from our English ancestors the legislative practice of creating corporate bodies, and till this day it has passed almost unquestioned.

.   .   .   .

From a review of the different attributes of corporations and partnerships, it is, I think, apparent that with regard to establishments where considerable capital is requisite, other things being equal, persons acting under a charter of incorporation would have great advantages over persons doing the same business under articles of copartnership. But while partnerships can be formed by all persons, without hindrance or restraint or the grant of any previous permission, corporations can only obtain existence (with the exceptions which I shall hereafter state) by a special grant from the Legislature. Charters of incorporations are therefore grants of privilege, to be exclusively enjoyed by the corporators. A charter of incorporation is therefore a grant of exclusive privilege, and every grant of exclusive privilege, strictly speaking, creates a monopoly; it carries on its face that the grantee has received facilities of making pecuniary or other gains from which the mass of his fellow citizens are excluded. This is the very substance of a monopoly. Every charter of incorporation, therefore, coming directly from the Legislature, and which can only be obtained by application to that body, is a monopoly grant; more or less objectionable, but still the creation of a monopoly.

[CORPORATE GRANTS MONOPOLISTIC]

It must necessarily follow, to every person whose mind is cast in that republican mold, the die of which is not yet, thank God, broken, that the principle of corporate grants is wholly adverse to the genius of our institutions; that it originates in that arrogant and interfering temper on the part of the Government which seeks to meddle with, direct, and control private exertions, and in that inefficient, petitioning, and suppliant temper necessarily engendered in a people taught not to rely upon their own exertions but to beg aid of their rulers. Every corporate grant is directly in the teeth of the doctrine of equal rights, for it gives to one set of men the exercise of privileges which the main body can never enjoy. Every such grant is equally adverse to the fundamental maxim of free trade, for it carries on its face that none but the corporators are free to carry on the trade in question with the advantages which the charter confers. The institutions so created owe their origin to the same policy which conceived a tariff and nearly sundered the Union.

It will consequently be admitted that corporate grants must have a vicious tendency unless the objects attained by them are of paramount public necessity and can be obtained in no other way; but I believe it is in my power to prove that these objects can in almost all cases be got at, not only in another, but far better mode; and as there is no such thing as an incorrect or unsafe theory accompanied by a correct or safe practice, we shall find the abstract evils that we might apprehend from a departure from the fundamental maxims of free trade and freedom more than realized in the existing state of things.

Great improvements have been made by us on the English system; but though the sore has been deeply probed, enough of the gangrene yet remains to taint the body politic.

We must not, however, lose sight of the important fact that the advantages resulting from acts of incorporation are such as, if fairly got, may be fairly enjoyed. There may be a difference of opinion on one point, the restricted liability of the corporators. This is an important point of the discussion, (though the principle is not essential to the existence of corporations, as in some of the neighboring States the members have been made liable in their separate property) and I shall consider it in a future part of these pages. As to the other attributes, I believe it will be readily conceded that they have about them nothing vicious but their exclusive origin; and that if they could be freely assumed by all, without license, no reasonable ground would be left for hostility to them. They would then be perfectly compatible with equality of rights and freedom of trade.

.   .   .   .

[REMEDY FOR MONOPOLY]

Let those rules which we have sanctioned in regard to religious corporations and limited partnerships, be combined and extended to every possible association for private purposes that it can enter into the head of man to form. Enact a general law providing for the creation of *Corporate Partnerships*, and declare that such corporate partnerships shall have all the powers now enjoyed by corporations. This name may be considered appropriate, as it presents to the mind the idea of a partnership endowed with the peculiar attributes of a corporation, which is the very object we are in quest of. . . . . There is but one ground on which I apprehend much diversity of opinion, and that is in relation to the restricted liability of the corporators. It may be said that they thus have an advantage not enjoyed by private individuals. This is a valid objection so long as corporate powers are given, as they are now, by exclusive and monopoly grant; but the moment they are obtained under a general law, it falls to the ground. Corporators will then have no advantage over the public at large, because any individual can become a corporator, when and for what purposes he pleases. This clause conflicts in no wise with the fundamental maxim of free trade. The corporator says to the world, "I own so many shares of such a corporate partnership; will you trust me on that security? for, understand, I have no other to give." Why not permit those who wish to deal with him on these grounds to do so? Apart from this, there is an intrinsic reason in the thing; for in these corporations a few persons manage the whole, and there would be much less readiness to invest, if capitalists knew they were to be liable for the acts of those over whom they have little control. I believe the restricted liability a just, wise, and equal provision; but it is not necessary to the existence of corporations; for in some of the neighboring States they have made corporators liable as partners. Such are the principles that I suggest, as applicable in relation to private corporations; and we have next to see how public corporations differ from private, and how far those which have heretofore been considered of a peculiar and exclusive character may be brought within the system which I propose to apply to all corporations created for the purposes of private traffic.

.   .   .   .

[PUBLIC CORPORATIONS]

Public Corporations, as they exist among us, are of two classes: banks whether of circulation, as the safety-fund banks, or of deposit, as the safety banks; and internal communication or internal improvement corporations, including those chartered for the purpose of making canals, railroads, turnpike roads, bridges, etc., etc.

It is necessary first to consider the subject as regards banks; for the questions which we have been thus far examining become more difficult of solution when that of currency is joined with them. It is requisite, however, to bear in mind the principles thus far established, viz., that corporate *grants* are grants of privilege, unequal, unjust, and limiting the freedom of trade; and that *corporate powers* may, if fairly obtained, be safely allowed to all persons desiring to use them for *private* purposes. To apply these principles correctly to banking, it is absolutely essential to comprehend what a bank is, and whether in its nature it differs from any private establishment of commerce.

Earliest history speaks of money as a currency or a circulating medium; and we now scarcely know of any people so utterly savage as to be in the habitual use of barter for their daily exchanges. Nor indeed, can we conceive of a state of things, in which, for want of money, or a medium of portable value, the farmer should be obliged to carry with him a bushel of potatoes to pay his gate-tolls, and a shoemaker, a package of shoes to discharge his travelling expenses, without also picturing to ourselves a state of complete barbarism. After supplying a man with food, clothing, and shelter, money is one of the earliest necessities that present themselves, and it may be classed among the positive wants.

We find, too, that from the earliest periods the precious metals, gold and silver, have been used as the chief circulating medium. Their beauty, great value with small bulk, susceptibility of coinage, ready cognition, and unchangeability have given them a universal reception. Until within a hundred years, no money was known but gold and silver among civilized nations.

Gold and silver coin, being, as I have said above, positively needed by every people who approach the civilized state, is needed to a certain amount, varying according to the respective activity of their enterprise and the character of their occupations. Just as a certain amount of household furniture is needed by a community, so is a certain amount of money. It is plain that a farmer needs less money than a shopkeeper, and an industrious people more than an indolent one. The total amount required by a nation, though it cannot be computed to a fraction, can be got at with very considerable accuracy.

Now it is unquestionable that every article of trade will flow in the great ocean of commerce where it is wanted and as it is wanted; and if government had done nothing to counteract this free action, the amount of gold and silver necessary for each country, they being strictly articles of trade, would always be found there; if more by any accident should be imported, a glut would ensue; its price compared with its price in other countries would fall, and the surplus would be exported; if, on the other hand, too much should go out, the price would rise as compared with its price in other countries, and enough would be imported to fill the vacuum. The fluctuations in the value of gold and silver would therefore be momentary and trifling, and the money want of the country would be regularly supplied, just as the want of woollens or cottons now is.

I have said that till within the last century no currency was known but that of specie. It is now a little more than a hundred years since the first bank empowered to issue notes was incorporated. The Bank of England was created about a century ago, for the purpose of enabling the government to borrow money with more facility. From this period dates the development of that lucrative business, the making of paper money.

The trading community is divided into borrowers and lenders. The lenders have a surplus capital beyond their wants, while the borrowers have not enough money to meet their necessities. The former, therefore, loan to the latter. But the lenders having capital have also credit, and derive the same advantage from their character as capitalists that men of truth do from their character for veracity. The assertions of the one will be believed without collateral evidence, and the other can lend though he has no money in his possession. He can give his promise to lend at a future day. This is lending credit.

A bank of circulation is an institution for the loan of money and the loan of credit. It is plain that this is the whole direct operation of such an institution. Its capital consists, we will say, of a million of dollars in money or specie. This is at once loaned out to the borrowers; so far it is a loan of money; now comes the credit. A merchant wishes to discount his note; that is to say, he wishes to obtain ready money in exchange for his promise to pay an equal sum at a future day. His own credit is not a matter of general notoriety, or, in other words, he is not generally known to pay all his just debts when due, and he has recourse to the bank, a public institution of large property, and the reputation of which is known to every one. The bank has however loaned all its own specie; what does it do? It investigates the business character of the applicant and, if satisfied, gives him the money in a roundabout, but sure mode: It takes the merchant's promissory note for the sum he wants, payable at a future day, and gives him its own promissory notes (deducting the discount or interest upon the sum, for the use of the money, up to the time when the merchant's note is due) payable at sight, and which, owing to the good standing of the bank, everybody will take as cash.

This then is all that a bank can do. It lends its money, and it lends its credit; but credit is nothing more than the expectation or certainty of money at some future period, and, therefore, a loan of credit is a promise to lend money when it shall be called for. A bank can consequently lend nothing but money. Its whole business is to make loans, either in cash, which is a loan of money in hand, or in paper notes,

which are promises to lend money at some future day. *Its whole
business is to lend money; such is the direct agency of a bank.* Is not
loaning money a private business?

We have next to consider the indirect results of these issues of
promissory notes. The promissory note of a private individual is
presented at its maturity, paid, and goes out of circulation. Not so
with a bank promissory note. Contrary to the expectation or design
of their first devisers, it has been found that the creation of banks of
circulation effects a complete revolution in circulating medium.

The reason is apparent. A certain quantity in value, it has been
said, is necessary for the exchanges of the country, and before the
institution of banks, gold and silver was used for the purpose; but
money is like everything else; any cheaper mode of making it drives
the dearer fabric from the market. So long as the bank is in good
credit its notes answer all the purposes of gold and silver coin, and
consequently, as paper is cheaper than specie, it is adopted in its
place. The specie, not being wanted, falls in price as compared with
other countries where paper is not used and is exported where it is
more in demand.

It may be set down as certain, then, that where there is a paper-
making institution in good credit, specie will not exist; that is to say,
the paper drives out the gold and silver to the extent that it is in good
credit. If its credit was absolutely beyond a question, not an ounce
of gold or silver would be seen. But there is always uncertainty, more
or less, from time to time, in regard to every bank, and specie is kept
in circulation to the extent of this suspicion. Indeed, if one could
devise a bank that would be without the possibility of breaking, and
if this state of things could be made to last, specie would not be wanted,
and a paper currency would then be the most economical invention
in the world; but unfortunately this cannot be realized. During the
summer season a people might be satisfied with a paper promise to
give each man a woollen suit when the first frost should come; but
when the frost comes, the paper clothing will not answer; so it is with
paper money. The frost is sure to come; over-trading, internal commotion, foreign aggression, any of those disturbances to which societies
are liable and which compel every one to suspect the solvency of his
neighbor, forces upon the holders of the bank promises the question
whether they are as good as specie. What then is the condition of

that country whose legislation is devised to favor paper money, and to give it an advantage over specie, and where the inevitable consequences of the introduction of the former medium are not counterbalanced by the operation of free and unlimited competition? In such a country bank paper has been well called, "suspicion asleep." The moment it wakes up, woe to the bank, and, unfortunately, woe to the holders also. What then is the first and only answer to the staggering question? Why, "*if* the bank is sound, I am safe," and you have the whole currency resting on an *if*. Away then to the bank, bad luck to the hindmost! And what can the bank do? It presses its debtors; they can afford no help; the specie has left the country; the notes cannot be paid; then comes a suspension of payments, a depreciation of the notes, a confusion of all the exchanges of the country, panic, failures, distress, and finally an importation of specie, that specie which never should have been exported; confidence then begins to reappear, the banks to resume payment, and things are gradually restored to their original state. This is no fancy sketch. This same disorder and suffering has taken place in England, in France, and in this country; it will take place everywhere where paper money has a legal advantage given to it over specie. . . . .

.   .   .   .

Another remarkable feature of the present mode of banking is the distribution of the legislative favors. In the city of New York we have twenty-three banks, with about twenty millions of capital. In Oneida, the second county of the state, there are but three, including a branch established at Utica, with a collective capital of seven hundred thousand dollars. Onondaga, the third, has but two banks, and Genesee, the fifth, but one, with a capital of one hundred thousand dollars; while large entire counties, such as Cattaraugus, Tioga, Alleghany, and Delaware, have not a bank within their limits. Some portion of these inequalities can be accounted for by the population not perfectly representing the ratio of trade; but there still remains more than can be explained, except by the natural tendency of monopoly and privilege to flow in narrow and partial channels.

Such is the result of the exclusive system, and how have we been obliged to patch and bolster it up? After setting scores of these institutions at work, the war came and blew them all to the sky. Then the General Government took the matter in hand and created a central bank to supervise and regulate the State institutions. The first exploit of the National Bank was to run within a hair's breadth of breaking, and its second to set about the deliberate creation of a general panic and distress. Here ended the reputation of the Federal regulator; but in the mean time the State banks had been considered in so precarious a situation that the Safety Fund act was thought necessary to secure their existence, and at a later day the credit of the State itself was called in to save them from ruin. We prop up a falling house with a cracked beam, and put a broken sleeper under the beam, without ever thinking of repairing the edifice itself.

The character of Mr. Van Buren's Safety Fund act is too remarkable to be passed over in silence. It was devised by a distinguished citizen and is perhaps an indispensable part of the present system. But how false in principle are its provisions: all the banks compelled to contribute towards the failures of the incompetent and dishonest, and the money dealings of the whole State subjected to the supervision of three commissioners! It is well understood that it is not the fund, but the investigation and report, which constitute the value of this system; yet what a system, which has to depend upon the sagacity and integrity of three men! How are these inquisitors to ascertain the goodness of the paper discounted, and who is to guarantee their honesty? I especially disclaim any allusion to the present incumbents; my business is with institutions, not individuals.

Is it not manifest that all these devices are as vicious as the system itself? No one imagines that the woollen trade must be put in the hands of privileged companies to ensure a sufficient supply in the country. Why, then, the money trade? It must not be forgotten that money is a commercial commodity; that it is needed for the purposes of traffic; and that Government has nothing to do with it but to fix the standard. Let it establish its mints and coin the bullion sent it; let it fix the standard of money as it does now of weights and measures; then leave the supply to that sovereign equalizer, *free trade*.

The moment you begin to place restrictions upon the money trade or banking, you derange every other operation of commerce, because the value of all things is computed in money. If you lay high duties upon foreign woollens, you create a fluctuation in the woollen business, but silks still remain of the same value. If you embrace silks in your restrictive system, still cottons are not affected; but the moment you alter the value of money, you alter the value of everything used by man and carry doubt and disorder into every private dealing. You may better play the fool with anything than money. That banks, privileged as at present, cause a fluctuation in the value of money, cannot be a matter of doubt. It is made their interest so to do. We have already said that a certain amount in value of paper is necessary to effect the exchanges of a country; consequently, the moment this amount is increased, the currency must begin to depreciate, for the plain reason that the surplus is not wanted. But the more paper issued by the banks, the greater their profits are. Their interest is to make a glut of paper money, which is in direct opposition to the interest of the community. Nor are we to lose sight of the fact that all fluctuations of the currency fall chiefly upon those who live by wages, the hard working poor. It is well settled that wages are the first to be affected by a depreciated medium, and the last to adapt themselves to it. The poor are therefore the first victims of over-issues.

By the present system, then, three distinct objects are effected, and it is a pity they were not introduced into every bank charter, as thus: "Whereas the rate of interest being but seven per cent, it is considered expedient to give the persons hereinafter named, the privilege of making twelve or fifteen; whereas it is considered expedient to export the specie from the country; and whereas it is deemed desirable to cause fluctuations in the value of money, therefore be it enacted ——" This would be a very popular preamble, and yet would only express the real end of every bank charter.

It is said that banks have made the country prosper. It is pure assertion without a shadow of proof. What does it mean that institutions created to lend money have made money? That they have caused a rapid circulation, and have stimulated enterprise, is true, and so would free private banking to an infinitely greater extent. But they have, in fact, caused great public and private injury to the community. It is not by means of them, but in spite of them, that the country has prospered. It has prospered, as did England, before the reform bill; as did America, under the tariff. Yet not for that are rotten boroughs, manufacturing bounties, and monopoly corporations great national blessings.

The Bank Commissioners, in their Report of January, 1835, say, "Banks have justly been esteemed as among the most powerful agents in developing the resources and stimulating the industry of the country. Actual capital could not have spread half the canvass which now whitens the ocean, or given motion to half the spindles which are now in operation. Credit, as a substitute for capital," has done it. All this comes from an ignorance of the true character of banks and the real meaning of credit. Every accumulation and addition to the mass of property is effected by the means of capital and labor. There is no such thing as credit distinct from capital. The only peculiarity of this country is that the idle capital has been freely invested in the hands of needy and industrious borrowers. This is the effect of credit, or credit itself. Does any one suppose that we wanted *chartered* banks for this object? Will it be said that money would not have been loaned if the legislature had not granted any exclusive privilege of doing it to a certain small number of individuals. No! *as compared with what would have been effected under a free trade system*, the banks have been a clog upon the industry of this country; they have embarrassed the transfers of money, and any assertion to the contrary is unsupported by facts, and flies in the face of first principles.

To the evils already enumerated, are to be added the pernicious political and moral effects of the system; the lobbying and intriguing at Albany; the bonuses thus placed in the hands of the legislature, (of ten or fifteen per cent upon every bank capital granted, for that is the amount which they almost invariably rise above par, immediately upon distribution) to be parcelled out among political adherents; the bribes of stock to the members; the commissionerships given to partisan friends, that the stock may be allotted to those well known for party devotion. Look at the manner in which the time of the legislature is spent. During the sessions of 1832, three hundred and thirty-three acts were passed, of which one hundred and fifty were acts of incorporation, and nine bank charters. In 1833, out of three hundred and twenty-three acts, one hundred and twenty-six were corporate grants, and eight bank charters. In 1834, where three hundred and twenty acts were made, one hundred and thirty-three were charters, eleven creating banks. Thus nearly one-half of the time of the legislature, chosen for public objects, is consumed in satisfying the demands of private interest.

.   .   .   .

[PROPOSED REMEDIES]

And now what can be done to remedy these evils? The measure of last winter was a positive and decided improvement. By abolishing the bills under five dollars, and carrying up the prohibition to bills of ten if not twenty dollars, we shall add much to the specie and drive a quantity of worthless paper from circulation. A restriction of bank issues to the amount of their respective capitals would be another valuable measure, for we find all those with capitals of less than $200,000 issuing from 150 to 200 per cent on them.

These are, however, but temporary and partial expedients. They render further reform more easy but not less indispensable. These remedies partake, too, of the narrow and restrictive character of the system. The whole system itself must be done away. Let the same axe which strikes at corporate grants be laid deep into the root of privileged banking; let this lucrative business be thrown open to universal competition. What would be the necessary consequence if these two reforms went hand in hand, and banking were placed under the provisions of the general law of *corporate* partnerships, already suggested.

In the first place, the business of lending money, discounting paper, and issuing notes would be immediately taken up and carried on by private individuals, and more particularly by corporate partnerships, in which persons of the most moderate means might make investments.

Secondly, the banks would have a more local character and credit, and their issues a more restricted circulation than they have now. Large institutions would immediately spring up (such as Messrs. Prime, Ward and King might establish tomorrow) which would have a national reputation; but we should not see bills, like the Chatauque notes, issued by companies insignificant in point of wealth, traveling hundreds of miles from where those who issue them are known, and owing their currency solely to two cabalistic words, *"safety fund,"* inscribed on them by the State.

Thirdly, the profits on this business would be reduced to an equality with those on every other branch of trade by the universal competition.

Fourthly, a sufficient amount of specie would be kept in the country. Each bank or banking partnership would be pressing on its neighbors driving back its notes, and from the impossibility of any concert between them, they would be compelled to keep on hand specie enough to prevent all danger of panic. It has been thought that the effect of this reform would be to banish absolutely all paper currency; but with much respect for those who entertain this idea, I apprehend that though the amount will be exceedingly diminished, it would not be completely done away by the free trade system. Paper is cheaper than specie to the amount that gold and silver are economized by its use, and they may be economized to a considerable extent compatible with the soundness of a paper medium.

Fifthly, for the very same reasons, the fluctuations of the currency would be done away with to the greatest possible extent.

Sixthly, the temptation of participating in unequal profits would be taken away from the members of the legislature, and the means of corruption placed beyond their reach.

In conclusion, it is scarcely necessary to say that I look upon banking as belonging, absolutely, to the class of private dealings, and that as such, it should be left under the provisions of a general partnership law, such as I have already suggested. It has been doubted whether, under such a law, small notes should not be prohibited, and landed security required. Neither provision is necessary. Leave the matter to be regulated by competition, and you would have such notes issued by such persons as the public convenience required, and the public confidence allowed. There can be no reason why the lenders of money should be obliged to give real security, any more than the importers of woollens. The paper of a large commercial house is often afloat to a greater amount than the issues of many a bank. If we could but imbue ourselves with the idea that banking is only the lending of money and that lending money is a matter between man and man, government would be saved a world of trouble.

.   .   .   .

Summary

I have thus completed my examination of the different kinds of corporations, and it may be well to make a brief summary of the principles which have, I believe, been established.

Corporations are legitimate for political objects, in the case of towns and counties, under the provisions of a general law in which villages and cities should also be included.

Corporate powers may be safely granted by a general law to all persons desiring to form those associations which I have classed under the head of private corporations.

Banking or lending money, being strictly a private traffic, ought to be left to the provisions of the same general law and should be thrown open to the competition of private partnerships and individuals.

Exclusive corporations for transportation by water are unreasonable monopolies, and corporations as they are now created by legislative grant are only legitimate for the purpose of internal communications by land.

We can now also make a scale of corporate evils which will give us a more accurate idea of what we have to dread. First, then, in evil, come the *banks*, as controlling the currency and affecting all other business.

Next the *ferry or water companies*, acting as restraints upon intercourse.

The *insurance companies* monopolizing a lucrative branch of business.

Then the *private companies*, only obnoxious on account of the trouble and expense to which individuals are put to obtain a charter.

The *town incorporations*, vicious only in theory.

And lastly, the *internal improvement land corporations*, where the speculative evils are counteracted by the fact that an object of immense importance can be attained in no other way.

Here, then, I have set forth the views of those who style themselves anti-monopolists, and these, with the single exception of the difference of opinion as to railroad and canal corporations, are their sole objects. It is not difficult to decide with what justice they have been termed agrarians and jacobins. It is not difficult to say whether those who labor for an equality of right are, in truth, working for a community of property. Property, in itself, is respectable, and the energy and industry by which it is acquired worthy of respect. They are the best friends of property and of men of property who would abolish every unequal and unrighteous means of acquiring it. It is those unequal and unrighteous modes of acquiring it which stimulate the jealousy and arouse the indignation of the less fortunate classes.

I propose, in the remainder of this treatise, briefly to investigate the means most likely to bring about the end at which we aim.

In doing this, it becomes necessary to abandon the field of economy and to enter upon that of politics, the various views here represented having been put forward as the creed and rallying-point of a strong section of the Democratic party in this city; and men eminent in the ranks of the administration having avowed their entire approbation of them. The ground so manfully taken by Mr. Cambreleng in the House of Representatives, last winter, is well known; and Mr. Senator Benton has made an equally positive exposition of his accordance with the views contained in these pages. In his St. Louis speech of June last, he said, "he had pleasure in responding to the sentiments which ascribed to him a dislike and opposition to chartered monopolies and exclusive privileges. He was thoroughly opposed to such things, and looked upon corporations, and especially moneyed corporations, as the legislative vice and opprobrium of the age and country in which he lived."

In this position of affairs, it behooves the members of this section of the Democratic party to proceed as if certain of ultimate success; but at the same time to recollect that however formidable their strength, they are still in the minority; they should remember what infamous efforts have been made to misrepresent their motives and falsify their opinions by those who denounce them as agrarians and infidels; and reflecting how difficult it is to simplify to the popular comprehension all the speculative points laid down in these pages, they should put forward as their watchword those tangible propositions which can be made intelligible to the humblest intellect. They should not, therefore, pledge their candidates, as was done last year, to oppose "all monopolies," because the phrase means anything or nothing; they should not send Representatives to Albany so little comprehending the subject as to vote, under such a pledge, against village charters; they should not declaim against all corporations whatever, because an immense number of these institutions are, in point of fact, harmless; they should not waste their force in attacking railroad and canal companies, because, as yet, no sufficient substitute for the present mode of making these works has been suggested. They should confine themselves to the subject of banks.

These are, in fact, the most mischievous offspring of our vicious legislation. In regard to these corporations, the points of attack are simple and manifest. The popular mind can be made to appreciate the real character of exclusive privileges which confer such enormous profits, and to understand the pernicious tendency which they exert upon the currency. Nor is it to be forgotten that it is the interest of these institutions which opposes the only formidable obstacle to the progress of reform. If the privileged banks are routed, all the other corporations united could make no head against the advocates of free trade.

Let then those opposed to monopoly set their faces against the increase of banks; let them insist upon the repeal of the restraining law which prohibits private banking, and the passage of an act authorizing the formation of corporate partnerships. These are plain, intelligible propositions; there will be no possibility of misunderstanding or misrepresenting them. They rest on the same immutable basis which supports the entire fabric of our government.

The suggestions here presented are urged by one who has no interest whatever in the contest now pending, and whose most ardent wishes will be satisfied, if, by anything in these pages, he shall have contributed to the success of the friends of free trade.

As to the allegation that those who maintain these views do so to the injury and division of the Democratic party, it is too low a consideration to be taken into view. If there be anything to which that party stands committed, it is hostility to privileged banking; and shall it be said that they who, while they acknowledge their devotion to that party, still demand its adherence to its original principles are false to their first professions?   To this, the best answer can be made in the words of Milton: "He who freely magnifies what hath been nobly done, and fears not to declare as freely what might be done better, gives ye the best covenant of his fidelity, and that his loyalist affection, and his hope waits on your proceedings."

17

GILBERT VALE

POLITICAL ECONOMY[1]

INTRODUCTION

POLITICAL ECONOMY is necessarily a part of Government, because it treats of the "Wealth of Nations" and the object of government is chiefly protection, individual and national, without which no accumulations of wealth will take place. We need not observe that government regards or should regard the *happiness* of the people, while political economy only regards the wealth of the nation. We hold no system of political economy sound that would sacrifice the happiness of the community to the acquisition of wealth or to the splendor of the government, just as we should hold no domestic economy good which should merely regard the accumulation of wealth at the expense of moral principles, health, or rational refinement of the family. Wealth is nothing but with a view to enjoyments: the *greatest quantity, for the longest time, with the least means.* There is an intimate connection between individual wealth and national; indeed, the latter chiefly consists of the associated properties of the former. Individual wealth may be acquired honorably, without the violation of any one social virtue, and in perfect harmony with the rights and interests of the community; it then not only benefits the possessor, but even in acquisition contributes to the wealth and happiness of others; this is the case with the planter or farmer, the manufacturer, and the trader and merchant, when the trader saves expenses both to the producer and consumer or offers facilities not to be had without him. While the merchant, if he import valuable foreign articles of consumption for that which has little or no value at home, performs a service which conduces to the wealth and happiness of individuals and to the community, equal to the producer. To exchange

[1] [From the Supplement to *The Diamond* (New York), Series II, April to August, 1841. This was an enlarged and improved version of a series of articles published by Vale in the *Sunday Reporter*, "a small paper then but little known," as early as 1832 — Abridged.]

our native ice or lumber for foreign silks or wine certainly adds to our comforts and increases our wealth, while the articles exchanged effect the same benevolent purpose for those who receive them, for ice is a luxury in the East Indies and lumber of great utility in Italy, where the tall pine has yielded to the more profitable vine. It is clear, too, that the acquisition of wealth by such honest means carries with it a blessing and necessarily involves a host of principals and assistants who participate in such wealth during the acquisition; but if individuals seek wealth merely by a transfer of property from one to another by trick, fraud, or violence, such wealth, so acquired, is a curse to a country, for it impoverishes many to make one rich, and adds nothing to the wealth of the nation; and if such accumulators have aids, principals, and assistants, however splendid they may appear, they blight the country in which they live and curse it in proportion to their numbers and success. Neither can they have an equal enjoyment in the acquisition with those of more honest and useful purpose. Their fame is the fame of a *quack;* in success they excite a sneer, and in misfortune, or failure of their schemes, where is the sympathiser? "There goes to destruction an oppressor," catches the ear of a *falling* speculator. In the acquisition of national wealth, whatever is based on selfish principles has too a wrong foundation and finally falls. The idea of one nation making money or property out of another without giving a suitable return is the unprincipled conceit of a little politician. Men of like minds frequently fancy themselves wiser than other people, more cunning, and they are generally caught in playing some mean trick in which they gain nothing but contempt. The politician who should gravely propose measures based on selfishness disgraces his country and gains *nothing* in the end but the reputation of a swindler; and if he succeeds for a time, he acquires for the country in whose name he has acted a disrespectful *sobriquet* and a reputation which awakens in a foreigner the feelings that he is transacting business with a sharper, a *yankee;* for one man is as wise as another, and he who is cheated once does not trust the party a second time. Political economy shows the means of honorably acquiring national wealth; it shows the resources of a nation, and its exercise is compatible with the well being of every other country; for national industry, while it enriches the natives, affords also, by its surplus produce, the means of importation; a profitable foreign trade, such as the Dutch once carried on, does the same; while to avail ourselves of the natural advantages of mines, fisheries, etc., effects the same object; *enough* is used, and the surplus given to foreigners for an equivalent satisfactory to both parties.

There is a branch of political economy merging indeed into government which has not received the attention it ought by economists; while sectarians, by their want of judgment and injudicious zeal, have placed the subject in an unenviable light. We refer to the Community System, which as a source of national wealth deserves our consideration, and as a means of happiness or the abatement of misery to some classes deserves additional attention. All we have to do at present, however, is to separate between the merely theoretical and untried parts of the system and which require a subversion of human nature or self interest, as now exhibited, and that which is practicable, has been tried, and found to answer; we may leave the theoretical parts for the future experiments of associated individuals who have confidence in the principles, while we avail ourselves of those portions which have been tried and found to succeed, and which is compatible with human nature as we now find it, and which is of immense national advantage both in saving and husbanding the wealth of the country and in an equal proportion advancing its happiness.

It was shown many years ago at New Lanark, by Mr. R. Owen that children in association, from eight years of age and upwards, could earn their own living, be highly educated, and enjoy abundance of time for infantile and useful sports, so necessary to cheerfulness and the proper and healthy development of the faculties both of body and mind. What then prevents a nation taking charge of the whole of the destitute and degraded children and by a proper cultivation of their feelings, as well as their understandings and bodily faculties, making of them a class equal to the *very best citizens?* The ancient Spartans valued themselves on their *public* education, and where were there more honorable or devoted citizens according to the prevailing opinions of those times? The effect of such a measure would be to remove pauperism and crime from those who are now *doomed* to it by being born in poverty, crime, and misery, to which alone they seem heirs, by their present mode of bringing up. This disposition of the destitute children would, too, stimulate private citizens, academies, and colleges, for if the poorest and most degraded were made *happy*, industrious, intelligent, and learned in all that was useful and even ornamental, private citizens must at least keep pace with them, and the whole nation would receive a vastly civilizing impulse.

Again, a successful experiment was made in Holland of giving to a company of poor destitute families a quantity of waste land, which land was too poor to be valued or purchased for cultivation. The government furnished the company with instruments, and till a scanty crop could be raised, with rations; they built each other *huts*, and as the land was *their own*, they applied *extra* labor; they kept pigs at first, and afterwards cows, and carefully preserved and applied all the manure they could collect, till this barren spot became well cultivated fields, and the huts gave way to cottages; and the nation was relieved from a mass of paupers, who merely wanted a small capital and union, and the meager gift of *poor* land, to emerge from their poverty. It is clear that while they were all destitute, their poverty contributed to their union, and while they wanted the necessaries and comforts of life, their own interest and that of the community was one. Whether they have now divided the property or continue in community, we have never learned; but the success was complete, as far as the fact that after the first year they were no longer a burden to the government. Now this experiment shows clearly that a government can provide for the whole of the poor, especially where they have good land instead of poor land to bestow, and whether they continue in community or afterwards quarrel and divide when they have property to quarrel about will not affect the question; the nation is relieved and the families made good citizens by industry. An industrial school would require a superintendent, and a poor community, while needing the assistance and using the property of the nation, would also require a governor, whose authority should cease with the rations, for each family would then have property in a hut and cultivated grounds to defend, and might therefore be trusted with the simple instruments of cultivation. It is clear that political economy may be enlarged to embrace these practical portions of the community system by which national savings are made and property created.

. . . .

[Of Wealth]

Political economy treats of Wealth, its source, means of increase, its distribution and ultimate object. As a science, it is intimately connected with politics; it was perhaps the original cause of government, and now the subject of the greatest number of laws. Its principles, like those of every science, are to be discovered, not created; they exist in the nature of man as a social being, and will necessarily overcome all laws opposed to them, but may be nourished and assisted by judicious legislation or impeded by the harassing measures of ignorance, either in law makers or in the people exercising an influence over them. As a proof of this statement, we may observe that the Spanish Government, ignorantly confounding money with wealth, conceived that a country would be the richer and more powerful the more money it had; it therefore, while it was importing large quantities of silver from its colonies in South America, and from that silver making coin, passed laws prohibiting the exportation of its precious metals; yet in defiance of those laws the Spanish dollars spread over the whole world and became the common money medium of foreign commerce; Spain did not grow rich, was not powerful, and the laws were evaded; nay, so striking were the effects of these ill conceived laws that, while Spain had yet her colonies, she was perhaps the poorest and weakest government in the world, with a most miserable population. The direct cause of this will appear when we come to speak of coin and currency. We proceed now to consider the nature of wealth.

Of Wealth. — What is wealth? Fifty different answers may be given, notwithstanding the apparent simplicity of the question. The difficulty consists in being able to give one that is free from objections, and to this we shall not pretend. The answer we select as subject to least objection is this: *Wealth is the produce of Labor.* This is not true when the produce is of no utility, yielding neither pleasure nor profit, but such labor will always be discontinued. It is not strictly true of Land yielding herbage and fruits spontaneously, but the difference between the product of cultivated and uncultivated land is so great as to render the small produce of the latter scarcely an exception, especially when we consider that some labor is necessary to gather the fruits and enclose the pasturage. With these and some other trifling exceptions, we shall find the definition is good which we shall now endeavor to illustrate.

In the earliest stages of society, the hunter must obtain his bow and arrows and the fisherman his implements by direct labor, and this is the first species of property or wealth; the former obtains his food and clothing from the animals he catches by the labor of pursuit, and this is all his wealth. If now the hunter should come in contact with civilized man, and should desire a rifle, it is clear that he can obtain it only by increased labor, or by procuring skins, that is, by killing more animals than he otherwise needed. Thus the rifle is property, and is the produce of labor to the hunter, to the person who previously possessed it, if he gave an equivalent for it, as well as the original maker. We shall not pursue the consequences of this transaction of the hunter any further for the present, for it is now evident that the hunter possesses the means of increasing his wealth, and this would lead us to the consideration of what is called capital employed in implements, while the exchange of skins for the rifle would lead us to consider the nature of trade in reference to wealth. These we leave as distinct parts. In examining any other species of property, you will find it to consist substantially in the produce of labor.

We will proceed to one or two objections.

Land has been stated to be wealth, but all its value, with the exception before made, is derived from cultivation, and if it yields large rent as in old countries, it does so by the superior state of its cultivation in comparison to that which merely yields a bare remuneration for labor.

The precious metals, as *coin*, are not wealth, but the medium of exchange; if a tailor sells clothes and buys shoes, he might as well exchange clothes for shoes, but for the conveniency of the medium which enables him to sell to one man and buy of another. Money, as coin, serves no other use; you neither eat, drink, nor wear it; indeed you put it to no other use; and if money is forced into circulation beyond the natural demand as a medium, it immediately sinks below the intrinsic value of the metal, and then leaves the country in spite of laws, or is thrown into the melting pot, as was done in Spain.

The Object of Wealth

Before we enquire into the laws of its increase and decrease, we shall first ascertain its object. This may briefly be stated to be in its consummation or enjoyment. The object then of political economy is to produce the greatest quantity of happiness which can flow from wealth. This object is not however obtained by two classes, both extremely eager. They who from a fear of want never enjoy the present; and they who so enjoy the present as to deprive themselves of future supplies. In the middle path lies our happiness.

The man who would enjoy wealth to the greatest extent will have two rational objects: one, to render his enjoyment permanent; the other, to enlarge his sphere; for no man is comfortable in feasting today with the prospect of fasting tomorrow; and the ingenuity of the human mind will always discover some rational want which it desires to have gratified. Philosophy in the use of wealth consists then in the enjoyment of the present, the perpetuation of that enjoyment, and in obtaining others which may be desirable; and if we include among our joys the luxury of doing good, we know no quantity of wealth that may not be disposed of.

The cause of poverty, except from malgovernment, is generally the immediate consumption of all that is procured by labor. Thus the laborer and the mechanic, who procure no more than they consume or consume as much as they procure, frequently suffer extreme distress, and the least interruption in their income, which will necessarily arise, occasionally involves them in difficulties. It is then necessary to perpetuate enjoyments, to spare something from the present, which savings form capital which may be applied either to increase wealth or as a fund for future necessities. We shall afterwards find that all capital arises from savings.

To be rich is merely to live below your income, and this pursued through a long life, without much energy, talent, or ingenuity, generally succeeds; but the object thus obtained is a misery, and aside from the wiser object of political economy, viz., the enjoyment of wealth. To extend this enjoyment, it is, however, necessary to make savings of a very considerable proportion to your income, which savings must be employed as a capital to increase wealth; and persons not accustomed to think on the subject will really be much surprised at the immense sums appropriated to this purpose. Mere industry will do but little in the increase of wealth, without the assistance of capital or savings. In vain would the farmer rise early and spend the day in labor without good *instruments* of husbandry: oxen or horses to assist in working them, or machinery to aid his exertions; but instruments, horses, and machinery must be procured by capital or savings. The mechanic, too, wants his instruments and his materials to work on, without which he cannot even make a beginning; and unless he can make savings to procure these, he must remain a journeyman and perhaps poor all his life. Thus to obtain the greatest happiness from wealth, we must make judicious savings to be employed as capital to perpetuate that happiness and to increase its sphere.

THE MEANS OF ACQUIRING WEALTH

The wealth of a nation is made up of the wealth of the individuals composing that nation; the increase of an individual's wealth is, therefore, a national benefit, provided such increase is not made at the expense of other individuals. There are three principal sources of wealth: Agriculture, Manufacture, and Commerce. I shall not enquire which of these is of the most importance, because I think them all of importance, and varying in different countries; nor do I see that there need be conflicting interests. There is a point in every country to which each may be carried with success, at which point they will assist each other; and this will be obtained generally better without legislation than with it.

Leave us alone is, generally speaking, the language of the merchant, the manufacturer, and the farmer; or, at least, do no more than remove impediments.

Superabundant produce becomes wealth only in proportion as it is exchangeable; thus, if a farmer raises more stock or grows more grain than his family can consume, the surplus is of no value, but as it will exchange; and if he is so situated that he can make no exchange, he is usually extremely poor; he is under the necessity of making his own garments and constructing his own utensils, and these he makes badly, at a great loss of time. In fact, in such a situation he is but one step removed from the uncivilized savage. His comforts or wealth begin when he can exchange his surplus produce with the blacksmith, the shoemaker, the storekeeper, the housecarpenter, the millwright, etc., to which we may perhaps paradoxically add the physician, the lawyer, and the parson. Thus it would appear that the farmer's happiness or enjoyment of wealth is intimately connected with manufacturers and traders. It must be equally evident that the manufacturer and storekeeper must be in part dependent on the farmer; I say in part, because in cities which have foreign trade, the manufacturer and storekeeper could do without the farmer, as they have done partly in Holland.

We shall now notice the part the manufacturer and storekeeper take in exchange, by which we may ascertain the point at which they and the farmer mutually assist each other. The manufacturer supplies the farmer, the storekeeper, and other manufacturers with what he makes, and receives in return, provisions, raw materials, and the manufactured goods of others. The storekeeper supplying whatever the farmer and neighboring manufacturers could not. The storekeeper's part then, is already expressed, viz., to supply all deficiencies. By his exertions the farmer and the manufacturer obtain materials, necessaries, and luxuries, at a much less expense than they could otherwise obtain them. While therefore the storekeeper obtains wealth by his profits he distributes the means of happiness around *him*, and if not a producer, is the cause of very considerable production; thus, the farmer would not grow a surplus if he had no means of disposing of it, but finding he can procure the means of increased happiness, at a moderate expense, by exchange with the storekeeper, he produces for that purpose, and thus the storekeeper is a party in causing production. In the same manner he causes production in manufactured goods, by facilitating the sale. Before an article can be consumed, the raw material must be procured, it must be manufactured, and a customer must be found. If the manufacturer had to seek his materials and each consumer, he must sell dear to cover the expenses; and if the consumer had to seek a manufacturer upon every purchase, he would go without many things and suffer the loss of time on the purchase of others.

PRODUCERS AND CONSUMERS OF WEALTH

All men are necessarily consumers of wealth, and most men producers. The object of this essay will be to point out the distinctions. The farmer and mechanic are direct producers of wealth, and the storekeeper, by rendering services to both, causes the production of wealth. We shall now examine the claims of the physician, the lawyer, and the parson, who have no existence in the patriarchal state of society. In order to get rid of a great deal of matter, not necessarily connected with political economy, we assume, and we think the assumption will be granted, that the services of the above classes are *desired* by those who employ them; and then it will be found that they cause the production of wealth nearly in the same manner as the storekeeper. Thus the prudent farmer grows enough to pay his family physician, his lawyer, and his parson, if he need them. The mechanic produces more, for the same purpose, than he otherwise would do. Thus these classes are the immediate cause of a production equal to their consumption; and if in addition to their immediate services, they make for, and communicate to the public, *useful* discoveries in physics, legislation, or divinity, so that they add to the enjoyments of life or decrease its evils, they substantially and permanently cause an increase in national wealth, which consists in everything from which we derive enjoyments.

With the physician, the lawyer, and the clergy, as it regards political economy, we must place the musician, the dancing master, the actor, and indeed all whose services are *desired*, and for which the other classes are willing to pay. They are all the cause of production equal to their own consumption and frequently far beyond it, as it is manifested by the fortunes which some of these individuals accumulate; and if the mechanics can be induced to work harder, that is, to produce more, for the pleasure of seeing a Kean, in all his favorite characters, both Kean and the public are benefited by the expenditure. If, however, the mechanic make the expenditure without producing more than his usual quantity, it is clear that he must forego some other enjoyment, and then there is no increase of wealth, but a mere transfer.

We now come to speak of mere consumers. Among these may be classed: An established clergy, a standing army, pensioners, unnecessary place men, gamblers and cheats, in fact all whose services are *not desired* but who, nevertheless, derive their support from the public; if these grow rich, others must grow poor or work for their support without receiving an equivalent. If therefore public money is paid for services desired by a part of the people only, the rest are robbed to the amount of their proportion. There is an error upon this subject which supposes that all who grow rich, who are not producers in the direct form, necessarily do so at the expense of others; the reverse is frequently true. The merchant who buys of the manufacturer, benefits him to the extent of his profits, especially if the merchant has discovered a new vent for that particular kind of goods. He benefits those to whom he sells, because they give him in exchange what they value less. A successful merchant will frequently make a large fortune with very small profits, merely by the extent of his business. The difference is that the laboring mechanic cannot add much to his income by mere increase of labor, but the merchant may increase his trade without a proportionate increase of personal labor. The merchant who collects skins from the Indians and gives them in exchange manufactured goods may very fairly get rich himself upon small profits and enrich those to whom he sells and from whom he buys merely by the extent of his transactions.

LABOR, THE DEMAND FOR IT, AND ITS PRICE

By labor we mean employment of every kind, from the most refined to the coarsest. We shall first consider its price, as it will be a natural introduction to its demand, and a subject not yet generally understood, or there would not be attempts to regulate the price of labor by legislation, which always proves abortive. Riots would never have occurred upon that subject if the parties had been acquainted with the fact that wages will always be in proportion to the demand for labor, and that that demand is always in proportion to the progress of national wealth or general prosperity; for national wealth is the wealth of the individuals forming a nation. The price of labor will be high in times of prosperity, low in times of adversity, and stationary when the progress of wealth is stationary; in the spite of legislation to keep the prices low or combinations to make it high, although these measures may effect a temporary change.

If the demand for labor is great, no power on earth will make men work for low wages, and the only inducement employers can offer to get men to produce largely is high wages; yet high wages generally reduce the profits of employers, and do not always increase the price of the manufactured articles, because as the employer chiefly lives upon profits, he can afford to lessen them with the increase of his sales. As high wages are the only inducement to increased exertion on the part of the laborer when labor is in great demand, it is clear that he will obtain them in times of prosperity and that such increase of wages will not necessarily affect the price of the manufactured article but the profits of the employer.

If there is very little demand for labor, the competition among the laborers will necessarily reduce the price, as employers have a direct interest in employing those who will work for the least sum, their profits being in the inverse proportion to the price of labor; and taking human nature as it is, we find the mass of mankind governed by their interests; but if *some* only are influenced to employ cheap labor, these will gradually influence the rest, because employing cheaper labor than others, they can, if they choose, forego higher profits and under-sell those who pay more than themselves for labor. No combination of men will prevent a reduction of wages if labor is not in demand; for at that time employers are bent upon saving expenses, and they will employ more apprentices, women, or men drawn from other employments less profitable, or more disagreeable, or altogether suspend their work if necessary. By the concurrence of both employers and employed, in the times of adversity, an intermediate state has been introduced with partial success. The whole of the men have been employed for a *part* of the time in each week, at the fair or usual wages.

If it be a fact that wages depend upon supply and demand of labor, it becomes an interesting enquiry, "What regulates that?" and if the answer is that the demand is in proportion to the increase of national wealth or a general prosperity, then "What regulates that?" The increase of wealth is the increase of produce, affording comfort and gratifications. If a shoemaker introduce his shoes for the first time, and they become an object of general desire as affording increased comfort, all who desire to partake of them must produce something in exchange; for money is the mere medium of exchange or representative of produce; but this increased produce is wealth, and this produce is the reward of labor, and the cause of its demand; and one man employs another when he has the means of exchange. A merchant imports some new and desirable article or commodity; it is clear, to enjoy this the people must produce something more than usual for exchange; here again is an increase of produce or wealth, and this increase of produce gives employment, first in its own creation, and then as the wages for something else.

On the Increase of Wealth

A voluntary union of ten, a thousand, ten thousand, or as many millions of men forms a nation. By this union they give up a portion of their natural rights for acquisitions which they deem more valuable, viz., protection of person and property; and this security operates upon production, because none would labor beyond his immediate necessities if he could not enjoy his produce in security. There is scarcely any end to consumption, either of quantity or variety, and consequently there is abundant encouragement to production. Man can do with very little but his desires are boundless; to satisfy these desires he taxes both his invention and his exertions, and if he produces largely of what he cannot consume, he does it that he may obtain what he can consume, and this explains a maxim in political economy that *there cannot be a general glut of goods or productions*, or in other words, too much of everything, because whenever a man wants to sell anything, he does it that he may purchase something else of the same value.

The value of an article is the cost of production: that is, the value of the raw material added to the price of the labor; and this value necessarily limits the use of the article; if therefore the cost of production can be reduced, an extensive use of that article will necessarily follow; or in other words, produce or wealth will be increased. This reduction is first effected by a division of labor, and, again, by improved implements or machinery, and these are assisted by commerce, which introduces the best materials at the lowest price; or it imports instruments to facilitate agriculture or manufactures.

The advantage gained by division of labor is chiefly in saving time lost in the change from one employment to another and in the facility of performing any employment acquired by constant practice.

The advantage gained by improved instruments or machinery is only limited by the cost of such implements; thus, a machine doing the work of ten men, which would be worn out in a year, would be no gain, if it cost the wages of ten men for the same period. The gradual and general introduction of improved implements and machinery must be a general good, because a greater produce would be obtained for the community; and the cost of production being less, the price of the produce would be decreased, and its increased consumption insured; but if the improvement in implements and machinery is rapid and partial in their application from their great cost, or any other cause, the public will be generally benefited and individuals greatly so, but at the expense of other individuals; for those who cannot procure the improved instruments or machinery will suffer the loss of their business which will be gained by those who can employ the less expensive mode of production. A remedy for this inconvenience might be found in the combination of the poorer classes of workmen in order to procure implements or machinery for their own benefit; but as machinery increases production, that is, forms wealth, if it be not a national benefit the fault is in the government.

Commerce is necessarily connected with manufactures. It equalizes the produce of the world by transporting the surplus of one part to another where it is wanted, and bringing back something useful in exchange. Commerce is in fact an extension of the principle of the division of labor, and the profits which it affords is the remuneration for the labor of transporting the objects of commerce to the consumers. The whole value of an article sometimes consists in this, as lumber transported from the waters of America to Italy, which has been frequently done by some of our friends *down East*.

It is evident that there may be a *general* increase of wealth if no obstructions are placed in the way of an industrious people, and that an individual may benefit the community and himself by introducing an improvement that shall lessen the cost of production or by discovering a new source of commerce.

.   .   .   .

FACTS IN RELATION TO MACHINERY MANUFACTURES AND TRADE

Machinery.— We have no interest, except that which is common to all the citizens, either in the question of machinery or commerce, to which latter we shall soon have to refer, as the one we have now taken up will necessarily lead to the other. The errors of men very frequently arise from their coming to conclusions at a jump, without a knowledge of existing facts, and a series of fair reasoning on those facts. Facts must be the foundation of reasoning, and from just reasoning on these alone can we arrive at sound conclusions.

.   .   .   .

Effects of Obstructing Machinery.— If a method is discovered of abridging the labor in any manufacture, the workmen in this trade immediately raise their voices against it; but they should recollect that if they do really prevent persons in their immediate neighborhood from using it, they cannot exercise a similar control over those that live at a distance, who will, undoubtedly, bring it into operation, and thus undersell their work, which is produced without the assistance of the improved processes and consequently considerably dearer. . . . .

But perhaps it may be asked would not you consider it a great evil if, in a large manufacturing town, two-thirds of the population should be suddenly bereft of work and left to shift for themselves? I answer undoubtedly it would; indeed so great as almost to overbalance the good which might hereafter result from the change, but such could not *possibly* happen; persons are too much attached to old methods, too unwilling to relinquish the course they have been accustomed to, to permit us to entertain the idea that a body of men would *suddenly* make such a change in their established practices as to discharge two-thirds of their workmen, even on the fairest prospect of advantage. The change, if it take place at all, must be gradual, and indeed so gradual as entirely to remove those inconveniences which sudden innovation would produce; prejudice opposes it; and here, prejudice, so much vilified, has its advantages, since the struggle which it creates leads, in the end, to a dispassionate spirit of inquiry, which rejects all the hare-brained schemes which ignorance and folly daily beget, which separates the metal from the dross and admits no novel contrivances as substitutes for the ancient but whose utility have been sanctioned by experiments, and their superiority over the old, incontestably demonstrated.

Effects of Machinery upon National Wealth

Machinery is never introduced into any manufacture but to effect work better, quicker, or cheaper, than by the labor of the hands only, but the produce of labor is wealth; the produce of machinery is, therefore, wealth too; for upon that supposition only is machinery used. Machinery can then be called contrivances to make property. The direct consequence of goods being made cheaper, better, or quicker is an increased consumption, but what is the meaning of an increased consumption but either the same individuals use more of the same articles or that the article upon which machinery has been employed become common to a larger portion of the people; that is, property which machinery has made cheap comes within the use of a large and increasing number of persons. Where machinery is not used, the inhabitants want the comforts and elegancies of life, and the mass of them necessarily remain in an uncivilized or barbarous state; for nearly the whole of every individual's time must be occupied with procuring and preparing the most common necessaries of life. Go back to the time when corn was ground between two small stones, the one concave, and the other convex, where one woman was engaged in putting corn into the concave, and another rubbing round the convex stone. What must be the state of society when time was thus employed, and when the other arts, which have properly been called the civilizing arts, were equally at a low ebb. History, but especially old tales, songs, law, and other records, informs us: huts without boarded floors or chimneys supplied the place of houses; and skins or coarse cloth, loosely hung about the body, were substitutes for beautiful broadcloth and a neat fit from a scientific tailor. Or if we go into the boyhood of the arts, when machinery was used, as some people think it ought to be, a *little*, and which happened, almost, within our memory, what do we find? Why men with leather breeches which would serve in duration father and son, *hung* upon the hips, with upper garments of any shape, coarse worsted stockings, knit at an immense loss of time, and heavy shoes, which gradually drew the calves of the legs within them; women clothed in woollen in one uniform garb, with house and household furniture equally plain, and intelligence on a par with their garb and furniture; then was the reign of witchcraft, charms, ghosts, goblins, superstitions, all of which have fled before the civilizing arts, chiefly aided by machinery. Instead of which, what do we find? The actual laboring people decreased in number, and all better clothed, fed, and educated than before, excepting where other counteracting causes prevailed, to induce poverty, etc., as *excessive taxation* in England. The same with absenteeism and the support of *two* churches in Ireland, etc.

We are levellers, agrarians, or anything else that means the same thing; but then we are disposed to level *upwards*, not downwards. We should be glad to see machinery do all the work, which is not necessary for health of body and mind. We should be glad to see universal abundance and the civilizing arts, and every man a philosopher in mind, a gentleman in purpose, and a workingman in body, without his ill shape, rude habits, and limited information, generally the effect of bad education, bad habits, or bad government, and which the *civilizing* arts chiefly impelled by machinery are great means of correcting.

Objections to Machinery Considered

[The first Objection:] *Machinery reduces wages, throws men out of employ, and buries children alive in factories.*— It does all this, some part unnecessarily, the rest a necessary evil, accompanying a greater good. Machinery reduces wages till the manual artisans have died off or changed their employment; this is usually done gradually; while the machinery is arriving at perfection, those employed in making the machine and in superintending its operation are as well paid at least as formerly, and much more rationally employed than in doing the work of a machine, by which the man is levelled with a mere brute or inanimate piece of workmanship. We do not think the firemen of New York would be less useful if their engines were drawn or driven by horses or steam. The same cause which reduces wages at first throws men out of employ, but when the machinery is fairly established we believe in *every case* it puts into employment a greater number of persons than it ever throws out; this we know to be the case in the manufacture of cotton, china, porcelain, silk, and many iron works, and printing (since stereotyping was introduced) etc., indeed in *all* cases we have had an opportunity of examining, and of those also where we have been enabled to catechise others in relation to their particular trades. As to the employment of children, we recommend industrial schools, where they may spend pleasantly and profitably a few hours in work, a few in study, and a few in open air juvenile sports. This subject is no longer one of theory; it has been tested by experiment, and proved that *four* hours judicious labor of a child is sufficient to support it. Were the government to erect industrial schools, the employment of children in future for thirteen hours a day would cease, or legislative measures should attempt the correction of so great an evil; we say attempt, for direct acts, which oppose the interests of manufacturers and the parents of the children, would probably fail.

Objection the second: *Machinery will produce too much of everything.* — Every political economist will at once perceive that this is the objection of ignorance, that amongst men who understood the subject, the fact is indisputable that *too much of everything will not and cannot exist.* The objection is, however, repeatedly urged, and that in public, with assurance, and therefore demands attention, though we deprecate the practice of those men who, through ignorance, oblige their opponents first to teach them a science before they can convince them of their errors. There cannot be too much of everything, because no man produces an article which he does not wish, and is willing to exchange for something else produced by another of the same value, or whose cost of production is the same. Now as this is universally the case, as everybody is willing to exchange what he has produced, it follows that there cannot be too much of everything. If too much of any one thing is produced it will not exchange for its ordinary value, and then the producer will cease his operation or produce something else. There will be some danger of producing too much when men have *enough;* we have never yet met with one man who had enough; indeed enough means as in the Scotchman's prayer, a little more than we have. It is clear that as there is *no limit* to expenditure, there can be no having enough; we might be content with a biscuit, a glass of water, homespun, and independence, but we could very well spend any amount.

Objection the third: *Expensive machinery requires large capitals; men of small capitals cannot therefore compete with men of large capitals; the little man is therefore crushed by the larger.*— We know that big fishes will eat little ones, but we know also that the big fish is sometimes caught in the meshes of a net which will allow the little ones to pass through. No arrangement will prevent all the advantages of capital over those who have none, or of great capitals over those who have small ones, though a combination of small capitals *might* (we say might, for we are doubtful of the result, excepting for short periods) compete with a large one. The evil, however, will be remedied by the *improvement and simplification of machinery,* and subdivisions of manufactures. Thus in the business of printing, the invention of stereotyping has led to a new business, and therefore lessened the amount of capital required by the printer. In the same business the introduction of power presses has led to a new business, and the printer can now do without a press and get his work done cheaper and more expeditiously by those who keep a power press and work for the public than he could do it. In this way are nearly all the newspapers worked in cities; and thus the printer, and especially newspaper printers, employ less capital than formerly by the introduction of an expensive machine. In the case of mills of every description this is strikingly the case. The first man who possessed a flour mill must have an advantage over every other and appear to impose the expense of a mill on every farmer, but the desire of every one to have a mill suggested the advantage to some capitalists to build one for the public. So of a saw mill and perhaps of every other. The improvement of machinery then and the introduction of expensive machinery, too, in its course serves to subdivide business and consequently to divide capital.

FOREIGN TRADE FURTHER CONSIDERED

Foreign trade differs but little from domestic trade; and domestic trade but little from individual traffic. All trade consists in mutual advantage; each gives what he values less for what he values most. Individuals and communities necessarily find out their own interest, and political legislation has generally proved abortive. The question in this country has generally been discussed more with party feelings and local interests than with philosophical acumen.

. . . .

In individual exchange, if one man puts a high price on his goods the other may do the same; but not so in national commerce, or foreign trade; for those who buy do it where they can get the articles the cheapest and the best. In foreign trade no price is fixed by the merchant, who sends his goods at his own risk; but it is sold at the market price, whether he gain enormously or lose, as from experience it is found that no loss can equal that of bringing back goods sent out for sale.

The Balance in Trade.— The difference between the whole amount of the invoices of goods imported and exported is called the balance in trade, and this balance is sometimes remitted in cash; but when the difference is considerable, it causes increased demand for bills of exchange on that country which has most to receive, and this increased demand gives rise to a premium on them which increases with their scarcity. The amount of this premium, while below a given sum, shows the state of trade; and gives to statesmen and politicians a very correct knowledge of the relative value of the exports and imports of the merchants; but after the premium rises to a sum equal to the expense and risk of sending cash, cash will be sent to save the premium. Writers on political economy formerly gave a very improper importance to this balance as if it were of very great consequence that a nation should have the balance in its favor. We shall examine this subject. If the balance is in favor of one country, the exchange is also in its favor, and against the other country or their customers; the consequence is that the one orders less goods who pays the premium, for his profits are lessened, which always discourages trade; and the other nation orders more, because he receives the premium; and in this way the balance of trade is frequently restored, after a short interruption with very little profit on the one side or disadvantage on the other, and in which the bill broker is often the most interested; but if the balance should be paid in cash, this will scarcely injure one nation nor benefit the other; for if a nation receives more cash than it wants for circulation and uses it as money, it depreciates a little its own circulation (see a late number on this subject) and if it export the money again for other goods, it is no better off than if it had imported goods at first instead of cash. The nation too which pays the balance is not *impoverished*, because it has given cash for what it *valued more* than cash. If by exporting the coin a deficiency can be made up precisely as any other deficiency is made up, that is by sending for bullion to those countries which have gold or silver mines, where produce or manufactures of some kind must be sent in payment, because none will exchange gold for gold, or silver for silver.

Thus in *all* cases a nation *must* have the sum of her imports nearly equal to that of her exports and the contra.

It is by *importations* that a nation is enriched. The Connecticut captain of a small vessel who took out lumber to Italy, and brought back fruit, straw hats, etc., much more valuable than lumber, enriched his country by what he brought, not by what he gave. In all other cases of commerce the same thing occurs; something of little value is given, and something more desirable is obtained; and the benefit is precisely the same whether the commerce is carried on by those at a distance, or those near, friends or foes. A general advantage arises from a free trade throughout these States, and the same advantage would exist if the states were separated, but continued to traffic; yet should such an event ever happen, the old women, or our imbecile legislators, would instantly begin to form a *tariff* for each state, and foolishly think to benefit one at the expense of another; in fact legislative interference in general may do a great deal of mischief and very little good, excepting in a few cases, and some such may exist in the United States.

. . . .

An Error in Legislation

There is something very discouraging to the political philanthropist in the fact that generations have passed away one after another without establishing *truths* known to many in each generation. A man may leave his property to his successors, but he cannot his information, and the most valuable truths are suffered to die, and are again eternally brought forward as something *new*, when they are really old, and ought to have been acted upon, successively, since the first formation of society.

The truths we refer to are that political society is, or ought to be, a *voluntary association for mutual protection*, for the good of the whole; and that all legislation should be upon those subjects, in which they have a common interest. The object then of legislation should be the protection of the *natural rights* of a man, as far as those rights do not interfere with the *natural rights* of other men. These principles appear self evident, and so we think they did to some of our forefathers several thousand years ago. But are they established? Do the history of nations and the records of legislation show that these principles have been well understood, and uniformly acted upon? Would not these principles lead generally to a *negative,* rather than to a positive legislation? Would not laws be prohibitory of individuals invading the natural rights of others, and would they not impose penalties on such violations? Yet investigation upon this subject brings to light a long list of facts in direct opposition to these principles, and even other principles are set up in violation of these; both cannot be correct. We find it gravely asserted, and almost uniformly acted upon, that the *majority should govern the minority;* and this is the key to all the miserable legislation in the world, and the foundation of most of the evils; this is the father of the religious and political persecutions, and the grand impediment to improvement. We have before published some such sentiments as these, and we may again do so; the subject is too important and too much neglected to render repetition a fault.

What is this governing majority but a subversion of all justice; the uprooting of the very foundation of political society, and establishing *club law,* with the sanction of forms. What need of written laws at all, if a majority is the rule and questions affecting partial interest be decided by numbers. What matters it to the sufferer whether he is persecuted *according* to law or *contrary* to law? Look the monster full in the face, and we shall see the evil it inflicts on society. Admit the right of legislators to legislate upon *any* subject and to decide by a *majority,* then *any* religious body which could obtain a majority could and would oppress the rest, and persecute *according to law.* And this object has been attempted by a union of the self-styled orthodox parties.[2] To a division of sects do we now evidently owe our religious liberty, and not to sound principles of politics or morals. To the curse of assuming the right of a majority to legislate for a minority do we owe the blundering upon the Tariff question. To this doctrine do we owe the electioneering trickery, each party attempting to get a majority, in order to control or mold society to *its standard;* but what is to be done, will some ask, who have read too fast. Why, *deny the right of legislating at all* upon such subjects in which a common interest does not exist, or in which one party goes beyond the defense of their own *natural rights* and invades the *natural rights* of another; or if necessary, let each individual systematically break or

[2][The reference here is to an unsuccessful attempt led by the Rev. Ezra Stiles Ely of Philadelphia to promote a union of orthodox sects under the name of the "Christian Party in Politics."]

disregard laws thus oppressive. There is more *honor in the breach than the observance of such laws*, and an appeal to the *constitution* will in these states generally support the resistance.

Agrarianism.— It appears to us that the above reasoning applies to agrarianism in every form; that it requires legislation on subjects about which nobody on earth has a right to legislate. We are agrarians if by that is meant the removal of all partial laws which *bestow privileges or deny rights* to one man which another enjoys; but every kind of agrarianism which we have known goes beyond this and, we think, invades the rights of others. The modified agrarianism was advocated in New York, and as set forth in Skidmore's *Rights of Man to Property*, is not exempt from this charge.

First, it advocates an actual division of property.

Secondly, to avoid a recurrence to such violence, it recommends securing personal acquisitions to the acquirer, but making the state the heir to all such acquired property.

.   .   .   .

As to the notion of the state becoming the heir of every man's property and doling out proportional parts to each individual as he becomes of age, we must say we have the same objection to it; it is giving to the state, to governors or to legislators, what never ought to belong to them. This scheme, to which we know the author attached the greatest importance, we consider as one of the wildest schemes that ever entered the brain of man; and the only thing that can be said in its favor is that it has never been tried. The legitimate object of legislators and governors is to *protect* the natural rights of man, and not to take the control of the property of society. The scheme appears big with mischief in every way we can conceive of it and calculated to raise up a set of men to *dispense* the public property instead of *adding* to public wealth. It would probably be abused, as all almoners of long standing that we ever heard of ever did abuse their trust. It would defeat itself, for many would not accumulate for the *public*, and others would dispose of their accumulation *just before death*, as is now done in England merely to avoid a tax. It would thus in one case prevent the growth of wealth, and in the other, cause secret hoards; and then would come *penalties*, and these could be but partially enforced; and if vigorously enforced on one side and resisted on the other, suffering and persecution, *according to law*, would be the consequence; and the whole arising from a *majority* assuming to rule a minority; instead of a government confining itself to its legitimate object, that of protecting the rights of every individual. In point of experience it is found that individuals do that best and cheapest which they are capable of doing at all; but this scheme would take from man the principal excitement to well being and well doing. The scheme would require violence *according to law* to put it into order, and would be out of joint at the end of every week after its commencement, and never in joint after a three months trial, because it would have to contend against the nature of man in social life which moves easier when left alone, and the best aid that can be given to it is to remove obstructions of every kind; society is harassed and vexed by too much legislation.

THE COMMUNITY SYSTEM *vs.* THE COMPETITION SYSTEM

The community system combining common property, equal rights, and mutual labor under the direction of elected officers, according to rules made or agreed to by the whole community, has never been tried, that we know of, on an extended scale. Some one has always appeared in the character of a *Dictator*, which adds to the facility, harmony, and prosperity of such a society, but it violates equal rights, and is a foundation on which despotism, tyranny, and fraud will *necessarily* be built, and the community either destroyed or turned to private benefit. Such a community will have abundance of the physical comforts of life; such comforts have Rapp's community, and the Shaking Quakers, except in the case of matrimony, on which subject the rulers have imposed a painful and unnatural restraint. Abundance without such restraint would no doubt follow Mr. Owen's plan, but Mr. Owen is a dictator, and that will succeed under his immediate direction which might, nay, has failed in other hands; any plan which denies individual property and demands continued common services must restrain individual liberty, and fail to bring out talents, energies, and virtues peculiar to a competitive state.

A community of equal rights where officers are elected and where no dictators exist will necessarily be divided into factions, as other societies similarly governed are; and when employment is dictated, genius will frequently be overlooked, and not properly estimated, for genius is not always observed on the surface, and generally brings itself out, in spite of family, friends, and early failures; as did Demosthenes, Patrick Henry, Kean, Arkwright, Belzoni, and all the eminent men in the American and French Revolutions.

A community system offers comfortable maintenance for moderate labor, care in sickness, a liberal education, equality (except from cliques, intrigue, etc.), and thus removes anxiety; and it offers a splendid public establishment, assembly rooms, public conveniences etc.; and, applied to the English laborer, in his present circumstances, would be a moral and humane relief.

The drawbacks are a temptation to apathy, divisions, intrigue, and supposed neglect, common to all societies with a restraint on personal liberty, *unbearable* to thousands who always go straight when left alone, but are uneasy in harness, and who, following a feeling *natural* to sheep and some men, leap a barrier merely to indulge their love of liberty, and the wisest men are directed by their judgments and *feelings;* the latter, an instinct less liable to err than reason, subject to various influences.

Now, a *good* government will secure all the above advantages, encourage genius, and preserve individual liberty; for it will *comfortably* maintain its poor, the aged, and the sick in need; an ample provision will be made for education; and the children whose parents cannot or will not provide and educate them will be made the children of the State; liberally educated, and taught agriculture, mechanism, with the arts and sciences, including even the rudiments of the *fine arts*, so that to be a child of the State should be a recommendation. A good government, by equal laws and favoring the distribution of wealth, will promote industry, and, by judicious laws, the harassing credit system might be destroyed; and the *one price* cash system can at any time become popular, for it is safe for an individual, or for numbers to try, as in Turkey; and then the worst feature in the competitive system is destroyed, and a liberal self-interest shown to be a social virtue; for "self-interest and social are the same." A *good* government, having the authority of a Dictator over the criminal, the idle, the unemployed and the destitute children, could to *advantage* apply the community system to them; while individuals in a free government, who imagine they could live in peace under the restraints of a community, can at any time so associate to their fancy, and might be happy; but to bring out the energies of a whole nation, requires the powerful motive of "self-interest," enlightened by a liberal education, which then becomes a national blessing and a source of individual and social happiness.

PART THREE

Social Criticism

18

GEORGE BANCROFT

THE OFFICE OF THE PEOPLE
IN ART, GOVERNMENT AND RELIGION[1]

[MAN'S PROGRESSIVE SPIRIT]

THE MATERIAL WORLD does not change in its masses or in its powers. The stars shine with no more lustre than when they first sang together in the glory of their birth. The flowers that gemmed the fields and the forests, before America was discovered, now bloom around us in their season. The sun that shone on Homer shines on us in unchanging lustre. The bow that beamed on the patriarch still glitters in the clouds. Nature is the same. For her no new forces are generated, no new capacities are discovered. The earth turns on its axis and perfects its revolutions and renews its seasons without increase or advancement.

But a like passive destiny does not attach to the inhabitants of the earth. For them the expectations of social improvement are no delusion; the hopes of philanthropy are more than a dream. The five senses do not constitute the whole inventory of our sources of knowledge. They are the organs by which thought connects itself with the external universe; but the power of thought is not merged in the exercise of its instruments. We have functions which connect us with heaven, as well as organs which set us in relation with earth. We have not merely the senses opening to us the external world, but an internal sense, which places us in connection with the world of intelligence and the decrees of God.

There is a *spirit in man* — not in the privileged few; not in those of us only who by the favor of Providence have been nursed in public schools. *It is in man;* it is the attribute of the race. The spirit, which is the guide to truth, is the gracious gift to each member of the human family.

[From *Literary and Historical Miscellanies* (New York, 1855), pp. 408–35 unabridged.]

Reason exists within every breast. I mean not that faculty which deduces inferences from the experience of the senses, but that higher faculty which from the infinite treasures of its own consciousness originates truth and assents to it by the force of intuitive evidence; that faculty which raises us beyond the control of time and space, and gives us faith in things eternal and invisible. There is not the difference between one mind and another which the pride of philosophers might conceive. To them no faculty is conceded which does not belong to the meanest of their countrymen. In them there can not spring up a truth which does not equally have its germ in every mind. They have not the power of creation; they can but reveal what God has implanted in every breast.

The intellectual functions, by which relations are perceived, are the common endowments of the race. The differences are apparent, not real. The eye in one person may be dull, in another quick, in one distorted, and in another tranquil and clear; yet the relation of the eye to light is in all men the same. Just so judgment may be liable in individual minds to the bias of passion, and yet its relation to truth is immutable and is universal.

In questions of practical duty, conscience is God's umpire, whose light illumines every heart. There is nothing in books which had not first and has not still its life within us. Religion itself is a dead letter wherever its truths are not renewed in the soul. Individual conscience may be corrupted by interest or debauched by pride, yet the rule of morality is distinctly marked. Its harmonies are to the mind like music to the ear; and the moral judgment, when carefully analyzed and referred to its principles, is always founded in right. The Eastern superstition which bids its victims prostrate themselves before the advancing car of their idols springs from a noble root and is but a melancholy perversion of that self-devotion which enables the Christian to bear the cross and subject his personal passions to the will of God. Immorality of itself never won to its support the inward voice; conscience, if questioned, never forgets to curse the guilty with the memory of sin, to cheer the upright with the meek tranquillity of approval. And this admirable power, which is the instinct of Deity, is the attribute of every man; it knocks at the palace gate; it dwells in the meanest hovel. Duty, like death, enters every abode and delivers its message. Conscience, like reason and judgment, is universal.

.   .   .   .

[RESPECT FOR MAN AS SUCH]

I speak for the universal diffusion of human powers, not of human attainments; for the capacity for progress, not for the perfection of undisciplined instincts. The fellowship which we should cherish with the race receives the Comanche warrior and the Kaffir within the pale of equality. Their functions may not have been exercised, but they exist. Immure a person in a dungeon; as he comes to the light of day, his vision seems incapable of performing its office. Does that destroy your conviction in the relation between the eye and light? The rioter over his cups resolves to eat and drink and be merry; he forgets his spiritual nature in his obedience to the senses. But does that destroy the relation between conscience and eternity? "What ransom shall we give?" exclaimed the senators of Rome to the savage Attila. "Give," said the barbarian, "all your gold and jewels, your costly furniture and treasures, and set free every slave." "Ah," replied the degenerate Romans, "what then will be left to us?" "I leave you your souls," replied the unlettered invader from the steppes of Asia, who had learnt in the wilderness to value the immortal mind, and to despise the servile herd that esteemed only their fortunes and had no true respect for themselves. You cannot discover a tribe of men, but you also find the charities of life and the proofs of spiritual existence. Behold the ignorant Algonquin deposit a bow and quiver by the side of the departed warrior, and recognize his faith in immortality. See the Comanche chieftain, in the heart of our continent, inflict on himself severest penance; and reverence his confession of the needed atonement for sin. The Barbarian who roams our Western prairies has like passions and like endowments with ourselves. He bears within him the instinct of Deity, the consciousness of a spiritual nature, the love of beauty, the rule of morality.

And shall we reverence the dark-skinned Kaffir? Shall we respect the brutal Hottentot? You may read the right answer written on every heart. It bids me not despise the sable hunter that gathers a livelihood in the forests of Southern Africa. All are men. When we know the Hottentot better, we shall despise him less.

[THE CERTAINTY OF POPULAR JUDGMENT]

If it be true that the gifts of mind and heart are universally diffused, if the sentiment of truth, justice, love, and beauty exists in every one then it follows, as a necessary consequence, that the common judgment in taste, politics, and religion is the highest authority on earth and the nearest possible approach to an infallible decision. From the consideration of individual powers I turn to the action of the human mind in masses.

If reason is a universal faculty, the universal decision is the nearest criterion of truth. The common mind winnows opinions; it is the sieve which separates error from certainty. The exercise by many of the same faculty on the same subject would naturally lead to the same conclusions. But if not, the very differences of opinion that arise prove the supreme judgment of the general mind. Truth is one. It never contradicts itself. One truth cannot contradict another truth. Hence truth is a bond of union. But error not only contradicts truth, but may contradict itself; so that there may be many errors, and each at variance with the rest. Truth is therefore of necessity an element of harmony; error as necessarily an element of discord. Thus there can be no continuing universal judgment but a right one. Men cannot agree in an absurdity; neither can they agree in a falsehood.

If wrong opinions have often been cherished by the masses, the cause always lies in the complexity of the ideas presented. Error finds its way into the soul of a nation only through the channel of truth. It is to a truth that men listen; and if they accept error also, it is only because the error is for the time so closely interwoven with the truth that the one cannot readily be separated from the other.

Unmixed error can have no existence in the public mind. Wherever you see men clustering together to form a party, you may be sure that however much error may be there truth is there also. Apply this principle boldly, for it contains a lesson of candor and a voice of encouragement. There never was a school of philosophy nor a clan in the realm of opinion but carried along with it some important truth. And therefore every sect that has ever flourished has benefited Humanity, for the errors of a sect pass away and are forgotten; its truths are received into the common inheritance. To know the seminal thought of every prophet and leader of a sect is to gather all the wisdom of mankind.

.   .   .   .

[GOVERNMENT OF THE PEOPLE GODLIKE]

In like manner the best government rests on the people and not on the few, on persons and not on property, on the free development of public opinion and not on authority; because the munificent Author of our being has conferred the gifts of mind upon every member of the human race without distinction of outward circumstances. Whatever of other possessions may be engrossed, mind asserts its own independence. Lands, estates, the produce of mines, the prolific abundance of the seas may be usurped by a privileged class. Avarice, assuming the form of ambitious power, may grasp realm after realm, subdue continents, compass the earth in its schemes of aggrandizement, and sigh after other worlds; but mind eludes the power of appropriation. It exists only in its own individuality; it is a property which cannot be confiscated and cannot be torn away; it laughs at chains; it bursts from imprisonment; it defies monopoly. A government of equal rights must, therefore, rest upon mind; not wealth, not brute force, the sum of the moral intelligence of the community should rule the State. Prescription can no more assume to be a valid plea for political injustice. Society studies to eradicate established abuses and to bring social institutions and laws into harmony with moral right, not dismayed by the natural and necessary imperfections of all human effort, and not giving way to despair, because every hope does not at once ripen into fruit.

The public happiness is the true object of legislation, and can be secured only by the masses of mankind themselves awakening to the knowledge and the care of their own interests. Our free institutions have reversed the false and ignoble distinctions between men; and refusing to gratify the pride of caste, have acknowledged the common mind to be the true material for a commonwealth. Everything has hitherto been done for the happy few. It is not possible to endow an aristocracy with greater benefits than they have already enjoyed; there is not room to hope that individuals will be more highly gifted or more fully developed than the greatest sages of past times. The world can advance only through the culture of the moral and intellectual powers of the people. To accomplish this end by means of the people themselves is the highest purpose of government. If it be the duty of the individual to strive after a perfection like the perfection of God, how much more ought a nation to be the image of

Deity. The common mind is the true Parian marble, fit to be wrought into likeness to a God. The duty of America is to secure the culture and the happiness of the masses by their reliance on themselves.

The absence of the prejudices of the Old World leaves us here the opportunity of consulting independent truth, and man is left to apply the instinct of freedom to every social relation and public interest. We have approached so near to nature that we can hear her gentlest whispers; we have made Humanity our lawgiver and our oracle; and, therefore, the nation receives, vivifies, and applies principles which in Europe the wisest accept with distrust. Freedom of mind and of conscience, freedom of the seas, freedom of industry, equality of franchises — each great truth is firmly grasped, comprehended, and enforced; for the multitude is neither rash nor fickle. In truth, it is less fickle than those who profess to be its guides. Its natural dialectics surpass the logic of the schools. Political action has never been so consistent and so unwavering as when it results from a feeling or a principle diffused through society. The people is firm and tranquil in its movements, and necessarily acts with moderation, because it becomes but slowly impregnated with new ideas; and effects no changes except in harmony with the knowledge which it has acquired. Besides, where it is permanently possessed of power, there exists neither the occasion nor the desire for frequent change. It is not the parent of tumult; sedition is bred in the lap of luxury, and its chosen emissaries are the beggared spendthrift and the impoverished libertine. The government by the people is in very truth the strongest government in the world. Discarding the implements of terror, it dares to rule by moral force and has its citadel in the heart.

Such is the political system which rests on reason, reflection, and the free expression of deliberate choice. There may be those who scoff at the suggestion that the decision of the whole is to be preferred to the judgment of the enlightened few. They say in their hearts that the masses are ignorant; that farmers know nothing of legislation; that mechanics should not quit their workshops to join in forming public opinion. But true political science does indeed venerate the masses. It maintains, not as has been perversely asserted, that "the people can make right," but that the people can *discern* right. Individuals are but shadows, too often engrossed by the pursuit of shadows; the race is immortal. Individuals are of limited sagacity; the common mind is infinite in its experience. Individuals are languid and blind; the many are ever wakeful. Individuals are corrupt; the race has been redeemed. Individuals are time-serving; the masses are fearless. Individuals may be false; the masses are ingenuous and sincere. Individuals claim the divine sanction of truth for the deceitful conceptions of their own fancies; the Spirit of God breathes through the combined intelligence of the people. Truth is not to be ascertained by the impulses of an individual; it emerges from the contradictions of personal opinions; it raises itself in majestic serenity above the strifes of parties and the conflict of sects; it acknowledges neither the solitary mind nor the separate faction as its oracle, but owns as its own faithful interpreter the dictates of pure reason itself, proclaimed by the general voice of mankind. The decrees of the universal conscience are the nearest approach to the presence of God in the soul of man.

Thus the opinion which we respect is, indeed, not the opinion of one or of a few, but the sagacity of the many. It is hard for the pride of cultivated philosophy to put its ear to the ground and listen reverently to the voice of lowly humanity; yet the people collectively are wiser than the most gifted individual, for all his wisdom constitutes but a part of theirs. When the great sculptor of Greece was endeavoring to fashion the perfect model of beauty, he did not passively imitate the form of the loveliest woman of his age; but he gleaned the several lineaments of his faultless work from the many. And so it is that a perfect judgment is the result of comparison, when error eliminates error, and truth is established by concurring witnesses. The organ of truth is the invisible decision of the unbiased world; she pleads before no tribunal but public opinion; she owns no safe interpreter but the common mind; she knows no court of appeals but the soul of humanity. It is when the multitude give counsel that right purposes find safety; theirs is the fixedness that cannot be shaken; theirs is the understanding which exceeds in wisdom; theirs is the heart of which the largeness is as the sand on the seashore.

It is not by vast armies, by immense natural resources, by accumulations of treasure, that the greatest results in modern civilization have been accomplished. The traces of the career of conquest pass away, hardly leaving a scar on the national intelligence. The famous battle grounds of victory are, most of them, comparatively indifferent to the human race; barren fields of blood, the scourges of their times but affecting the social condition as little as the raging of a pestilence. Not one benevolent institution, not one ameliorating principle in the Roman state was a voluntary concession of the aristocracy; each useful element was borrowed from the democracies of Greece or was a reluctant concession to the demands of the people. The same is true in the modern political life. It is the confession of an enemy to Democracy, that *"all the great and noble institutions of the world have come from popular efforts."*

It is the uniform tendency of the popular element to elevate and bless humanity. The exact measure of the progress of civilization is the degree in which the intelligence of the common mind has prevailed over wealth and brute force; in other words, the measure of the progress of civilization is the progress of the people. Every great object connected with the benevolent exertions of the day has reference to the culture of those powers which are alone the common inheritance. For this the envoys of religion cross seas and visit remotest isles; for this the press in its freedom teems with the productions of maturest thought; for this the philanthropist plans new schemes of education; for this halls in every city and village are open to the public instructor. Not that we view with indifference the glorious efforts of material industry; the increase in the facility of internal intercourse; the accumulations of thrifty labor; the varied results of concentrated action. But even there it is mind that achieves the triumph. It is the genius of the architect that gives beauty to the work of human hands, and makes the temple, the dwelling, or the public edifice, an outward representation of the spirit of propriety and order. It is science that guides the blind zeal of cupidity to the construction of the vast channels of communication which are fast binding the world into one family. And it is as a method of moral improvement that these swifter means of intercourse derive their greatest value. Mind becomes universal property; the poem that is published on the soil of England finds its response on the shores of Lake Erie and the banks of the Missouri, and is admired near the sources of the Ganges. The defense of public liberty in our own halls of legislation penetrates the plains of Poland, is echoed along the mountains of Greece, and pierces the darkest night of Eastern despotism.

[THE RIGHTS OF MEN TO EDUCATION]

The universality of the intellectual and moral powers and the necessity of their development for the progress of the race proclaim the great doctrine of the natural right of every human being to moral and intellectual culture. It is the glory of our fathers to have established in their laws the equal claims of every child to the public care of its morals and its mind. From this principle we may deduce the universal right to leisure; that is, to time not appropriated to material purposes, but reserved for the culture of the moral affections and the mind. It does not tolerate the exclusive enjoyment of leisure by a privileged class, but, defending the rights of labor, would suffer none to sacrifice the higher purposes of existence in unceasing toil for that which is not life. Such is the voice of nature; such the conscious claim of the human mind. The universe opens its pages to every eye; the music of creation resounds in every ear; the glorious lessons of immortal truth that are written in the sky and on the earth address themselves to every mind, and claim attention from every human being. God has made man upright that he might look before and after; and he calls upon everyone not merely to labor, but to reflect; not merely to practise the revelations of divine will, but to contemplate the displays of divine power. Nature claims for every man leisure, for she claims every man as a witness to the divine glory, manifested in the created world.

.   .   .   .

The right to universal education being thus acknowledged by our conscience not less than by our laws, it follows that the people is the true recipient of truth. Do not seek to conciliate individuals; do not dread the frowns of a sect; do not yield to the proscriptions of a party; but pour out truth into the common mind. Let the waters of intelligence, like the rains of heaven, descend on the whole earth. And be not discouraged by the dread of encountering ignorance. *The prejudices of ignorance are more easily removed than the prejudices of interest; the first are blindly adopted; the second wilfully preferred.* Intelligence must be diffused among the whole people; truth must be scattered among those who have no interest to suppress its growth. The seeds that fall on the exchange or in the hum of business may be choked by the thorns that spring up in the hotbed of avarice; the seeds that are let fall in the salon may be like those dropped by the wayside which take no root. Let the young aspirant after glory scatter the seeds of truth broadcast on the wide bosom of humanity; in the deep, fertile soil of the public mind. There it will strike deep root and spring up and bear a hundredfold, and bloom for ages and ripen fruit through remote generations.

It is alone by infusing great principles into the common mind that revolutions in human society are brought about. They never have been, they never can be, effected by superior individual excellence.

. . . .

[The People the Agents of Progress]

Yes, reforms in society are only effected through the masses of the people and through them have continually taken place. New truths have been successively developed and, becoming the common property of the human family, have improved its condition. This progress is advanced by every sect, precisely because each sect, to obtain vitality, does of necessity embody a truth; by every political party, for the conflicts of party are the war of ideas; by every nationality, for a nation cannot exist as such till humanity makes it a special trustee of some part of its wealth for the ultimate benefit of all. The irresistible tendency of the human race is therefore to advancement, for absolute power has never succeeded, and can never succeed, in suppressing a single truth. An idea once revealed may find its admission into every living breast and live there. Like God it becomes immortal and omnipresent. The movement of the species is upward, irresistibly upward. The individual is often lost; Providence never disowns the race. No principle once promulgated has ever been forgotten. No "timely tramp" of a despot's foot ever trod out one idea. The world cannot retrograde; the dark ages cannot return. Dynasties perish; cities are buried; nations have been victims to error or martyrs for right; humanity has always been on the advance, gaining maturity, universality, and power.

Yes, truth is immortal. It cannot be destroyed; it is invincible, it cannot long be resisted. Not every great principle has yet been generated; but when once proclaimed and diffused, it lives without end in the safe custody of the race. States may pass away; every just principle of legislation which has been once established will endure. Philosophy has sometimes forgotten God; a great people never did.

The skepticism of the last century could not uproot Christianity because it lived in the hearts of the millions. Do you think that infidelity is spreading? Christianity never lived in the hearts of so many millions as at this moment. The forms under which it is professed may decay; for they, like all that is the work of man's hands, are subject to the changes and chances of mortal being. But the spirit of truth is incorruptible; it may be developed, illustrated, and applied; it never can die; it never can decline.

No truth can perish; no truth can pass away. The flame is undying, though generations disappear. Wherever moral truth has started into being, humanity claims and guards the bequest. Each generation gathers together the imperishable children of the past and increases them by new sons of light, alike radiant with immortality.

19

RICHARD M. JOHNSON

SUNDAY OBSERVANCE AND THE MAIL[1]

T HE COMMITTEE ON POST-OFFICES AND POST-ROADS, to whom the memorials were referred, for prohibiting the transportation of mails, and the opening of post offices on Sunday, report that the memorialists regard the first day of the week as a day set apart by the Creator for religious exercises, and consider the transportation of the mail and the opening of the post offices on that day the violation of a religious duty, and call for a suppression of the practice. Others, by counter-memorials, are known to entertain a different sentiment, believing that no one day of the week is holier than another. Others, holding the universality and immutability of the Jewish Decalogue, believe in the sanctity of the seventh day of the week as a day of religious devotion; and, by their memorial now before the Committee, they also request that it may be set apart for religious purposes. Each has hitherto been left to the exercise of his own opinion; and it has been regarded as the proper business of government to protect all, and determine for none. But the attempt is now made to bring about a greater uniformity, at least in practice; and, as argument has failed, the Government has been called upon to interpose its authority to settle the controversy.

Congress acts under a Constitution of delegated and limited powers. The Committee look in vain to that instrument for a delegation of power authorizing this body to inquire and determine what part of time, or whether any, has been set apart by the Almighty for religious exercises. On the contrary, among the few prohibitions which it contains is one that prohibits a religious test; and another which declares that Congress shall pass no law respecting an establishment of religion, or prohibiting the free exercise thereof. The Committee might here rest the argument, upon the ground that the question referred to them does not come within the cognizance of Congress;

[1] [*Report of the Committee on Post-Offices and Post-roads of the United States Senate* (January, 1829) — Text complete.]

but the perseverance and zeal with which the memorialists pursue their object seems to require further elucidation of the subject. And as the opposers of Sunday mails disclaim all intention to unite Church and State, the Committee do not feel disposed to impugn their motives; and whatever may be advanced in opposition to the measure will arise from the fears entertained of its fatal tendency to the peace and happiness of the nation. The catastrophe of other nations furnished the framers of the Constitution a beacon of awful warning, and they have evinced the greatest possible care in guarding against the same evil.

The law, as it now exists, makes no distinction as to the days of the week, but is imperative that the postmasters shall attend at all reasonable hours in every day to perform the duties of their offices; and the postmaster-general has given his instructions to all postmasters that, at post offices where the mail arrives on Sunday, the office is to be kept open one hour or more after the arrival and assorting of the mail. But, in case that would interfere with the hours of public worship, the office is to be kept open for one hour after the usual time of dissolving the meeting. This liberal construction of the law does not satisfy the memorialists. But the Committee believe that there is not just ground of complaint, unless it be conceded that they have a controlling power over the consciences of others. If Congress shall by the authority of the law sanction the measure recommended, it would constitute a legislative decision of a religious controversy in which even Christians themselves are at issue. However suited such a decision may be to an ecclesiastical council, it is incompatible with a republican legislature, which is purely for political and not religious purposes.

In our individual character we all entertain opinions and pursue a corresponding practice upon the subject of religion. However diversified these may be, we all harmonize as citizens, while each is willing that the other shall enjoy the same liberty which he claims for himself. But in our representative character our individual character is lost. The individual acts for himself; the representative acts for his constituents. He is chosen to represent their religious views, to guard the rights of man; not to restrict the rights of conscience. Despots may regard their subjects as their property and usurp the divine prerogative of prescribing their religious faith; but the history of the world furnishes the melancholy demonstration that the disposition of one man to coerce the religious homage of another springs from an unchastened ambition rather than a sincere devotion to any religion. The principles of our Government do not recognize in the majority any authority over the minority, except in matters which regard the conduct of man to his fellow man. A Jewish monarch, by grasping the holy censer, lost both his scepter and his freedom. A destiny as little to be envied may be the lot of the American people who hold the sovereignty of power, if they, in the person of their representatives, shall attempt to unite, in the remotest degree, Church and State.

From the earliest period of time religious teachers have attained great ascendancy over the minds of the people; and in every nation, ancient or modern, whether pagan, Mahommedan, or Christian, have succeeded in the incorporation of their religious tenets with the political institutions of their country. The Persian idols, the Grecian oracles, the Roman auguries, and the modern priesthood of Europe have all in their turn been the subject of popular adulation and the agents of political deception. If the measure recommended should be adopted, it would be difficult for human sagacity to foresee how rapid would be the succession or how numerous the train of measures which might follow, involving the dearest rights of all, the rights of conscience. It is perhaps fortunate for our country that the proposition should have been made at this early period, while the spirit of the Revolution yet exists in full vigor. Religious zeal enlists the strongest prejudices of the human mind and, when misdirected, excites the worst passions of our nature under the delusive pretext of doing God service. Nothing is so incessant in its toils, so persevering in its determinations, so appalling in its course, or so dangerous in its consequences. The equality of right secured by the Constitution may bid defiance to mere political tyrants, but the robe of sanctity too often glitters to deceive. The Constitution regards the conscience of the Jew as sacred as that of the Christian, and gives no more authority to adopt a measure affecting the conscience of a solitary individual than that of a whole community. That representative who would violate this principle would lose his delegated character and forfeit the confidence of his constituents. If Congress shall declare the first day of the week holy, it will not convince the Jew nor the Sabbatarian. It will dissatisfy both and, consequently, convert neither. Human power may extort vain sacrifices, but Deity alone can command the affections of the heart. It must be recollected that, in the earliest settlement of this country, the spirit of persecution, which drove the pilgrims from their native homes, was brought with them to their new habitations; and that some Christians were scourged and others put to death for no other crime than dissenting from the dogmas of their rulers.

With these facts before us, it must be a subject of deep regret that a question should be brought before Congress which involves the dearest privileges of the Constitution, and even by those who enjoy its choicest blessings. We should all recollect that Catiline, a professed patriot, was a traitor to Rome; Arnold, a professed Whig, was a traitor to America; and Judas, a professed disciple, was a traitor to his Divine Master.

With the exception of the United States, the whole human race consisting, it is supposed, of eight hundred millions of rational human beings, is in religious bondage; and in reviewing the scenes of persecution which history everywhere presents, unless the Committee could believe that the cries of the burning victim and the flames by which he is consumed bear to Heaven a grateful incense, the conclusion is inevitable that the line cannot be too strongly drawn between Church and State. If a solemn act of legislation shall in one point define the God or point out to the citizen one religious duty, it may with equal propriety define every part of divine revelation and enforce every religious obligation, even to the forms and ceremonies of worship, the endowment of the church, and the support of the clergy.

It was with a kiss that Judas betrayed his Divine Master, and we should all be admonished, no matter what our faith may be, that the rights of conscience cannot be so successfully assailed as under the pretext of holiness. The Christian religion made its way into the world in opposition to all human governments. Banishment, tortures, and death were inflicted in vain to stop its progress. But many of its professors, as soon as clothed in political power, lost the meek spirit which their creed inculcated and began to inflict on other religions and on dissenting sects of their own religion persecutions more aggravated than those which their own apostles had endured. The ten persecutions of pagan emperors were exceeded in atrocity by the massacres and murders perpetrated by Christian hands; and in vain shall we examine the records of imperial tyranny for an engine of cruelty equal to the holy inquisition. Every religious sect, however meek in its origin, commenced the work of persecution as soon as it acquired political power. The framers of the Constitution recognized the eternal principle that man's relation with God is above human legislation and his rights of conscience unalienable. Reasoning was not necessary to establish this truth; we are conscious of it in our own bosoms. It is this consciousness which, in defiance of human laws, has sustained so many martyrs in tortures and in flames. They felt that their duty to God was superior to human enactments and that man could exercise no authority over their consciences; it is an inborn principle which nothing can eradicate.

The bigot, in the pride of his authority, may lose sight of it; but strip him of his power, prescribe a faith to him which his conscience rejects, threaten him in turn with the dungeon and the faggot, the spirit which God has implanted in him rises up in rebellion and defies you. Did the primitive Christians ask that government should recognize and observe their religious institutions? All they asked was toleration; all they complained of was persecution. What did the Protestants of Germany and the Huguenots of France ask of their Catholic superiors? Toleration. What do the persecuted Catholics of Ireland ask of their oppressors? Toleration.

Do not all men in this country enjoy every religious right which martyrs and saints ever asked? Whence, then, the voice of complaint? Who is it that, in the full enjoyment of every principle which human laws can secure, wishes to wrest a portion of these principles from his neighbor? Do the petitioners allege that they cannot conscientiously participate in the profits of the mail contracts and post offices because the mail is carried on Sunday? If this be their motive, then it is worldly gain which stimulates to action, and not virtue and religion. Do they complain that men, less conscientious in relation to the Sabbath, obtain advantages over them by receiving their letters and attending to their contents? Still their motive is worldly and selfish. But if their motive be to make Congress to sanction by law their religious opinions and observances, then their efforts are to be resisted as in their tendency fatal both to religious and political freedom. Why have the petitioners confined their prayer to the mails? Why have they not requested that the government be required to suspend all its executive functions on that day? Why do they not require us to exact that our ships shall not sail, that our armies shall not march, that officers of justice shall not seize the suspected, or guard the convicted? They seem to forget that government is as necessary on Sunday as on any other day of the week. It is the Government, ever active in its functions, which enables us all, even the petitioners, to worship in our churches in peace. Our Government furnishes very few blessings like our mails. They bear, from the center of our Republic to its distant extremes, the acts of our legislative bodies, the decisions of the justiciary, and the orders of the executive. Their speed is often essential to the defense of the country, the suppression of crime, and the dearest interests of the people. Were they suppressed one day of the week, their absence must often be supplied by public expresses, and, besides, while the mail bags might rest, the mail coaches would pursue their journey with the passengers. The mail bears, from one extreme of the Union to the other, letters of relatives and friends, preserving a communion of heart between those far separated and increasing the most pure and refined pleasures of our existence. Also, the letters of commercial men convey the state of markets, prevent ruinous speculations, and promote general as well as individual interest; they bear innumerable religious letters, newspapers, magazines, and tracts, which reach almost every house throughout this wide republic. Is the conveyance of these a violation of the Sabbath? The advance of the human race in intelligence, in virtue and religion itself, depends, in part, upon the speed with which a knowledge of the past is disseminated. Without an interchange between one country and another and between different sections of the same country, every improvement in moral or political science, and the arts of life, would be confined to the neighborhood where it originated. The more rapid and the more frequent this interchange, the more rapid will be the march of intellect and the progress of improvement. The mail is the chief means by which intellectual light irradiates to the extremes of the republic. Stop it one day in seven, and you retard one-seventh the improvement of our country. So far from stopping the mail on Sunday, the Committee would recommend the use of all reasonable means to give it a greater expedition and a greater extension. What would be the elevation of our country if every new conception could be made to strike every mind in the Union at the same time! It is not the distance of a province or state from the seat of government which endangers its separation, but it is the difficulty and unfrequency of intercourse between them. Our mails reach Missouri and Arkansas in less time than they reached Kentucky and Ohio in the infancy of their settlements; and now, when there are three millions of people, extending one thousand miles west of the Alleghany, we hear less of discontent than when there were a few thousands scattered along their western base.

To stop the mails one day in seven would be to thrust the whole western country and other distant parts of this Republic one day's journey from the seat of government. But were it expedient to put an end to the transmission of letters and newspapers on Sunday because it violates the law of God, have not the petitioners begun wrong in their efforts? If the arm of government be necessary to compel man to respect and obey the laws of God, do not the state governments possess infinitely more power in this respect? Let the petitioners turn to them, and see if they can induce the passage of laws to respect the observance of the Sabbath; for if it be sinful for the mail to carry letters on Sunday, it must be equally sinful for individuals to write, carry, receive, or read them. It would seem to require that these acts should be made penal to complete the system. Traveling on business or recreation, except to and from church; all printing, carrying, receiving, and reading of newspapers; all conversations and social intercourse, except upon religious subjects, must necessarily be punished to suppress the evil. Would it not also follow, as an inevitable consequence, that every man, woman, and child should be compelled to attend meeting; and, as only one sect, in the opinion of some, can be deemed orthodox, must the law not determine which that is and compel all to hear these teachers and contribute to their support? If minor punishments would not restrain the Jew or the Sabbatarian or the Infidel, who believes Saturday to be the Sabbath, or disbelieves the whole, would not the same system require that we should resort to imprisonment, banishment, the rack, and the faggot to force men to violate their own consciences or compel them to listen to doctrines which they abhor? When the state governments shall have yielded to these measures, it will be time enough for Congress to declare that the rattling of the mail coaches shall no longer break the silence of this despotism. It is the duty of this

Government to affirm to all — to Jew or Gentile, Pagan, or Christian — the protection and the advantages of our benignant institutions on Sunday, as well as every day of the week. Although this Government will not convert itself into an ecclesiastical tribunal, it will practice upon the maxim laid down by the Founder of Christianity that it is lawful to do good on the Sabbath day. If the Almighty had set apart the first day of the week as time which man is bound to keep holy and devote exclusively to his worship, would it not be more congenial to the prospects of Christians to appeal exclusively to the great Lawgiver of the universe to aid them in making men better, in correcting their practices by purifying their hearts? Government will protect them in their efforts. When they shall have so instructed the public mind and awakened the consciences of individuals as to make them believe that it is a violation of God's law to carry the mail, open post offices, or receive letters on Sunday, the evil of which they complain will cease of itself, without any exertion of the strong arm of civil power. When man undertakes to be God's avenger he becomes a demon. Driven by the frenzy of a religious zeal, he loses every gentle feeling, forgets the most sacred precepts of his creed, and becomes ferocious and unrelenting.

Our fathers did not wait to be oppressed when the mother country asserted and exercised an unconstitutional power over them. To have acquiesced in the tax of threepence upon a pound of tea would have led the way to the most cruel exactions; they took a bold stand against the principle, and liberty and independence were the result. The petitioners have not requested Congress to suppress Sunday mails upon the ground of political expediency, but because they violate the sanctity of the first day of the week.

This being the fact, and the petitioners having indignantly disclaimed even the wish to unite politics and religion, may not the Committee reasonably cherish the hope that they will feel reconciled to its decision in the case? especially as it is also a fact that the countermemorials, equally respectable, oppose the interference of Congress, upon the ground that it would be legislating upon a religious subject and therefore unconstitutional.

20

FRANCES WRIGHT

ON EXISTING EVILS AND THEIR REMEDY[1]

[AMERICA STILL CULTURALLY EUROPEAN]

The result of my observation has been the conviction that the reform commenced at the Revolution of '76 has been but little improved through the term of years which have succeeded; that the national policy of the country was then indeed changed, but that its social economy has remained such as it was in the days of its European vassalage.

In confirmation of this I will request you to observe that your religion is the same as that of monarchical England, taught from the same books, and promulgated and sustained by similar means — viz., a salaried priesthood set apart from the people; sectarian churches in whose property the people have no share, and over whose use and occupancy the people have no control; expensive missions, treasury funds, association; and, above all, a compulsory power, compounded at once of accumulated wealth, established custom, extensive correspondence, and a system of education imbued with its spirit and all pervaded by its influence.

Again, in proof of the similarity between your internal policy and that of monarchical England, I will request you to observe that *her law is your law*. Every part and parcel of that absurd, cruel, ignorant, inconsistent, incomprehensible jumble styled the common law of England — every part and parcel of it, I say, not abrogated or altered expressly by legislative statutes, which has been very rarely done — is at this hour the law of revolutionized America.

Further, in proof of the identity of your fabric of civil polity with that of aristocratical England, I will request you to observe that the system of education pursued in both countries is, with little variation, one and the same. There you have endowed universities, privileged

---

[1] [From Frances Wright, *A Course of Popular Lectures* (New York, 1829), pp. 150-170 — Abridged.]

by custom, enriched by ancient royal favor, protected by parliamentary statutes, and devoted to the upholding, perpetuating, and strengthening the power and privilege to which they owe their origin. There, too, you have parish schools under the control of the parish priest, and a press everywhere coerced by law, swayed, bribed, or silenced by ascendant parties or tyrannous authority. And *here*, have we not colleges with endowments still held by the royal charters which first bestowed them; and colleges with lands and money granted by American legislatures, not for the advantage of the American people, but for that of their rulers, for the children of privileged professions upon whom is thus entailed the privilege of their fathers, and that as certainly as the son of a duke is born to a dukedom in England? *Here*, have we not also schools controlled by the clergy; nay, have we not all our public institutions, scientific, literary, judicial, or humane, ridden by the spirit of orthodoxy and invaded, perverted, vitiated, and tormented by opiniative distinctions? And *here*, have we not a press paralyzed by fear, disgraced by party, and ruled by loud tongued fanaticism, or aspiring and threatening sectarian ambition? And more, my friends: see we not, in this nation of confederated freemen, as many distinctions of class as afflict the aristocracies of Britain or the despotism of the Russias, and more distinctions of sect than ever cursed all the nations of Europe together, from the preaching of Peter the hermit to the trances of Madame Krudner or the miracles of Prince Hohenlohe?

Surely all these are singular anomalies in a republic. Sparta, when she conceived her democracy, commenced with educational equality; when she aimed at national union, she cemented that union in childhood at the public board, in the gymnasium, in the temple, in the common habits, common feelings, common duties, and common condition. And so, notwithstanding all the errors with which her institutions were fraught and all the vices which arose out of those errors, did she present for ages a wondrous sample of democratic union and consequently of national prosperity.

[NATIONAL EDUCATION THE REMEDY]

What, then, is wanted here? What Sparta had: *a national education*. And what Sparta, in many respects, had not: *a rational education*.

Hitherto, my friends, in government as in every branch of morals, we have but too much mistaken words for truths and forms for principles. To render men free, it sufficeth not to proclaim their liberty; to make them equal, it sufficeth not to call them so. True, the Fourth of July, '76, commenced a new era for our race. True, the sun of promise then rose upon the world. But let us not mistake for the fulness of light what was but its harbinger. Let us not conceive that man, in signing the declaration of his rights, secured their possession; that having framed the theory he had not, and hath not still, the practice to seek.

Your fathers, indeed, on the day from which dates your existence as a nation, opened the gates of the temple of human liberty. But think not they entered, nor that you have entered, the sanctuary. They passed not, nor have you passed, even the threshold.

Who speaks of liberty while the human mind is in chains? Who of equality while the thousands are in squalid wretchedness, the millions harassed with health-destroying labor, the few afflicted with health-destroying idleness, and all tormented by health-destroying solicitude? Look abroad on the misery which is gaining on the land! Mark the strife and the discord and the jealousies, the shock of interests and opinions, the hatreds of sect, the estrangements of class, the pride of wealth, the debasement of poverty, the helplessness of youth unprotected, of age uncomforted, of industry unrewarded, of ignorance unenlightened, of vice unreclaimed, of misery unpitied, of sickness, hunger, and nakedness unsatisfied, unalleviated, and unheeded. Go! mark all the wrongs and the wretchedness with which the eye and the ear and the heart are familiar, and then echo in triumph and celebrate in jubilee the insulting declaration: *all men are free and equal.*

.   .   .   .

[NATIONAL EDUCATION OR COMMON SCHOOLS]

This measure, my friends, has been long present to my mind as befitting the adoption of the American people; as alone calculated to form an enlightened, a virtuous, and a happy community; as alone capable of supplying a remedy to the evils under which we groan; as alone commensurate with the interests of the human family, and consistent with the political institutions of this great confederated Republic.

I had occasion formerly to observe, in allusion to the efforts already made and yet making, in the cause of popular instruction, more or less throughout the Union, that as yet the true principle has not been hit, and that until it be hit all reform must be slow and inefficient.

The noble example of New England has been imitated by other States until all not possessed of common schools blush for the popular remissness. But, after all, how can *common schools*, under their best form and in fullest supply, effect even the purpose which they have in view?

The object proposed by common schools — if I rightly understand it — is to impart to the whole population those means for the acquirement of knowledge which are in common use: reading and writing. To these are added arithmetic and, occasionally perhaps, some imperfect lessons in the simpler sciences. But, I would ask, supposing these institutions should even be made to embrace all the branches of intellectual knowledge, and thus science offered gratis to all the children of the land, how are the children of the very class for whom we suppose the schools instituted to be supplied with food and raiment, or instructed in the trade necessary to their future subsistence, while they are following these studies? How are they, I ask, to be fed and clothed, when, as all facts show, the labor of the parents is often insufficient for their own sustenance and, almost universally, inadequate to the provision of the family without the united efforts of all its members? In your manufacturing districts you have children worked for twelve hours a day; and, in the rapid and certain progress of the existing system, you will soon have them, as in England, *worked to death*, and yet unable, through the period of their miserable existence, to earn a pittance sufficient to satisfy the cravings of hunger. At this present time, what leisure or what spirit, think you, have the children of the miserable widows of Philadelphia, realizing, according to the most favorable estimate of your city and county committee, sixteen dollars per annum for food and clothing; what leisure or what spirit may their children find for visiting a school, although the same should be open to them from sunrise to sunset? Or what leisure have usually the children of your most thriving mechanics, after their strength is sufficiently developed to spin, sew, weave, or wield a tool? It seems to me, my friends, that to build schoolhouses nowadays is something like building churches. When you have them, you need some measure to ensure their being occupied.

But, as our time is short and myself somewhat fatigued by continued exertions, I must hasten to the rapid development of the system of instruction and protection which has occurred to me as capable, and alone capable, of opening the door to universal reform.

In lieu of all common schools, high schools, colleges, seminaries, houses of refuge, or any other juvenile institution, instructional or protective, I would suggest that the state legislatures be directed (after laying off the whole in townships or hundreds) to organize, at suitable distances and in convenient and healthy situations, establishments for the general reception of all the children resident within the said school district. These establishments to be devoted, severally, to children between a certain age. Say, the first to infants between two and four, or two and six, according to the density of the population, and such other local circumstances as might render a greater or less number of establishments necessary or practicable. The next to receive children from four to eight, or six to twelve years. The next from twelve to sixteen, or to an older age, if found desirable. Each establishment to be furnished with instructors in every branch of knowledge, intellectual and operative, with all the apparatus, land, and conveniences necessary for the best development of all knowledge; the same, whether operative or intellectual, being always calculated to the age and strength of the pupils.

To obviate, in the commencement, every evil result possible from the first mixture of a young population, so variously raised in error or neglect, a due separation should be made in each establishment, by which means those entering with bad habits would be kept apart from the others until corrected. How rapidly reform may be effected on the plastic disposition of childhood has been sufficiently proved in your houses of refuge, more especially when such establishments have been under *liberal* superintendence, as was formerly the case in New York. Under their orthodox directors, those asylums of youth have been converted into jails.

It will be understood that, in the proposed establishments, the children would pass from one to the other in regular succession; and that the parents, who would necessarily be resident in their close neighborhood, could visit the children at suitable hours but in no case niterfere with or interrupt the rules of the institution.

In the older establishments, the well-directed and well-protected labor of the pupil would, in time, suffice for and then exceed their own support, when the surplus might be devoted to the maintenance of the infant establishments.

In the beginning, and until all debt was cleared off and so long as the same should be found favorable to the promotion of these best palladiums of a nation's happiness, a double tax might be at once expedient and politic.

First, a moderate tax per head for every child, to be laid upon its parents conjointly or divided between them, due attention being always paid to the varying strength of the two sexes and to the undue depreciation which now rests on female labor. The more effectually to correct the latter injustice, as well as to consult the convenience of the industrious classes generally, this parental tax might be rendered payable either in money or in labor, produce, or domestic manufactures; and should be continued for each child until the age when juvenile labor should be found, on the average, equivalent to the educational expenses, which, 1 have reason to believe, would be at twelve years.

This first tax on parents to embrace equally the whole population, as, however moderate, it would inculcate a certain forethought in all the human family, more especially where it is most wanted: in young persons who, before they assumed the responsibility of parents, would estimate their fitness to meet it.

The second tax to be on property, increasing in percentage with the wealth of the individual. In this manner I conceive the rich would contribute, according to their riches, to the relief of the poor and to the support of the state, by raising up its best bulwark: an enlightened and united generation.

Preparatory to or connected with such measures, a registry should be opened by the state, with offices through all the townships, where, on the birth of every child, or within a certain time appointed, the same should be entered, together with the names of its parents. When two years old, the parental tax should be payable and the juvenile institution open for the child's reception, from which time forward it would be under the protective care and guardianship of the state, while it need never be removed from the daily, weekly, or frequent inspection of the parents.

Orphans, of course, would find here an open asylum. If possessed of property, a contribution would be paid from its revenue to the common educational fund; if unprovided, they would be sustained out of the same.

In these nurseries of a free nation, no inequality must be allowed to enter. Fed at a common board; clothed in a common garb, uniting neatness with simplicity and convenience; raised in the exercise of common duties, in the acquirement of the same knowledge and practice of the same industry, varied only according to individual taste and capabilities, in the exercise of the same virtues, in the enjoyment of the same pleasures, in the study of the same nature, in pursuit of the same object — their own and each other's happiness — say! would not such a race, when arrived at manhood and womanhood, work out the reform of society, perfect the free institutions of America?

I have drawn but a sketch; nor could I presume to draw the picture of that which the mind's eye hath seen alone, and which it is for the people of this land to realize.

In this sketch, my friends, there is nothing but what is practical and practicable, nothing but what you yourselves may contribute to effect. Let the popular suffrage be exercised with a view to the popular good. Let the industrious classes and all honest men of all classes unite for the sending to the legislatures those who will represent the real interest of the many, not the imagined interests of the few; of the people at large, not of any profession or class.

To develop further my views on this all-important subject at the present time would be to fatigue your attention and exhaust my own strength. I shall prosecute this subject in the periodical of which I am editor, which, in common with my public discourses, have been and will ever be devoted to the common cause of human improvement and addressed to humankind without distinction of nation, class, or sect. May you, my fellow beings, unite in the same cause, in the same spirit! May you learn to seek truth without fear! May you further learn to advocate truth as you distinguish it; to be valiant in its defense, and peaceful while valiant; to meet all things, bear all things, and dare all things for the correction of abuses and the effecting, in private and in public, in your own minds, through the minds of your children, friends, and companions, and, above all, *through your legislature*, a radical reform in all your measures, whether as citizens or as men!

21

ELY MOORE

ON LABOR UNIONS[1]

WE HAVE ASSEMBLED, on the present occasion, for the purpose of publicly proclaiming the motives which induced us to organize a general union of the various trades and arts in this city and its vicinity, as well as to defend the course and to vindicate the measures we deign to pursue. This is required of us by a due regard to the opinions of our fellow men.

We conceive it, then, to be a *truth*, enforced and illustrated by the concurrent testimony of history and daily observation, that man is disposed to avail himself of the possessions and services of his fellow man, without rendering an equivalent, and to prefer claims to that which of right belongs to another. This may be considered a hard saying; but we have only to turn our eyes inward and examine ourselves, in order to admit, to the full extent, the truth of the proposition that man, by nature, is selfish and aristocratic. *Self-love* is constitutional with man, and is displayed in every stage and in all the diversities of life; in youth and in manhood, in prosperity and in adversity. It not only discovers itself in the strifes and contentions of states and empires, but in the smallest fraternities, in the factory and the workshop, in the village school and the family circle. In fact, wherever society exists, however small the number or rude the members, you will find self-love stimulating to a contest for power and dominion. This prevailing disposition of the human heart, so far from being an evil in itself, is one of the elements of life and essential to the welfare of society. The *selfish* generate the social feelings. It is only pernicious in its tendency and operation, therefore, when it passes its true and natural bounds and urges man to encroach upon the rights and immunities of man.

In order to mitigate the evils that ever flow from inordinate desire

[1] [From *Address delivered before the General Trades' Union of the City of New York at the Chatham Street Chapel, Monday, December 2, 1833* (New York, 1833) — Abridged.]

and unrestricted selfishness, to restrain and chastise unlawful ambition, to protect the weak against the strong, and to establish an equilibrium of power among nations and individuals, conventional compacts were formed. These confederative associations have never been fully able to stay the march of intolerance, of mercenary ambition, or of political despotism. Even in this fair land of freedom, where liberty and equality are guaranteed to all, and where our written constitutions have so wisely provided limitations to power and securities for rights, the twin fiends, *intolerance* and *aristocracy*, presume to rear their hateful crests! But we have no cause to marvel at this. Wherever man exists, under whatever form of government, or whatever be the structure or organization of society, this principle of his nature, selfishness, will appear, operating either for evil or for good. To curb it sufficiently by legislative enactments is impossible. Much can be done, however, towards restraining it within proper limits by unity of purpose and concert of action on the part of the *producing* classes. To contribute toward the achievement of this great end is one of the objects of the "General Trades' Union." Wealth, we all know, constitutes the aristocracy of this country. Happily no distinctions are known among us save what wealth and worth confer. No legal barriers are erected to protect exclusive privileges or unmerited rank. The law of primogeniture forms no part of American jurisprudence, and our revolution has converted all feudal tenures into allodial rights. The greatest danger, therefore, which threatens the stability of our Government and the liberty of the people is an undue accumulation and distribution of wealth. And I do conceive that real danger is to be apprehended from this source, notwithstanding that tendency to distribution which naturally grows out of the character of our statutes of conveyance, of inheritance, and descent of property; but by securing to the producing classes a fair, certain, and equitable compensation for their toil and skill, we insure a more just and equal distribution of wealth than can ever be effected by statutory law.

Unlike the septennial reversion of the Jews or the agrarian law of Rome, the principle for which we contend holds out to individuals proper motives for exertion and enterprise. We ask, then, what better means can be devised for promoting a more equal distribution of wealth than for the producing classes to *claim*, and by virtue of union and concert, *secure their claims* to their respective portions? And why should not those who have the toil have the enjoyment also? Or why should the sweat that flows from the brow of the laborer be converted into a source of revenue for the support of the crafty or indolent?

It has been averred, with great truth, that all governments become cruel and aristocratical in their character and bearing in proportion as one part of the community is elevated and the other depressed, and that misery and degradation to the many is the inevitable result of such a state of society. And we regard it to be equally true that, in proportion as the line of distinction between the employer and employed is *widened*, the condition of the latter inevitably verges toward a state of vassalage, while that of the former as certainly approximates toward supremacy; and that whatever system is calculated to make the many dependent upon or subject to the few not only tends to the subversion of the natural rights of man, but is hostile to the best interests of the community, as well as to the spirit and genius of our Government. Fully persuaded that the foregoing positions are incontrovertible, we, in order to guard against the encroachments of aristocracy, to preserve our natural and political rights, to elevate our moral and intellectual condition, to promote our pecuniary interests, to narrow the line of distinction between the journeyman and employer, to establish the honor and safety of our respective vocations upon a more secure and permanent basis, and to alleviate the distresses of those suffering from want of employment have deemed it expedient to form ourselves into a "General Trades' Union."

It may be asked, how these desirable objects are to be achieved by a general union of trades? How the encroachments of aristocracy, for example, are to be arrested by our plan? We answer, by enabling the producer to enjoy the full benefit of his productions, and thus diffuse the streams of wealth more generally and, consequently, more equally throughout all the ramifications of society. This point conceded, and conceded it must be, it is not requisite we conceive that the line of investigation should be dropped very deep, in order to bring it up tinged with proof that the verity of our other positions necessarily follow. But for the particular means by which the several objects just enumerated are to be attained, we beg leave to refer to our constitution and to our general plan of organization.

There are, doubtless, many individuals who are resolved, right or wrong, to misrepresent our principles, impeach our measures, and impugn our motives. Be it so. They can harm us not. Let them, if they please, draw the vengeful bow to the very double and let fly the barbed arrows; the temper and amplitude of the shield of the Union, we trust, will be found sufficient to ward off the stroke. Their shafts, though winged by hate, and hurled with their utmost strength, will scarcely reach the mark, but, like the spent javelin of aged Priam, fall to the ground without a blow. We have the consolation of knowing that all good men, all who love their country, and rejoice in the improvement of the condition of their fellow men, will acknowledge the policy of our views and the purity of our motives. The residue, I trust, will not defame us with their approbation. Their censure we can endure, but their praise we should regard as an eternal disgrace. And why, let me ask, should the character of our Union be obnoxious to censure? Wherefore is it wrong in principle? Which of its avowed objects reprehensible? What feature of it opposed to the public good? I defy the ingenuity of man to point to a single measure which it recognizes that is wrong in itself or in its tendency. What, is it wrong for men to unite for the purpose of resisting the encroachments of aristocracy? Wrong to restrict the principle of selfishness to its proper and legitimate bounds and objects? Wrong to oppose monopoly and mercenary ambition? Wrong to consult the interests and seek the welfare of the producing classes? Wrong to attempt the elevation of our moral and intellectual standing? Wrong to establish the honor and safety of our respective vocations upon a more secure and permanent basis? I ask — in the name of heaven I ask — can it be wrong for men to attempt the melioration of their condition and the preservation of their natural and political rights?

I am aware that the charge of "illegal combination" is raised against us. The cry is as senseless as 'tis stale and unprofitable. Why, I would inquire, have not journeymen the same right to ask their own price for their own property or services that employers have? or that merchants, physicians, and lawyers have? Is that equal justice which makes it an offense for journeymen to combine for the purpose of maintaining their present prices or raising their wages, while employers may combine with impunity for the purpose of lowering them? I admit that such is the common law. All will agree, however, that it is neither wise, just, nor politic, and that it is directly opposed to the spirit and genius of our free institutions and ought therefore, to be abrogated.

It is further alleged that the General Trades' Union is calculated to encourage *strikes* and *turnouts*. Now, the truth lies in the converse. Our constitution sets forth that "Each trade or art may represent to the Convention, through their delegates, their grievances, who shall take cognizance thereof, and decide upon the same." And, further, that "No trade or art shall strike for higher wages than they at present receive, without the sanction of the Convention." True, if the Convention shall, after due deliberation, decide that the members of any trade or art there represented are aggrieved and that their demands are warrantable, then the Convention is pledged to sustain the members of such trade or art to the uttermost. Hence, employers will discover that it is idle, altogether idle, to prolong a contest with journeymen when they are backed by the Convention. And journeymen will perceive that in order to obtain assistance from the Convention, in the event of a strike or turnout that their claims must be founded in justice, and all their measures be so taken as not to invade the rights or sacrifice the welfare of employers. So far, then, from the Union encouraging strikes or turnouts, it is destined, we conceive, to allay the jealousies and abate the asperities which now unhappily exist between employers and the employed.

We all know that whenever journeymen stand out for higher wages the public are sufferers, as well as the parties more immediately concerned. The Trades' Union, we conceive, will have a tendency to correct this evil.

Again, it is alleged that it is setting a dangerous precedent for journeymen to combine for the purpose of coercing a compliance with their terms. It may, indeed, be dangerous to aristocracy, dangerous to monopoly, dangerous to oppression, but not to the general good or the public tranquillity. Internal danger to a state is not to be apprehended from a general effort on the part of the people to improve and exalt their condition, but from an alliance of the crafty, designing, and intriguing few. What! tell us, in this enlightened age, that the welfare of the people will be endangered by a voluntary act of the people themselves? That the people will wantonly seek their own destruction? That the safety of the state will be plotted against by three-fourths of the members comprising the state! O how worthless, how poor and pitiful, are all such arguments and objections!

Members of the "General Trades' Union," permit me at this time and before I leave this part of my subject to caution you against the wiles and perfidy of those individuals who will approach you as friends but who, in reality and in truth, are your secret enemies. You will know them by this sign: an attempt to excite your jealousy against certain individuals who, peradventure, may stand somewhat conspicuous among you, by insinuations that these men have ulterior designs to accomplish, that political ambition lies at the root of the whole matter, and all that. This will be done, recollect, not so much to injure the individuals against whom the insinuations are ostensibly directed as to abuse you by impairing your confidence in the Union. It is the heart of the Union at which these assassins aim the stroke! 'Tis the Union, your political safeguard, that they would prostrate! 'Tis the Union, the citadel of your hopes, that they would sack and destroy! I entreat you, therefore, to shun such counselors as you would the pestilence. Remember the tragedy in the garden of Eden and hold no communion with the adversary. But why caution you thus, when your own good sense would so readily teach you that the very attempt to deceive you was an insult to your understandings? Because, did they not presume upon your ignorance and credulity, they would never attempt to alienate your affections from the Union. Remember, then, fellow mechanics, that the man who attempts to seduce you from your duty to yourselves, to your families, and your brother mechanics by misrepresenting the objects of the Union, offers you not only an insult but an *injury!* Remember that those defamers would exult at your misfortunes, would "laugh at your calamity, and mock when your fear cometh." Aye, would trample down your liberties and rejoice at beholding

> The seal of bondage on your brows —
> Its badge upon your breasts!

You will not regard it as ill-timed nor irrelevant to the present occasion, my friends, should I invite your attention for a moment to the important bearing which the useful arts have upon the welfare of society. In order to estimate their importance correctly, it is necessary to contemplate the condition of man as we find him in a state of nature, where the arts are unknown and where the lights of civilization have never dawned upon his path. Wherever man is thus situated, we find him a creature of blind impulse, of passion, and of instinct, of groveling hopes and of low desires; and his wants, like those of the brute, supplied only by the spontaneous productions of nature, his only covering a scanty supply of hair, his food the acorn and the loathsome insect; the cavern his dwelling, the earth his couch, and the rock his pillow! The superiority of man's condition, therefore, over that of other animals is attributable solely to the influence of the mechanic arts. Without their aid, the native powers of his mind, however great, could never have been developed; and the physical sciences, which he has been enabled to master in a state of civilization, would have still been numbered among the secrets of nature. What progress, for example, could he have made in the science of astronomy without the aid of the telescope? In chemistry without the retort and receiver? In anatomy and surgery, without the knife and the tourniquet? In agriculture without the hoe and the mattock, the spade and the plough, the scythe and the pruning hook?

Contrast *civilized* with *savage* man. Compare, for example, the Bushmen of Southern Africa, whose chief supply of food consists of the locust and the ant, or the Eskimos, who feast and fatten upon train oil and seals' blubber, with the inhabitants of those countries where the useful arts are known and cultivated, and you will be enabled to estimate more correctly their influence upon the welfare of man. The condition of the Eskimos, although wretched and degraded, is far preferable to that of the Bushman. Physiologists tell us that their physical structures and capacities are about the same. The comparative elevation, therefore, of the one is ascribable directly to the fact of the arts having been partially introduced among them. The Eskimo has been taught to construct the boat, to string the bow, and to fashion the spear. But the Bushmen are utterly ignorant of the arts and, consequently, strangers to civilization and improvement; their moral and intellectual features, therefore, have been the same through the succession of ages and the lapse of centuries. No improvement, no melioration in their condition has taken place; but, through the transition of generations, sires and sons have lived and died alike degraded!

Various philosophers have attributed the differences which exist between nations to various causes. Hippocrates, for example, with regard to the Scythians, and Strabo, as respecting the Medes and Armenians, took it for granted, that climate alone causes the distinctions or similitudes, whether physical or moral, which characterize various people. This ancient hypothesis has been adopted to the full extent, by thousands, notwithstanding its manifest absurdity. La Mothe adopted the puerile and chimerical theory of natural *sympathies* and *antipathies*, and contended that to their influence was ascribable the difference which distinguishes one nation from another. While Bayle, with much more propriety and truth, attributed those differences to political interests and institutions of state. That climate and government exert great influence over the character and conduct of man and create striking national distinctions is admitted. It is a combination of those two causes which makes the Frenchman loquacious, gay, volatile; the Spaniard taciturn, staid, and solemn; the Ottoman dull, languid, and listless; the German hardy, diligent, and contemplative. But, however opposite and distinctive the habits and principles which the influence of climate and government may generate, and however those causes operate upon the character and condition of man, yet they affect his happiness and welfare but remotely and partially indeed, when compared with the influence exercised by the mechanic arts. For although men of different nations may be opposed in fundamental opinions and the elements of their thoughts and actions be at variance, yet, where the arts are practiced, man is *civilized* and, therefore, comparatively blessed; but where the arts are unknown — no matter what be the climate, the form of government, or the circumstances that surround him — man is a *savage*, and degraded to the level of the brute that resembles him in form and in habits. Civilized man, therefore, is what he is by means of the mechanic arts.

Who were the pioneers of the West? What class of society prepared the way for the agriculturist, the merchant, and the professional man? Were they not artificers? Was not the forest made to bow beneath the stroke of the axe, the stubborn glebe to yield to the hoe and the ploughshare? Was not the harvest gathered with the rake and the reaping hook; the grain converted into flour by the mill or the mortar; and the raw material into fabrics by the wheel and the loom, and fashioned into garments with the shears and the needle; the game of the forest and of the prairie secured with the trap and the rifle; the habitation erected by means of the trowel, the hammer, and the saw? Unquestionably, without the agency of the arts, the adventurer must have returned disappointed or perished in the enterprise. Place man, without a knowledge of the arts and their uses, in a country with a rigid climate, a stubborn and ungrateful soil, and want, starvation, and death must be his destiny. No country can be cleared or settled, nor colony founded, without the aid of the mechanic arts. First settlers, therefore, are as much dependent upon the useful arts for their subsistence, comfort, and welfare as are the plants of the field for their life and growth upon the light of the sun and the dews of heaven!

I will no longer detain you on this part of my subject but, in conclusion, will merely observe that the culture of the mechanic arts are not only calculated to elicit, expand, and invigorate the inventive faculties of man, to strengthen his natural imbecility, inform his natural ignorance, and enrich his natural poverty, but also to advance his morals, refine his manners, and elevate his character.

My object in inviting you to a consideration of this subject at the present time is to impress upon your minds the importance of the situation which you, in reality, ought to occupy in society. This you seem to have lost sight of in a very great degree; and, from some cause or other, have relinquished your claims to that consideration to which, as mechanics and as men, you are entitled. You have, most unfortunately for yourselves and for the respectability of your vocations, become apparently unconscious of your own worth, and been led to regard your callings as humble and inferior, and your stations as too subordinate in life. And why? why is it so? Why should the producer consider himself inferior to the consumer? Or why should the mechanic, who builds a house, consider himself less important than the owner or occupant? It is strange, indeed, and to me perfectly unaccountable that the artificer, who prepares the accommodations, the comforts, and embellishments of life, should consider himself of less consequence than those to whose pleasure and convenience he ministers.

It was observed by someone of the olden time that "A man's pretensions was the standard by which the world judged of his merits." Were you to be judged by this standard, my friends, your merits, I apprehend, would be somewhat difficult to find. Do not consider, from these observations, however, that I would urge you to put forth claims that are not well founded or make pretensions to that which you are not entitled to. Far from it. I merely wish you to take a

fair estimate of your worth and importance, but not to overrate yourselves or your callings. I would have you remember, however, that
when a man sinks in his own estimation, he is sure to sink also in the
estimation of the world. And just so in relation to any occupation or
calling in life. If those who follow it confess it to be degrading, the
world is sure to consider it in no better, but generally in a worse light.

In order to be convinced of the blessings conferred upon society by
means of the useful arts, we have only to look around us for a moment.
But, like all blessings familiar to us, they are not properly appreciated;
and the services of those who practice them, like the services of all
common benefactors, are vastly underrated. It is not my intention,
as I have already intimated, to go into detail or to attempt a comparison between the relative merits, or rather utility, of the various
arts practised among us. Such a course would be neither gratifying,
instructive, nor ingenuous. I will briefly allude, however, to some of
those modern inventions and discoveries in mechanical philosophy
which I conceive to be of the greatest importance to the world.

The *art of printing* has, perhaps, contributed more essentially to the
welfare of mankind, to the advancement of society, and to the promotion and diffusion of political, physical, and ethical truths than all
the arts beside. It is, in fact, an art that is *"preservative* of all arts."
Wherever it is known and encouraged, the progressive improvement
of society is certain, and the march of mind secure and unembarrassed.
But where the press has never shed its light or dispensed its intellectual
treasures, the night of ignorance and the gloom of superstition rests
upon the soul and obscures the intellect of man; and should it be
struck from existence, with its rich treasures of instruction, the world,
ere long, would be merged in night and barbarism.

The invention of the *mariner's compass* or rather, the discovery of
that mystic and incomprehensible law which gives polarity to the
needle, claims to be ranked, on account of its importance, next to the
press. The navigator is no longer compelled to keep the coast within
view in order to steer his course aright, but now seeks the middle of
the ocean with confidence and security; nor does it require a period
of ten years, as in the days of Ulysses and Aeneas, to make a voyage
from Ilium to the island of Ithaca or to the shores of Italy. Neither
does the modern navigator require a Palinurus, as did the pious
Trojan of old, to stand at the helm and observe the stars of heaven.

He possesses, in the compass, a safer guide than either Orion or Arcturus. But for the compass those geographical limits which from the dawn of creation had concealed one half of the world from the other had never been passed; and America perhaps at this moment would have been a pathless world of woods, made vocal by the serpent's hiss, the panther's scream, and the wild man's terrific yell, and perchance here even on this consecrated spot, where now stands the temple of the living God, the wild fox would have made his den, or the red man his habitation!

The *steam engine* next takes rank in point of importance. Its effects on the condition of society are of incalculable importance. In almost every branch of the arts it is hailed as an auxiliary. Its application to nautical purposes is of greater utility and of deeper concernment to the world than the world at present imagines. It is an agent whose power and influence will be most beneficially felt in contributing toward the preservation of the American Union by overcoming those physical barriers that have isolated one section of our country from the other. By means of its power, space is annihilated, and the inhabitants from the extremes of the Union are now brought into frequent and friendly intercourse. Let it be borne in mind, however, that neither the printing press nor the mariner's compass nor the steam engine could have been produced without the aid of the common mechanic. The toil and skill of the artificers in wood and iron and steel were requisite to their completion. The square and the compass, the axe and the plane, the hammer and the anvil were all indispensable to their production.

. . . .

So far from the government under which we live being unfavorable to our interests as artists and mechanics, it is, in every respect, most propitious! There never was a land under heaven where the intellectual powers of man had so fine a field and such fair play as they have in our own country and in our own times. If our march, therefore, is not onward to honor, competency, and fame, the fault is all our own.

Will you meet me with the excuse that your early opportunities in life were limited? that you have no time for improvement? that it is too late to enter the lists for distinction? and that you must, therefore, be content to live and die in obscurity? Such are the common apologies of the indolent, the spiritless, and the dissolute. Let no such pretexts, therefore, be made by members of the trades' union.   Would you have your ambition fired, your hopes elevated, or your resolution strengthened by glorious example?   Then contemplate for a moment the history of those illustrious men, whose names stand as "landmarks on the cliffs of fame," who were the artificers of their own fortunes, and who, like yourselves, were mechanics and artists.   Franklin, who astonished, and confounded the schoolmen of Europe and with impunity dallied with the lightnings of heaven, was once an obscure journeyman printer! His elevation was the result of his own efforts.   Roger Sherman, one of the most extraordinary men in the extraordinary age in which he lived, and William Gifford, the immortal author of the Baviad and Maeviad, were both shoemakers.   George Walton, the distinguished patriot and jurist of Georgia, acquired his education by torchlight during the term of his apprenticeship to a carpenter! General Knox was a bookbinder, and General Greene (the second Washington), a blacksmith.   But we are not limited to the past for examples. Our distinguished townsman, Frazee, was a common stonemason.   As a sculptor he now stands unequalled in this country, and as a self-taught artist unsurpassed by any in the world.

Would you enjoy the fame of those illustrious men? Then follow their example and imitate their virtues.   Like them, be diligent, be honest, be firm, be indefatigable.   Pursue knowledge with a diligence that never tires and with a perseverance that never falters; and honor and glory and happiness will be your reward! You have no longer an excuse why you should not prosper and flourish, both as a body and as individuals.   You know your rights and, consequently, feel your strength.   If mortification and defeat should attend you, blame not your fellowmen; the cause will be found within yourselves.   Neither blame your country; the fault will not be hers! No, Land of Genius, Land of Refuge, Land of the Brave and Free! thy sons have no cause to reproach thee! All thy deserving children find favor in thine eyes, support on thy arm, and protection in thy bosom!

22

ORESTES AUGUSTUS BROWNSON

THE LABORING CLASSES[1]

[The Chartist Movement]

THE SUBJECT of the little work before us is one of the weightiest which can engage the attention of the statesman or the philanthropist. It is, indeed, here discussed only in relation to the working classes of England, but it in reality involves the condition of the working classes throughout the world — a great subject, and one never yet worthily treated. Chartism, properly speaking, is no local or temporary phenomenon. Its germ may be found in every nation in Christendom; indeed wherever man has approximated a state of civilization, wherever there is inequality in social condition and in the distribution of the products of industry. And where does not this inequality obtain? Where is the spot on earth in which the actual producer of wealth is not one of the lower class, shut out from what are looked upon as the main advantages of the social state?

Mr. Carlyle, though he gives us few facts, yet shows us that the condition of the workingmen in England is deplorable and every day growing worse. It has already become intolerable, and hence the outbreak of the Chartists. Chartism is the protest of the working classes against the injustice of the present social organization of the British community, and a loud demand for a new organization which shall respect the rights and well-being of the laborer.

The movements of the Chartists have excited considerable alarm in the higher classes of English society and some hope in the friends of humanity among ourselves. We do not feel competent to speak with any decision on the extent or importance of these movements. If our voice could reach the Chartists, we would bid them be bold and determined; we would bid them persevere even unto death; for their cause is that of justice, and in fighting for it they will be fighting

<hr />

[1] [From "*The Laboring Classes,*" *a review of Thomas Carlyle's Chartism, originally published in the Boston Quarterly Review for 1840* (Boston, 1840) — Abridged.]

the battles of God and man. But we look for no important results from their movements. We have little faith in a John Bull mob. It will bluster and swagger, and threaten much; but give it plenty of porter and roast beef, and it will sink back to its kennel, as quiet and as harmless as a lamb. The lower classes in England have made many a move since the days of Wat Tyler for the betterment of their condition, but we cannot perceive that they have ever effected much. They are doubtless nearer the day of their emancipation than they were, but their actual condition is scarcely superior to what it was in the days of Richard the Second.

[Middle Class Enemies of the Workers]

There is no country in Europe in which the condition of the laboring classes seems to us so hopeless as in that of England. This is not owing to the fact that the aristocracy is less enlightened, more powerful, or more oppressive in England than elsewhere. The English laborer does not find his worst enemy in the nobility but in the middling class. The middle class is much more numerous and powerful in England than in any other European country and is of a higher character. It has always been powerful, for by means of the Norman Conquest it received large accessions from the old Saxon nobility. The Conquest established a new aristocracy and degraded the old to the condition of Commoners. The superiority of the English Commons is, we suppose, chiefly owing to this fact.

The middle class is always a firm champion of equality when it concerns humbling a class above it, but it is its inveterate foe when it concerns elevating a class below it. Manfully have the British commoners struggled against the old feudal aristocracy, and so successfully that they now constitute the dominant power in the state. To their struggles against the throne and the nobility is the English nation indebted for the liberty it so loudly boasts and which, during the last half of the last century, so enraptured the friends of humanity throughout Europe.

But this class has done nothing for the laboring population, the real *proletarii*. It has humbled the aristocracy; it has raised itself to dominion, and it is now conservative — conservative in fact, whether it call itself Whig or Radical. From its near relation to the workingmen, its kindred pursuits with them, it is altogether more hostile to them than the nobility ever were or ever can be. This was seen in the conduct of England towards the French Revolution. So long as that Revolution was in the hands of the middle class and threatened merely to humble monarchy and nobility, the English nation applauded it; but as soon as it descended to the mass of people and promised to elevate the laboring classes, so soon as the starving workman began to flatter himself that there was to be a revolution for him too as well as for his employer, the English nation armed itself and poured out its blood and treasure to suppress it. Everybody knows that Great Britain, boasting of her freedom and of her love of freedom, was the life and soul of the opposition to the French Revolution; and on her head almost alone should fall the curses of humanity for the sad failure of that glorious uprising of the people in behalf of their impre- scriptible and inalienable rights. Yet it was not the English monarchy nor the English nobility that was alone in fault. Monarchy and nobility would have been powerless, had they not had with them the great body of the English Commoners. England fought in the ranks, nay, at the head of the allies, not for monarchy, not for nobility, nor yet for religion; but for trade and manufactures, for her middle class, against the rights and well-being of the workingman, and her strength and efficiency consisted in the strength and efficiency of this class.

Now this middle class, which was strong enough to defeat nearly all the practical benefit of the French Revolution, is the natural enemy of the Chartists. It will unite with the monarchy and nobility against them, and spare neither blood nor treasure to defeat them. Our despair for the poor Chartists arises from the number and power of the middle class. We dread for them neither monarchy nor nobility. Nor should they. Their only real enemy is in the employer. In all countries is it the same. The only enemy of the laborer is your employer, whether appearing in the shape of the master mechanic, or in the owner of a factory. A Duke of Wellington is much more likely to vindicate the rights of labor than an Abbot Lawrence, although the latter may be a very kind-hearted man and liberal citizen, as we always find *Blackwood's Magazine* more true to the interests of the poor than we do the *Edinburgh Review*, or even the *London and Westminster*.

[WEAKNESS OF CARLYLE'S RECOMMENDATIONS]

Mr. Carlyle, contrary to his wont, in the pamphlet we have named, commends two projects for the relief of the workingmen, which he finds others have suggested: universal education, and general emigration. Universal education we shall not be thought likely to depreciate; but we confess that we are unable to see in it that sovereign remedy for the evils of the social state as it is which some of our friends do, or say they do. We have little faith in the power of education to elevate a people compelled to labor from twelve to sixteen hours a day and to experience for no mean portion of the time a paucity of even the necessaries of life, let alone its comforts. Give your starving boy a breakfast before you send him to school and your tattered beggar a cloak before you attempt his moral and intellectual elevation. A swarm of naked and starving urchins crowded into a schoolroom will make little proficiency in the "Humanities." Indeed, it seems to us most bitter mockery for the well-dressed and well-fed to send the schoolmaster and priest to the wretched hovels of squalid poverty, a mockery at which devils may laugh but over which angels must weep. Educate the working classes of England; and what then? Will they require less food and less clothing when educated than they do now? Will they be more contented or more happy in their condition? For God's sake beware how you kindle within them the intellectual spark, and make them aware that they too are men, with powers of thought and feeling which ally them by the bonds of brotherhood to their betters. If you will doom them to the external condition of brutes, do in common charity keep their minds and hearts brutish. Render them as insensible as possible, that they may feel the less acutely their degradation and see the less clearly the monstrous injustice which is done them.

General emigration can at best afford only a temporary relief, for the colony will soon become an empire and reproduce all the injustice and wretchedness of the mother country. Nor is general emigration necessary. England, if she would be just, could support a larger population than she now numbers. The evil is not from overpopulation, but from the unequal repartition of the fruits of industry. She suffers from overproduction, and from overproduction because her workmen produce not for themselves but for their employers. What then is the remedy? As it concerns England, we shall leave the

English statesman to answer. Be it what it may, it will not be obtained without war and bloodshed. It will be found only at the end of one of the longest and severest struggles the human race has ever been engaged in, only by that most dreaded of all wars, the war of the poor against the rich, a war which, however long it may be delayed, will come, and come with all its horrors. The day of vengeance is sure; for the world after all is under the dominion of a just Providence.

[THE COMING CRISIS OF CAPITALISM]

No one can observe the signs of the times with much care without perceiving that a crisis as to the relation of wealth and labor is approaching. It is useless to shut our eyes to the fact, and like the ostrich fancy ourselves secure because we have so concealed our heads that we see not the danger. We or our children will have to meet this crisis. The old war between the King and the Barons is well nigh ended, and so is that between the Barons and the Merchants and Manufacturers, landed capital and commercial capital. The business-man has become the peer of my Lord. And now commences the new struggle between the operative and his employer, between wealth and labor. Every day does this struggle extend further and wax stronger and fiercer; what or when the end will be God only knows.

In this coming contest there is a deeper question at issue than is commonly imagined, a question which is but remotely touched in your controversies about United States banks and sub-treasuries, chartered banking and free banking, free trade and corporations, although these controversies may be paving the way for it to come up. We have discovered no presentiment of it in any king's or queen's speech, nor in any President's message. It is embraced in no popular political creed of the day, whether christened Whig or Tory, *Juste-milieu* or Democratic. No popular Senator or deputy or peer seems to have any glimpse of it; but it is working in the hearts of the million, is struggling to shape itself, and one day it will be uttered, and in thunder tones. Well will it be for him who, on that day, shall be found ready to answer it.

What we would ask is, throughout the Christian world, the actual condition of the laboring classes, viewed simply and exclusively in their capacity of laborers? They constitute at least a moiety of the human race. We exclude the nobility, we exclude also the middle class, and include only actual laborers, who are laborers and not proprietors, owners of none of the funds of production, neither houses, shops, nor lands, nor implements of labor, being therefore solely dependent on their hands. We have no means of ascertaining their precise proportion to the whole number of the race, but we think we may estimate them at one half. In any contest they will be as two to one, because the large class of proprietors who are not employers but laborers on their own lands or in their own shops will make common cause with them.

Now we will not so belie our acquaintance with political economy as to allege that these alone perform all that is necessary to the production of wealth. We are not ignorant of the fact that the merchant, who is literally the common carrier and exchange dealer, performs a useful service and is therefore entitled to a portion of the proceeds of labor. But make all necessary deductions on his account, and then ask what portion of the remainder is retained, either in kind or in its equivalent, in the hands of the original producer, the workingman? All over the world this fact stares us in the face: the workingman is poor and depressed, while a large portion of the non-workingmen, in the sense we now use the term, are wealthy. It may be laid down as a general rule, with but few exceptions, that men are rewarded in an inverse ratio to the amount of actual service they perform. Under every government on earth the largest salaries are annexed to those offices which demand of their incumbents the least amount of actual labor either mental or manual. And this is in perfect harmony with the whole system of repartition of the fruits of industry which obtains in every department of society. Now here is the system which prevails, and here is its result. The whole class of simple laborers are poor and in general unable to procure any thing beyond the bare necessaries of life.

[CHATTEL SLAVERY SUPERIOR TO WAGE SLAVERY]

In regard to labor two systems obtain: one that of slave labor, the other that of free labor. Of the two, the first is, in our judgment, except so far as the feelings are concerned, decidedly the least oppressive. If the slave has never been a free man, we think, as a general rule, his sufferings are less than those of the free laborer at wages. As to actual freedom one has just about as much as the other. The laborer at wages has all the disadvantages of freedom and none of its blessings, while the slave, if denied the blessings, is freed from the disadvantages. We are no advocates of slavery; we are as heartily opposed to it as any modern abolitionist can be; but we say frankly that, if there must always be a laboring population distinct from proprietors and employers, we regard the slave system as decidedly preferable to the system at wages. It is no pleasant thing to go days without food, to lie idle for weeks, seeking work and finding none, to rise in the morning with a wife and children you love, and know not where to procure them a breakfast, and to see constantly before you no brighter prospect than the almshouse. Yet these are no unfrequent incidents in the lives of our laboring population. Even in seasons of general prosperity, when there was only the ordinary cry of "hard times," we have seen hundreds of people in a not very populous village, in a wealthy portion of our common country, suffering for the want of the necessaries of life, willing to work, and yet finding no work to do. Many and many is the application of a poor man for work, merely for his food, we have seen rejected. These things are little thought of, for the applicants are poor; they fill no conspicuous place in society, and they have no biographers. But their wrongs are chronicled in heaven. It is said there is no want in this country. There may be less than in some other countries. But death by actual starvation in this country is, we apprehend, no uncommon occurrence. The sufferings of a quiet, unassuming but useful class of females in our cities, in general sempstresses, too proud to beg or to apply to the almshouse, are not easily told. They are industrious; they do all that they can find to do, but yet the little there is for them to do, and the miserable pittance they receive for it is hardly sufficient to keep soul and body together. And yet there is a man who employs them to make shirts, trousers, etc., and grows rich on their labors. He is one of our respectable citizens, perhaps is praised in the newspapers for his liberal donations to some charitable institution. He passes among us as a pattern of morality and is honored as a worthy Christian. And why should he not be, since our *Christian* community is made up of such as he, and since our clergy would not dare question his piety lest they should incur the reproach of infidelity and lose their standing and their salaries? Nay, since our clergy are raised up, educated, fashioned, and sustained by such as he? Not a few of our churches rest on Mammon for their foundation. The basement is a trader's shop.

We pass through our manufacturing villages; most of them appear neat and flourishing. The operatives are well dressed and, we are told, well paid. They are said to be healthy, contented, and happy. This is the fair side of the picture; the side exhibited to distinguished visitors. There is a dark side, moral as well as physical. Of the common operatives, few, if any, by their wages, acquire a competence. A few of what Carlyle terms not inaptly the "body-servants" are well paid, and now and then an agent or an overseer rides in his coach. But the great mass wear out their health, spirits, and morals without becoming one whit better off than when they commenced labor. The bills of mortality in these factory villages are not striking, we admit, for the poor girls when they can toil no longer go home to die. The average life — working life, we mean — of the girls that come to Lowell,[2] for instance, from Maine, New Hampshire, and Vermont, we have been assured, is only about three years. What becomes of them then? Few of them ever marry; fewer still ever return to their native places with reputations unimpaired. "She has worked in a factory," is almost enough to damn to infamy the most worthy and virtuous girl. We know no sadder sight on earth than one of our factory villages presents when the bell, at break of day, or at the hour of breakfast or dinner, calls out its hundreds or thousands of operatives. We stand and look at these hard-working men and women hurrying in all directions and ask ourselves where go the proceeds of their labors? The man who employs them and for whom they are toiling as so many slaves is one of our city nabobs, reveling in luxury; or he is a member of our legislature, enacting laws to put money in his own pocket; or he is a member of Congress, contending for a high tariff to tax the poor for the benefit of the rich; or in these times he is shedding crocodile tears over the deplorable condition of the poor laborer, while he docks his wages twenty-five per cent; building miniature log cabins, shouting Harrison and "hard cider." And this man too would fain pass for a Christian and a republican. He shouts for liberty, stickles for equality, and is horrified at a Southern planter who keeps slaves.

---

[2] [Lowell, Mass., was one of the early mill-towns, the development of which signalized the end of Jefferson's idyllic agrarian picture of the United States.]

One thing is certain: that, of the amount actually produced by the operative, he retains a less proportion than it costs the master to feed, clothe, and lodge his slave. Wages is a cunning device of the devil for the benefit of tender consciences who would retain all the advantages of the slave system without the expense, trouble, and odium of being slaveholders.

The slave system, however, in name and form, is gradually disappearing from Christendom. It will not subsist much longer. But its place is taken by the system of labor at wages, and this system, we hold, is no improvement upon the one it supplants. Nevertheless the system of wages will triumph. It is the system which in name sounds honester than slavery and in substance is more profitable to the master. It yields the wages of iniquity, without its opprobrium. It will therefore supplant slavery and be sustained, for a time.

Now, what is the prospect of those who fall under the operation of this system? We ask, is there a reasonable chance that any considerable portion of the present generation of laborers shall ever become owners of a sufficient portion of the funds of production to be able to sustain themselves by laboring on their own capital — that is, as independent laborers? We need not ask this question, for everybody knows there is not. Well, is the condition of a laborer at wages the best that the great mass of the working people ought to be able to aspire to? Is it a condition — nay, can it be made a condition — with which a man should be satisfied, in which he should be contented to live and die?

In our own country this condition has existed under its most favorable aspects and has been made as good as it can be. It has reached all the excellence of which it is susceptible. It is now not improving but growing worse. The actual condition of the workingman today, viewed in all its bearings, is not so good as it was fifty years ago. If we have not been altogether misinformed, fifty years ago, health and industrious habits constituted no mean stock in trade, and with them almost any man might aspire to competence and independence. But it is so no longer. The wilderness has receded, and already the new lands are beyond the reach of the mere laborer, and the employer has him at his mercy. If the present relation subsist, we see nothing better for him in reserve than what he now possesses, but something altogether worse.

.   .   .   .

[The Establishment of Social Democracy]

Now the great work for this age and the coming is to raise up the laborer, and to realize in our own social arrangements and in the actual condition of all men that equality between man and man which God has established between the rights of one and those of another. In other words, our business is to emancipate the proletaries as the past has emancipated the slaves. This is our work. There must be no class of our fellow men doomed to toil through life as mere workmen at wages. If wages are tolerated it must be, in the case of the individual operative, only under such conditions that, by the time he is of a proper age to settle in life, he shall have accumulated enough to be an independent laborer on his own capital, on his own farm or in his own shop. Here is our work. How is it to be done?

Reformers in general answer this question, or what they deem its equivalent, in a manner which we cannot but regard as very unsatisfactory. They would have all men wise, good, and happy; but in order to make them so, they tell us that we want not external changes, but internal. And therefore, instead of declaiming against society and seeking to disturb existing social arrangements, we should confine ourselves to the individual reason and conscience, seek merely to lead the individual to repentance and to reformation of life, make the individual a practical, a truly religious man; and all evils will either disappear, or be sanctified to the spiritual growth of the soul.

.   .   .   .

For our part, we yield to none in our reverence for science and religion; but we confess that we look not for the regeneration of the race from priests and pedagogues. They have had a fair trial. They cannot construct the temple of God. They cannot conceive its plan, and they know not how to build. They daub with untempered mortar, and the walls they erect tumble down if so much as a fox attempt to go up thereon. In a word they always league with the people's masters, and seek to reform without disturbing the social arrangements which render reform necessary. They would change the consequents without changing the antecedents, secure to men the rewards of holiness, while they continue their allegiance to the devil. We have no faith in priests and pedagogues. They merely cry peace, peace, and that too when there is no peace, and can be none.

We admit the importance of what Dr. Channing in his lectures on the subject we are treating recommends as "self-culture." Self-culture is a good thing, but it cannot abolish inequality nor restore men to their rights. As a means of quickening moral and intellectual energy, exalting the sentiments, and preparing the laborer to contend manfully for his rights, we admit its importance and insist as strenuously as anyone on making it as universal as possible; but as constituting in itself a remedy for the vices of the social state, we have no faith in it. As a means it is well, as the end it is nothing.

The truth is the evil we have pointed out is not merely individual in its character. It is not, in the case of any single individual, of any one man's procuring, nor can the efforts of any one man, directed solely to his own moral and religious perfection, do aught to remove it. What is purely individual in its nature, efforts of individuals to perfect themselves may remove. But the evil we speak of is inherent in all our social arrangements, and cannot be cured without a radical change of those arrangements. Could we convert all men to Christianity in both theory and practice, as held by the most enlightened sect of Christians among us, the evils of the social state would remain untouched. Continue our present system of trade, and all its present evil consequences will follow, whether it be carried on by your best men or your worst. Put your best men, your wisest, most moral, and most religious men, at the head of your paper money banks, and the evils of the present banking system will remain scarcely diminished. The only way to get rid of its evils is to change the system, not its managers. The evils of slavery do not result from the personal characters of slave masters. They are inseparable from the system, let who will be masters. Make all your rich men good Christians, and you have lessened not the evils of existing inequality in wealth. The mischievous effects of this inequality do not result from the personal characters of either rich or poor, but from itself, and they will continue just so long as there are rich men and poor men in the same community. You must abolish the system or accept its consequences. No man can serve both God and Mammon. If you will serve the devil, you must look to the devil for your wages; we know no other way.

[PRIESTHOOD AND PROGRESS]

Mankind came out of the savage state by means of the priests. Priests are the first civilizers of the race. For the wild freedom of the savage, they substitute the iron despotism of the theocrat. This is the first step in civilization, in man's career of progress. It is not strange then that some should prefer the savage state to the civilized. Who would not rather roam the forest with a free step and unshackled limb, though exposed to hunger, cold, and nakedness, than crouch an abject slave beneath the whip of the master? As yet civilization has done little but break and subdue man's natural love of freedom, but tame his wild and eagle spirit. In what a world does man even now find himself when he first awakes and feels some of the workings of his manly nature? He is in a cold, damp, dark dungeon, and loaded all over with chains, with the iron entering into his very soul. He cannot make one single free movement. The priest holds his conscience, fashion controls his tastes, and society with her forces invades the very sanctuary of his heart and takes command of his love, that which is purest and best in his nature, which alone gives reality to his existence, and from which proceeds the only ray which pierces the gloom of his prison house. Even that he cannot enjoy in peace and quietness, nor scarcely at all. He is wounded on every side, in every part of his being, in every relation in life, in every idea of his mind, in every sentiment of his heart. O, it is a sad world, a sad world to the young soul just awakening to its diviner instincts! A sad world to him who is not gifted with the only blessing which seems compatible with life as it is: absolute insensibility. But no matter. A wise man never murmurs. He never kicks against the pricks. What is is, and there is an end of it; what can be may be, and we will do what we can to make life what it ought to be. Though man's first step in civilization is slavery, his last step shall be freedom. The free soul can never be wholly subdued; the ethereal fire in man's nature may be smothered, but it cannot be extinguished. Down, down deep in the center of his heart it burns inextinguishable and forever, glowing intenser with the accumulating heat of centuries, and one day the whole mass of Humanity shall become ignited and be full of fire within and all over, as a live coal; and then slavery and whatever is foreign to the soul itself shall be consumed.

But, having traced the inequality we complain of to its origin, we proceed to ask again what is the remedy? The remedy is first to be sought in the destruction of the priest. We are not mere destructives. We delight not in pulling down; but the bad must be removed before the good can be introduced. Conviction and repentance precede regeneration. Moreover, we are Christians, and it is only by following out the Christian law, and the example of the early Christians, that we can hope to effect anything. Christianity is the sublimest protest against the priesthood ever uttered, and a protest uttered by both God and man, for he who uttered it was God-man. In the person of Jesus both God and man protest against the priesthood. What was the mission of Jesus but a solemn summons of every priesthood on earth to judgment and of the human race to freedom? He discomfited the learned doctors and with whips of small cords drove the priests, degenerated into mere money changers, from the temple of God. He instituted himself no priesthood, no form of religious worship. He recognized no priest but a holy life and commanded the construction of no temple but that of the pure heart. He preached no formal religion, enjoined no creed, set apart no day for religious worship. He preached fraternal love, peace on earth, and good will to men. He came to the soul enslaved, "cabined, cribbed, confined," to the poor child of mortality, bound hand and foot, unable to move, and said in the tones of a God, "Be free; be enlarged; be there room for thee to grow, expand, and overflow with the love thou wast made to overflow with."

.   .   .   .

The priest is universally a tyrant, universally the enslaver of his brethren, and therefore it is Christianity condemns him. It could not prevent the re-establishment of a hierarchy, but it prepared for its ultimate destruction by denying the inequality of blood, by representing all men as equal before God, and by insisting on the celibacy of the clergy. The best feature of the Church was in its denial to the clergy of the right to marry. By this it prevented the new hierarchy from becoming hereditary, as were the old sacerdotal corporations of India and Judea.

We object to no religious instruction; we object not to the gathering together of the people on one day in seven, to sing and pray, and listen to a discourse from a religious teacher; but we object to everything like an outward, visible church; to everything that in the

remotest degree partakes of the priest. A priest is one who stands as
a sort of mediator between God and man; but we have one mediator,
Jesus Christ, who gave himself a ransom for all, and that is enough.
It may be supposed that we Protestants have no priests, but for ourselves we know no fundamental difference between a Catholic priest
and a Protestant clergyman, as we know no difference of any magnitude, in relation to the principles on which they are based, between
a Protestant church and the Catholic church. Both are based on the
principle of authority; both deny in fact, however it may be in manner,
the authority of reason and war against freedom of mind; both substitute dead works for true righteousness, a vain show for the reality
of piety, and are sustained as the means of reconciling us to God
without requiring us to become godlike. Both therefore ought to go
by the board.

We may offend in what we say, but we cannot help that. We
insist upon it that the complete and final destruction of the priestly
order, in every practical sense of the word "priest," is the first step
to be taken towards elevating the laboring classes. Priests are, in
their capacity of priests, necessarily enemies to freedom and equality.
All reasoning demonstrates this, and all history proves it. There
must be no class of men set apart and authorized, either by law or
fashion, to speak to us in the name of God or to be the interpreters of
the word of God. The word of God never drops from the priest's lips.
He who redeemed man did not spring from the priestly class, for it is
evident that our Lord sprang out of Judea, of which tribe Moses spake
nothing concerning the priesthood. Who in fact were the authors of
the Bible, the book which Christendom professes to receive as the
word of God? The priests? Nay, they were the inveterate foes of
the priests. No man ever berated the priests more soundly than did
Jeremiah and Ezekiel. And who were they who heard Jesus the most
gladly? The priests? The chief priests were at the head of those
who demanded his crucifixion. In every age the priests, the authorized
teachers of religion, are the first to oppose the true prophet of God
and to condemn his prophecies as blasphemies. They are always a
let and a hindrance to the spread of truth. Why then retain them?
Why not abolish the priestly office? Why continue to sustain what
the whole history of man condemns as the greatest of all obstacles to
intellectual and social progress.

.   .   .   .

[THE NEED FOR A REVIVAL OF TRUE CHRISTIAN IDEALS]

The next step in this work of elevating the working classes will be to resuscitate the Christianity of Christ. The Christianity of the Church has done its work. We have had enough of that Christianity. It is powerless for good, but by no means powerless for evil. It now unmans us and hinders the growth of God's kingdom. The moral energy which is awakened it misdirects, and makes its deluded disciples believe that they have done their duty to God when they have joined the Church, offered a prayer, sung a Psalm, and contributed of their means to send out a missionary to preach unintelligible dogmas enough already, and more than enough. All this must be abandoned, and Christianity, as it came from Christ, be taken up and preached, and preached in simplicity and power.

According to the Christianity of Christ, no man can enter the kingdom of God who does not labor with all zeal and diligence to establish the kingdom of God on the earth — who does not labor to bring down the high and bring up the low; to break the fetters of the bound and set the captive free; to destroy all oppression, establish the reign of justice, which is the reign of equality, between man and man; to introduce new heavens and a new earth, wherein dwelleth righteousness, wherein all shall be as brothers, loving one another, and no one possessing what another lacketh. No man can be a Christian who does not labor to reform society, to mold it according to the will of God and the nature of man, so that free scope shall be given to every man to unfold himself in all beauty and power, and to grow up into the stature of a perfect man in Christ Jesus. No man can be a Christian who does not refrain from all practices by which the rich grow richer and the poor poorer, and who does not do all in his power to elevate the laboring classes, so that one man shall not be doomed to toil while another enjoys the fruits; so that each man shall be free and independent, sitting under "his own vine and fig tree with none to molest or to make afraid." We grant the power of Christianity in working out the reform we demand; we agree that one of the most efficient means of elevating the workingmen is to Christianize the community. But you must Christianize it. It is the gospel of Jesus you must preach, and not the gospel of the priests. Preach the gospel of Jesus, and that will turn every man's attention to the crying evil we have designated, and will arm every Christian with power to effect those changes in social arrangements which shall secure to all men the equality of position and condition which it is already acknowledged they possess in relation to their rights. But let it be the genuine gospel that you preach, and not that pseudo-gospel which lulls the conscience asleep and permits men to feel that they may be servants of God while they are slaves to the world, the flesh, and the devil, and while they ride roughshod over the hearts of their prostrate brethren. We must preach no gospel that permits men to feel that they are honorable men and good Christians, although rich and with eyes standing out with fatness, while the great mass of their brethren are suffering from iniquitous laws, from mischievous social arrangements, and pining away for the want of the refinements and even the necessaries of life.

.   .   .   .

We cannot proceed a single step with the least safety, in the great work of elevating the laboring classes, without the exaltation of sentiment, the generous sympathy and the moral courage which Christianity alone is fitted to produce or quicken. But it is lamentable to see how, by means of the mistakes of the Church, the moral courage, the generous sympathy, the exaltation of sentiment Christianity does actually produce or quicken is perverted, and made efficient only in producing evil or hindering the growth of good. Here is wherefore it is necessary on the one hand to condemn in the most pointed terms the Christianity of the Church, and to bring out on the other hand in all its clearness, brilliancy, and glory the Christianity of Christ.

[Reform by Legislative Enactment]

Having, by breaking down the power of the priesthood and the Christianity of the priests, obtained an open field and freedom for our operations, and by preaching the true Gospel of Jesus, directed all minds to the great social reform needed, and quickened in all souls the moral power to live for it or to die for it, our next resort must be to government, to legislative enactments. Government is instituted to be the agent of society, or more properly the organ through which society may perform its legitimate functions. It is not the master of society; its business is not to control society, but to be the organ through which society effects its will. Society has never to petition government; government is its servant and subject to its commands.

Now the evils of which we have complained are of a social nature. That is, they have their root in the constitution of society as it is; and they have attained to their present growth by means of social influences, the action of government, of laws, and of systems and institutions upheld by society, and of which individuals are the slaves. This being the case, it is evident that they are to be removed only by the action of society, that is, by government, for the action of society is government.

But what shall government do? Its first doing must be an *un*doing. There has been thus far quite too much government, as well as government of the wrong kind. The first act of government we want is a still further limitation of itself. It must begin by circumscribing within narrower limits its powers. And then it must proceed to repeal all laws which bear against the laboring classes, and then to enact such laws as are necessary to enable them to maintain their equality. We have no faith in those systems of elevating the working classes which propose to elevate them without calling in the aid of government. We must have government and legislation expressly directed to this end.

[BREAK THE POWER OF THE BANKS]

But again what legislation do we want so far as this country is concerned? We want first the legislation which shall free the Government, whether State or Federal, from the control of the banks. The banks represent the interest of the employer, and therefore of necessity interests adverse to those of the employed; that is, they represent the interests of the business community in opposition to the laboring community. So long as the Government remains under the control of the banks, so long it must be in the hands of the natural enemies of the laboring classes, and may be made, nay, will be made, an instrument of depressing them yet lower. It is obvious then that, if our object be the elevation of the laboring classes, we must destroy the power of the banks over the Government and place the Government in the hands of the laboring classes themselves or in the hands of those, if such there be, who have an identity of interest with them. But this cannot be done so long as the banks exist. Such is the subtle influence of credit and such the power of capital that a banking system like ours, if sustained, necessarily and inevitably becomes the real and efficient government of the country. We have been struggling for ten years in this country against the power of the banks, struggling to free merely the Federal Government from their grasp, but with humiliating success. At this moment, the contest is almost doubtful, not indeed in our mind, but in the minds of no small portion of our countrymen. The partisans of the banks count on certain victory. The banks discount freely to build "log cabins," to purchase "hard cider," and to defray the expense of manufacturing enthusiasm for a cause which is at war with the interests of the people. That they will succeed, we do not for one moment believe; but that they could maintain the struggle so long and be as strong as they now are at the end of ten years' constant hostility proves but all too well the power of the banks and their fatal influence on the political action of the community. The present character, standing, and resources of the bank party prove to a demonstration that the banks must be destroyed or the laborer not elevated. Uncompromising hostility to the whole banking system should therefore be the motto of every workingman and of every friend of humanity. The system must be destroyed. On this point there must be no misgiving, no subterfuge, no palliation. The system is at war with the rights and interest of labor, and it must go. Every friend of the system must be marked as an enemy to his race, to his country, and especially to the laborer. No matter who he is, in what party he is found, or what name he bears, he is, in our judgment, no true democrat, as he can be no true Christian.

[RESTRICT INHERITANCE OF PROPERTY]

Following the destruction of the banks, must come that of all monopolies, of all privilege. There are many of these. We cannot specify them all; we therefore select only one, the greatest of them all, the privilege which some have of being born rich while others are born poor. It will be seen at once that we allude to the hereditary descent of property, an anomaly in our American system, which must be removed or the system itself will be destroyed. We cannot now go into a discussion of this subject, but we promise to resume it at our earliest opportunity. We only say now that as we have abolished hereditary monarchy and hereditary nobility we must complete the work by abolishing hereditary property. A man shall have all he honestly acquires, so long as he himself belongs to the world in which he acquires it. But his power over his property must cease with his life, and his property must then become the property of the State, to be disposed of by some equitable law for the use of the generation which takes his place. Here is the principle without any of its details, and this is the grand legislative measure to which we look forward. We see no means of elevating the laboring classes which can be effectual without this. And is this a measure to be easily carried? Not at all. It will cost infinitely more than it cost to abolish either hereditary monarchy or. hereditary nobility. It is a great measure, and a startling. The rich, the business community, will never voluntarily consent to it, and we think we know too much of human nature to believe that it will ever be effected peaceably. It will be effected only by the strong arm of physical force. It will come, if it ever come at all, only at the conclusion of war, the like of which the world as yet has never witnessed, and from which, however inevitable it may seem to the eye of philosophy, the heart of Humanity recoils with horror.

We are not ready for this measure yet. There is much previous work to be done, and we should be the last to bring it before the legislature. The time, however, has come for its free and full discussion. It must be canvassed in the public mind, and society prepared for acting on it. No doubt they who broach it, and especially they who support it, will experience a due share of contumely and abuse. They will be regarded by the part of the community they oppose or may be thought to oppose as "graceless varlets," against whom every man of substance should set his face. But this is not, after all, a thing to disturb a wise man nor to deter a true man from telling his whole thought. He who is worthy of the name of man speaks what he honestly believes the interests of his race demand and seldom disquiets himself about what may be the consequences to himself. Men have, for what they believed the cause of God or man, endured the dungeon, the scaffold, the stake, the cross; and they can do it again, if need be. This subject must be freely, boldly, and fully discussed, whatever may be the fate of those who discuss it.

23

FREDERICK ROBINSON

A PROGRAM FOR LABOR[1]

[THE NECESSITY FOR REFORM]

IT BECOMES US, fellow citizens, to rejoice on the anniversary of that day when freedom and equality was promulgated as the natural birthright of man. It is the people's day and should ever be devoted to their service, to the keeping alive in them the knowledge of their rights, and it ought never to be appropriated to any other purpose. It should always be regarded as the epoch of our political emancipation from a foreign power and the commencement of a new era in the social and political condition of the people. But while we rejoice on this occasion over the advantages acquired for the human race by the labors and sacrifices of our fathers, let us not suppose there is nothing left for *us* to do but to glory in their achievements and boast of being their descendants. It behooves us rather, on every annual return of this day, to examine what progress we have made in knowledge and virtue and enquire what steps we have taken in the promotion of human happiness; what we have done for the general diffusion of truth, and the dissemination of a just knowledge of their own rights among the great mass of the people; in what way we have improved our social and political condition, and to devise means for a more perfect enjoyment of that liberty and equality which our fathers purchased for us with their blood.

The condition of the people can never remain stationary. When not improving they are sinking deeper and deeper into slavery. Eternal vigilance alone can sustain them, and never ceasing exertion is necessary for their social and political improvement. For the interests of the thousands are always contrary to the interests of the millions. The prosperity of the one always consists in the adversity of

---

[1] [From *An Oration delivered before the Trades' Union of Boston and Vicinity, July 4, 1834* (Boston, 1834) — Abridged.]

the other.[2] As the millions become intelligent, united, and independent, the thousands are divested of their power, importance, and wealth. The few have always understood this and seen the necessity of the closest union among themselves in order to maintain their ascendency, while the many have not only been ignorant of this fact, but have always regarded the few as their benefactors, protectors, and friends. Hence we are doomed to never-ceasing exertion for the enjoyment of our rights and the improvement of our condition until we work out the reform of society, and by the complete enjoyment of the blessings of equality, the common good of all the people shall constitute the interest of all.

[REFORM MUST COME FROM THE PEOPLE]

Our destiny, fellow citizens, is in our own hands, and we must rely upon ourselves alone for the improvement of our republican institutions, the reform of our laws, and the bettering of our social and political condition. And if we sink into slavery, to ourselves alone must the calamity be charged. For the governments, the constitutions, the laws, and all the institutions of the country are in our hands, and we have the power to mold them to our will.   In this respect we have the advantage of all the rest of the world. Before the industrious, democratic portion of the people in other countries will be able to enjoy all the rights and exercise all the powers guaranteed to us by our constitutions, many revolutions are to take place, either silently and peaceably in the lapse of time, or more suddenly by convulsions, bloodshed, and civil war. We cannot be judged therefore in comparison with the people of other nations. If we are not in every respect far before them in knowledge and in virtue, no less than in abundance and all the blessings of social life, we show ourselves vastly less deserving. For every institution, every law, every action of our government emanates from ourselves; we are responsible for all the evils arising from bad laws, defective constitutions, evil administrations, or whatever in society tends to the injury of the people. But our fathers

---

[2] In saying that the interests of any two portions of the community are distinct, we speak of them in the same worldly and selfish view, in which they are usually considered among men. An enlarged and beneficent view of human happiness, would teach us that no permanent benefit could be gained to any one, by an encroachment upon the natural rights of a fellow creature.

have purchased for us political rights and an equality of privileges which we have not yet had the intelligence to appreciate, nor the courage to protect, nor the wisdom to enjoy. For although it cannot be denied that in this country there can be no advantages, powers, or privileges which everyone has not an equal right to enjoy, yet do we not see everywhere around us, privileges, advantages, monopolies enjoyed by the few which are denied to the many; indeed do we not see all the same machinery in operation among us which has crowded the great mass of the people of other countries down into the grossest ignorance, degradation, and slavery. While we have been comparing our condition with the miserable slavery of other nations, and boasting of our advantages, and glorying in the achievements of our fathers, ignorantly supposing that we were already in the possession of the highest degree of liberty and in the enjoyment of the most perfect equality, the enemy have been silently encroaching upon our rights. But this delusion has passed; the enchantment is broken. The people are beginning to awake. Every day brings to our ears the pleasing intelligence that the industrious classes, which always constitute the democracy of the country, are beginning to bestir themselves and are enquiring what they shall do to be saved, not from the threatened evil of another world, but from the evils which they begin to see impending over them and their children here.

But how shall we avoid these evils, how improve our condition and scatter the blessings of equality over the land? We must do it, fellow citizens, by union among ourselves and by acting in concert with the democracy of the country. While the few can contrive means to keep the people divided among themselves, they fall an easy prey. There are but two great political divisions in the world: those who are in favor of a government of the people, and those who are in favor of a government over the people; of a government of the many, and a government of the few; of liberty and slavery. But it has often been shown by reasons and arguments not to be controverted, that a government over the people has not a right to exist, because there is not one man in a hundred whose interests, to say nothing of his duty, would not lead him to oppose such a government, and as it is impossible for one man forcibly to govern a hundred, a government over the people can only exist with ignorance, corruption, and fraud.

[THE PARTIES OF THE COUNTRY]

The aristocracy of our country are well aware that their notions of government are unsound, and in order to prevent the true appellation of aristocracy from being attached to them, they continually contrive to change their party name. It was first Tory, then Federalist, then no party, then amalgamation, then National Republican, now Whig, and the next name they assume perhaps will be republican or democrat. But by whatever name they reorganize themselves, the true democracy of the country, the producing classes, ought to be able to distinguish the enemy. Ye may know them by their fruit. Ye may know them by their deportment toward the people. Ye may know them by their disposition to club together, and constitute societies and incorporations for the enjoyment of exclusive privileges and for countenancing and protecting each other in their monopolies. They are composed in general of all those who are, or who believe themselves to be favored by some adventitious circumstances of fortune. They are those, with some honorable exceptions, who have contrived to live without labor, or who hope one day to do so, and must consequently live on the labor of others. But there is not one man in a hundred whose interests, if he knew his own true interests, would lead him to join this party. Their numbers would be very small and truly contemptible, were it not for the ignorance, the foolish pride and vanity of many, who are continually itching to get into 'good society,' always ready to cringe with spaniel-like sycophancy to the rich, following wherever they lead, and careless of the liberty and happiness of others provided they are favored slaves themselves and receive some little notice from their masters. Every individual attached to this party from interest, from vanity, or pride, should justly receive the epithet of partisan. But it is impossible for a true democrat to be a party man, or for those favorable to democracy to constitute a party. For how can he be a partisan, who looks upon all men as equal and contends that there is no power, no advantage, no privilege, which can be enjoyed by any one man or class of men, which does not equally belong to all, and ought not equally to be enjoyed by every other man in the nation.

How indeed can that be called a party which embraces and equalizes all citizens. But we have often been deceived by those whom we have raised to power; and it is therefore difficult to know on which side the people's interests lie. This is a part of the policy of the aristocracy.

They divide themselves into all parties, and by contriving to obtain the ascendency in all, endeavor to bring all into equal contempt with the people. How often have we in this way been deceived. Some ambitious, learned, and talented demagogue, finding it the cheapest way to power and wealth, courts the people, "the rabble," whom he at heart despises, and after making great hypocritical pretensions to democracy, is raised to office by the people. Being now raised to distinction by the many, he begins to court the favor of the few. Having political authority, he now longs for riches, titles, and family alliances with the proud and the wealthy. He begins to interest himself in all the exclusive policy of the aristocracy, promotes the establishment of all kinds of moneyed combinations, favors the chartering of all kinds of monopolies, and finally becomes identified with the exclusive policy of the few. Their opposition in the mean time gradually softens down. Their papers become less virulent, then seem half way to approve; and in order to deceive the people, pretend to be converted to their cause, and speak in high terms of their intelligence in choosing so good a man. He is now the candidate of the aristocracy, and the people being in this way deceived continue also to support him. But experience ought to teach us that when opposition towards any one begins to abate, it is time to watch him closely; and when this opposition is changed into favor, it is time to desert him. For the aristocracy of our country, under all the different names which they have assumed, have never failed to receive with open arms all traitors to the cause of the people, and have always put them forward in the warfare which they have unremittingly waged against free principles. They do this from the same policy which induces armies to push forward in battle the traitors and deserters from the opposite camp. Because they know that traitors and deserters have already passed the Rubicon, have put everything at stake, and must therefore fight with the most reckless and desperate fury, knowing that if the party to which they have deserted fail, they must lose all, becoming contemptible in the eyes of those to whom they have deserted, while held in abhorrence by the party they had betrayed. In all their schemes to deceive us, patriotism and love of country is forever upon their tongues. The rich merchant, whose whole soul is absorbed in profits and losses, and instead of laboring to render the condition of his species more equal, comfortable, and happy, endeavors to impress his dependents with a sense of the great difference between his situation and theirs, to make his superiority discernible and their inferiority insupportable, will notwithstanding boast much of patriotism. The sentimentalist, the poet, may deem the love of country to be an attachment to the hills and valleys, the mountains and cataracts, the bubbling springs and purling streams, the rivers and oceans, the far extended prospect, the luxuriant verdure; and while absorbed in these things, and regardless of whatever affects the human race, if charged with want of patriotism would be offended; for his local attachment, his love of mountains, vales, and streams, he mistakes for patriotism. And the capitalist, if he loves the banks, the insurance companies, and all the incorporate joint stock institutions of "our country, our whole country," thinks, perhaps, that this love is patriotism. But real patriotism consists not in a love of the soil, the climate, the scenery, because these may be found in other countries, equal, and in some superior to our own. Neither does it consist in an attachment to governments, constitutions, and laws; if it did, the inhabitant of Turkey would be unpatriotic if he loved not the laws which enable the Grand Turk at any time to strike off his head. But patriotism consists in nothing but a brotherly affection, an extensive love toward the whole human family, and a constant desire, a never-ceasing exertion to subserve the interests and promote the happiness of all.

The true lover of his country will consequently feel an attachment to the constitutions and laws of his country while he believes them to be subservient to the happiness, interests, rights, and liberties of the whole people; and he will have an utter abhorrence, a perfect hatred for all institutions which have a contrary effect, which tend to raise one man above another or in any way to keep the great mass of the people in ignorance and slavery. For whatever exalts the few, humbles the many; and luxury and splendor grow from poverty and want. Some must be poor, that others may be rich. And wherever we find the few possessed of excessive riches, we find, as a consequence, the many reduced to excessive poverty. For riches can no more exist without poverty than mountains without valleys. If there were not a single rich man in the world, there would be no less wealth in the world than there is now; but then it would be spread equally over the whole surface of society, diffusing equal abundance, comfort, and happiness among all.

Neither can poverty exist without riches. In communities, where the whole people are in want of many conveniences, living among rocks and mountains, like the Swiss, far removed from commerce; where the soil is so hard and sterile, that all must labor to procure the necessaries of life; yet, since equality in some degree prevails, the people are contented and happy.

.   .   .   .

[THEORY OF DEMOCRACY]

All mankind are one great family, and the Almighty Father of us all has made our common mother earth to produce bountifully, and more than enough, to feed, and clothe, and shelter all. He spreads his great table before us and loads it with abundance. He gives all an equal right to partake, and yet a few gormandizers devour the whole and leave the rest to want. Equality comprises everything that is good; inequality everything that is evil. Equality is liberty. Liberty without equality is dead. It is a word without meaning, mere "sounding brass, and a tinkling cymbal." Equality is democracy. Everyone who truly loves the human race will favor such governments, constitutions, laws, and administrations as he believes to be productive of equality. Equality will be the test, the measure of every question on which he is to act. In all his intercourse with his fellow men, in all his dealings, it will be his governing principle to do unto others, as he would that others should do unto him. This is the rock on which democracy is founded. The man that indulges himself in ostentation; that feels the pride of wealth or of birth; that plumes himself on his talents, learning, or professional skill, and looks down with contempt on what he calls the ignorant and the vulgar; that feels himself better than the laborer, the mechanic, or the fisherman, and is not free to take him by the hand and treat him as a brother — whatever he may call himself, he is not a democrat. For the spirit of democracy, which is equality, teaches us that the laborer, the producer, and not the talented, the rich, and the learned, are the benefactors of mankind. It is the laborer that provides us with food and clothing, that builds our houses, ships, and factories, digs the canals, levels the railroads, and procures for us all the necessaries, conveniences, and luxuries of life. How foolish then is pride and haughtiness; how childish, how thoughtless it is for men to presume that, because they can live at ease on hereditary wealth, because they can issue a writ, plead a cause, make a speech, administer a dose, or expound the mysteries of religion, that they are better than their neighbors. For which is of the most importance to society, to be able to make a speech, or a hob nail, to issue a writ, or manufacture a shoe, to provide food and clothing and shelter for the healthy, or drugs for the sick. But the law of nature, in what is called civilized society, is reversed. This law declares that industry is honorable and idleness disgraceful, that the laboring man shall have abundance and the idle shall be in want. But experience shows us everywhere the idle living in palaces, caressed, honored, surrounded with all the beauties and luxuries of life, and the laborer continually reduced to wretchedness and starvation. Nearly all the evils of life, treachery, fraud, and crime, may be traced to the perversion of this law of nature. For when honest labor is looked upon as so disgraceful that men often know and feel that to bend themselves to operative industry would injure their subsequent prospects in the world, is it strange that so many contrive to live without labor? And when we see the idle living in luxury and the laborer in want and disgrace, ought we to wonder that so many prefer to live by fraud, theft, robbery, or by any means rather than by honest industry? But let everyone know and feel that in exact proportion as he labors industriously in some useful employment will he improve his condition and increase his respectability; and that no one can enjoy the fruits of labor, which are wealth and respectability, without industry; and most of the fraud, hypocrisy, cunning, crime, and villainy of the world would come to an end; for misery, degradation, and want, the cause of all crime, would be removed. But the thousands live upon the millions, and these things will continue until the millions see the evil and contrive to enjoy the fruit of their own industry.

[REFORM OF LAW AND THE JUDICIARY]

In the savage state each individual produces for himself whatever he consumes, and of course no union with others is required to protect his labor. But in a state of society where no one labors for his own consumption alone, but each receives the labor of others in exchange for his own, the price of labor in each division of labor, to prevent fraud, ought to be fixed by agreement among the laborers themselves. The right of the producer to fix the price of his own labor is unquestionable; for its denial admits the right of slavery. But every effort which the producing classes have ever made for the enjoyment of this most obvious right has always met with the most determined opposition of the aristocracy. Wherever they have held all political power, laws have been enacted inflicting fines, imprisonment, and transportation on those that attempt by unions among themselves to fix the price of their labor. Where they have not all political power, they have recourse to everything within their reach, to every argument, to every quibble, every sophistry, in order to flatter the people to relinquish, or drive them to renounce this right. Those that have not the unblushing confidence to deny this right altogether contend that it is an individual and not a social right. For although each individual may fix the price of his own labor, yet no two or more individuals have a right to agree among themselves to fix the price. But when men enter into a state of society, all those rights which it is impossible to enjoy without the aid of others become social rights and must be enjoyed, if at all, by concert with others. It is unreasonable to suppose that we are possessed of rights which we have not the power to enjoy. But if we have not the social right to fix the price of our own labor, it is perfectly useless to allow us the right at all. For how can an unaided individual without wealth, without education, ignorant of the world, and even of the value of his own labor, who must command immediate employment or starve, enjoy this right as an individual right? If he enjoy it at all, the interests of others engaged in the same or other employments must secure it to him. No law has ever been enacted in this country in relation to this subject. But the aristocracy have notwithstanding attempted to frighten the people with the semblance of law. The judiciary in this State, and in every State where judges hold their office during life, is the headquarters of the aristocracy. And every plan to humble and subdue the people originates there. One of the most enormous usurpations of the judiciary is the claim and possession of common law jurisdiction. Common law, although contained in ten thousand different books, is said to be unwritten law, deposited only in the head of the judge, so that whatever he says is common law, *must be* common law, and it is impossible to know, before the judge decides, what the law is. But still in order to justify the judge in all iniquitous decisions, they have recourse to precedents, or previous decisions. And however unjust and wicked any decision may be, if a previous decision of the same kind can be found, either in ancient or modern times, in Great Britain or in any of the States in this Union, the judge justifies himself before the public and escapes with impunity.

Now, common law is said to consist of all the precedents or practices of the courts of Great Britain and of all acts of Parliament up to the time of the formation of our government. Previously to the Revolution, acts of Parliament had been passed to prevent unions of the people to fix the price of labor. Although these laws have since been repealed in Great Britain, and since the year 1824 there has been no law in England in relation to this subject, the aristocracy contend that these laws, which we have never enacted, have not been repealed by our legislature, although the power that made them has since destroyed them, are, notwithstanding, in full force among us. We ought not therefore to be surprised if we soon hear of indictments on these old and repealed English laws, if juries can be found ignorant and servile enough to follow the dictation of lawyers and judges. Indeed attempts have already been made for this purpose. One of the judges in this city, not long since, charged the grand jury to indict the working men who attempt by unions to fix the price or regulate the hours of labor; although this judge, and indeed all the judges, are members of a secret trades union of lawyers, called the bar, that has always regulated the price of their own labor and by the strictest concert contrived to limit competition by denying to everyone the right of working in their trade, who will not in every respect comply with the rules of the bar.

All prices fixed by bar rules are in the *minimum*, allowing no one to take less than a fixed sum for each service; but everyone may take as much more as he can. What then ought we to think of the man who, being a member of the secret trades union of the bar, calls upon the jury to indict the members of the open Trades Union of the people, who join not for the purpose of injuring others, but for the enjoyment of their most inestimable right, to be deprived of which must always keep them in want, ignorance, and slavery? Does it not become us, fellow citizens, when we see the enemies of the equal rights of man everywhere combined to maintain their ascendency, to unite and employ our power of numbers against the power of their wealth and learning, for the recovery and protection of our rights?

Who are they who complain of trades unions? Are they not those whose combinations cover the land and who have even contrived to invest some of their combinations with the sanctity of law? Are they not those who are the owners of all kinds of monopolies, who pass their lives in perpetual caucuses, on 'change, in halls connected with banks, composing insurance companies, manufacturing companies, turnpike, bridge, canal, railroad, and all other legalized combinations? Do not each of the learned professions constitute unions among themselves to control their own business? And have they not fortified their unions by alliance with each other and with the rich, and thus established a proud, haughty, overbearing, fourfold aristocracy in our country? Well may the capitalists, monopolists, judges, lawyers, doctors, and priests complain of trades unions. They know that the secret of their own power and wealth consists in the strictest concert of action; and they know that when the great mass of the people become equally wise with themselves and unite their power of numbers for the possession and enjoyment of equal rights, they will be shorn of their consequence, be humbled of their pride, and brought to personal labor for their own subsistence. They know from experience that unions among themselves have always enabled the few to rule and ride the people; and that, when the people shall discover the secret of their power and learn to use it for their own good, the scepter will fall from their hands and they themselves will become merged in the great "vulgar" mass of the people.

The judge knows this. He knows that he is a member of a combination of lawyers, better organized, and more strict and tyrannical in the enforcement of their rules than even masonry itself. He knows that when the dispositions in the community to investigate and destroy secret societies turns itself upon the bar, abuses will be discovered so enormous as completely to eclipse those of every other combination. We shall then discover that we have been "fishing for minnows and let slip the leviathan." We shall discover that by means of this regularly organized combination of lawyers throughout the land the whole government of the nation has always been in their hands, that the laws have always been molded to suit their purposes, and what are called Courts of Justice are only engines to promote their interests and secure their ascendency in the community. The judges know that this combination has enabled them to usurp one entire branch of our government and to turn all the rest of the citizens out of doors. For who dares to go into our public courts and attend to his own concerns or to perform the business of his neighbor? We all know that this preposterous state of things could only have been brought about by union among lawyers and by their combination to involve the laws and the practice of the law in inexplicable obscurity and formality, by the adoption of all the cumbrous learning of British courts.

It is for the interest of this trades union of lawyers to have the laws as unintelligible as possible, since no one would pay them for advice concerning laws which he himself could understand. Can we believe that our laws would be the dark chaos they now are if our legislators had been disinterested men, of only common education and good understanding? Instead of living under British laws after we had thrown off the government which produced those laws, we should have adopted republican laws, enacted in codes, written with the greatest simplicity and conciseness, alphabetically arranged in a single book, so that every one could read and understand them for himself. "Ignorance of the law," it is said, "excuseth no man." Can we then, who call ourselves freemen, any longer live under laws which it is impossible to understand?. Without a knowledge of the laws under which we live, are we not deceiving ourselves if we suppose ourselves to be freemen? The people of Rome in the most corrupt ages justly considered it the most intolerable tyranny when one of their despots had the laws written in a small hand and posted up so high that the people could not conveniently read them. But shall we, who claim to be free and equal, voluntarily continue in a state of almost total ignorance, with laws so multiplied, so obscure, and so contradictory, as to render the general knowledge of them impossible?

But we can easily conceive how this state of things is perpetuated, by means of the quarterly meetings of bar unions in every county throughout the nation. After having consulted together on the best way of fortifying themselves in their illegal and unconstitutional monopoly, they very naturally enter into social conversations and agreements as to what individuals among them would be most likely to succeed in any election for the principal officers of the government; for President, members of Congress, governors, and state legislators. Having agreed on what course to be pursued, they dissolve and distribute themselves in the different cities, towns, and villages, throughout the nation. Each performs his individual part; and, by acting in concert, by secret confidential communications, by speaking publicly and privately in favor of their candidates, they have generally succeeded in electing the men predestined to office by the bar. Having in this way succeeded in electing the appointing officers, where will the appointments be most likely to fall? In what way besides this can we account for the fact that almost every office of honor and profit remains in the hands of members of the bar? But the evil of the secret trades union of the bar does not stop here. When the legislature assembles, every senator and every representative of the bar is prepared. They are all acquainted with each other; they feel that it is for their interest to act in concert. United efforts are always made by this fraternity to choose the president of the Senate and the speaker of the House of Representatives from the bar. This effected, the whole business of legislation is completely in their hands. The president of the Senate and the speaker of the House have the appointing of all committees, and, being lawyers, they are always careful to put a majority of their brethren on every committee which has anything to do with the laws; and in this way laws are drafted, introduced, and *talked through* the legislature by members of the bar. While the people submit to these abuses, it is easy to account for the continued existence of the dark and intricate labyrinth of our laws.

Of all the reforms which we have pledged ourselves to accomplish the reform of the judiciary and of the laws is the most important. Let us then go about the work with never ceasing efforts, until the great mass of our fellow laborers, who always constitute an overwhelming majority, shall see the necessity of a thorough law reform. In the first place judges should be made responsible to the people by periodical elections. The boast of an independent judiciary is always made to deceive you. We want no part of our government independent of the people. Those who are responsible to nobody ought to be entrusted by nobody. But to whom are the judges responsible? The aristocracy always center around power placed beyond the reach of the people; and until we can fill the bench with men of learning, good sense, and sound judgment who do not belong to the secret fraternity of the bar, all attempts to simplify the laws and the practice of the law will be in vain. For why need we attempt to legislate, while the judges hold legislative power and can nullify our laws at their pleasure?

[ABOLITION OF CORPORATE MONOPOLY]

Of all the contrivances of the aristocracy, next to the usurpation of the judiciary, and thus turning the most potent engine of the people's government against themselves, their unions in the shape of incorporate monopolies are the most subtle, and the best calculated to promote the ends of the few, the ignorance, degradation, and slavery of the many. This hydra of the adversary has within a few years grown up around us, until the monster covers the whole land, branching out annually into new heads of different shape, each devouring the substance and destroying the rights of the people. But the most potent and deadly is the bank, a monopoly which takes everything from the people and gives them nothing in return. The whole value of paper money consists in the consent of the people to give it currency, and all the advantages of such a currency of right should accrue to the people. A bank monopoly consists in the exclusive power of issuing notes of hand without interest and receiving the notes of hand of others bearing interest with good security. And whatever notes of hand the banks may issue more than the gold and silver which they have to redeem them is an absolute cheat upon society, as much so as it would be to forge the same notes. But it has been shown of late by bank returns that there is not in the possession of all the banks specie enough to pay more than twelve and a half per cent on the whole bank circulation, which shows that the banks taken together are recovering an annual interest of six cents on every ninepence they possess. How completely then by the means of bank unions have the aristocracy nullified the people's law against usury; and yet the judges, who are the sworn and salaried guards of the constitutional rights of the people, are silent on this subject! What is the difference whether I let one dollar for forty-eight cents, or split it in eight parts and let each of them under the name of a dollar for six cents? Money was designed as a measure of value, as a medium of exchange of labor, like weights and measures; and like the fair regulation of weights and measures, the coining and regulating of the value of money is one of the most important prerogatives of sovereignty. For whatever tends to derange the currency either by increasing or diminishing its quantity, has the same effect upon the community, as, without the knowledge of the people, to enlarge or to reduce the common weights and measures. Some would find themselves growing rich they know not how, and some notwithstanding every effort would sink deeper and deeper into poverty. The people would, as they now do, regard every thing as under the control of fortune, luck, chance; and a sense of the uncertainty of the result of their efforts would paralyze their exertions. Such is the effect of banking. It enlarges and contracts the value of this medium of exchange of labor, as the interests of the few require. It now issues large quantities of paper money, and a kind of delusive prosperity succeeds. The capitalist, the merchant, the lawyer, and all who live without labor, and all who are possessed of property, find their condition improving from day to day. But what sensibly enriches the thousands, although abstracted from the millions, seems at first so small, and so indirect as not immediately to excite alarm. The producer complains not, the money market is easy, and all allow that times are good. The husbandman finds his farm gradually increasing in value; and what was formerly valued at a thousand, is now worth two or three or four thousand dollars according to the increase of paper currency. The farmer wonders to find himself becoming rich. But pride and wants grow with riches. He pulls down his old house and barn and builds anew, and thus becomes in debt; his farm is now worth five thousand dollars, and his debts amount to three. He soon goes to the bank and mortgages his farm for three thousand dollars. And although he is now worth nominally twice as much as before, even if his masters suffer the currency to remain where it is, he becomes a slave for life; since the annual interest will absorb the whole profit of his farm and labor, and when he has worn himself out in their service, his portion of our mother earth, by the addition of lawyers' fees and court expenses, will pass into other hands. But if the banks withdraw the paper trash, his farm will fall immediately down to its original value, and he will be deprived of all and find himself besides in debt, thrown out of employment, his family broken up, and his children obliged to fly to the factories, "those principalities of the destitute, and palaces of the poor," for sustenance.

Thus banking, both by issuing and by withdrawing its paper, disturbs the equality of society, and only serves to make the rich richer, and the industrious portion of the people still more dependent and wretched. It is a two-edged sword in the hands of the enemy, whichever way it is wielded destroying the people. But the great monopoly has of late received a shock which it is our interest and our duty to make fatal. Now is the time to destroy the evil; and we should do it so unanimously as completely to obliterate every hope of raising another in its place. Kill the great monster, and the whole brood which are hatched and nourished over the land will fall an easy prey. But if we suffer it to escape with life, however wounded, maimed, and mutilated, it will soon recover its wonted strength, its whole power to injure us, and all hope of its destruction must be forever renounced. The enemy are everywhere coming to the rescue and rallying to sustain it, beseeching and petitioning us to spare its life. But let us turn a deaf ear to their entreaties, and its destruction is sure.

[OTHER REFORMS]

We have pledged ourselves also to the world as opposed to all legislation and all laws relating to religion. In this we recognize the rights of the mind to be individual rights. We accord to each individual the right of thinking, understanding, judging, and believing for himself, and the right of communicating his notions, opinions, or belief, and enforcing them by every argument and with all the power and ingenuity of which he is capable. And no man should be blamed, injured, or molested on account of his opinions whether right or wrong on any subject. For we always suppose our own opinions to be right, or we should renounce them. And with respect to belief everyone must be the judge for himself. A person may be blamable for so conceited, so bigoted an attachment to his own opinions as not to hear and rationally weigh all the reasons, proofs, and arguments against them. Everyone is justly blamable and answerable to himself for erroneous opinions conceived or retained for want of such impartial examination as his situation enables him to use, or from an obstinate conviction of their infallibility. And this is all the blame that can reasonably be attached to anyone on account of his belief, because the opinions of men are above their control. Everyone comes to a conclusion on any given subject when a certain weight of evidence has been received, enough to produce conviction on his mind, although perhaps to another individual, whose mind is differently constituted, the same evidence is quite insufficient. So that one man may believe and another disbelieve the same thing, having the same evidence, and both be equally sincere and guiltless. Our opinions are not subject to our will. We cannot believe and disbelieve as we please. And, consequently, it is as unjust to make men accountable for their belief as for their personal appearance; for the features of their opinions as for the features of the face; both the one and the other are formed by circumstances not within their voluntary control. And it is as wicked, as absurd, as tyrannical, to hate, to punish, to oppose, and persecute men for the one as for the other. The only effect, therefore, which laws, punishments, penalties, and disabilities can possibly have is to render it prudent for individuals, if they entertain unpopular or unlawful belief, to conceal it, and in self-defense, and against their own will, to cover themselves in the garb of hypocrisy. For if, as formerly, we had laws to scourge, imprison, torture, burn, behead, or hang everyone who would not agree to a certain belief, everyone must certainly perceive that if he wanted to live, he must assume that belief. There is no subject too high or too holy to be investigated. It is fraud and falsehood alone that ever desire to be shielded from public scrutiny. Let truth and error meet each other in broad day. We have nothing to fear, but much to hope, from the contest. Show them fair play, and truth will always come off victorious. And those that would take the law as a shield of their opinions prove that they themselves, at least, are distrustful of their soundness and truth.

We have also pledged ourselves to the world in favor of the repeal of the militia laws and the abolition of imprisonment for debt. And we have reason to believe that the unequal and odious militia service which had been thrown from the aristocracy upon the shoulders of the producers has already been meliorated by our exertions. And the pledge which we gave the world for the abolition of imprisonment for debt, we have the satisfaction of knowing, *is this day redeemed*.[3]

Our success in these measures should encourage us to persevere until all the reforms which we have proposed are accomplished. United, continued efforts will carry them all; for in all these great reforms the democracy of the country is with us. We have the satisfaction of knowing that we are pioneers in the great cause; and we must be willing to expose ourselves to the shot of the enemy, while clearing the way for the whole army to come up and carry the works.

[3] [The Massachusetts law prohibiting imprisonment for debt, in whose passage Robinson had been most active and influential, went into operation on July 4, 1834.]

[THE NEED FOR UNIVERSAL EDUCATION]

The cause of the people, I trust and believe, is now progressing. And it only needs for us to carry the first, the great reform which we have proposed, the equal mental and physical education of all, at the expense of all, and our emancipation from the power of aristocracy will be effectual and eternal.

We are as yet but a half educated and half civilized people. The few are educated in one half of their faculties, and the people in the other half. The few have been educated mentally, at an expense sufficient for the entire education of all; and the many have been obliged to devote their whole time to bodily labor, while the powers of the mind have been almost entirely neglected. But the human race can never arrive to that state of knowledge, equality, and happiness of which they are capable until all are educated both mentally and physically alike, at the common expense of all. This great idea of equal, universal education has gone abroad. Its practicability has been proved, and the enemies of the equal rights of man cannot refute it. It has been shown that there is time enough between the ages of five years and twenty years, for every child to acquire as much intellectual knowledge as can now be obtained in the colleges of the rich, and at the same time to learn a mechanical trade, or skill in some productive employment, by which to maintain himself independently in after life, and nearly or quite support himself during the time. When the great mass of the laboring people become wise enough to establish institutions for the equal education and maintenance of their children in every neighborhood throughout our country, and furnish them with instructors in every branch of knowledge, with all the books, apparatus, land, machinery, and labor-saving power best calculated for the development of the mind and their own support, the reign of equality will then commence. For when the intellectual faculties of all shall be enlarged by education, and the productive powers of all shall be brought into action, a state of independency, comfort, wealth, happiness, and benevolent feeling will ensue of which we have not now the power to conceive.

.   .   .   .

[THE NEED FOR LABOR UNIONS]

It is certain that the productive power of man even in his rudest state is equal to his comfortable subsistence, by the devotion of something less than his whole time and strength to personal labor. To suppose that he could only live by constant exertion and that no time could be afforded to relaxation, contemplation, and study is to charge creative power with injustice. From the whole analogy of nature we learn that such active labor alone as is conducive to his happiness and health has always been sufficient to supply the wants of man. But the productive power of man is continually increasing. His ingenuity has taught the brute creation and even the elements to labor for him. Yet every contrivance to increase the amount of his production, instead of easing the burthen of his labor, bettering his condition, or affording him more leisure for relaxation, amusement, and the acquirement of knowledge, has only enabled a few more to live without labor; and instead of benefiting the people at large, still farther disturbs the equality of society. We have reason to believe from late investigations on this subject that the productive power of man is now increased by steam and other kinds of labor-saving machinery at least twenty-fold, so that what the unaided power of man could only accomplish in twelve hours is now produced in thirty-eight minutes.

These startling facts ought to lead us to enquire how it is that in the midst of such wonderful improvements the condition of the producer continues the same; and to search out the law or the principle that divides to the producer and the nonproducer their respective shares of the fruit of labor.

For everything in this world is governed by laws or principles which no unions can alter, or even no legislation affect. Wherever anything is produced in greater abundance than is wanted for immediate consumption, its value will depreciate below the costs of its production. The least surplus injures the producer, and excessive abundance is his destruction. But when the market is but scantily supplied, the producer receives a more adequate return for his labor, and the nonproducer is obliged to part with a larger portion of his funds to command the necessaries, conveniences, and luxuries of life. In such times things tend to equality. But in times of great abundance the competition of laborers reduces their produce often below the means of supporting life; and the nonproducing part of society speculate upon it, hoard the surplus in storehouses, and thus control the market and become rich at the expense of the laborer. While the one is rolling in wealth and living in luxury and splendor, the real producer of his wealth is reduced to the most deplorable poverty, wretchedness, and want. It becomes us then to learn the law that governs our productions and to live in such accordance therewith as to secure our own happiness and avoid the evils which the violation of this law has inflicted upon the great majority of the human race, in all nations, and in every age. For while the productive classes remain ignorant of this principle, the law of individual competition will prevail; and everyone supposing that the more he produces, the more he will receive in return for his produce, is stimulated on until the market is full; prices now begin to fall; he is obliged to labor harder in order to supply his accustomed enjoyments; and thus the market is still farther overstocked and the prices still more reduced, until his greatest exertions fail to supply him with the necessaries of life. What misery now stares him in the face. He sees his wife and little ones famishing for bread, which again stimulates him to still greater exertion. But like the man in the morass, every effort to extricate himself sinks him deeper and deeper into the mire, until his continued and excessive productions have entirely glutted the market, and he has completely worked himself out of employment; like Tantalus up to his chin in water, perishing with thirst, in the midst of excessive abundance, he is dying with hunger. He sees his children one after another sicken and die around him for want of nourishment, his body is worn with labor and weakened by abstinence, and his mind distracted with his numerous troubles, until at last he sinks under the weight of his accumulated misery. In this way alone the market relieves itself, by working the destruction of the producer. In countries where all the occupations of life are full, unless the government or the people have recourse to some countervailing principle, these periods of famine from excessive production would be periodical, and as regular in their return as the return of the seasons. In England the producer retreats to the almshouse, and by living without producing, helps the sooner to relieve the market of its repletion. In China infanticide forever regulates the number of the producers to the produce required.

How important then are trades unions, not for the purpose of controlling the price of labor while the market is glutted, for this is impossible. The nonproducer laughs at your every effort, while his storehouses are bursting with the fruit of your labor. But how important for the purpose of seeing that no more is produced than barely enough to supply the demand. It should be the first object of the members of every productive employment to ascertain the actual daily and yearly consumption of the articles of their produce, and to regulate their hours of labor in such accordance therewith as nearly as possible to supply the demand. When the market is not oversupplied, the producer has the power of setting any reasonable price on his own labor. But it is impossible for trades unions or any other power to keep up prices when the market is glutted; for, in such case, the producer loses his natural and rightful control over the price of his own labor, and the nonproducer fixes the price.

[THE POWER OF THE PEOPLE]

All legislative power, fellow citizens, is in our hands. And by this power, if we are wise, we can meliorate our condition. But in whatever way we labor for the protection and enjoyment of our own rights and interests, let us not forget that we are the natural guardians and protectors of the other, the weaker and the better half of our own species; of those who have borne us in the womb, have loved, protected, and nourished us in infancy, and led us through the bright and flowery but dangerous path of childhood; who are the companions of our manhood, who rejoice with us in our prosperity and desert us not in the hour of our greatest adversity, who smooth for us the bed of sickness, and even comfort us in the hour of death. But they are the weaker portion of our species, and weakness and ignorance have always been the legitimate prey of the aristocracy. However much *we* have borne from them in every age, our mothers, our wives, our sisters, our daughters have been still more abused. Their sufferings call for our immediate interposition, and we ought never to rest until we regulate the hours of their labor in factories by direct legislation; until we make it a crime to work our daughters or our children in the mills of these Philistines more than six hours a day. Who can read the account of the sufferings of the most innocent, the most beautiful and helpless part of our species, in these great workshops of monopolists, both in Europe and our own country, without bursting into tears? What must be the feelings of full grown men who can live in idleness and splendor at the expense of the slavery of innocent females and even boast of fat dividends obtained from fourteen hours daily labor of young women and children. England has already been legislating on this subject, and shall we see our sisters and daughters oppressed without making an effort for their relief?

It becomes us also to make provision by law for the relief of fatherless children and orphans, allowing to each a weekly sum from the public purse, enough to supply them with the necessaries of life and afford them means of instruction until they are able to support themselves. The condition of the widows and fatherless children of the producing classes in this country, I know from my own experience, is most deplorable. Left without property, often with several infant children, the very care of which seems too great a burden to many; without even a house or a room for shelter, what must the feelings of the inno- cent, bereaved, and helpless widow be? Thrown upon the world, she must either submit to the ruin and degradation of an almshouse, or her feeble hands must provide food and clothing and shelter and fuel for herself and little ones. How can we cling to any of the superfluities of life or even enjoy the homely meal while we hear the widow and fatherless crying for food? By what tenure do we hold the breath of our lives? Tomorrow our wives may be widows and our children orphans without bread. We are all embarked upon the great ocean of life. Some of us must sink in every stage of the voyage. We know not who, nor when, nor where. It becomes us then to make provision ere we sink for the rescue of our wives and children from the waves.

It would be easy, fellow citizens, to suggest to you improvements for the relief of the wretched, the instruction of the ignorant, the reform of the vicious, the exaltation of the humble, and the humiliation of the proud, until the shades of night envelope the hemisphere. For what have we yet done in these respects, since our fathers wrought out for us political independence and equality of privileges, and put into our hands the power of perfecting our government and securing our happiness? The millions have been lulled into a fatal security, while the thousands have been active in promoting their own interests. Yet we have still reason to rejoice that, while we have been sleeping on our post, the enemy have not yet completely subdued us; that, although we have been inactive, while they have been busy in dividing our ranks, bribing our officers, and filling their army with the venal and profligate; that, while we have been at ease within the walls of the citadels erected for our safety by the toil of our fathers, they have been silently sapping the foundations, preparing their engines, building their arsenals, rearing their fortifications, digesting their plans, and providing their great financial institutions for the payment of their troops, and the corrupting of our sentinels. Yet we have reason to rejoice that our weapons are still in our hands; that the ballot box, the wooden scepter of the sovereignty of the people, has not yet been wrested from our possession; that our citadels are yet in our own keeping, although the enemy have found means to send in their ass loads of gold. And, if we gird on our armor, heal the divisions in our own ranks, expel the corrupt and the disaffected, we can easily regain the vantage ground, and on the day of battle sally forth, destroying their engines, leveling their fortifications, breaking up their strongholds, scattering their forces, demolishing their monopolies, and triumphantly restore the liberties of the people into their own hands.

24

LANGDON BYLLESBY

PROPOSED REMEDIES FOR UNEQUAL WEALTH[1]

THE SAGE OF MONTICELLO has put it on record, in a shape that will not speedily be obliterated, "that mankind are more disposed to suffer, while evils are sufferable, than to right themselves by abolishing the forms to which they are accustomed." How near or how distant the verity of this dogma may place the remedy of the evils of unequal wealth which it has herein been attempted to array and expose remains to be seen; and, perhaps, a conclusion could only be obtained by determining the point to which these evils will continue sufferable, and this must be one of two cases: either,

First, When the evils result in general distresses that cannot be resisted or repaired under the existing forms; or,

Second, When the conviction becomes general that such distresses *must* ensue unless the existing forms are abolished and replaced by better kinds.

Reform, under the first circumstances, is mostly accompanied with violence and disorder, owing to the distress coming, partially, by surprise, and the urgency for relief not being able to brook the delay necessary for digesting the plans which are abundantly suggested for obtaining it or to overcome the interests that may be adverse to reform. In the second case the same wisdom and foresight that perceives the approaching dilemma deliberately provides its remedy, and avoids the worst by timely stepping out of its course into the newly prepared forms.

However, whatever amelioration in this matter takes place, there can be no fear but that it will proceed in the latter manner; for ages of experience, and abundance in late years, demonstrate that though violence may change the operation of oppressive circumstances, yet the very means of violence plant anew the seeds from which it must again spring up and grow with renewed vigor. But there is good

[1] [From *Observations on the Sources and Effects of Unequal Wealth* (New York, 1826), Chapter III, pp. 81-105 — Abridged.]

reason to believe that the germ of peaceful reform has already sprouted and will in good time shower its fruit around us.

.   .   .   .

[THE REMEDY SUGGESTED]

What will be the precise features of a system that shall supplant the existing systems of unequal wealth and individual privation will probably require some experiment to disclose; yet, with the aid of the light shed on it by that distinguished philanthropist, Mr. Robert Owen, and his coadjutors, we may venture to say the most prominent ones will certainly be:

First, Such an arrangement as will secure to the producer the full products and control of the fruits of his labor, from the incipience to their consumption;

Second, That all exchanges of products will be based on principles of reciprocity, or equal quantities of labor for other equal quantities;

Third, That no one consume the products of labor without yielding exact compensation therefor, in some shape or other, unless incapacitated; and,

Fourth, The consequent evasion of those uses of money from which it has been customary to derive interest.

It has not yet been demonstrated, that a perfect community or state of *measured equality* can permanently exist, even when its objects are confined to the pursuit of the arts of life alone; but that they are not likely to, when enthralled by any extraneous observances or prerequisites, has already been assumed and argued. Indeed, there seems to be something in the human disposition or temper that revolts at the idea of a *pure* community, as well as an intermixture of injustice in their practice, which it is difficult to reconcile with the common notions of the "rights of things." If it could so happen that some persons should be born with *four* eyes and the perfect use thereof, they would have as just a right to see all that they qualified them to see, as they who are born with only *two*. So also it would seem if natural strength, acquired dexterity, or more vivid intellect enabled one to ply his labor with such effect as to produce a greater quantity than another, he would have as fair a right to the larger as the other to the lesser quantity, provided such superiority be not used to the depression of another; and, altogether, extended capacity admits of extended enjoyments, and it has a right to such enjoyments, so far as it fabricates them for itself in conformity to the general good. But that something approaching the nature of a community or, more properly, an association for securing equal advantages could be made to procure those results for every department of Productive Industry, the elucidations of the subject by the experiments and disquisitions of Mr. Owen and others already adverted to leave no room to doubt; and, with modifications suited to each particular kind, would be easily put to practice, though it cannot be said that more than the fundamental principles have yet been laid out, and they must depend much on experience for their perfection.

Nevertheless, whatever be the power of such establishments as they have projected to effect general comfort and happiness by equalizing interests throughout both agricultural and manufacturing affairs, and in the efficiency of which we have the most implicit belief, yet we do not perceive how the means they propose, to wit, the erection of limited and independent villages, comprising a variety of concerns, are to include the immense and important interests, with valuable uses, embraced in the composition of large cities, in which an equalization of advantages in order to obtain the same benefits is full as desirable as in other situations. However, we believe it practicable to come at a similar result by the most feasible means, and at the same time preserve from desolation, by turning to account, the stupendous quantity of the products of labor which are there bestowed in the variety of buildings accommodated to the present systems of inequality and deprivation, in conjunction with maintaining and confining the precious metals to their legitimate and happy uses, in the form of a circulating representative of labor performed or wealth actually produced; for which purposes the felicity of the contrivance seems to fall little short of divine inspiration, apart from its profanation and abuse to the devices of injustice and oppression, through the operations of unfair profits, usury, and stock institutions. We will therefore refer, for the merits of the propositions for the former purpose, to the plans themselves, introduced in an appendix to this book, under the title of Practical Illustrations, and proceed to offer some ideas towards the latter object.

The term Equality, unfortunately, from its association with other words of similar force and value in recent transactions that have left recollections of horror on men's minds, ever comes before them with suspicious aspect; and when plans for equalizing the condition of mankind are spoken of, the unreflecting, measuring things to be with things that were, accompany them with apprehensions of commotion, disorder, irreligion, rapine, and destruction; when, at the same time, they are as foreign to its establishment, as is unequal wealth to that of sound morality, strict honesty, and unaffected piety. The establishment of forms that shall effect a system of equal advantages would, in their very progress, offer additional security against irruptions on any man's property and never cost either the wealthy or needy the contribution of a single cent which they did not cheerfully give, however it might, by its peaceful operations, interfere with the revenues of a few of the former class, though the circumstances of nineteen-twentieths of society would be vastly improved. But in order to obtain this result, it is proper that all distinctly first understand the origin of the insecurity and inconveniences with which they are burdened, and then unite in concert of action to cultivate the means of relief for which there are multitudes of imperfect models around them. Small capitalists have discernment enough to join, in companies of greater or less numbers, to give effect to their operations; and the greater ones have sufficient ingenuity to combine their wealth for a mutual profitable investment, in the shape of stock, for the erection of some institution, as a bank, insurance office, or other establishment professing to be a public benefit, and, by their processes, contrive to forward and uphold each other in the advantages they have become possessed of, until the insecurity inseparable from the dishonesty of the present systems, may happen to prostrate them. Now, it wants nothing more than the institution of associations on almost the identical principles of any of those, to complete the object; except that instead of *money* composing the stock, it should consist of the *productive labor* of its members, properly adjusted and applied; and a short course of discreet application would demonstrate to every man that the ability to perform the manipulations and labor of any handicraft or art, in connection with the assistances that ingenuity has already devised, would be of similar value to him as the dividend on a capital of many tens of thousand dollars, under the prevailing forms.

The character and nature of such an institution would, perhaps, be best expressed by a title like this: "Association for Securing Equal (or Mutual) Advantages (or Interests)," preceded by the appellation of such particular kind of mechanics, or other departments of industry who adopt it; the objects and operation of which will be best illustrated by an outline of some articles proper for organizing an association of the kind contemplated, and which might, with alterations to suit circumstances, be found applicable to every branch of productive industry and even commercial and maritime pursuits. However, to display it more familiarly, we will adapt it generally to mechanical businesses of permanent location, as, they are commonly practised in cities, by the following

EXEMPLIFICATION

WE, whose names are hereunto annexed, in order and with intent to secure to ourselves the full profits and benefits of our labor and application, as also to escape the inconvenience and distress of unsteady employment arising from the practices and arts of competition or from the caprice of those who have obtained the management and control of the exercise of our craft; and further with an intention to equalize the value of labor when devoted to the production of different articles of necessity or convenience, and also to avail ourselves of such devices to relieve our toil and increase our ease as our craft has been, or from time to time may be found susceptible, RESOLVE, to unite and organize ourselves into a coöperative body, under the title of "The ——'s Association of Mutual Advantages, of the city of ——;" to pursue which objects severally and collectively,

We do agree, To advance, in shares of —— dollars each, the sum of —— dollars, to be appropriated to the providing of such buildings and the purchase of such materials as will be necessary for the prosecution and exercise of our craft, and to appoint certain of our number whose abilities may be competent to apportion the work and superintend the sales of our products.

We do agree, That no other requisite shall be necessary for admission to this association than being a reasonably good workman and paying the amount of a share into the general stock. But if an applicant be not a competent workman, he shall submit himself to the instruction of a member who is, on such terms as they can accommodate, until he may be so acknowledged.

We do agree, That while we freely admit to the advantages of this association all whose handicraft and wishes accord with ours, we will likewise unreservedly discard all whose conduct may tend to injure or dishonor its character and views, after due admonition and notice.

We do agree, That every member, so far as practicable, shall be supplied with that kind of work at which he is most expert or that may be most agreeable; and to arrange compensation in such order as will best equalize the avails of equal dexterity and industry.

We do agree, So to divide what work is to be done that all may have an equal chance to receive a fair share of the profits, provided that in no case work shall be retarded on account of the negligence or indolence of anyone to whom it may be apportioned.

We do agree, That every Saturday evening a return shall be made to the members, by those appointed for that purpose, of the amount sold; and, after paying therefrom for all the work done the past week, after a fixed rate, the overplus shall remain in hand, as a fund for defraying of necessary expenses and supplying of materials; and, at the end of every three months, such division of the said fund shall be made among the stockholders as the prospects of the association will justify.

We do agree, That, as the prosperity of the association and applications for admission may increase, those who may hold a number of shares shall be obligated to sell to new applicants, until the whole be reduced to one share each; and finally to pay the whole entirely off; after which time new members shall be excluded from the quarterly division first ensuing their admission but be equal partakers ever after.

We do agree, That whenever anyone may wish to withdraw from the association or ill conduct compels expulsion, a fair account of his interest in the funds and property of the association shall be made and paid, either immediately, or at the next quarterly division.

We do agree, That for the careful instruction of apprentices to our craft, when such are offered, they shall be put under the tuition of the most expert and accomplished workmen, either by appointment or in rotation, and there continue until they may be proved incapable of sufficiently acquiring the art, or capable of working alone; his said instructor the while receiving the whole profits of his labor; after which, for the remainder of his apprenticeship, the apprentice shall receive one-half the proceeds of his labor for his maintenance, and the funds of the association the other half, and, on the expiration of the stipulated time, the apprentice shall be admitted an equal member of the association.

We do agree, That the most effectual means for ascertaining the value of our labor, as compared with the processes of other arts and with agriculture, as also the proportion of operatives in each mechanic or other art that will best comport with the free and general supply of all, shall be inquired after, and, when ascertained, that we will endeavor to adjust and conform ours, and admit all others to an equality.

We do agree, That in the purchase of all articles for the supply of our necessities or gratification of our inclinations, whether of domestic or foreign production, we will give the preference to the establishments of associations similar to our own, and obligate ourselves to adhere to such preference whenever it can be done, especially where they will admit equal quantities of labor to balance each other.

We do agree, That whenever any member shall discover an art, process, or machine that will have the power of expediting or ameliorating our labor or improving the quality of our manufacture, he shall have liberal reward therefor, in proportion to its value, either by immunity, or gratuity from the funds; and we do bind ourselves, each to the others, that if anyone shall make any such discovery, he shall forthwith disclose it for the general benefit of the association; and if any one conceives a plan that to him appears likely to have such effect, he may communicate it to a committee appointed for the purpose, and if to them it appears reasonable and likely to answer, the expense of the necessary experiments to test it shall be paid from the funds of the association.

We do agree, That in order to subvert all factitious distinctions of merit or honor between the members of different callings or trades, believing all labor, the tendency of which is to add to the comfort and happiness of mankind, to be equally honorable and reputable, and that such distinctions are only due to the accomplishments of the mind and the usefulness of the individual, we will give all possible attention to the improvement of our understanding and knowledge, by providing such books and assistances to education and intelligence for the free use of the members and apprentices as from time to time shall be convenient, and circumstances shall show fit and necessary, and to encourage such lectures and efforts as any members may volunteer, directed to that end.   And further, that after the expiration of——years, a moderately good acquaintance with the principal branches of science and at least one living or dead language shall be requisite for admission to our association.

We do agree, That we will endeavor to promote and effect a general system of conference and interchange of opinions between this and other similar associations, by means of delegates, in such manner as shall hereafter be determined, in order to effect the objects contemplated in the preceding articles, to establish and uphold each other, and to promote the extension of the system by such aid and assistances as we shall be able to contribute.

[DEFENSE OF THE FOREGOING PLAN]

The foregoing, it is believed, will be found to contain the fundamental principles for an association that would have the power of securing to its members the products of their labor, though some variations and numerous additions would be required to suit it to every kind of manufacture as the circumstances of each have need, particularly in the case of builders, comprising masons, carpenters, etc.   But all mechanics, traffickers, mariners, and others will have no great difficulty in perceiving by what modifications it might be made applicable to their condition and pursuits.

It will readily occur to any who consider of the project that the amount of capital for erecting such an institution should be confined within as moderate bounds as possible, as well as being divided into shares of a very small compass, in order that the whole trade may be enabled to fall in; for the more nearly the whole are embraced, the more decisive and certain will be its success and the necessity for the remainder acceding, as also their ability to contend with competition from without.   If an association comprise the whole of the workmen of a particular species of manufacture in a certain locality, the bone and muscle of it belongs to that association; therefore, an individual who might persist in maintaining an exclusive establishment could only supply it with his own labor; but, as the attendant burdens of rent, etc. would be proportionably greater, he would persevere to disadvantage, if not finally sink.   It can likewise scarcely escape notice, that the establishment of such associations would relieve its members and their business from the oppressive charges for rents, in situations where the artificial circumstances of the existing systems have rendered the position more valuable; for any location within a convenient distance of the center of consumption would answer equally well, there being no attraction to particular places by competitors, all being involved in this establishment. Hence, in proportion as similar institutions should be adopted by other manufacturers whose accommodation would be equally untrammelled by arbitrary location, the inequality of wealth arising from disparity in the value of houses and position would at once fall to the ground; for while the principles of such institutions should be conformed to and persevered in, none could have any superiority over others; and the immense sums yearly extracted from the labor of mechanics in the form of rents would be saved them; for the high rate of the value of property in cities, or rather in particular parts of cities, arises wholly from the artificial circumstances attending the existing systems of competition and exclusion, in the production of necessaries and conveniences and in the monopolizing control of exchanging and distributing them by the agency of extensive capital. But under a system of equalization they would descend to a value corresponding with the labor expended in their erection, except occasionally some little advance on account of the preferences for a city, or superior situation for domestic enjoyments or other satisfactions.

In this fact will be perceived a long step towards subverting the derivation of interest from money; but when to it is added the relief from maintaining a large stock by numerous independent establishments and escape from the expedients and assistance the proprietors are compelled to subsidize, in order to maintain a standing beside competitors who are better provided with capital and resources, the complete escape from the system of taking interest, or taxing the labor of the industrious, will be apparent. Concert and coöperation by an association will bear no comparison with any other mode in the power it possesses of rapidly creating an immense stock of the most valuable articles, over the supply of present consumption or demand; and when the accumulation becomes cumbersome from excess, its fabricators, like a hive of bees, can leisurely enjoy themselves on the fruit of their labor.

But foremost among the benefits of such an alteration in the prosecution of the arts of life will be the power of calling into useful operation the dormant ability for labor which everywhere is visible and which, owing to the instability of employment and the check on demand we have shown to follow an increased power of production, together with the tendency of the arts of competition of which we shall presently speak, under the existing systems, cannot be applied with advantageous effect, whereby both vast quantities of the products of labor and the uses of consumption are lost, will at least be greatly obviated, or more probably wholly removed. There are at all times, in all places, large proportions of the productive classes unemployed, and, though it might seem that they are, notwithstanding, aiding the consumption to the fullest extent, such is not the fact. A person can exist on no more than one-third of what he can in his own person consume; or rather, what full health, strength, and comfort require for their support, both in food and habiliments; and to this limit of mere existence the proportion of which we speak are confined, as also a large portion of those who are actually employed, through the restricting nature of competition.

.   .   .   .

[Claims to Consideration] [2]

At first view, it might seem that if competition really had this power of curtailing the consumption, it ought, in time, to acquire an increased violence of action that should almost entirely suppress production. And so indeed it would; but at a particular point of its operation what are called "poor rates," or taxes, are interposed; and according to the modulation of their pressure on the competitors, is the effect varied and prevented from becoming insupportable. Poor rates and other imposts are actually the friction weight which has prevented the machinery of the present system of competition from acquiring a motion that would long ago have destroyed itself.

What the average result would be as to the extent of the means of comfort and enjoyment which each individual would possess in the event of a general change of systems cannot yet be distinctly determined; but there is sufficient data to warrant the assertion that each can have abundance, with ample leisure to enjoy it; and though some

[2] [*Ibid.*, pp. 113–117 — Text complete.]

may, possibly, have greater affluence, if the term will apply, than others, yet poverty would become an obsolete word.

The tables annexed to Morse's Gazetteer are incomplete, giving the amount of manufactures, etc. of the United States in 1810, but not the number of persons engaged in them; and for 1820, the number of persons engaged, but not the amount of manufactures or products; and we at present have neither knowledge of, nor access to, an authority to resolve the difficulty. But the kingdom of Great Britain, the situation of which presents the best opportunities for determining statistical questions, gives the following particulars by which to form a conclusion. According to Colquhoun's work, on its Wealth and Resources, the population, in 1812, was 17,096,803 persons; and the whole product, income, etc. of all classes, 430,521,372 pounds sterling, or about 1,800,514,900 dollars, being something more than 105 dollars for each individual in the kingdom, or 525 dollars for a family of five persons. This immense sum, however, was produced by 7,897,531 of the inhabitants, which, if it had all accrued to the producers, would have been about 228 dollars for each individual, or 1,140 dollars for every family of five persons; and when it is considered that under a system of equal advantages there would, in the end, be but trifling rent charges, two-thirds of this sum, rated by its present capacity, would afford a comfortable living; leaving the other third for such purposes as the public exigencies might require. But when it is further recollected that the prevailing practices of competition, as we have just shown, expel more than one-half of the existing productive powers from useful action, leaving out of view those that it is yet possible to devise, it must be evident that if all could be so circumstanced as to have free exercise, an application of labor not exceeding four or five hours per day would surround everyone with an abundance of all things that the most voluptuous now enjoy, accompanied with the happy feeling of its certain continuance, so long as the promise that "seed time and harvest, summer and winter, and day and night, shall not cease," may endure; which assurance, no possible situation under the present institutions can ever give.

It is unnecessary to expatiate on the immense deduction from, or rather total barrier to, human happiness that is consequent on the irresistible propensity, perhaps necessity, of "taking thought for the morrow"; every one of mature age has felt it and observed its effect on health, the courtliness of social demeanor, its power of destroying the enjoyment of present comforts, and its unfriendliness to strict integrity. "The health of the body is greatly dependent on the health of the mind; and there is no doubt that, by introducing a system which would abolish everything resembling pecuniary distress, and with it the calamitous effects of extreme poverty, as well as the thousands of anxious cares and fears among all classes, bodily health would be nationally improved." Altogether, there has never anything of a temporal kind been presented to the mind of man attended by so many inducements for an earnest attention, and at least an experimental examination of its practicability, as an equalization of the advantages of industry and labor; and we repeat the conviction that its test cannot be much longer delayed, consistently with the welfare of the world.

Though we would not presume to say that it *cannot* be, yet we do not think it probable that society at large will ever be completely resolved into these associations, as many useful occupations in the hands of individuals extend their influence over a large surface, and their usefulness would be damaged by being concentrated. But likely, as in the Egyptian pyramids, while one kind represents the great stones that compose their bulk, the other will form the cement which binds them in the edifice, with the same power to resist the causes of destruction to which other forms are subject.

25

THOMAS SKIDMORE

A PLAN FOR EQUALIZING PROPERTY [1]

W HOEVER LOOKS at the world as it now is will see it divided into two distinct classes: proprietors, and non-proprietors; those who own the world, and those who own no part of it. If we take a closer view of these two classes, we shall find that a very great proportion even of the proprietors are only nominally so; they possess so little that in strict regard to truth they ought to be classed among the non-proprietors. They may be compared, in fact, to the small prizes in a lottery, which, when they are paid, leave the holder a loser.

If such a phenomenon in the history of man, for such is the situation in which we find him in all countries and in all ages, could have possibly found an existence under a system that should have given *each individual* as he arrived at the age of maturity as much of the property of the world as any contemporary of his was allowed to possess at a similar age; I say, if under such a system, such an unhappy result should have arisen as we now see afflicting the human race, there would be nothing to hope. We might despair of seeing things better than they now are and set ourselves down in quiet content that there was no remedy. But when we see that the system which has prevailed hitherto and prevails to this moment is not of this description; that it acts on principles in direct opposition to it; that it gives to some single descendant of some holder of property under William Penn possessions of the value perhaps of a million of dollars, while, it may be, an hundred thousand other inhabitants of Pennsylvania, collectively, have not half that sum; *and all this, merely because of a few beads having been given to some Indians some two hundred years ago;* how is it possible to have had a different result? The system is one

[1] [From *The Rights of Man to Property! being a Proposition to make it equal among the adults of the present generation: and to provide for its equal transmission to every individual of each succeeding generation, on arriving at the age of maturity* (New York, 1829), Chapter IV, pp. 125–144 — Abridged.]

that *begins* by making whole nations paupers; and why should it not be expected that they would *continue* so?   Indeed it would be a miracle, exceeding everything of the kind that has ever been supposed to have happened, if we had seen from such an organization of things anything but what we now see.

The truth is, *all* governments in the world have begun wrong: in the *first appropriation* they have made or suffered to be made of the domain over which they have exercised their power and in the *transmission* of this domain to their posterity.   Here are the two great and radical evils that have caused all the misfortunes of man.   These and these alone have done the whole of it.   I do not class among these misfortunes the sufferings with which sickness afflicts him, because these have a natural origin, capable, however, of being nearly annihilated by good governments but greatly aggravated by those that are bad.

If these remarks be true, there would seem, then, to be no remedy but by commencing anew.   And is there any reason why we should not?   That which is commenced in error and injustice may surely be set right when we know how to do it.   There is *power* enough in the hands of the people of the State of New York or of any other State to rectify any and every thing which requires it, when they shall see wherein the evil exists and wherein lies the remedy.   These two things it is necessary they should see before they can possess the moral power and motive to act.   I have succeeded, I think, in showing, for that is self-evident, that man's *natural* right to an equal portion of property is indisputable.   His artificial right, or right in society, is not less so.   For it is not to be said that any power has any right to make our artificial rights unequal any more than it has to make our *natural* rights unequal.   And inasmuch as a man in a state of nature would have a right to resist, even in the extremity of death, his fellow or his fellows, whatever might be their number, who should undertake to give him less of the property common to all than they take each to themselves; so also has man now, in society, the same right to resist a similar wrong done him.   Thus, today, if property had been made equal among all present, right would have taken place among them; but if tomorrow a new member appear, and provision be not made to give him a quantity substantially equal with all his fellows, injustice is done him, and if he had the power, he

would have the perfect right to dispossess all those who have monopo-
lized to themselves not only their own shares but his also. For it is
not to be allowed even to a majority to contravene equality, nor, of
course, the right, even though it be of a single individual. And if,
alone, he has not power sufficient to obtain his rights, and there be
others also in like condition with him, they may unite their efforts,
and thus accomplish it if within their power. And, if this may be
lawfully done, upon the supposition that yesterday, only, a government was made, and an equal enjoyment of property guaranteed to
all, how much more proper is it when, unjust government existing,
it has never been done at all. When the whole mass of people, as it
were, ninety-nine out of every hundred, have never had this equal
enjoyment, in any manner or shape whatever? If still there be those
who shall say that these unjust and unequal governments ought not
to be destroyed, although they may not give to man in society the
same equality of property as he would enjoy in a state of nature;
then I say that *those are the persons* who, in society, *if anybody*, should
be deprived of all their possessions, inasmuch as it is manifestly as
proper for them to be destitute of property as it is for any one else.
If slavery and degradation are to be the result, they are the proper
victims. After an equal division has been once made, there seems
nothing wanting but to secure an equal transmission of property to
posterity. And to this there is no irremovable objection. For I
think I have succeeded in showing that the right of a testator to give
and of an heir to receive is a mere creature of the imagination; and
that these rights, as they are called, ought to be abolished as interfering
with the real rights of the succeeding generation. Had it not been
for these, we should not have seen a Van Rensellaer possessing that
which would make hundreds and perhaps thousands of families as
happy as they could wish to be, and to which they have as good a
natural right and ought to have as good an *artificial title* as himself.
It would be of no consequence for him to say that he derived his right
from some old Dutch charter obtained some twenty years after
Hudson's first discovery of the river which now bears his name. The
rights of nature which can never be alienated, which can never pass
out of our hands but through ignorance or force, and which may be
claimed again whenever ignorance and force disappear, are superior
to any and to all chartered rights, as they are called, let them be of

what government they may, even of our own government, and much
more so to those of any that is or was foreign.

.   .   .   .

Instead, therefore, of this gentleman or any other person in similar
circumstances having any right to complain of any dispossession of
vast estates thus coming to him by what is called descent, one would
naturally think that he ought to congratulate himself that he has
enjoyed the sweets they have afforded him so long; and that gratitude
to as well as a proper consideration for the rights of each individual
around him should make him acquiesce in the decree of this community, if they should think proper so to order, to surrender it up,
preparatory to its being divided equally among the whole, himself,
of course, being one of the number.

So, also, if there be any individual who has had any connection
with the gentleman whose name I have taken the liberty of using, in
the way of the common transactions of business, and who has thereby
been able to appropriate to himself more than his natural and equal
share of the property of the globe, such person, if he does justice to
the forbearance of the community, is also under the necessity of
feeling the same sentiment of gratitude that they have permitted
him to enjoy so long a greater proportion of the blessings of the earth
than they have themselves tested, and *he* ought equally also to be
prepared to acquiesce in the same degree which shall forbid him to
riot in these superior enjoyments any longer.

It is of no avail, in the struggles of conscious self-interest, for such
a one to attempt to persuade himself that he would have a right to
disobey such a mandate of the community. In justification of himself, if he should say, "I was more industrious than others, more
temperate, more frugal, more ingenious, more skilful, had greater
bodily strength which I did not fail to exercise and therefore, for all
these reasons, I ought to be allowed to retain what I have," could
we not say it is not true? And admitting it to be true that he was
equally as industrious, etc., as many thousands of his fellow-citizens,
would it not be the most fatal argument that could be urged against
him? For if all these qualities are to be considered as giving him a
title to *his property*, as he calls it, why should it not give a title also
to them to an equal possession with him? And yet they have labored
all their lives, possessed all the qualities that he lays claim to, and

yet have nothing! Such is, at least, the case with the great mass of mankind. And *all* the rich, we certainly know, cannot pretend to be proportionally *more* virtuous than they. The mere accidental circumstance of having acquaintance with him from whom he has drawn his wealth, of having his confidence, of knowing how to take advantage of the situation of all the particulars in any way concerned in the operation of extracting such wealth from its former proprietor, is not of such importance as to give a right paramount over all other men, even if we were to admit such former proprietor to be a just and genuine owner. But such he evidently is not; and as such wealth derived from him, whoever may have it, must be delivered up to the community who are the rightful owners. A poisoned fountain cannot send forth sweet waters, nor he who holds a vicious title give a virtuous one to another.

But, in some respects, the reasoning in which I have allowed myself to indulge in the course of the present chapter is of a kind calculated to compel me to blend two things together which ought to be kept separate: that is, the injustice and enormity of unequal first possession, and the *effects* growing out of it. The reader will know what I call first possession; it is that which the governments of every country order to be given to him who is so fortunate as to have what is called a legator, whatever he shall have requested out of anything which he possessed at the termination of his life. The *effects* of which I spoke as growing out of it are the additions made to it by acquisition, through the operation of that state of things where a few have all and the many nothing. I use the word legator but the word donor is equally applicable, since the latter gives the property, it may be, a few years sooner; the difference being only in time. It will be better, therefore, to defer combating any further objections which will naturally arise to that which is yet to be proposed until a full view can be had by all of the features it will exhibit.

So much has been said as to what really is not and should not be that the reader is, no doubt, prepared to anticipate in part what *should* be; to foresee the modification which it is necessary our state government should undergo before the rights of property which belong to man in his natural state can be secured to him in the artificial state in which society finds him; and before the rights of posterity can be preserved to them, as they should have been to us, for their own exclusive use and benefits.

This modification will be accomplished by pursuing the following

PLAN

1. Let a new State Convention be assembled. Let it prepare a new constitution, and let that constitution, after having been adopted by the people, decree an abolition of all debts, both at home and abroad, between citizen and citizen, and between citizen and foreigner. Let it renounce all property belonging to our citizens, without the State. Let it claim all property within the State, both real and personal, of whatever kind it may be, with the exception of that belonging to resident aliens, and with the further exception of so much personal property as may be in the possession of transient owners, not being citizens. Let it order an equal division of all this property among the citizens, of and over the age of maturity, in manner yet to be directed. Let it order all transfers or removals of property, except so much as may belong to transient owners, to cease until the division is accomplished.

2. Let a census be taken of the people, ascertaining and recording in books made for the purpose the name, time when born, as near as may be, and annexing the age, the place of nativity, parentage, sex, color, occupation, domicile or residence, and time of residence since last resident in the State, distinguishing aliens from citizens, and ordering, with the exception of the Agents of Foreign Governments, such as Ambassadors, etc., that all such aliens shall be considered as citizens if they have been resident for the five years next previous to the time when the before mentioned division of property shall have been ordered.

3. Let each citizen, association, corporation, and other persons at the same time when the census is being taken give an inventory of all personal property, of whatever description it may be, and to whomsoever it may belong, in his, her, or their possession. Let also a similar inventory of all real property within the State be taken, whoever may be the owner of it. And from these data let a general inventory be made out of all the real and personal property within the State which does not belong to alien residents or transient owners. To this let there be added all property in the possession of our tribunals of law and equity, and such State property as can be offered up to sale without detriment to the State.

4. Let there be next a dividend made of this amount among all such citizens who shall be of and over the age of eighteen, if this should be fixed as I am inclined to think it should be as the age of maturity; and let such dividend be entered in a book for the purpose to the credit of such persons, male and female.

5. Let public sale be made, as soon after such dividend is made as may be practicable, to the highest bidder of all the real and personal property in the State. Care must be taken that the proper authority be required to divide all divisible property that shall require it into such allotments or parcels as will be likely to cause it to bring the greatest amount at the time of sale.

6. All persons having such credit, on the books before mentioned, are authorized and required to bid for an amount of property falling short not more than ten per cent. of the sum placed to their credit and not exceeding it more than ten per cent. Delivery may be made of the whole, if it be real property, and the receiver may stand charged with the overplus. If it be personal property, delivery to be made only to the amount of the dividend unless it be secured.

7. When property, real or personal, is offered for sale which is not in its nature divisible and in its value such as to be of an amount greater than would fall to the lot of any one person, then it shall be proper to receive a joint bid of two or more persons, and these may purchase in conjunction, giving in their names, however, at the time of sale.

8. As it regards personal property which may be secreted or clandestinely put out of the way, order should be given that from the time when any Inventory of any person's property of the kind is made out up to the completion of the General Sale, the owner should be answerable for the forthcoming of so much as may be left in his possession, at the peril of imprisonment for fourteen years, as is now the punishment for the crime of grand larceny, unless good cause were shown to the contrary. Similar punishment, also, should be visited upon everyone who knowingly gave in a false or defective statement of the property he had in his possession or who, having received his patrimony, goes abroad and receives debts or property which the State has renounced.

9. As the General Sales are closed, their amount should be ascertained, and a new dividend declared. It will then be seen how much

this dividend, which may be called a "patrimony," differs from the original dividend. By comparing the amount of each person's purchases with this patrimony, it will be seen whether he is creditor or debtor to the State, and how much, and he will be entitled to receive the same or required to pay it to the State accordingly.

10. There is one exception to the delivering of property to presons who may bid it off. It is to those for whom, from excessive intemperance, insanity, or other incapacitating cause, the law may provide, as it should, proper and suitable trustees or guardians. Under proper regulations, it should be entrusted to *them*.

11. While all this is transacting, persons already arrived at the age of maturity and before they can be put in possession of their own patrimony will die. Of these and others throughout the State, a daily register should be kept from this time forward forever; and so also should be kept another register of the births of those now in minority and of those that shall hereafter be born. The property intended to be given to those who shall thus have died and the property of those who shall have received their patrimony in consequence of the General Division and who shall die before the first day of January ensuing the completion of the General Sales shall be divided equally among all those who shall have arrived at the age of maturity between the time of taking the Census aforesaid and the first day of January just mentioned.

12. An annual dividend forever shall be made of the property left throughout the State by persons dying between the last day of every year and the first day of the next succeeding among those who throughout the State, male and female, shall have arrived at the age of maturity within such period; and it shall be at their option, after the dividend is made, to receive it in cash or to use the credit of it in the future purchase of other property which the State will have constantly on sale in consequence of the decease of other persons in the ensuing year.

13. Property belonging to persons not citizens, but transiently resident among us, and dying here, to abide by the laws which govern the state or nation to which such person belonged in the disposal of property in such a situation; provided such state or nation allows the property, or the value thereof, of our citizens dying there and leaving property to be sent home to abide by the operation of our own laws.

14. Other states or nations adopting a similar internal organization as it regards the transmission of property to posterity, and consenting to bestow patrimonies upon minors born in this State — and who shall prefer receiving them in any such foreign state — upon their producing documents certifying the fact of their nativity, age, etc., and that they have received no patrimony from their native state, shall have the favor reciprocated under like circumstances; otherwise, a minor born in another state must reside the last ten years of his minority in this before he can be considered as entitled to the patrimony of a native born citizen, and must moreover be liable to severe punishment if, either after he has received his patrimony, he accepts aught from his native or other state, by way of legacy or gift, or, before maturity, he receives such legacy or gift, and then accepts the patrimony in question.

15. All persons of full age from abroad, Ambassadors, etc., excepted, resident one year among us, are citizens and must give up all property over an amount equal to the patrimony of the State for the year being, unless such persons were citizens of a state acknowledging the equal rights of all men to property in manner the same as this State is supposed to do.

16. All native born citizens from the period of their birth to that of their maturity shall receive from the State a sum paid monthly or other more convenient installments equal to their full and decent maintenance according to age and condition; and the parent or parents, if living and not rendered unsuitable by incapacity or vicious habits to train up their children, shall be the persons authorized to receive it. Otherwise, guardians must be appointed to take care of such children and receive their maintenance allowance. They are to be educated also at the public expense.

17. When the death happens of either of any two married persons, the survivor retains one half of the sum of their joint property, their debts being first paid. The other half goes to the State, through the hands of the Public Administrator; this Office taking charge of the effects of all deceased persons.

18. Punishment by imprisonment for a term of fourteen years should be visited upon him who during his lifetime gives away his property to another. Hospitality is, of course, not interdicted but charity is, inasmuch as ample provision will be made by the State

for such persons as shall require it. The good citizen has only to inform the applicant for charity where his proper wants will be supplied.

19. All persons after receiving their patrimony will be at full liberty to reside within the State, or to take it or its avails to any other part of the world which may be preferred and there to reside as a citizen or subject of another state.

20. Property being thus continually and equally divided forever, and the receivers of such property embarking in all the various pursuits and occupations of life, these pursuits and occupations must be guaranteed against injury from foreign competition, or otherwise indemnity should be made by the State.

I have thus developed the principles of the modification which the Government of this State should undergo and the means necessary to accomplish it in order that every citizen may enjoy in a state of society substantially the rights which belong to him in a state of nature. I leave the reader therefore for the present to his own reflections, intending in the next chapter to offer such reasons as the subject admits for enforcing the propriety of adopting such modification and of the means proposed of accomplishing it.

26

RICHARD HILDRETH

HOPES AND HINTS AS TO THE FUTURE[1]

IN THE CURSORY VIEW taken in a preceding chapter of the history of Christendom for the last eight centuries, we have found that period divisible, without any very great forcing, into four ages of two centuries each, during which the Clergy, the Nobles, the Kings, and the Burghers successively enjoyed a certain headship and predominancy. But, besides these four ruling orders, we have also, during these centuries, caught some slight occasional glimpses of another order, to wit, the mass — the delvers, agricultural and mechanical, those who work with their hands — in numbers, at all times and everywhere, the great body of the people, but scarcely anywhere possessing political rights, and even where, by some fortunate chance, they have gained them, for the most part, speedily losing them again.

The clergy, the nobles, the kings, the burghers have all had their turn. Is there never to be an *Age of the People* — of the working classes?

Is the suggestion too extravagant, that the new period commencing with the middle of this current century is destined to be that age? Certain it is, that, within the last three quarters of a century, advocates have appeared for the mass of the people, the mere workers, and that movements, even during this age of the deification of money, and of reaction against the theory of human equality, have been made in their behalf such as were never known before.

We may enumerate first in the list of these movements the indignant protest against the African slave trade and the combination for its suppression into which the governments of Christendom have been forced, by the efforts of a few humane individuals appealing to the better feelings of their fellow-countrymen, and operating through

---

[1] [From *Theory of Politics; an Inquiry into the Foundations of Governments and the Causes and Progress of Political Revolutions* (New York, 1853), Concluding Chapter, pp. 267–274 — Text complete.]

them on the British and American governments. It has, indeed, become customary, among the advocates of money making, no matter by what means, in which category we must place some London newspapers of great pretensions, to sneer at the attempted suppression of the slave trade as a failure. It is true that, by the connivance of the Portuguese, Brazilian, and Spanish authorities with scoundrel merchants, British and American, the trade still exists. But what is it compared with what it would be did it enjoy, as formerly, the patronage and favor of all the flags? and how much longer is it likely to flourish?

We may mention next among these movements on behalf of the laboring class the abolition of chattel slavery in so many of the ultramarine offshoots from Europe; not alone by the strong hand of the slaves themselves, as in Haiti; not alone in consequence of protracted civil war — a consequence generally pretty certain to follow — as in the Spanish-American republics; but also from a mere sense of shame and wrong, as in the now (so called) free states of the North American Union; and from an impulse of humanity and justice, even at a heavy outlay of money, as in the British tropical colonies.

We may mention further the subdivision which has been carried so far, in France, of the lands of that country among the actual cultivators; a subdivision objected to by certain British economists as not so favorable to the production of wealth, a point, however, not to be hastily conceded, but which unquestionably does tend to give to the cultivators a certain social importance and political weight.

Let us add the system of savings banks, by which the English laborers for wages have been enabled to invest their savings in a comparatively safe and easy manner, and thus to share in that accumulation of wealth which forms so important an element of power.

Add further the constant advances and development of manufacturing industry, giving employment and high wages to a class of laborers vastly superior in intelligence to the stupid and thoughtless rustics by whom the fields of Europe are generally cultivated, a class among whom have arisen those Chartists and Socialists whom we have had occasion to notice, towards the close of our burgher age, as claimants for political rights; a class, in fact, from which the larger portion of the existing burgher class has itself derived its origin.

Such are some of the social changes which may be regarded as precursors and signs of the approaching Age of the People.

If the mass of the people are ever to be raised above the servile position in which they have been so long and so generally held, there would seem to be only one way in which it can be permanently and effectually done, viz., by imparting to them a vastly greater portion than they have ever yet possessed of those primary elements of power, sagacity, force of will, and knowledge, to be backed by the secondary elements of wealth and combination. Nor does the prospect of thus elevating them appear by any means one altogether so hopeless.

Whatever objections may be made to the existing distribution of riches, and to the artificial processes by which it is regulated, subjects which will form important topics of the "theory of wealth," this at least must be conceded, that no mere redistribution of the existing mass of wealth could effectually answer the proposed purpose of elevating the people. Any such redistribution, even if means could be found — and they could not — to prevent this equalized wealth from running back again, more or less, into masses, would still leave everybody poor, at the same time that it cut up by the roots a great mass of industrious occupations. What is vastly more important than the distribution of the actually accumulated wealth is the distribution of the annual returns of human industry. But no redistribution even of that, though it might sweep away the existing comfortable class, would suffice, very materially, to elevate the condition of the great body of the people. Above and beyond any of these schemes of redistribution, in order to redeem the mass of the people from poverty and its incidents, a great increase in the amount both of accumulated wealth and of annual products is absolutely essential.

Here, indeed, we discover one great reason of the state of social depression in which the mass of the people have been, and still are, so generally held. The good things which the combined efforts of any given community can as yet produce are not enough to give hardly a taste to everybody; and the masses have of necessity been kept at hard labor, on bread and water, while luxuries and even comforts have been limited to a few. Labor, the sole resource of the mass of the people, has been of little value, because labor has been able to produce but little; and the proceeds of the labor of production being so small, hence the greater stimulus to substitute in place of it fraud and violence as means of acquisition. The same man who will remorselessly cut your throat in the struggle for the scanty waters of a rivulet in the desert, not enough for the whole thirsty and gasping company, would readily share his cup with you did the stream only run a little fuller.

The first great necessity, then, of the human race is the increase of the productiveness of human labor. Science has done much in that respect within the last century, and in those to come is destined to do vastly more. Vast new fields are opening on our American continent on which labor can be profitably employed. So far from labor being the sole source of wealth, all-sufficient in itself, as certain political economists teach, nothing is more certain than that Europe has long suffered, and still suffers, from a plethora of labor, from being obliged to feed and clothe many for whom it has had nothing remunerative to do. The United States of America have now attained to such a development, that they are able easily to absorb from half a million to a million annually of immigrants from Europe. What is more, the laborers of Europe have found it out and are rapidly emigrating. In so doing, not only do they change a barren field of labor for a fertile one, and at the same time relieve the pressure at home, but, by becoming themselves consumers, far more so than ever they were able to be at home, of the more artificial products of the countries from which they emigrate, they contribute doubly to raise the wages of those whom they have left behind.

The development of productive industry seems then to be at this moment one of the greatest and most crying necessities of the human race. But what is more essential to this development than peace and social order? It is not pusillanimity, then, on the part of the people of Europe, but an instinct, more or less conscious, of what they need most, that prompts them to submit for the present, without further struggle, to the rulers who have shown themselves to possess, for the time being, the power to govern, a power, let it be noted, quite too unstable, however, not to require, even in the view of those who possess it, great circumspection and moderation in its exercise. War and civil commotions, though sometimes necessary to the preservation of popular liberties, have very seldom indeed been the means of their acquisition; conspiracies hatched abroad, never. When the fruit is ripe, it will fall almost without shaking the tree. What prompts to anticipate that period is much oftener individual or class suffering or ambition than the true interest of the mass of the people. The greatest obstacle at this moment to the comparative political freedom of Europe is the vast aggregation of power in the shape of standing armies. But how are these armies possibly to be got rid of, except by a certain interval of uninterrupted quiet, dispensing with their use, and such a contemporaneous increase in the value of labor as to make the maintenance in idleness of so many hands, instead of being, as it now is, a sort of substitute for a poor law, and a relief to the overstocked labor market, a useless sacrifice, and an expense too great for any community to submit to?

It surely is not from barricades and street insurrections provoking the murder of quiet citizens in their own houses, by fusillades and grape shot in the name of peace and order, but rather from a more careful, comprehensive, and profound study of social relations, joined to an interval of peaceful coöperation in the production of great economical results, that we are to hope for the dispersion and extinction of those unfortunate and unfounded antipathies, so rife at present between those who labor with their heads and those who labor with their hands; those who plan and those who execute; antipathies growing out of prevailing but mistaken theories of politics and political economy, which, by dividing the party of progress into two hostile sections, filled with jealousy, fear, and hatred of each other, have contributed so much more than anything else to betray Samson, shorn, into the hands of the Philistines; jealousies, fears, and hatreds not only the chief source of the discomfitures recently experienced by the popular cause, but which, so long as they shall continue, will render any further advancement of it hopeless.

This socialist question of the distribution of wealth once raised is not to be blinked out of sight. The claims set up by the socialists, based as they are upon philosophic theories of long standing, having, at least some of them, many ardent supporters even in the ranks of those who denounce the socialists the loudest, cannot be settled by declamations and denunciations and mutual recriminations, any more than by bayonets and artillery. It is a question for philosophers; and until some solution of it can be reached which both sides shall admit to be conclusive, what the party of progress needs is not action, for which it is at present disqualified by internal dissensions, but deliberation and discussion. The engineers must first bridge this gulf of separation before all the drumming and fifing and shouting in the world can again unite the divided column and put it into effectual motion.

BIOGRAPHICAL NOTES

GEORGE BANCROFT (1800 – 1891), a graduate of Harvard College and the University of Göttingen, after a brief career as a secondary school teacher, achieved his greatest and most lasting fame as a historian. As leader of the Democratic Party in Massachusetts, he was appointed Collector of the Port of Boston, an office he held for eight years, 1837-1845. He was briefly Secretary of the Navy in the cabinet of President Polk. From 1846 to 1849, he served as American minister to Great Britain; from 1867 to 1874, he was the minister to Germany. His chief publications were *History of the United States*, in various editions and revisions between 1834 and 1874; *History of the Formation of the Constitution of the United States* (1882); *Martin Van Buren to the End of His Public Career* (1889); *Literary and Historical Miscellanies* (1855); and an early volume of *Poems* (1823).

ORESTES AUGUSTUS BROWNSON (1803–1876), attended Norwich Academy, became an ordained Universalist minister, and was distinguished during his career as a liberal editor. From 1829 to 1830, he edited the *Gospel Advocate*, a Universalist publication in Auburn, New York. From 1830 to 1832, he was associate editor of the *Free Enquirer*. From 1838 to 1842, he edited the *Boston Quarterly Review*, which, after a year's merging with the *Democratic Review* (1842-1843), re-emerged as *Brownson's Quarterly Review* (1844–1865). Brownson's religious changes were rapid; he was successively a Presbyterian, a Universalist, a Freethinker, and a Unitarian before his conversion to Catholicism in 1844. Besides his journalistic writings, he was the author of an autobiography, *The Spirit Rapper* (1854), and a volume of autobiographical reminiscences, *The Convert* (1857), both somewhat fictionalized; several theological works; an early theologico-political treatise, *New Views of Christianity, Society, and the Church* (1836); and a systematic treatment of political theory, *The American Republic; Its Constitution, Tendencies, and Destiny* (1865).

WILLIAM CULLEN BRYANT (1794–1878), a graduate of Williams College, and a practising lawyer, achieved his greatest note as a poet. From 1826 to his death, he was one of the editors of the *New York Evening Post*. Besides his editorials and his poetry, he published a volume of *Letters of a Traveller*.

LANGDON BYLLESBY — Philadelphia printer, inventor, and journalist, remains an obscure figure. To him is attributed a satire, *Patent Right Oppression Opposed* (1813), as well as his *Observations on the Sources and Effects of Unequal Wealth* (1826).

JAMES FENIMORE COOPER (1789–1851), after two years at Yale and one year as a merchant seaman, became (1808–1811) a midshipman in the United States Navy. This experience and a deep interest in the subject led to the writing of his *History of the Navy of the United States of America* (1839) and *Lives of Distinguished American Naval Officers* (1846). From 1826 to 1833, he was United States Consul at Lyons, and traveled extensively in Europe. Besides his many novels, the basis of his reputation, his naval histories, and his travel sketches, he wrote *Notions of the Americans* (1828), *A Letter to His Countrymen* (1834), and *The American Democrat* (1838).

CHARLES STEWART DAVEIS (1788–1865), a graduate of Bowdoin College and a practising lawyer, was connected during his entire public life with the Maine boundary dispute. In 1827, he headed the state mission to New Brunswick in connection with this controversy; his report was published by the state legislature in 1828. In 1830, he was named special agent of the United States to present the evidence in the dispute to the King of the Netherlands, who was to act as arbitrator. In 1838, his state sent him to Washington as their agent to re-agitate the boundary claims, and in 1840, he was elected to the state senate where he acted as chairman of a special committee which prepared an extended report on the northeastern boundary, published in 1841 as a Senate Report.

WILLIAM EMMONS (1792-?) was a printer in Boston and one of the leading speakers for the radical wing of Massachusetts Democrats. Several of his orations have been published as well as his *Authentic Biography of Col. Richard M. Johnson of Kentucky* (1834) and *Biography of Martin Van Buren, Vice President of the United States* (1835). He published the very popular poem *The Battle of Bunker Hill, or The Temple of Liberty* (1839), written by his brother, Richard Emmons.

THEOPHILUS FISK (1801-1867), a graduate of Norwich Academy and a Universalist minister, served as editor of the freethinking *Priestcraft Unmasked* and the *New Haven Examiner*. In the latter periodical he espoused the workingmen's cause. In 1835, he edited the *Boston Reformer* (earlier called the *New England Artisan*). In 1844, he bought *Kendall's Expositor*, a fortnightly published in Washington. A very able and popular speaker, he made a lecture tour in England and Ireland in 1851. Later in his life he became a sponsor of the political career of Andrew Johnson of Tennessee

WILLIAM M. GOUGE (1796-1863), an editor and accountant, served in 1831 as reporter of debates in the convention for the revision of the state constitution of Delaware. In 1834, he became a clerk in the Treasury Department, a position he held for several years. In 1841-1842, he

edited *The Journal of Banking*, a Jacksonian publication. In 1854, he became special accounting agent of the United States Treasury Department, and in 1857-1858, he was one of two accountants for the State Bank of Arkansas. In addition to his published official reports, he wrote *A Short History of Money and Banking* (1833); *An Inquiry into the Expediency of Dispensing with Bank Agency and Bank Paper in the Fiscal Concerns of the United States* (1837); and *The Fiscal History of Texas* (1852).

BENJAMIN FRANKLIN HALLETT (1797-1862), a graduate of Brown University and member of the Rhode Island bar, was successively editor of the *Providence Journal*, the *Daily Advertiser* of the same city, and the *Boston Daily Advocate* from 1821 to 1838. He was an active leader of the Democratic Party in Massachusetts. In 1853, he was appointed District Attorney of Boston. He was the chairman of the Democratic National Committee in the 1856 presidential campaign. In addition to various political and patriotic orations, his publications included two extended legal briefs: *The Rights of the Marshpee Indians* (1834) and *The Right of the People to Establish Forms of Government* (1848).

DAVID HENSHAW (1791-1852) engaged in various business activities, including a drugstore, a bank and insurance company, railroads, and publishing. These activities made him a man of wealth. In 1826, he was elected to the Massachusetts State Senate. In 1827, he was defeated for election to Congress, but was appointed Collector of the Port of Boston, and thus patronage chief of the Massachusetts Democratic party. In 1839 he was elected to the state legislature. In an internal split for control of the national Democratic party, he opposed the Van Buren faction; rewarded by nomination July, 1843, as Secretary of the Navy, his nomination was rejected by the Senate (February, 1844). His chief publications were: *Remarks on the Bank of the United*

States (1831); *Remarks on the Rights and Powers of Corporations* (1837); *Letters on Internal Improvements and the Commerce of the West* (1839); and *The Exchequer and the Currency* (1842).

RICHARD HILDRETH (1807–1865), Harvard graduate and lawyer, wrote editorials for the *Boston Daily Atlas* early in his career, and the *New York Tribune* toward its close. His only public office was that of United States Consul at Trieste, 1861–1864. His major publications were: *The History of Banks* (1837); *Banks, Banking, and Paper Currency* (1840); *Despotism in America* (1840); *History of the United States* (1849–1852); *Theory of Morals* (1844); *Theory of Politics* (1853); *Japan as It Is and Was* (1855). His translation of Bentham's *Theory of Legislation* (1840, from the French of Etienne Dumont) is still used. His novel *The Slave; or, Memories of Archy Moore* (1836) influenced Harriet Beecher Stowe.

ANDREW JACKSON (1767–1845) qualified to practise law in Tennessee at the age of twenty-one. In 1789, he became prosecuting attorney for the district of Nashville and two years later, under the territorial government, he held the same office. He was a delegate to the Tennessee constitutional convention of 1796, and in the same year was elected to the House of Representatives. In 1797, he became a member of the United States Senate until, a little over a year later, he was elected one of the superior judges of Tennessee. In 1822, the Tennessee legislature nominated Jackson for the presidency, two years before the election. In 1823, he was again sent to the Senate. Jackson polled the highest popular vote in the presidential election of 1824, but the election was thrown into Congress and John Quincy Adams was selected. In 1828, and again in 1832, Jackson was elected to the presidency.

Jackson's military career began with his election in 1791 as judge advocate of the Davidson County Militia regiment.

He was elected major general of the Tennessee militia in 1802, and in 1812, he commanded the Tennessee forces in the war against the Creek Indians. He was commissioned as Major General in the army of the United States in 1814 and won distinction by the victory of his forces in the Battle of New Orleans in 1815. Given command in the Seminole War in 1818, he exceeded his instructions and entered Spanish Florida. When Florida became a United States territory, Jackson was named as its governor.

After his active career, he retired in 1836 to the Hermitage, a Tennessee estate purchased out of the profits of his ventures in land speculation, and there he died in 1845.

RICHARD MENTOR JOHNSON (1780–1850) was admitted to the Kentucky bar in 1802, and, two years later, elected to the state legislature. From 1807 to 1819, he served in the United States House of Representatives. During this period, he earned his military laurels as the colonel of a regiment of mounted Kentucky riflemen from 1812 to 1814. In 1814, he became chairman of the House Committee on Military Affairs. Elected to the Kentucky legislature in 1819, he was immediately named United States Senator, and in the Senate he remained for ten years. In 1829, he was again elected to the House of Representatives where he remained until elected to the vice-presidency in 1836, for a single term. From 1841 until 1850 he was politically inactive. His death in 1850 came shortly after he had again been chosen to serve in the Kentucky legislature.

WILLIAM LEGGETT (1801–1839) attended Georgetown College but did not graduate. After pioneering in Illinois, he served as midshipman in the United States Navy from 1822 to 1826. From 1829 to 1836, he was part-owner and assistant editor of the *New York Evening Post*. In 1836, he was editor of the *Plaindealer*, and, in 1837, of the *Examiner*. In 1839, he was appointed diplomatic agent of the United States in Guatemala, but his early death prevented his serving in this capacity. One of the hardest hitting of the radical Democrats, his chief writings are his editorials. In addition he wrote three books: *Leisure Hours at Sea* (1825); *Journals of the Ocean* (1826); and *Tales and Sketches by a Country Schoolmaster* (1829).

ELY MOORE (1798–1860) studied medicine for a time before becoming a printer. In 1833, he was elected president of the newly-formed General Trades' Union and edited the paper, *The National Trades' Union*. In the same year he served as a member of a state commission to investigate the competitive use of convict labor. In 1834, he was elected chairman of the convention of the National Trades' Union, a federation of unions from six eastern cities. With the support of Tammany Hall, he was elected to Congress in 1834 and 1836. In 1839, he became Surveyor of the Port of New York and, in 1845, United States Marshal for the Southern District of New York. About 1848, he edited the *Warren Journal* for a time, but soon migrated to Kansas, where, in 1853, he became an Indian agent for the Miami and other tribes, and, in 1855, register of the United States Land Office at Lecompton, Kansas, a post he held until his death.

JOHN L. O'SULLIVAN (1813–1895) received degrees from Columbia College in 1831 and 1834 before entering into the practice of law. In 1837, with his brother-in-law S. D. Langtree, he founded the *United States Magazine and Democratic Review*, and maintained his part-ownership and part-editorship until 1846. In 1841, he was elected to the New York State legislature. From 1844 to 1846, he edited the *New York Morning News*. He served as a member of the Board of Regents of the University of the State of New York from 1846 to 1854 and as United States chargé d'affaires in Portugal

from 1854 to 1858. From this time to his death he seems to have practised law.

FREDERICK ROBINSON (1799-?), journalist and leader of the Massachusetts Democratic Party, was a member of the Massachusetts State Legislature in 1834. He was a stalwart advocate of the General Trades' Union as an adjunct of Democratic politics. Later he held a political sinecure at the Boston Customs House. He left the Democratic Party in the 1850's because of his growing anti-slavery views. Several of his addresses were published in pamphlet form.

THEODORE SEDGWICK, JR. (1811–1859), was a graduate of Columbia College and a practising lawyer in the State of New York. He served as attaché of the United States Legation in Paris from 1833 to 1834. He declined an ambassadorship and an assistant secretaryship in the State Department in 1857, and was named in 1858 United States Attorney for the Southern District of New York. In addition to his contributions to *Harper's Monthly*, *Harper's Weekly*, and the *New York Evening Post*, he was the author of the following works: *Memoir of William Livingston* (1833); *What is a Monopoly?* (1835); *Constitutional Reform* (1843); *Thoughts on the Proposed Annexation of Texas* (1844); *The American Citizen* (1847); *A Treatise on the Measure of Damages, or an Inquiry into the Principles which Govern the Amount of Compensation Recovered in Suits at Law* (1847); and *A Treatise on the Rules which Govern the Interpretation and Application of Statutory and Constitutional Law* (1857).

STEPHEN SIMPSON (1789–1854), after an early career as a bank clerk and military service in the War of 1812, became in 1816 one of the editors of the *Portico*, published in Baltimore; this was but the first of many editorships which he held. He was a Jackson supporter as early as 1822 and an early leader in the Working-men's Party in Philadelphia, but when he received no patronage after Jackson's election he became disgruntled and in 1830 he ran for Congress as candidate of the "Federal Republicans," a Philadelphia faction which followed the program of the National Republicans. Later he became even more closely allied with the pro-Bank faction. After some dubious business dealings which left him with a tarnished reputation, he attached himself to the political fortunes of James Buchanan. In addition to *The Working Man's Manual: a New Theory of Political Economy, on the Principle of Production the Source of Wealth* (1831), he wrote a *Biography of Stephen Girard* (1832).

THOMAS SKIDMORE (?-1832) was a mechanic and one of the leaders of the New York Workingman's Party. He edited a daily paper, *The Friend of Equal Rights*, and was a candidate for election to the New York State Assembly. His only published work was *The Rights of Man to Property! Being a Proposition to Make it Equal among the Adults of the Present Generation* (1829).

GILBERT VALE (1788–1866), an Englishman educated for the ministry, became one of the leaders of the freethought movement in America after 1829. He taught, he lectured, and he wrote; he edited various papers, including *The Citizen of the World*, the *Sunday Reporter*, the *Beacon* and its continuation, the *Independent Beacon*. He invented a type of globe which was much used in simplifying the teaching of astronomy. An ardent disciple of Thomas Paine, he is best remembered by his *Life of Thomas Paine* (1841); his other published books include *Fanaticism; Its Source and Influence* (1835), and *The Astronomy and Worship of the Ancients* (1855).

MARTIN VAN BUREN (1782–1862), in 1800, at the age of eighteen, was a delegate to the congressional caucus at Troy, New York. Licensed to practise law in 1803, he served as surrogate of Hudson County from 1808 to 1813. Elected as New York State Senator in 1812, he was re-elected in 1816, but did not serve because of his appointment as attorney-general of the State of New York. He was elected to the United States Senate in 1821 and re-elected in 1827; in 1828, he became Governor of New York, a post he resigned in 1829 to become Secretary of State under President Jackson. His 1831 nomination as United States Minister to Great Britain was not confirmed by the Senate. During Jackson's second administration, he was Vice-President of the United States, and from 1837 to 1841, he was President. In 1848, as presidential candidate of the Free Soil Party, he failed of election. His *Inquiry into the Origin and Cause of Political Parties in the United States* was published posthumously in 1867.

JOHN W. VETHAKE — a physician, lectured in chemistry at Dickinson College in 1827, and taught the same subject at the Baltimore medical branch of Washington College in Pennsylvania. His brother, Henry Vethake, was a professor at the University of Pennsylvania. For a short time he edited the anti-Jacksonian *Poughkeepsie Anti-Mason*. He was an occasional contributor to the *New York Evening Post*. Some of his speculative papers on medical subjects were published, including *A Discourse on the Western Autumnal Disease* (1826).

WALT WHITMAN (1819–1892), after elementary education, became a printer's devil and later apparently a journeyman compositor. He taught various schools between 1836 and 1841, and during the same years began his editorial work with the *Long Islander*, and his practical politics by stumping Queens County for the Democratic party in 1840. Between 1841 and 1848 he was associated as editor or writer with at least ten newspapers and magazines including the *Democratic Review*, *Brother Jonathan*, and the *Brooklyn Eagle*. For a brief period he left New York and wrote for the *New Orleans*

Crescent. On his return he again moved from paper to paper until about 1862. His Civil War services led to a clerkship in the Department of the Interior for a very short time and then a clerkship lasting eight years (1865–1873) in the Attorney General's office. This was ended by a paralytic stroke, after which he retired to Camden, New Jersey. His major work, *Leaves of Grass,* appeared in ten editions during his life, each corrected and enlarged by the author (1855, 1856, 1860, 1867, 1871, 1876, 1881–1882, 1882, 1888–1889, 1891–1892). Other works published during his life were *Walt Whitman's Drum Taps* (1865), *Passage to India* (1871), *Democratic Vistas* (1871), *Memoranda During the War* (1875), and *Specimen Days and Collect* (1882–1883).

FRANCES WRIGHT (1795–1852), one of the leaders in the American freethought movement, ardent advocate of nationalized education and of the gradual emancipation of slaves, edited (with others) the *New-Harmony Gazette* and the *Free Enquirer.* She was one of the first women to deliver public lectures in the United States, on anticlerical themes. Her published books include: *Altorf* (1819); *Views of Society and Manners in America* (1821); *A Few Days in Athens* (1822); and *A Course of Popular Lectures* (1829).